12

D0078388

Encyclopedia of the Antebellum South

Encyclopedia of the Antebellum South

JAMES M. VOLO

and

DOROTHY DENNEEN VOLO

Greenwood Press
Westport, Connecticut • London

Library of Congress Cataloging-in-Publication Data

Volo, James, 1947–
   Encyclopedia of the antebellum South / James M. Volo and Dorothy
Denneen Volo.
     p. cm.
   Includes bibliographical references and index.
   Summary: Alphabetical entries present the culture, history, and
key figures of the American South in the half-century before the
Civil War.
   ISBN 0–313–30886–1 (alk. paper)
   1. Southern States—Civilization—1775–1865 Encyclopedias,
Juvenile. [1. Southern States—Civilization—1775–1865
Encyclopedias.] I. Volo, Dorothy Denneen, 1949– . II. Title.
F213.V65 2000
975'.03'03—dc21   99–28797

British Library Cataloguing in Publication Data is available.

Library of Congress Catalog Card Number: 99–28797
ISBN: 0–313–30886–1

First published in 2000

Greenwood Press, 88 Post Road West, Westport, CT 06881
An imprint of Greenwood Publishing Group, Inc.
www.greenwood.com

Printed in the United States of America

The paper used in this book complies with the
Permanent Paper Standard issued by the National
Information Standards Organization (Z39.48–1984).

10 9 8 7 6 5 4 3 2 1

Cover illustrations: Scene of the antebellum South, period bride and groom, and Southern
riverboat courtesy of the authors.

Contents

Introduction

The **antebellum South** conjures images of oversized verandas, lazy rivers churned by the paddle wheels of luxurious steamboats, exaggerated hoop skirts, and trees hung with Spanish moss. At first glance, the slower pace of the Civil War antebellum period (1810–1860) seems to have rendered it an era untouched by time. While the North was developing its modern industrial strength to meet the needs of an expanding nation, the South seemed to cling to an idyllic, if mechanically inefficient, simplicity, remaining suspended in the past—like Peter Pan in the false innocence of a perpetual childhood.

In reality, however, the antebellum South was exceedingly complex and replete with contradictions. It was at once chivalrous and crude, hospitable and harsh, bold and backward. It is difficult today to conceive of a society that could elevate civility, personal behavior, and honor to such high standards and yet perpetuate an institution that denied basic human status to a large portion of its population. It is equally difficult to understand a people who valued their own families, traditions, and heritage to the point of taking up arms to defend them, but who routinely disregarded the integrity of slave families and suppressed African religion and culture. Moreover, while the white South staunchly argued for its own political rights, many of its laws curtailed the personal liberty of all blacks, freemen and slaves alike.

While a characteristically extravagant hospitality was extended to all who shared in this Southern heritage, those from outside the region were highly suspect and kept at arm's length. Individual plantations were virtually self-sufficient city-states lacking little in the way of food or the means to provide for daily needs. Yet the region was almost totally dependent upon remote markets, manipulative agents, and Northern manufactures. The plantation aristocracy ruled like feudal lords. They were, nonetheless, critically starved for cash, and many were steeped in perpetual debt. Finally, the very climate that provided the South with a generous growing season, balmy breezes, and sweet-scented surroundings also spawned **epidemics** of cataclysmic proportions that cut short many lives.

The antebellum South was a time and place with its own integrity. Historians and writers have, all too frequently, treated it as a mere counterpoint to Northern accomplishment or as a necessary but unimaginative prelude to the "real" history found in the Civil War. The antebellum South had, however, its own culture, leaders, achievements, and history, and it deserves to be viewed as a distinct entity.

The authors of this encyclopedia have attempted to build a picture of the antebellum South through alphabetical entries; but, additionally, they have tried to convey throughout the work certain key concepts which they hope will bind together the people, places, movements, and attitudes of the antebellum period. Among these, **nullification, romanticism, states' rights**, and **manifest destiny** stand out. The South's "peculiar institution" of **slavery** and the **extension of slavery into the territories** have been examined not only as uniquely individual elements of antebellum Southern society, but also as themes that permeated the attitudes, beliefs, and actions of the antebellum Southerner.

The work is dedicated to the history of the South and of the Southern lifestyle as it was in the half-century before the Civil War. Additionally, it covers certain noteworthy events preceding or following this period to provide continuity and closure. For instance, the **Constitutional Convention** of 1787 and the death of **Abraham Lincoln** in 1865 are mentioned. Nonetheless, the vast majority of the entries deal with the period from 1810 to 1860 as it affected the South and Southern perceptions of society, culture, and politics in the years before **secession**. The criteria for inclusion in this encyclopedia have been determined with the help of input from historians teaching college level and graduate classes and librarians serving high school students.

Cross-references appear in the entries in **bold** type. Related entries are listed at the end of most entries. A short bibliography of suggested readings also follows every entry. An effort has been made to direct the reader to recent materials of high quality. However, some older volumes remain the definitive works in a given area. Because primary sources can provide profound insight, a number of primary source materials have also been suggested. Great care has been take to ascertain that these materials are readily available in public libraries and educational facilities. Extensive use has been made of illustrations drawn from period **newspapers** and instructional texts from the era. In addition to the visual information provided, they allow the reader to view events as they may have been seen by antebellum contemporaries. The selection process was also affected by the judgment and knowledge of the authors and editors of this work.

Personalities profiled include well-known statesmen, apologists, reformers, writers, entertainers, and soldiers—particularly those who were Southerners. Additionally, it is hoped that other entries on slaves, bankers, gamblers, prostitutes, laborers, and farmers give voice to the nameless individuals who often go unnoticed in standard histories while nonetheless making up the vast majority of the people who lived in the antebellum South.

Encyclopedia of the Antebellum South

ABOLITION (ABOLITIONISTS): No reform movement is more closely associated with the antebellum period than the abolition of **slavery**. Those who identified themselves as abolitionists generally crusaded for the immediate social and political equality of all blacks in the United States. Contrary to the common Southern perceptions of abolitionists, the use of violence to attain **emancipation** never had a great appeal to the mass of people in the North; and the more provocative tactics and strategies of the radicals rarely had any effect outside of New England. Anti-slavery, as a wider movement, was far too decentralized and subject to too many local variations to march in lockstep behind the radicals. Radical abolitionists—always a minority among anti-slavery advocates—were loath to accept the slow pace of gradual emancipation and became increasingly militant in their frustration. This militancy was not universally shared even among dedicated anti-slavery proponents.

Attacks on slavery in the early years of the Republic had been based on the ideals set forth in the Declaration of Independence and the incompatibility of slavery with the concept that "all men are created equal." Many Americans freed their slaves during and immediately after the American Revolution—a circumstance not confined to the North. Following the Revolution a large number of Southerners spoke about the abolition of slavery in abstract terms, and others were sufficiently dedicated to its ultimate eradication to provide for private manumission of their slave property—a formal emancipation process controlled by law. Yet early opposition to emancipation, including that of **Thomas Jefferson** and **Abraham Lincoln**, was based largely on the racist concept that the inherent inequality of the races would prevent their living in peace and prosperity together. Allegiance to slavery as an institution was rarely expressed. That was to come later in the turmoil over **states' rights**.

The realm of anti-slavery activity centered mainly on increasing the public's awareness of the plight of the slave and the degrading effects of slavery
on American society. Common activities included private and public meetings; correspondence in the form of letters, poems, and articles; and writing,
lectures, conventions, and the submission of petitions. The preparation and
circulation of anti-slavery petitions was a particularly popular public activity
among women, as their active participation in public gatherings, even for a
benevolent purpose, was widely considered improper, while the submission
of letters, poems, and articles for publication by women had only recently
gained public acceptance.

In the wake of the religious revival and evangelical movements of the
nineteenth century, the anti-slavery movement took on many of the characteristics of a Protestant-Abolition crusade. Proponents of the movement
helped to found the Lane Theological Seminary in Cincinnati, a stronghold
of the evangelical movement in the West, and they provided the financial
resources for an anti-slavery religious community at Oberlin College. Radicals, especially **William Lloyd Garrison** and Wendell Phillips, attacked
many of the religious institutions of the nation as supporters of slavery. They
disrupted religious services at pro-slavery churches and castigated the clergy
and the anti-slavery moderates as conspiring with Southern slave power.
Harriet Beecher Stowe warned her readers in *Uncle Tom's Cabin* that
God's vengeance would fall upon "both North and South . . . and the Christian Church," which had a heavy account of injustice for which to answer.

While many Northerners were against slavery, they were also remarkably
prejudiced against blacks. They were averse to having them live in their
communities and inclined to leave the issue of universal emancipation alone.
The treatment of blacks in Northern states was often brutish, and they were
despised and treated with contempt. Any plan for a general abolition of
slavery had to deal with the touchy problem of **free blacks** living in a white-
dominated, racist society. This led many sympathetic whites to fear for the
ultimate welfare and safety of a black population suddenly foisted on an
unfriendly America should the radicals attain their goal of universal emancipation.

The majority of the proponents of emancipation looked to the concepts
of gradualism and colonization, rather than immediate emancipation and
inclusion, to relieve the supposed incongruities of the races living peacefully
together. Gradual emancipation legislation in many Northern states provided that **children born as slaves** were freed on attaining maturity, having
been given a skill or **education** in the interim so that they might provide
for themselves. Similarly formed legislation had quietly obliterated slavery
throughout the New England states by mid-century. Private parties among
anti-slavery proponents favored the removal of free blacks to colonies established far from the Americas. The African city of Monrovia was founded as
a freemen's colony in 1821 in this manner. Less dramatic suggestions were

also made to remove freed blacks to the Indian territories, **Florida**, the Caribbean Islands, and Central America.

There was a growing recognition, however, that slavery was a great moral and social evil that must be ended soon. But it was also true that slavery had become uneconomical for the smaller planters. As early as 1816, several Southern states, **Virginia, Georgia, Maryland**, and **Tennessee** included, had asked the federal government to procure a site for colonization by freed blacks, and they had jointly petitioned for federal financial aid to offset the monetary loss involved in emancipating their slaves. The British government had successfully indemnified its slaveowners in the West Indies for their loss when the **Atlantic slave trade** was ended in 1808, but a similar arrangement was not possible in antebellum America either financially or politically.

In 1817 the American Colonization Society was formed to encourage free blacks to return to Africa. The organizational meeting was held in no less a prestigious place than the chambers of the House of Representatives. Among its founders were **Henry Clay, Andrew Jackson**, Francis Scott Key, and other notables from both the North and South. The society found support from all sections of the country and from both slavery and anti-slavery advocates.

African colonization was very popular politically. At the time, it was estimated by the proponents of colonization that slavery could be abolished by 1890. During the debates with **Stephen A. Douglas** in 1858, **Abraham Lincoln** had expressed both support for colonization and a belief in an inherent inequality among the races. True to his word, in 1862, one year before the Emancipation Proclamation, President Lincoln signed a congressional appropriation of $100,000 for the purpose of encouraging black colonization. A minority of free blacks espoused great interest in their African homeland.

But the radical abolitionists demanded immediate, unreimbursed emancipation, and integration of freed blacks into white society, not gradualism and separation. They felt that no price, including war and disunion, was too great to pay in the cause of ending slavery and racial prejudice. Active participation was held in high esteem among abolitionists, and many traveled to the South to speak out at meetings, denounce slavery proponents, and conduct escaping slaves along the **Underground Railroad**. The radical abolitionists berated the gradualists and colonialists as being less than completely dedicated to the cause of emancipation and went so far as to suggest that they were actually covert supporters of slavery by allowing free blacks to remain among them only as "inferior beings."

The rhetoric of the most outspoken radicals was often couched in inflammatory and unambiguous terms aimed at ending slavery. Many abolitionists openly endorsed the rebellion of **Nat Turner** and **John Brown**'s attempt to foment an armed slave rebellion in Virginia by attacking Harper's Ferry in 1859. In this the South saw a call for social chaos on a grand scale and perceived a very real physical threat by those "who whetted knives of butchery for our mothers, sisters, daughters, and babes" (Barton H. Wise, *The Life of Henry A. Wise of Virginia*, 1899). Against this background the writings and speeches of the radicals proved truly heavy rhetoric.

The impracticality of blacks being integrated into the fabric of American society in the antebellum period can best be measured by the resistance to racial integration seen in the South after a costly and painful war had forced emancipation upon it. With no solution to the perceived problems of free black participation in white society, and faced with economic ruin if forced to forfeit their considerable investment in black labor, Southerners were forced to turn any moderate attitudes they may have possessed toward gradual emancipation into a total defense of Southern society against any disruption from without. Impelled by a growing body of public opinion in the North that slavery must be abolished *at all costs*, Southern apologists launched an equally militant defense of the institution of slavery, portraying it as a positive good—a civilizing and caring medium for blacks who would otherwise revert to the brutality of their African origins. **Related Entries**: Atlantic Slave Trade; Douglass, Frederick; Garrison, William Lloyd; Republican Party.

SUGGESTED READING: Alice Dana Adams, *The Neglected Period of Anti-Slavery in America, 1800–1831* (1973); Ezekiel Birdseye, *An Abolitionist in the Appalachian South, 1841–1846* (1997); Henry Mayer, *William Lloyd Garrison and the Abolition of Slavery* (1998); Philip Spencer, *Three Against Slavery: Denmark Vesey, William Lloyd Garrison, Frederick Douglass* (1972).

ABORTION AMONG FEMALE SLAVES: Female slaves were condemned to work in the fields, leaving little time for the proper rearing of children. Older women with half a dozen children were expected to work as efficiently as young females in their prime with no offspring. A contemporary observer, **Fanny Kemble**, noted that "women were generally shown some indulgence for three or four weeks previous to childbirth . . . [and] they are generally allowed four weeks after the birth of a child, before they are compelled to go into the field, they then take the child with them." Female slaves were noted by white observers as being resourceful in preventing conception or in aborting unwanted pregnancies. A **Georgia** physician noted the complaints of the slaveowners concerning the tendency of female slaves to destroy their offspring and deprive their owners of the natural increase in their slave property. Miscarriages could often be brought on by a combination of herbal concoctions, violent exercise, and external and internal manipulation. Ironically, both the root and seed of the **cotton** plant were used as abortfacients. Catherine Clinton (1982) points out that "slave mothers who committed infanticide were judged guilty of murder. . . . and slave midwives and medicine men were warned [against] abetting such activities." Child mortality among slaves was very high, and ironically, it was largely responsible for the total death rate among slaves being higher than that of the general white population. **Related Entries**: Children Born as Slaves; Miscegenation.

SUGGESTED READING: Catherine Clinton, *The Plantation Mistress: Woman's World in the Old South* (1982); Frances A. Kemble, *Journal of a Residence on a Georgia Plantation, 1838–1839* (1863; 1984); Kenneth M. Stampp, *The Peculiar Institution* (1956).

ADAMS, JOHN QUINCY (1767–1848): politician, congressman, secretary of state, and sixth President of the United States (1825–1829). By the end of the second term of President **James Monroe** in 1824 there was only a single viable political party, the Jeffersonian Republicans. A series of presidential candidates came forth, each with his own minority of sectional backers, so that the party failed to unite behind a single person. Nonetheless, one-third of the members were able to compromise on William H. Crawford of **Georgia**, although Crawford had recently been stricken with a paralysis. Additional candidates were nominated at local party meetings and through state legislatures for a total of four. Among these were **Andrew Jackson, Henry Clay**, and John Quincy Adams of Massachusetts.

John Quincy Adams was an experienced secretary of state and was well equipped to be President. Unfortunately, he had inherited from his father, President John Adams, many of his less desirable characteristics, particularly a cold and calculating manner. In the bitter campaign that followed, the younger Adams proved a poor vote getter. Jackson had the largest number of popular votes and 90 electoral votes; Adams had 84 electoral votes from New England and New York; Crawford, with 41, carried most of the South; and Clay came in last with 37, mostly from the old Northwest. No one had the required majority to be elected.

This result meant that the election would be decided by the House of Representatives between the two leading candidates, Jackson and Adams. As he distrusted and disliked Jackson, Clay bargained his influence in the House to Adams in order to deprive Jackson of the presidency. Charges of corruption and quid pro quo were made and widely believed following Adams' election, and the selection of Clay as his secretary of state seemed to verify that a "corrupt bargain" had been made. Jackson never forgave either Adams or Clay, and he began his presidential campaign for 1828 almost immediately.

Adams' administration was little more than a list of failures. He called for huge outlays for **internal improvements at federal expense** and for enlarging the navy. Yet he ignored the National Republicans who had elected him, and the supporters of Jackson (now called Democratic Republicans, or just **Democrats**) gained control of Congress. They blocked almost all of

Adams' initiatives, favoring the tariff and supporting industry and the working class. Although the Jackson men did not plan to hurt the South, they did pass a remarkable new piece of legislation, the **Tariff of 1828**, called the "Tariff of Abominations" because it levied duty of 40 percent on most manufactured goods imported into the country.

Adams signed the Tariff of 1828 into law, winning the support of New England, **Delaware**, and **Maryland** in his reelection bid, but Jackson decisively won the electoral vote, making Adams a one-term President like his father. Like his father also, Adams left **Washington** for Massachusetts and private life. He was particularly depressed by his failure and wrote that he had "no plausible motive for wishing to live, when everything that I foresee and believe of futurity makes death desirable" (Lorant, 1951).

Nonetheless, in 1830 Adams rejoiced at being elected to Congress. His services in Congress well outweighed any of his failures as President. He flew into his role as congressman, taking strong positions against **slavery**. Adams presented no less than a dozen petitions to limit slavery in the District of Columbia, and he quickly became "the scourage of the South," defying not only the Southerners in Congress, but the President himself.

He found himself, once again, in the middle of the tariff issue, but he demonstrated that he had learned from his earlier failure by advocating a compromise tariff in 1833. The Adams Bill, shepherded through the legislature by Henry Clay, reduced many taxes while retaining the principle of protective legislation. Yet, it proved unsatisfactory to most Southern members.

In 1837, with both houses of Congress fighting over financial policy, Adams defiantly agitated on the slavery issue. He fought the **gag rule** limiting discussion of anti-slavery in Congress, and his demands to be heard on the question of slavery invariably produced an uproar. Still, he persisted, remonstrating against the admission of **Texas** into the Union, arguing for the prohibition of slavery in the territories, and defending the Africans seized aboard the *Amistad*. A growing number of **abolitionists** made him their hero, and he increasingly became preoccupied with little else. During a debate in 1847 Adams attempted to rise to speak but collapsed. He died at age eighty without regaining consciousness. **Related Entries**: *Amistad;* Clay, Henry; Jackson, Andrew.

SUGGESTED READING: Samuel Flagg Bemis, *John Quincy Adams and the Union* (1956); Stefan Lorant, ed., *The Presidency: A Pictorial History of Presidential Elections from Washington to Truman* (1951); Leonard L. Richards, *The Life and Times of Congressman John Quincy Adams* (1986); Jack Shepherd, *The Adams Chronicles: Four Generations of Greatness* (1975).

AFRICAN COLONIZATION: As early as 1816 several Southern states, **Virginia, Georgia, Maryland**, and **Tennessee** included, had asked the federal government to procure a site for colonization by freed blacks, and they had jointly petitioned the government for federal financial aid to offset the monetary loss involved in emancipating their slaves. In 1817 the American Colonization Society was formed to encourage **free blacks** to return to Africa. The society drew its initial support from all sections of the country and from both **slavery** and anti-slavery advocates.

Colonization societies outnumbered abolition societies in America right up to the opening of the war. Within two decades of its founding more than 140 branches of the American Colonization Society were formed in the Southern states, with the majority of chapters in Virginia, **Kentucky**, and Tennessee. In the North approximately 100 societies were formed—radical abolition seemingly stealing some of the colonialists' thunder—the majority established in the states of Ohio, New York, and Pennsylvania. Only in Massachusetts did immediate abolition have a greater following than colonization. Of all the states only Rhode Island and **South Carolina** had no colonization societies.

The Ohio Resolutions of 1824 recommended to the states that the federal government enact into law and provide financial support for a program by which all slaves born after enactment would be set free at the age of twenty-one with the provision that they agree to foreign colonization. Proponents of colonization estimated that slavery could be abolished by 1890. The plan lacked any indemnification to the slaveowners for their losses in terms of slave property, however. Although absolute values are impossible to ascertain, the total "property" value of slaves owned in the South has been estimated at $4 billion. Eight Northern states endorsed the plan, while the six Southern states, predictably, rejected it.

A minority of free blacks espoused great interest in their African homeland, yet a larger number were interested, not in Africa, but in other areas outside the United States. Canada, Central America, and Haiti were all mentioned as possible sites for black emigration. Several prominent free blacks, such as poet James M. Whitfield, the Rev. **Henry H. Garnet**, and Dr. Martin R. Delancy, called for an emphasis on black nationalism and militant black unity. It was feared that in the United States blacks could always expect to be crawling in the dust at the feet of their former oppressors.

Colonization was very popular politically. During the debates with **Stephen A. Douglas** in 1858, **Abraham Lincoln** had expressed support for colonization. In 1862, a year before the Emancipation Proclamation, he signed a bill appropriating $100,000 to encourage black colonization. **Related Entry**: Emancipation.

SUGGESTED READING: John W. Blassingame, *The Clarion Voice* (1976); David Brion Davis, *The Problem of Slavery in Western Culture* (1988); Joanne Pope Melish, *Disowning Slavery: Gradual Emancipation and Race in New England, 1780–1860* (1998).

AGRICULTURAL PRODUCTS: Although **cotton** was "King," the South produced a wide range of agricultural products. Corn was actually the most abundant crop, outstripping even cotton in quantity produced, but it was generally used for man and beast locally. Other items were grown in large enough quantities to allow for their export. These included rice, tobacco, **sugarcane**, indigo, bran, apples, molasses, wheat, and flour. **Livestock** provided lard, **bacon and pork**, ham, beef, leather, hides, wool, guano, eggs, and feathers. Beef was used only locally until the establishment of the western **railroads** of the post–Civil War era, and mutton had not tempted the tastes of the American public. The importance of any particular product in the export trade was closely allied to its ability to withstand shipping without spoilage. In the absence of refrigeration, meat, if not transported as live animals, had to be preserved. Salting and drying retarded the growth of bacteria, as did pickling, smoking, and sugar curing. Grains, vegetables, and fruits, if not for immediate consumption, had to be dried. **Related Entries**: Agriculture; Inventions; Plantation Economy.

SUGGESTED READING: Duncan Clinch Heyward, *Seed from Madagascar* (1937); F. L. Olmsted, *The Cotton Kingdom* (1861; 1996); Joseph C. Roberts, *The Story of Tobacco* (1949); Alice R. Huger Smith, *A Carolina Rice Plantation of the Fifties* (1936).

AGRICULTURE: In the antebellum period the most important crop in the South was **cotton**, yet in the colonial period it had been tobacco. Both were important cash crops. While tobacco remained an important product in **North Carolina** and **Kentucky** in the nineteenth century, the tobacco plantations of **Virginia** and **Maryland** were feeling the effects of depressed prices and depleted soils. The rice plantations of **South Carolina** and **Georgia** were still prosperous in the 1850s. Rice planters supplemented their incomes by growing indigo, which needed no work in the winter, when rice was most demanding of labor. Indigo was the basis for a highly valued blue dye. The **sugar** plantations of the delta country of **Louisiana** provided cash for an income-hungry **planter aristocracy**. The largest Southern crop (by quantity grown), in any case, was corn.

Nonetheless, cotton was the "King" of agricultural produce. Cotton production had originated in the tidewater region, but it quickly spread into the upcountry of South Carolina and Georgia and west into all the states that were to become the Confederacy. However, the lustrous, long-staple varieties could not be grown in all types of soil. Small farmers might raise an acre or two of low grade tobacco, several of grain, and possibly a few of cotton for sale. The staple food crops were Indian corn, sweet potatoes, and cowpeas in most places.

The vast majority of Southern farmers worked their own land and planned their lives around rural activities and seasonal chores. Family members usu-

The success of the plantation economy was dependent upon unpaid black labor, and financial success was vital to the continuation of the genteel Southern lifestyle. (From the authors' collection.)

ally cooperated in completing these chores, and this togetherness was thought to foster feelings of **kinship** and traditional family values. Fathers and mothers worked beside their children and grandchildren in an idyllic, if not a mechanically efficient, simplicity.

Small farmers rarely owned slaves but may have harbored a desire to accumulate enough money to buy one or two. The ownership of even a single slave raised one to a new social status. Nowhere was the equality between Southern whites so complete as in their ability to force Negroes to work; yet as the price of single slaves approached $2,000, the small farmers could no longer afford to buy them. Of the 10,000 plantations that came to rely on slave labor in the antebellum period, fewer than 10 percent had more than 100 slaves. It has been estimated that slaveowners represented as little as 6 percent of Southern whites. Half of these were small slaveholders who had fewer than five slaves and labored in the fields beside them.

The institution of **slavery** had been in a decline for some time before the war, particularly among the small tobacco planters who had worn out their soil. By mid-century cotton accounted for two-thirds of the exports of the country and had breathed new life into slavery by creating an unprecedented demand for agricultural laborers. Seventy-five percent of all cotton came from plantations, as did almost all of the rice, sugar, and tobacco. The success of the **plantation economy** depended on inexpensive black labor, and financial success was vital to the continuation of the genteel Southern life-style. Prosperous cotton planters wisely diversified their holdings into both rice and sugar, as had **Wade Hampton**, the richest man in the South on the eve of the Civil War, having plantations in South Carolina, **Mississippi**, and Louisiana. **Related Entries**: Agricultural Products; Cotton; Plantation Economy.

SUGGESTED READING: Joyce E. Chaplin, *An Anxious Pursuit: Agricultural Innovation and Modernity in the Lower South, 1730–1815* (1993); Paul R. Johnson, *Farm Inventions in the Making of America* (1976); John S. Otto, *The Southern Frontier, 1607–1860: The Agricultural Evolution of the Colonial and Antebellum South* (1989).

ALABAMA: Highlights of a description of the state taken from John Hayward's *Gazetteer of the United States* (1853) read as follows:

History and Early Settlement: Alabama was originally settled by French and Spanish immigrants. It was set off from **Georgia** in 1800 as a separate territory; which was again divided in 1817, the western portion forming the state of **Mississippi**. It was constituted as a state by act of Congress in March, 1819.

Surface and Soil: The face of the country exhibits much variety. In the northern quarter it is elevated and somewhat broken, but gradually improves in appearance and fertility as one proceeds southward where it settles into wide-spreading prairies and gently-swelling plains, profusely covered with grass and beautiful herbage. There are many large tracts which are remarkably productive. The most prominent crops are **cotton**, corn, wheat, and rice. Tobacco and **sugarcane** are also cultivated to some extent.

Rivers: Nearly every part of the state is amply watered by large streams admitting of extensive steamboat navigation. The most important rivers are the Tennessee, Chattahoochee, Alabama, and the Tombigbee. The bottom lands along the rivers, and the country lying in the neighborhood of Muscle Shoals, are usually considered unhealthy.

Education: The University of Alabama is located in Tuscaloosa and had 92 students in 1850 and 181 alumni. There are 30 public school libraries in the state holding 1000 volumes.

Internal Improvements: The state enjoys numerous facilities for intercommunication. Many miles of **railroads**, and several important canals, have already been constructed, and others are also contemplated.

Manufacture: Little attention has been given to the business of converting the principle [*sic*] staples of the state into fabrics for exportation. Nearly all the cotton produced is sent as raw material to markets beyond the state, and but a small portion of the population is engaged in the manufacture of other articles of domestic growth.

Indians: There are within the limits of Alabama several formidable tribes: Cherokees, Choctaws, Chickasaws, and Creeks. During the **War of 1812** the white settlers were much annoyed by the Indians, who were finally subdued by General **Andrew Jackson**.

Population: (1850) Northern Alabama—557,005 whites. Southern Alabama—214,666 whites. Slaves—342,892. Colored—2293. One of the chief causes of the unparalleled increase in the population along the Gulf Coast in the last forty years was the annexation of a part of **Florida** in 1812.

Related Entries: Geography; Plantation Economy.

SUGGESTED READING: Virginia Hamilton, *Alabama: A History* (1984); John Hayward, *Gazetteer of the United States* (1853); William Warren Rogers, *Alabama: A History of a Deep South State* (1994).

ALAMO (MISSION OF SAN ANTONIO DE BAJAR): In 1836 an army of Texans (Texicans) led by the former governor of **Tennessee, Sam Houston**, wrested all of the territory of **Texas** from the Mexican republic. While this army was being formed a small group of about 200 audacious Texans, under the leadership of William Travis, James Bowie, and **David "Davy" Crockett**, fortified and held the Alamo mission and its surrounding buildings in San Antonio for thirteen days against an overwhelming force of 3,000 Mexicans under General Antonio Lopez de Santa Anna. On the final day of the siege, Santa Anna's troops overran the defenders, killing all but a handful. The surviving men were executed. Three women, two white children, and a black boy were the only survivors.

The defense of the Alamo mission was foolhardy and doomed to failure. Nonetheless, almost 1,600 of Santa Anna's troops were killed at the Alamo, and the defense of the mission serves as one of the most glorious events in the short history of the Republic of Texas. The brutality of the siege's climax, taken together with the execution of more than 400 Texans at Goliad by Santa Anna shortly thereafter, created popular sympathy for Texas in the United States. Southerners (in fact all Americans) were quick to incorporate the defense of the Alamo into their own martial mythology—a circumstance that served as a factor in later disputes between the Southern states and the federal government. It was altogether fitting that Southerners felt as they did, as the majority of the Texans at the mission exulted in their own Southern heritage and ancestry. **Related Entries**: Houston, Samuel; Texas, Annexation of.

SUGGESTED READING: William C. Davis, *Three Roads to the Alamo: The Lives of David Crockett, James Bowie, and William Barret Travis* (1998); Olga W. Hall-Quest, *Shrine of Liberty: The Alamo* (1948); Lon Tinkle, *Thirteen Days of Glory: The Siege of the Alamo* (1958; 1996).

AMERICAN PARTY. *See* Nativists.

AMERICAN SYSTEM: In the years following the **War of 1812, Henry Clay** of **Kentucky** proceeded to develop his American System, a program characterized by an enhanced regard for nationalism. His proposals included an emphasis on **internal improvements at federal expense;** protective **tariffs;** a renewal of the national bank; a standing army, frigates for the navy,

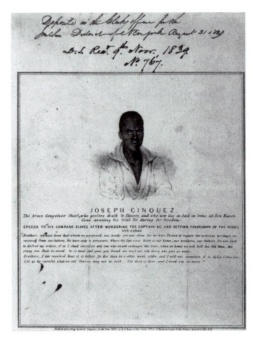

Cinque, leader of the Amistad Revolt. (Reproduced from the collections of the Library
of Congress.)

and federal control of the **militia;** and cooperation with other nations in
the Western Hemisphere. These proposals, with the conspicuous absence of
any change in the institution of **slavery**, served as the focus for some of the
most divisive issues in the antebellum period.

Although representing Kentucky, a border state with strong Southern
leanings, Henry Clay sought to cast its fortunes with the East rather than
with the South. His advocacy for internal improvements at the expense of
the national government were largely directed toward this end, and he was
instrumental in providing for the upkeep and extension of the Cumberland
Road into Kentucky. Nonetheless, he also proposed a series of **roads** and
canals to link Canada to **New Orleans**, but these plans were largely thwarted
by administrations unfriendly to the ideas. **Related Entries**: Clay, Henry;
Internal Improvements at Federal Expense.

SUGGESTED READING: Maurice G. Baxter, *Henry Clay and the American System* (1995); Clement Eaton, *Henry Clay and the Art of American Politics* (1957).

AMISTAD (**Supreme Court Decision**): The *Amistad* was a slave ship
belonging to Spanish owners that sailed from Havana in 1839 for another
Cuban port. The master of the ship had on board over fifty blacks, including
four children. All of these were so recently imported from Africa that most

spoke neither English nor any other European language. On the journey the blacks, under the leadership of a warrior named Cinque, overcame the crew and took control of the ship. In the process, they killed the captain and the ship's cook. With the coerced help of the surviving crew, they proceeded to sail north along the Atlantic coast of the United States.

Some months later, the vessel was found at anchor off the shore of Long Island, New York. A boarding party from the *USS Washington* commanded by Lt. Cmdr. T. R. Gedney, USN, took the *Amistad* into the port of New London, Connecticut, along with the blacks. Gedney brought a case in the U.S. District Court in New Haven for the salvage rights to the ship, which included the fair market value of the "slaves" on board.

John H. Hyde, an **abolition** sympathizer and the editor of the New London *Gazette*, wrote a story about the incident, making the blacks instant celebrities. The Anti-Slavery Society in Connecticut contacted Roger S. Baldwin, a New York attorney, to defend the rights of the Africans found aboard the *Amistad*. With financing arranged by **Louis Tappan**, the Committee of Friends of the Amistad Africans was formed. The abolitionists brought suit in the Connecticut state courts before Judge Andrew T. Judson, claiming the freedom of the Africans under existing U.S. law, as the United States had joined with Britain to prohibit the slave trade in 1808. Under several treaties between 1817 and 1830, the Spanish had also made the slave trade illegal.

The abolitionists' lawyers argued, and the district court agreed, that the blacks had the status of free men on the grounds that they were free-born Africans, not subjects of Spain or any other country. They were in fact of the Mendi tribe and had been kidnapped as free men from their homeland in Sierra Leone and illegally transported to a Spanish possession. They were therefore free under Spanish law as well. Since the treaties between the United States and Spain did not require that the Africans be returned to Spanish territory, the court ruled that they were at liberty to return to Africa if they wished.

Abolitionist forces were initially elated but quickly became alarmed when it was learned that President Martin Van Buren's administration in **Washington** was determined to overturn the decision so as not to offend the sensibilities of the South in the election of 1840. Even ex-President **John Quincy Adams**, now a congressman, weighed in on the side of the Africans. The case was appealed to the **Supreme Court**, where Justice Joseph Story delivered his opinion in 1841. The Court awarded Lt. Cmdr. Gedney the salvage rights to the ship and its cargo, but freed the Africans on the grounds that they had always been free men and had never become slaves under Spanish law. This was deft footwork if ever there was any. By declaring that the Africans were free by the laws of Spain, the Court was able to side-step any accusations of freeing slaves or setting precedents for the **emancipation** of American-born black slaves under U.S. law.

It had taken almost three years for the Africans on board the *Amistad* to

Riding was a passion for both Southern men and women. (From *Godey's Lady's Book,* 1858.)

regain their freedom. In the interim, they were housed in Westville, Connecticut, about two miles outside New Haven. Under the care of the abolitionists, many of the Africans learned to speak and write English, studied the Bible, and became "civilized Christian Men." One was later to serve as an English interpreter in an African mission in Sierra Leone, and one of the female children became a teacher. On November 27, 1841, with money raised for the purpose among interested British abolitionists, thirty-five of the surviving Africans were returned to their homeland, accompanied by five white missionaries and teachers. A Christian mission to Africa was established there and remained prosperous for many decades. It is interesting to note that little money was raised among American abolitionists for the return trip to Africa. **Related Entries**: Abolition; Supreme Court of the United States; Tappan, Arthur and Lewis.

SUGGESTED READING: Howard Jones, *Mutiny on the Amistad* (1987; 1997); David Pesci, *Amistad* (1998).

AMUSEMENTS AND DIVERSIONS: The isolation of the **plantation economy** made Southerners accustomed to a self-contained life. It is perhaps only natural, then, that their entertainments and amusements were self-generated. Those of lesser means and in the most rural areas found diversion in hunting, fishing, riding, shooting matches, and social gatherings at home, church, and county court. Yet, even as they amassed their wealth, the Southern gentry remained a working aristocracy and, like their less affluent neighbors, enjoyed activities that kept them outdoors. They did not participate in organized games in the modern sense. Spectator sports were basically limited to **horseracing** and cock fighting, and the majority of the animals were owned and bred by the spectators themselves. Indoors, pastimes were rooted in the Southerners' basic convivial nature and centered on such simple pleasures as congenial company surrounded by bounteous food and good drink.

Dancing was particularly well loved by Southerners. Music was often supplied by family members. Young women of wealth were commonly accomplished on the piano. Young men often possessed skill on the flute or violin. Many slaves were also talented musicians and were often asked to play for their master's amusement.

Equal to the Southern woman's passion for clothes was the Southern gentleman's passion for **gambling**. No deed or topic of conversation was too trivial to spawn a wager. Games of cards, dice, and table games that involved luck were extremely fashionable. Other popular games included cribbage, checkers, tangrams, and lotto. A forerunner of bingo, lotto was played with cards placed in three horizontal and nine vertical rows. Five numbers from one to ninety appeared on the cards, with the remaining spaces blank. Children's versions of the game were developed to teach spelling, multiplication, botany, and history.

Evenings were often spent **reading**. Oral presentation, with an articulate reader, often enhanced the literature and allowed the women, in particular, to do other chores such as sewing and embroidery. Reading aloud became an activity with many of the characteristics of **theater**. While instructional or improving literature might be encouraged, novels provided women with an almost pure escape from the isolation of plantation life.

Women engaged in a variety of needlework crafts including tatting, knitting, crocheting, and netting. Ladies' magazines carried a profusion of patterns for trims, fashion accessories, and small household items for these handicrafts. Patchwork quilts were another popular activity. Women worked on quilts alone for their families and in group quilting bees as community activities. The social standing of the quilter often dictated the pattern style, with rural women selecting more practical designs and urban or more affluent women favoring more complex and fashionable patterns. **Related Entries**: Gambling; Horseracing.

SUGGESTED READING: Dorothy Denneen Volo and James M. Volo, *Daily Life in Civil War America* (1998).

ANNEXATION OF TEXAS. *See* Texas, Annexation of.

ANTEBELLUM SOUTH: The antebellum South is normally considered to be the geographical region south of the **Mason-Dixon Line** and east of

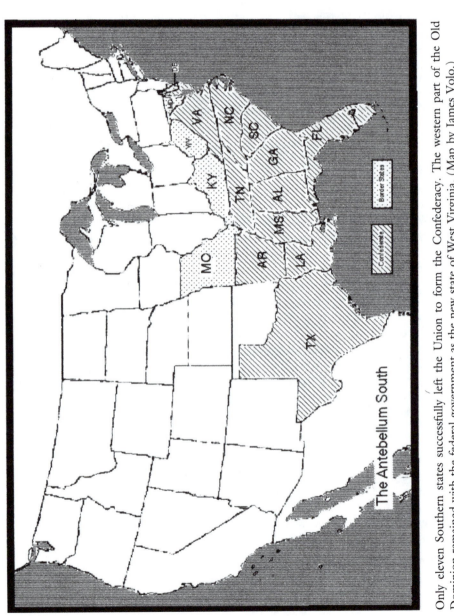

The Antebellum South

Only eleven Southern states successfully left the Union to form the Confederacy. The western part of the Old Dominion remained with the federal government as the new state of West Virginia. (Map by James Volo.)

the 98th meridian. It is specifically identified with the eleven states that were to become the Confederates States of America in 1861 and generally includes the border states of **Missouri, Kentucky, Maryland**, and **Delaware**. The adjective "antebellum" is used to describe a period of about fifty years before the outbreak of the Civil War—approximately from 1810 to 1860. The term is somewhat inappropriate, as two wars were fought by the United States during those years: the **War of 1812** and the **Mexican War of 1846**. Nonetheless, the period is socially and politically a continuum leading directly to the Civil War. A study limited to the period between the wars—1848 through 1860—would be altogether too narrow to explain those characteristics of the South that led to its **secession** from the Union.

During the 1810–1860 period the South became increasingly aware of the widening gap between its unique cultural and economic lifestyle and that of the North. Persistent disputes over the issues of **states' rights** and **slavery** hardened Southern attitudes toward the North and caused Southern moderates to abandon compromise. As Southern traditions and values increasingly came under attack by Northern radicals, the South clung to the past for validation. A "Southern consciousness" emerged during the antebellum period which drew its strength from the ideals of medieval chivalry and aristocracy. If the antebellum period did nothing else, it at least developed in Southerners a sense of group identity. **Related Entries**: Confederate Government; Kinship; Plantation Economy; Planter Aristocracy.

SUGGESTED READING: William W. Freehling, *Prelude to Civil War: The Nullification Controversy in South Carolina, 1816–1836* (1966); Drew Gilpin Faust, *The Creation of Confederate Nationalism: Ideology and Identity in the Civil War South* (1988); James R. Kennedy and Walter D. Kennedy, *The South Was Right* (1995).

ANTI-MASONIC PARTY: The anti-Masonic movement of the 1820s exhibited a substantial degree of anti-aristocratic sentiment. Freemasons were accused of being, and in many cases were, wealthy and prominent men holding substantial positions in government and society even though they came from outside the circle of America's first families. The anti-Masonic movement saw in the Fraternal Order of Freemasons a conspiracy of dangerous persons holding high Masonic office and placing the good of the order above the needs of the country. The total secrecy that cloaked the order added a sense of collusion to their activities.

In 1826 a man named William Morgan was abducted and probably murdered near Niagara, New York. The episode was an odd one, but it led almost immediately to the establishment of the first third party in American political history, the Anti-Masonic Party. Morgan, an apostate Freemason, had threatened to write a tell-all book exposing the secrets of the Masons. Morgan's disappearance at the hands of a gang of Masons, and the subsequent publication of an anti-Masonic book by his friend David Miller, led to a fierce wave of anti-Masonic sentiment in western New York that spread to Vermont and all of New England.

In the late colonial period prominent Americans like George Washington, Henry Lee, James Otis, John Hancock, and John Adams had met in Masonic chapters whose rituals had been carried over from their British predecessors. Although Freemasonry was popular among the upper classes, it had about it a taint of heresy and preferment for members of the order when applied to local government. Freemasons were known to be pledged to aid their fellows, yet the dedication of so many highly placed members of society to the order was an anomaly in a largely Christian country such as the United States.

The Anti-Masonic Party was a single-issue organization, and its adherents were united only in their hatred of the Masons. The movement was largely Northern in character, with many of its members abandoning the order. This put them at odds with the many Southerners among the **planter aristocracy** who remained dedicated Freemasons. Historian Page Smith (*The Nation Comes of Age*, Vol. 5, 1981) suggests that the appeal of the order for Southerners was one of "associational activity" which served to counteract the ongoing disintegration of traditional American life.

The founding of the Anti-Masonic Party had profound effects on American politics. In the space of four years the Anti-Masonic Party, the first viable third party in the United States, became a considerable political power. The party served as a vehicle for aggressive young politicians who chose to show that they were no longer willing to tolerate the "politics as usual" attitude of the established parties. In 1831, at the first political nominating convention ever held, William Wirt was chosen as a candidate for President of the United States. He received a substantial 8 percent of the popular vote. Thereafter, third parties were essentially reactionary: the Masons had given rise to the Anti-Masons, the Catholics to the **Nativists**, and the slaveowners to the **Republicans. Related Entries**: Nativists; Suffrage.

SUGGESTED READING: John Quincy Adams, *Letters from the Honorable John Quincy Adams to Edward Livingston, Grand High Priest of the General Grand Royal Arch Chapter of the United States* (1834); William L. Stone, *Letters on Masonry and Anti-Masonry, Addressed to the Honorable John Quincy Adams* (1832); William P. Vaughn, *The Anti-Masonic Party in the United States, 1826–1843* (1983).

ARCHITECTURE: While the South developed no distinctive style of architecture, it was very successful in adapting existing modes from Europe, and even from the North, to its own needs and inclinations.

From colonial times, upland Southern homes continued Anglo-Saxon traditions. Buildings can be found that show Jacobean, Tudor, and Stuart influences. It was, however, the Georgian style that really took hold during colonial times and reigned until the Greek Revival style came into favor

Bellevue Plantation in Tennessee typifies the Southern plantation house. Its grand white columns support a two-story porch, which provides perpetual shade and comfortable space for outdoor living. (Photo by James Volo.)

during the 1830s. Even then, early Greek Revival houses often bear traces of a lingering Georgian influence.

Yet the mention of the **antebellum South** invariably brings to mind the image of stately porticoed mansions, balconies, and ballrooms. The grand, white-columned Greek Revival plantation house has become so symbolic of the antebellum South that many people think it was developed there. Actually, the earliest example of note of Greek Revival styling was Latrobe's Bank of Pennsylvania, built in Philadelphia in 1798. The style then began to spread across the country, ironically taking hold in the South more slowly at first, and penetrating the Deep South at the very last. Greek Revival, however, so came to be the embodiment of the paternalistic, chivalric, and aristocratic ideals of the South that it remained an integral part of the conservative Southern culture in a time when the industrialized North moved forward. As the gap between Northern and Southern beliefs widened, the Greek temple form of architecture symbolized stability and authority in a time when the lifestyle and rights of the South were under attack. It was a physical manifestation of the ideal of Greek democracy.

Regions in the lower South had ties to France and to Spain. A blend of these two influences was adapted to the subtropical climate of the lower Mississippi and **Louisiana**. Houses were constructed high off the ground, away from dampness and potential flooding. Walls were thick to keep out the heat, and long, sloping roofs extending over two-story porches provided perpetual shade and a comfortable space for outdoor living. High-ceilinged rooms with full-length windows allowed for the circulation of the cooled porch air and gave the rooms a sense of dignity and scale unlike those found in any other region. Rounded colonnades extended from ground to roof, providing a classical dignity. The central building was frequently flanked by two pavilions. Often external staircases divided and curved gracefully to the center of the house. Dormer windows, which added light to the attic, were also common.

Inside the Southern plantation home, there was frequently a large center hall with grand rooms to the side allowing for good air circulation and ventilation. Regularity of design was carried from the main house to the outbuildings that made up the entire plantation, creating a sense of symmetry and pleasant arrangement. A typical domestic complex included a detached kitchen about the size of a single-room house, a dairy for the cool storage of milk products, a smokehouse to preserve meats, a laundry, and sometimes an icehouse, schoolroom, or storehouse. Slaves and servants were often quartered in these work buildings or, in larger operations, provided with separate housing. Northern travelers compared the resulting scene to small villages.

Not all white residents of the South lived in plantation manors. The vernacular architecture of the Upland South was characterized by the log cabin, constructed of horizontal courses notched together at the corners. This technology was brought to the area with the migration of Scotch-Irish and Germans who came from central Pennsylvania in the early nineteenth century.

Many cabins of the white yeoman farmer varied little in construction from those of slaves. What set them apart were the unique additions and porches that personalized these homes in a way the uniformity of slave housing would not permit. The porches of these cabins were used as extended workrooms of the house and to that end were generally furnished with tables and some kind of seating. One popular style of cabin was the dogtrot, which could be described as two two-room cabins joined together by a central breezeway onto which each of the rooms opened.

Wood was the characteristic building material in the Lowland South due to the abundance of timber. Post buildings assembled with basic mortise and tenon joints or notch joints were versatile enough to be used for outbuildings and farmhouses alike. Exterior walls were usually shingled or sided with planks. Interior walls might be finished in lath and plaster. Wood framing, requiring the use of pit-saws or water-powered sawmills, was generally reserved for large homes. These building techniques changed little before the Civil War. **Related Entry**: Slave Dwellings.

SUGGESTED READING: Wayne Andrews, *Pride of the South: A Social History of Southern Architecture* (1979); D. Clayton James, *Antebellum Natchez* (1993); Clay Lancaster, *Antebellum Architecture in Kentucky* (1991); Mills Lane, *Architecture of the Old South* (1987); Lisa C. Mullins, ed., *Early Architecture of the South* (1987).

ARKANSAS: Highlights of a description of the state taken from John Hayward's *Gazetteer of the United States* (1853) read as follows:

History and Early Settlement: Originally within the limits of **Louisiana**, it was set off with **Missouri** under the name, Missouri Territory, soon after the purchase of the former by the United States. In 1819, Missouri was divided and the southern portion became the Territory of Arkansas. It was elevated to the rank of an independent state in 1836.

Surface and Soil: As a whole the state cannot be considered as a region of great fertility, some three fourths of its surface being unproductive. The staple products are **cotton** and Indian corn. [C]onsiderable quantities of wheat, oats, sweet potatoes and tobacco are also raised. Immense plains afford facilities for the growth of cattle, and the forests and prairies abound with buffalo, deer elk, wild turkeys, geese, quails & c. Indigenous fruits such as grapes and plums, are found in profusion. The peach is cultivated with great success.

Education: Although large provision for the support of public **education** has been made, the subject has occupied little public attention. There are comparatively few common schools and only some eight or ten academies or high schools. There are no colleges.

Rivers: There is scarcely a spot that has not some navigable watercourse within a distance of 100 miles.

Internal Improvements: Little interest has been manifested on this subject.

Manufacture: Manufacturing has amounted to nothing beyond the fabrication of articles for household use and consumption.

Minerals: Salt is abundant, being found upon the surface of several large prairies to a depth of four to six inches and in many remarkable springs.

Indians: Many tribes have their abodes still within the state, most of which are the Cherokees, Choctaws, Osages, Quapas, Camanches, & c.

Population: Between 1810 and 1820 the population increased from 1,000 to 15,000. In 1830, it doubled and in 1840 had risen to nearly 100,000, one fifth of whom were slaves. In 1850 it was 209,639.

Other: Slaves are entitled by law to trial by jury and in capital cases no differences on account of color are made in the imposition of penalties.

Related Entry: Geography.

SUGGESTED READING: Harry S. Ashmore, *Arkansas: A History* (1984); John Hayward, *Gazetteer of the United States* (1853).

ARTISTS. *See* Painters.

ATLANTIC SLAVE TRADE: Between 1701 and 1808 no fewer than 2 million Africans were imported into the North American continent as slaves. They were brought in by slavers working the triangular route—from Europe with trade goods, to the west coast of Africa for slaves, and to the American slave markets for **sugar** and valuable **raw materials**. The identity of the slavers is a largely unexplored aspect of the slave trade, but it is known that

THE AFRICANS OF THE SLAVE BARK "WILDFIRE."—[FROM OUR OWN CORRESPONDENT.]

THE SLAVE DECK OF THE BARK "WILDFIRE," BROUGHT INTO KEY WEST ON APRIL 30, 1860.—[From a Daguerreotype.]

Africans were taken from their homes and kept
under the most cruel and crowded conditions
across the Atlantic. (From *Harper's Weekly*, 1860.
Reproduced from the collections of the Library of
Congress.)

the British, Spanish, Portuguese, and Americans were most heavily involved
before the trade was banned in 1808. It is estimated that between 13 and
33 percent of the slaves loaded aboard slave ships died during the transatlantic leg of the voyage, with the lower number finding favor among recent
researchers. Although the records are incomplete on both sides of the Atlantic, the total of slaves sold in America seems to be about 13 percent lower
than that purchased in Africa.

The majority of the blacks imported before the first decade of the nineteenth century were members of about one dozen largely agricultural tribes
from northwest Africa. Slave purchasers preferred slaves that came to their
plantations with a tradition of farming practices rather than those with a
hunting or warrior background. Approximately 59 percent of the Africans
brought to America came from West Africa, while the remainder were
Bantu-speaking peoples of the central portion of the continent. As slaves
were brought to the Atlantic for sale, more is known about the coastal point
of departure of these people than of their ethnic or tribal origin. Slaves were
imported from a number of coastal regions: Senegambia, Sierra Leone, the

Windward Coast, the Gold Coast, the Bight of Benin, the Bight of Biafra, Angola, Mozambique, and Madagascar.

In 1805 Denmark abolished the slave trade, and in 1808 the United States and Great Britain agreed to end the Atlantic trade, by force if necessary. The other European nations agreed to some form of curtailment in the next few years. The Portuguese and Spanish continued to legally import African slaves into Brazil and Spanish America for several decades. The United States, Britain, and France kept naval squadrons on patrol near the West African coast and in American waters to intercept slavers. Those Africans who were rescued were returned to the coast of Africa, but rarely to their point of origin (Sierra Leone being the most frequent point of return).

Nonetheless, historians disagree about the number of slaves imported into the United States between 1808 and 1861. Certainly some slaves were imported, as the anti-slave trade legislation was very weak, and continuously enforced only by the Royal Navy as a matter of foreign policy. However, the admittedly sporadic enforcement of the law by the United States at sea does not automatically translate into an increased importation of slaves.

Estimates of total illegal importation of slaves ranging from 250,000 to 1 million individuals during the half century before the Civil War were widely believed and repeated for many years. Recent scholarship, however, suggests that even the lower estimate may be high. It appears that historians have paid too great attention to the number of slaving vessels built in the United States during the antebellum period, presuming that they were outfitted to circumvent the law. It seems more likely that these vessels were used in the Cuban or Brazilian slave trade. Indeed, even if all the slavers built by 1850 had brought Africans to the United States, they could not have imported the numbers that have been suggested. Moreover, **abolitionists** would certainly have made criticism of continued importation an important part of their agenda. They did not. This suggests that only moderate numbers of Africans were being imported in contravention of the law. **Related Entry**: Value of Slaves.

SUGGESTED READING: Philip D. Curtin, *The Atlantic Slave Trade: A Census* (1969); Hugh Thomas, *The Slave Trade: The Story of the Atlantic Slave Trade, 1440–1870* (1997).

BACON AND PORK: Razorback hogs, running free in the brush and foraging for themselves, provided even the poorest Southern families with nourishing, if stringy, meat and had done so since colonial times. Nonetheless, a sizable and more determined effort at pork production was initiated by Southern farmers in the antebellum period. Prior to the introduction of **railroads**, long legs were a desirable breeding factor in these hogs, as they were expected to walk to market. With the advent of rail shipping, however, breeders began to focus on tastier meats and fatter hogs.

Bacon was a common foodstuff used in Southern home cooking. Bacon was made from the sides or flanks of the hog, kept in a slab, soaked in brine, and smoked in a building known as a smokehouse designed for the purpose. Fruit woods and hardwoods such as apple and hickory lent bacon their distinctive flavors. This operation cured the meat and retarded the growth of bacteria so that bacon could be stored in a cool, dry location for long periods of time. Slabs of bacon wrapped in cloth sacks were hung in a cool, dry cellar or outbuilding. Thick slices could be cut from a single slab for several days with no noticeable deterioration of the remainder.

Fresh pork, sugar- and honey-cured hams, and sausage made from the less desirable cuts of pork were also keenly desired by the Southern palate. Pork was chosen for these processes because it kept well when so treated. Other meats did not fare so well. Pork products also proved acceptable to the needs of the export market as they resisted spoilage during transportation. **Related Entries**: Agricultural Products; Food.

SUGGESTED READING: James Trager, *The Food Chronology* (1995); Waverly Root and Richard de Rouchemont, *Eating in America* (1976); Dorothy Denneen Volo and James M. Volo, *Daily Life in Civil War America* (1998).

BANK OF THE UNITED STATES: Through more than two dozen branches and agencies, the Second Bank of the United States, or National

Bank, ruled the commerce and industry of the young nation. By expanding or contracting credits, the Bank could virtually control the money supply of the country. Only the independent banks of New England, which were well financed and well managed, could expect to act with any degree of autonomy.

The original Bank of the United States, established in 1791, had not been rechartered in 1811, but in 1816 it was reestablished as a means to lift the country from the financial chaos surrounding the **War of 1812**. The new institution's charter favored a revival of Alexander Hamilton's ideal of concentrating the affairs of the people of the United States in the hands of a few talented or well-born men. There were twenty-five directors of the National Bank, seven appointed by the President of the United States and the remainder by outside stockholders.

Initially capitalized with $35 million, of which the government subscribed $7 million, the Bank was designated as the sole repository of federal funds. No interest was paid on these funds. The secretary of the treasury could authorize the member branches to issue currency as long as the notes were redeemable in **specie** and signed by the president of the institution. These notes were actually drafts drawn on the parent bank and endorsed "to the bearer." Nonetheless, the government honored them in payment for public obligations, and they circulated as money. The National Bank simplified the operations of the Treasury and proved a good investment for both the government and the stockholders.

The Bank's directors generally avoided politics, and initially their policies were not widely mentioned as an issue. However, in the depression of 1819, the Bank had foreclosed on more than 50,000 acres of farmland in **Kentucky** and Ohio, creating popular resentment against it in the South and West. **Andrew Jackson** had opposed the Bank in 1817 on the grounds that it was unconstitutional, yet his political ambitions had temporarily overruled his outspoken antipathy for it for almost a decade. In 1826 a large body of anti-Bank politicians from Kentucky and **Alabama** became Jackson's supporters, taking their hatred of the monopolistic Bank with them. During the campaign of 1827–1828 Jackson returned to his earlier position and began speaking against the Bank. Ultimately, his tone became very hostile, and Jackson added to the charges of unconstitutionality an objection to the great power wielded by the directors, calling them a danger to liberty. By the presidential election of 1832 Jackson's refusal to recharter the Bank had become the primary political issue between himself and his major opponent, **Henry Clay**.

Jackson showed his understanding of the public mind when he simplified this complex and impersonal issue into one sentence: "Shall the rights of the common man be respected or shall the rich rule the country again?" His crushing defeat of Clay was widely seen as a mandate to dismantle the Bank. Jackson's attempt to kill it proved a rallying point for moneyed interests, manufacturers, and merchants who gathered together in the new **Whig Party**. The financial management of the National Bank under Nicholas

Biddle was brought into question in 1836, and the Bank's charter was not renewed. Nonetheless, it continued its existence until 1841, and then failed, its whole capital being lost. **Related Entries**: Clay, Henry; Jackson, Andrew.

SUGGESTED READING: Jonathan R.T. Hughes, *American Economic History* (1998); Robert V. Remini, *Andrew Jackson and the Bank War* (1967).

BANKING INSTITUTIONS: In the antebellum period banking was constantly under attack. During the administration of **Andrew Jackson** the financial management of the National Bank (**Bank of the United States**) under Nicholas Biddle came into question, and the Bank's charter was not renewed. When the Bank failed in the 1840s its whole capital was lost. Certainly the elimination of the National Bank hampered the future growth of central banking in the United States for decades.

The **specie** controversy of 1837 brought on an economic **panic**. A large number of private banks in the West and South were not able to weather the requirements of specie payments and went into liquidation in the 1830s. Nonetheless, others, especially in New England, gradually resumed business. This resilience came, in large part, from an extraordinary increase of banking capital during the period. In 1830 there were 329 banks and branches in the United States with a capital of $145 million; in 1840, despite the Panic of 1837, there were 901 banks and branches with $358 million in capital. Although the banking capital had more than doubled, the number of institutions actually reached its peak in 1837 and fell through 1846.

By 1850 the number of banks and branches had contracted by 30 percent, with almost 200 institutions going out of business due to financial failure. Yet the banking failures of this period were largely sectional in nature, with Northern institutions weathering the bad economic times. However, banks in **Mississippi, Alabama**, Illinois, and parts of other Western states lost almost their entire capital. In 1852 there were 349 banks in New England, 363 institutions in the Middle States, 95 in the South, 83 in the Southwest, and 80 in the Northwest (see table).

Moreover, the availability of banking capital in proportion to population ran from a high of almost $29 per person in New England to as little as $2.27 in the Northwest. The Southern states of **Virginia, North Carolina, South Carolina**, and **Georgia** had $10.30 per person, and those states that would form the rest of the Confederacy in 1861 a mere $6.49 per head. It can be seen that the limited capital available to Southerners made them dependent on the good will and good credit of **cotton** and **sugar** buyers, and victims of a cash-starved **plantation economy. Related Entries**: Bank of the United States; Jackson, Andrew; Plantation Economy.

SUGGESTED READING: Richard B. Du Boff, *Accumulation and Power: An Economic History of the United States* (1988); Matthew St. Clair Clarke, *Legislative*

A Summary of Banking Institutions in the U.S. in 1852

New England States

Maine	37
New Hampshire	28
Vermont	31
Massachusetts	137
Rhode Island	69
Connecticut	47
Total	349

Middle States

New York	244
New Jersey	26
Pennsylvania	54
Delaware	9
Maryland	26
District of Columbia	4
Total	363

Southern States

Virginia	38
North Carolina	22
South Carolina	14
Georgia	21
Total	95

Southwestern States

Alabama	2
Louisiana	25
Tennessee	23
Kentucky	26
Missouri	6
Mississippi	1
Total	83

Western States

Ohio	58
Indiana	14
Michigan	6
Wisconsin	1
Iowa	1
Total	80

Source: John Hayward, *A Gazetteer of the United States* (1853).

and Documentary History of the Bank of the United States, Including the Original Bank of North America (1967).

BARKESDALE, WILLIAM (1821–1863): politician, secessionist, and Confederate officer. William Barkesdale of **Mississippi** was a true **Fire-eater** and had been a vociferous and effective proponent of **secession** for many years prior to the outbreak of the Civil War. Few of the prominent Fire-eaters went on to serve in battle, choosing rather to remain in politics; however, he was a notable exception. The Confederate War Office made him a brigadier general, and he proved one of the most effective political commanders in the war. The tenacity and opposition posed by his Mississippi regiments to the river crossing of federal troops during the Battle of Fredericksburg won him great renown. During the Battle of Gettysburg, Barkesdale was killed as he fought in The Peach Orchard. **Related Entries**: Fire-eaters; Secession.

SUGGESTED READING: Emory M. Thomas, *The Confederacy as a Revolutionary Experience* (1991); Dorothy Denneen Volo and James M. Volo, *Daily Life in Civil War America* (1998).

BELL, JOHN (1797–1869): congressman, senator, secretary of war, and presidential candidate (1860). John Bell was a prominent attorney and politician who served for fourteen years in the U.S. Congress. Bell was originally a follower of **Andrew Jackson**, but he split with the Jacksonians to become a leader of the **Whig Party**. He was partly responsible for the successful election of the ill-fated **William Henry Harrison** in 1840, but he could not abide Harrison's successor, **John Tyler**. Bell, as secretary of war, resigned from Tyler's cabinet in 1841 and remained out of active politics for almost six years.

Thereafter, he was elected to the U.S. Senate, where he was recognized as a pro-Southern member. As a large slaveowner he had no love for **abolitionists**, but he supported moderation on the question of **slavery** and its extension in the territories. His vote against the admission of Kansas in 1857 under the pro-slavery Lecompton Constitution was sharply criticized by the South but was praised by the North for its moderation. In this regard Bell's position was illustrative of the disruption of the entire Whig Party after 1854. A serious misreading of the tempter of the voters had taken place, and many Whigs were turning to the moderate wing of the new **Republican Party**.

With the death of the Whigs, Bell cast around for some new alliance. In 1860 a group composed mostly of old Whigs and **Nativists**, called the Constitutional Union Party, nominated Bell for the presidency. The fine speaker Edward Everett was his running mate. They ran on a platform of upholding the constitutional legitimacy of slavery, the Union, and the rule of law, but slavery and the fear of disunion remained the pivotal questions. When it became obvious to the candidates, based on the results of two gubernatorial elections in Pennsylvania and Indiana, that Lincoln was going to win, Bell proclaimed a new dedication to **secession**. He captured the states of **Kentucky, Tennessee**, and **Virginia** and received only 13 percent of the popular vote. Once it became obvious that Lincoln was going to use force to preserve the Union, Bell advised Tennessee to ally itself with the Confederacy in order to fight the Northern invasion of Southern soil. He survived the war as a broken man with no remaining political aspirations. **Related Entry**: Lincoln, Abraham.

SUGGESTED READING: Joseph H. Parks, *John Bell of Tennessee* (1950).

BENJAMIN, JUDAH P. (1811–1884): lawyer, senator, cabinet member in the **Confederate government**. Very little is known about Judah P. Benjamin. His biographer, Pierce Butler, has noted that "he did not leave behind him half a dozen pieces of paper." Benjamin rose from being a nearly penniless immigrant to become a successful lawyer and planter, a senator representing **Louisiana**, and the occupant of three cabinet posts in the Confederate government. Finally, having abandoned America for Britain after the Civil War, he rose to lead the London bar and served as Queen's Counsel.

Although his ancestral roots were Jewish, Benjamin was neither orthodox nor observant of his religion. He married outside of his religion and seems to have become a **Catholic**. Nonetheless, he was able to overcome the ethnic and religious prejudice of a Gentile world to become one of the most capable members of the Confederate cabinet and a respected and loyal friend of President **Jefferson Davis**.

Benjamin invested the profits of his successful law practice in a **sugar** plantation at Bellechasse, a few miles from **New Orleans**. While a senator, he worked valiantly for the sugar planters of his chosen state, and strove to spread American influence throughout the Western Hemisphere. His view of **manifest destiny** extended to Mexico, Central America, and the Caribbean.

In the antebellum period Benjamin championed the most extreme Southern positions on **states' rights, slavery**, and **secession**. In his final speech before the Senate, he rose to the peak of his political power and personal prestige. "You may carry desolation into our peaceful land," he told the Senate. "You may set our cities in flames . . . but you can never subjugate us." In 1860 Benjamin joined Jefferson Davis in **Washington** to speed disunion, and he called for the Southern states to seize all federal property within their domain.

With his radicalism as a recommendation, Judah Benjamin was an obvious choice for the Confederate cabinet. Nonetheless, he was offered only the uninspiring post of attorney general. However, he quickly proved to be one of the ablest men in a generally ineffective group, and Davis was forced to find other employment for him. Briefly as secretary of war, and then as secretary of state for four years, Benjamin proved to be the brains of the Confederacy, working unremittingly both day and night. Although he was hounded from the War Department because of the quick loss of New Orleans, the Southern public was generally content with his performance as secretary of state.

During the war years Benjamin became personally committed to Jefferson Davis—a devotion that seems to have been reciprocated. He did all in his power to prevent any shortcoming in the governance of the nation and to rectify any disaster that befell it on the battlefield. At a most critical period in the life of the Southern nation Judah Benjamin proved a statesman of intellect, diplomacy, and genius. **Related Entry**: Confederate Government.

SUGGESTED READING: Pierce Butler, *Judah P. Benjamin* (1907); Eli N. Evans, *Judah P. Benjamin: The Jewish Confederate* (1989); Burton J. Hendrick, *Statesmen of the Lost Cause* (1939).

BENTON, THOMAS HART (1782–1858): editor, politician, and senator. Although born and educated in **North Carolina**, Thomas Hart Benton is most closely associated with Western interests. In 1809 he was elected a state senator in **Tennessee**, to which he had moved as a young man. As a state senator, Benton expressed a great interest in safeguarding land tenure for settlers and securing the rights of slaves in capital cases. In 1815 Benton abandoned his excellent prospects in Tennessee to become the editor of the *Missouri Enquirer* in St. Louis.

Missouri took to Benton and elected him to the U.S. Senate in 1820. Although Benton was a moderate in most things, he was a radical advocate when it came to the interests of the West. He championed the extension of the telegraph and the **railroad;** a reduction in the cash price of government lands; the grant of free homesteads in the West; a national highway to New Mexico; and the free navigation of the **Mississippi River**. In fostering these issues he anticipated the growth of the American West by many decades. Benton's lifelong political interest was in sound money, and he was a leader in the war on the **Bank of the United States**.

While in 1820 Benton had opposed all restriction on **slavery** in Missouri, a decade later, viewing slavery as a hindrance to the settlement of the West, he had come to favor gradual **emancipation**. Yet he scorned **abolitionists**. Whatever support he gave slavery was based entirely on his desire to maintain the Union. In the **nullification** crisis he stood against the offensive **tariffs**, but wished to see the issue more clearly resolved than it was.

Benton's attitude toward the **annexation of Texas** was somewhat puzzling. He felt that the issue should have been resolved decades earlier. In 1846, although he supported the effort, he viewed the war as an unnecessary affront to the Mexican government. As a proponent of the acquisition of the **Oregon Territory**, Benton nevertheless had no fondness for the "Fifty-four Forty or Fight" slogan of most expansionists, including his son-in-law, **John C. Fremont**, and he was willing to accept a compromise settlement at the 49th parallel rather than create tension with Great Britain. His overriding wish seems to have been that of maintaining peace.

Unfortunately Benton destroyed the good will of his constituents in espousing a moderate position in the debates over the **Compromise of 1850**. Disregarding the personal risk of his position—during the debate Senator Henry S. Foote of Missouri threatened Benton with a pistol in the Senate chamber—he maintained his opposition to the agreement because it made too many concessions to the **secessionists**. His constituents turned him out of his Senate office in 1850, but he was able to secure a seat in the House of Representatives. In 1856 he failed to gain the governorship of his state, and he supported **James Buchanan** rather than Fremont for the presidency. His death from cancer in 1858 spared him having to witness the violence that resulted from a disunion he had worked so hard to avoid. **Related Entries**: Compromise of 1850; Fremont, John C.

SUGGESTED READING: Theodore Roosevelt, *Thomas Hart Benton* (1886; 1984); William M. Miegs, *The Life of Thomas Hart Benton* (1904).

BIRNEY, JAMES G. (1792–1857): lawyer, **abolitionist**, and twice candidate for President of the United States. In the history of the anti-slavery movement James G. Birney occupies an unusual position. Although he was an active anti-slavery leader, he owned and sold slaves. Birney was born in Danville, **Kentucky**, graduated from the College of New Jersey at Princeton, and read law in Philadelphia. Birney's Irish family had advocated a free state constitution for Kentucky and had favored the **emancipation** of slaves. In 1816, however, his marriage into Kentucky society brought him some slaves, and two years later he moved with his wife and his slaves to a plantation in **Alabama**. Here he was elected to the first General Assembly of Alabama, but his opposition to **Andrew Jackson** made him unpopular, and he was not reelected.

Although successful at law, Birney found that his plantation brought him financial embarrassment. He was forced, reluctantly, to sell the property and his slaves. This last task was very difficult for Birney, who had an "almost insuperable repugnance to selling slaves," making it necessary in his future campaigns to justify his disposal of the few that he had possessed.

A visit to the Northeast in 1829 convinced Birney of the superiority of **free labor**. In 1832 he joined the American Colonization Society and traveled throughout the South for some time as a lecturer for that organization. On several occasions his meetings were interrupted by unfriendly mobs, and he was exposed to personal danger a number of times. Ironically, the response to his lectures convinced him that colonization would simply cause slaveowners to sell their slaves south, thereby increasing the interstate slave trade. Birney therefore came to the position that abolition must be secured by any constitutional means. He had slowly passed from slaveowner to gradualist to abolitionist.

As a presidential candidate, Birney received a mere 7,000 votes in 1840, but in 1844 he amassed more than 62,000. He garnered no electoral votes in either campaign, however. Horace Greeley reported in the *New York Times* that Birney had sought the Democratic nomination for 1844, but this seems unlikely. In 1845 Birney suffered a severe fall from his horse, resulting in partial paralysis. Now an invalid, he closed his public career and devoted himself to an examination of legal cases involving **slavery**. At mid-century he produced an *Address to the Free Colored People* of the United States advising them to move to Liberia in the face of **Fugitive Slave Laws** strengthened by the **Compromise of 1850**. Birney thereafter voted **Republican**. **Related Entry**: Abolition.

SUGGESTED READING: William Birney, *James G. Birney and His Times* (1890); Betty L. Fadeland, *James Gillespie Birney: Slaveholder to Abolitionist* (1969).

BLACK ANTI-SLAVERY ACTIVISTS: From 1841 to 1860, **Frederick Douglass** was the most prominent black **abolitionist**, "filled by his escape to freedom with noble thoughts and thrilling reflections" (*Narrative of the Life of an American Slave, Written by Himself,* 1845). Yet, among black activists there were several equally eminent success stories. These included Charles Lenox Remond, the first black anti-slavery activist to address the Massachusetts legislature; Sarah Parker Remond (his sister), a lecturer and practicing physician; **Williams Wells Brown**, the nation's first black playwright; Frances E.W. Harper, a prominent poet; Henry Bibb, a former slave and editor of a Canadian newspaper; John Mercer Langston, a free black lawyer from Ohio; Dr. Martin R. Delancy, a Harvard-trained black physician; and **Rev. Henry Highland Garnet**, the first black man to speak in the U.S. House of Representatives.

Several black newspapers were printed in the antebellum period that vied for prominence in anti-slavery circles with **William Lloyd Garrison**'s *Liberator*. The *Impartial Citizen* was printed in Syracuse, New York, beginning in 1848; the *Colored Man's Journal* was popular in the 1850s in New York City; San Francisco had the *Mirror of the Times* in the 1850s; and the *Alienated American* was published briefly in Cleveland, Ohio. One of the earliest papers was *Freedom's Journal*, established in 1827 by John B. Russwurm, the first Negro to received a degree from an American college.

One of the most popular black papers of the 1850s was *Frederick Douglass' Paper*, later called *Douglass' Monthly Magazine*. Unlike the other black papers, which were locally popular and short-lived, Douglass' work was circulated through eighteen states and two foreign countries. It had more than 4,000 subscribers and survived for more than thirteen years. Not only did these papers showcase the ability of blacks to write and edit, but they also hinted at the large number of blacks among their subscribers who could read. **Related Entry**: Douglass, Frederick; Garnet, Henry Highland; Tubman, Harriet.

SUGGESTED READING: John H. Bracey, Jr., ed., *Blacks in the Abolitionist Movement* (1971); Editors of Time-Life Books, *Perseverance, African Americans: Voices of Triumph* (1993); Shirley J. Yee, *Black Women Abolitionists: A Study in Activism, 1828–1860* (1992).

BLACK CODES: The British colony of **Virginia** was the first to compile Black Codes into a single statute in 1680, thus becoming a model for the other colonies. Specifics varied from colony to colony, but all were essentially similar. The basic foundation of the codes defined slaves as property, not people, and as such they were subject to sale at any time. Only **Louisiana** forbade the sale of slave children under the age of ten from their mothers. Slaves were forbidden to strike a white person at any time, even in self-defense. They could not visit or be visited by whites or **free blacks**, and unauthorized religious services were forbidden. Other prohibitions abridged the ability of slaves to sue, to testify in court against whites, to marry the mate of their choice, to learn to read or to write, and to leave home without written permission.

Not all of the restrictions laid down in the codes were strictly observed by the slavemasters. The literacy and wedlock bans were often ignored by lenient slaveholders. Yet during times when the **fear of slave revolts** increased, the codes were more likely to be strictly enforced. The codes made demands upon masters under penalty of fine or imprisonment, and the community demanded that slaveowners adhere to them in times of social unrest.

Notwithstanding the harsh realities of living under such strictures, the Black Codes also provided some protection to the slaves from particularly unethical masters. Slaveowners were required by law in most states to provide adequate **food**, clothing, and shelter for their workers. Slaves could not be worked on Sundays except in emergency situations. Moreover, support for the elderly and infirm was also usually mandated. Enforcement of this group of requirements was difficult at best, since slaves could not testify against their masters, and in any case few Southern courts would have ruled against a white master if such a suit could be brought by a slave. **Related Entry**: Federal Laws Governing Slavery.

SUGGESTED READING: Helen Tunnicliff Catterall and James J. Hayden, *Judicial Cases Concerning American Slavery and the Negro* (1968); William B. Scott, *Criminal Proceedings in Colonial Virginia* (1984); Kenneth M. Stampp, *The Peculiar Institution* (1956).

BLACK HAWK WAR OF 1832: During **Andrew Jackson**'s two terms as President, ninety-four Indian treaties were signed. Some of them were legitimate, and the tribes agreed to various amounts of compensation to give up their lands and move west. Other agreements were questionable, with agents misrepresenting the intent or meaning of the treaties or with tribes selling rights to lands that they did not possess. Some tribes went peacefully to the lands west of the **Mississippi River**, but others dared to fight against the troops of the United States.

In 1832 a few hundred Sauk and Fox Indians under the leadership of Black Hawk attempted to return to their ancestral lands in Illinois and Wisconsin. They were pursued by a force of regulars and **militia**, and defeated at the Battle of Bad Axe in August 1832. During the war a postmaster by the name of **Abraham Lincoln**, who had been elected captain of his local militia unit, helped to chase Black Hawk and his Indians back into the Wisconsin wilderness. This was to be Lincoln's only military experience, yet when the Civil War began, he consistently interfered with his generals in the field. **Related Entry**: Indian Removal.

SUGGESTED READING: Cecil D. Eby, *That Disgraceful Affair: The Black Hawk War* (1973).

BLACK REPUBLICANISM: The **Republican Party** was from its inception the party of **abolition**. It came into being in response to the passage of the **Kansas-Nebraska Act of 1854** with the purpose of ending race-based **slavery**. The radicals who joined the Republican Party did so largely because of the slavery issue. They generally were absorbed by the concept of the immediate abolition of slavery and the granting of full civil and social rights to blacks. They saw no compromise position in these matters and were willing to destroy the party, if such was necessary, to attain their goals. If the Union did not stand for liberty, it was also expendable.

Nonetheless, moderates made up the majority of those who wished to end slavery. There was a wider variety in their beliefs than among the radicals. They emphasized that slavery was a territorial issue, and were willing to leave slavery long established in areas of the South alone. Many believed in gradual **emancipation** and foreign colonization efforts by black freemen. They did not foresee blacks living in equality in a white society, but rather a free black community somehow physically separated from it.

In 1854 **Abraham Lincoln** gave the most radical speech of his entire life—his famous "House Divided" speech, calling for the country to become all free or all slave. Never again did he express such radical views. His words were widely interpreted as a declaration of war on Southern institutions. By failing to center himself within the anti-slavery spectrum, Lincoln essentially drove the moderates in his party toward the radical position. Certainly this is the light in which the South viewed the Republicans and Lincoln during the 1860 election. Southern apologists invented the concept of Black Republicanism as a counterpoint to the anti-slavery charges of a "slave power conspiracy." They saw possible Republican success in the 1860 presidential election as "an alarming indication" of the ripening schemes of abolitionists to "plunder" and "outrage" the Southern way of life with their growing fanaticism. The Southerners were so successful in this propaganda campaign that they forced Lincoln to disclaim any hopes for "social and political equality of the White and Black races" and to disavow any plan to make "voters or jurors of Negroes, [or] of qualifying them to hold office, [or] to intermarry with white people." The abolitionists exacerbated the seriousness of the situation by taunting the South with threats of black retribution. **Related Entries**: Lincoln, Abraham; Republican Party.

SUGGESTED READING: Richard M. Abbott, *The Republican Party and the South, 1855–1877: The First Southern Strategy* (1986).

BLACK SLAVEOWNERS: On the eve of the Civil War there were blacks in the South, themselves free, who owned slaves, used slave labor in their businesses, and condoned **slavery**. Black slavemasters—especially shippers, tradesmen, and artisans—owned many of their fellow Negro workers, an arrangement often entered into in lieu of an apprenticeship agreement. Incredibly, many of these free Negro tradesmen and artisans invested heavily in slaves. This was especially true of free Negroes who owned shipping concerns where slaves served as shipwrights, sailmakers, and stevedores. It has been documented that in 1830 more than 2,000 black slaves were owned by free Negro masters in **New Orleans** alone.

The campaign to emancipate these slaves raised interesting questions about the wartime sympathies of free Negroes who owned slaves. Black masters, who sometimes also owned the members of their families, had their rights recognized by law in most states. They could therefore stabilize their work force and provide a modicum of legal protection for their loved ones. These men were highly educated, cultured, and sophisticated in their outlook, and they were decidedly against any form of gradual **emancipation** without indemnification. At the beginning of the war many of them were openly Confederate in their outlook. **Related Entry**: Free Blacks.

SUGGESTED READING: John W. Blassingame, *Black New Orleans* (1973); Ervin L. Jordan, Jr., *Black Confederates and Afro-Yankees in Civil War Virginia* (1995).

BLEEDING KANSAS: In 1853 the House of Representatives decided to designate a large portion of the unorganized land in the Midwest into the Territory of Nebraska. With the support of **Stephen A. Douglas** and the **Democrats**, the **Kansas-Nebraska Act of 1854** revised the division of this territory into two parts, repealing the provisions of the **Missouri Compromise** regarding the **extension of slavery into the territories** and replacing them with the doctrine of **popular sovereignty**, which allowed the settlers of Nebraska and Kansas, respectively, to decide the question of **slavery** by majority vote. As it was anticipated that Nebraska would be a free area, anti-slavery forces, thinly disguised as the Massachusetts Emigrant Aid Society and similar organizations, sent hundreds of anti-slavery settlers to Kansas in an attempt to influence the outcome of the vote. Hundreds of thousands of dollars were raised for the Kansas crusade, and firearms, including new breechloading Sharps rifles, were sent to the territory disguised as crates of bibles and religious tracts. Concurrently, pro-slavery forces spilled over the border from **Missouri** with the same goal in mind. The Society of Missourians for Mutual Protection pledged to keep the **abolitionists** out of Kansas.

By 1855 popular sovereignty had made Kansas a literal battleground of opposing forces. Armed companies of hastily organized **militia** and small quasi-military gangs intimidated settlers, overturned wagons, scattered stock, and smashed opposition presses. In 1856 President Franklin Pierce recognized a legislature for Kansas Territory organized by the pro-slavery forces led by the chief justice of the territorial court, Samuel Dexter Lecompte. These pro-slavery delegates drew up a constitution protecting slavery known as the Lecompton Constitution.

Abolition forces in Topeka, Kansas, elected a free state legislature with its own constitution. Pierce declared the abolitionist aid societies the cause of all the trouble and replaced the territorial governor with a pro-slavery man, Wilson Shannon. Judge Lecompte declared the Topeka government an unlawful organization even though it was headed by his predecessor, the original territorial governor, Andrew Reeder.

Meanwhile, **James Buchanan** succeeded Pierce as President. Before long, Missouri "border ruffians" had crossed into Kansas to attack and burn the free state stronghold of Lawrence. Radical abolitionist **John Brown**, with his four sons, reacted quickly by killing five pro-slavery men at Pottawatomie Creek. Murder, lawlessness, and violence filled the territory.

Ultimately, federal troops were sent into Kansas Territory to restore peace, and the free state forces were in the ascendancy by late 1858. Although Buchanan declared for the Lecompton Constitution, the voters soundly rejected it, and Kansas became a free territory. In 1861 a free Kansas was admitted to the Union as the thirty-fourth state. **Related Entries**: Brown, John; Kansas-Nebraska Act of 1854.

SUGGESTED READING: George W. Brown, *False Claims of Kansas Historians Truthfully Corrected* (1902); James C. Malin, *John Brown and the Legend of Fifty-Six* (1942); James Redpath, *The Public Life of Captain John Brown* (1860); Marc Simmons, *Murder on the Santa Fe Trail* (1987).

BRECKINRIDGE, JOHN C. (1821–1875): soldier, statesman, Vice President, and presidential candidate. John C. Breckinridge was an enigma.

In 1846 the call for volunteers to fight in the **Mexican War** failed to stir any enthusiasm in Breckinridge, who was practicing law in **Kentucky**. Nonetheless, he was called upon in 1847 to give a memorial speech at a great military funeral for a score of Kentuckians killed in action at Buena Vista. His speech, given before 20,000 people, brought him recognition as an orator and a commission in the 3rd Kentucky Volunteers, whom he led to Mexico. It is unclear how Breckinridge talked himself into the army, but he arrived in Mexico only after the campaign had reached its climax.

Breckinridge entered politics at a time when **slavery** was a hotly contested issue, and as a Southern **Democrat** he opposed **abolition**. In 1851 he won a congressional seat from which he established his leadership in the party. He stood publicly as a Unionist and against the intervention of Congress on the subject of the **extension of slavery into the territories**. In the 1856 presidential election, he was chosen as the running mate for **James Buchanan**. As Vice President, Breckinridge was noted for his poise and decisiveness.

As the **secession** hysteria surged toward disunion, Breckinridge pleaded for the preservation of the nation. He initially had his name removed from the Democratic nomination for the presidency in 1860, but when the Southern faction disrupted the convention and selected him as their candidate, he accepted.

Abraham Lincoln probably would not have won the presidency in 1860 had the election not become a four-way race. The Democratic Party split between pro-slavery Breckinridge and **Stephen A. Douglas**, a moderate. The fourth candidate was **John Bell** of **Tennessee**.

Lincoln won the election with just under 40 percent of the popular vote and 59 percent of the electoral votes. He carried eighteen states, yet, with the exception of coastal California, not one of them was below the **Mason-Dixon Line**. Significantly, Douglas, who beat both Breckinridge and Bell with 30 percent of the popular vote, received a mere 4 percent of the electoral votes. Breckinridge, with 18 percent of the popular vote, carried every state that would come to be in the Confederacy except **Mississippi** and **Virginia**. The former Vice President also carried **Maryland** and **Delaware**. Bell received 13 percent of the popular vote.

Although he lost the presidential election, Breckinridge had been elected as a senator from Kentucky, a state that initially declared its neutrality in the secession crisis. As a senator he opposed Lincoln's war policy, refusing to vote for men or money to wage war against the South. With the firing on Fort Sumter, Breckinridge declared that the Union no longer existed and that Kentucky was once again a sovereign entity. In September 1861, Kentucky abandoned its neutrality, having been invaded by armies from both sides. The federal military immediately began to arrest suspected Confederate sympathizers, and Breckinridge fled to the Southern army. On December 2, 1861, the Senate declared him a traitor and formally expelled him.

Breckinridge was given the rank of brigadier general in the Confederate

Army. Although he had no military training other than that gained in the Mexican War, he seems to have been an able commander. He took part in several battles, seeing particular activity in the battles of Murfeesboro, Chickamauga, and the final threat to **Washington, DC**, led by General Jubal Early. Thereafter, he was recalled to **Richmond** to serve as secretary of war. At war's end he escaped the country and remained in Canada until 1869. Thereafter, he returned to Kentucky to practice law, foregoing any further political activity. **Related Entries**: Democratic Party; Lincoln, Abraham; Secession.

SUGGESTED READING: William C. Davis, *Breckinridge: Statesman, Soldier, Symbol* (1992); Frank H. Heck, *Proud Kentuckian: John C. Breckinridge, 1821–1875* (1976).

BROAD CONSTRUCTION OF THE CONSTITUTION. *See* Constitutional Interpretation.

BROOKS, PRESTON S. (1819–1857): congressman. Although he gave only two or three notable speeches in Congress, Preston S. Brooks remains one of the best known Southern representatives from the antebellum period because of his attack on Senator Charles Sumner of Massachusetts in the Senate Chamber.

Brooks was educated at South Carolina College, graduating in 1839. Thereafter, he practiced law for a short time and served for two terms in the state legislature. During the **Mexican War**, Brooks served as captain in the Palmetto Regiment with little distinction other than that of being an admirable drill instructor and disciplinarian. After the war, he turned to **agriculture**.

In 1852 he was elected to the U.S. Congress and in 1854 was reelected for a second term. Brooks was incensed by a vitriolic speech given during the 1856 debates in which Sumner denounced Brooks' uncle, Senator A. P. Butler of **South Carolina**. Two days later, Brooks, who later claimed that he had given Sumner time to reconsider his rhetoric and apologize, found Sumner at his desk in the Senate Chamber and struck him repeatedly over the head with a cane. Sumner was left insensible on the floor and never completely recovered from his injuries.

Northerners fiercely denounced Brooks' actions. He was brought before the House for expulsion, but survived on a party line vote. Nonetheless, he resigned after a speech in his own justification and was reelected by his constituents. Southerners applauded Brooks. Communities and state legislatures passed resolutions in his favor. He was presented with a number of symbolic gold-headed canes. Brooks lived for less than a year after his attack. **Related Entry**: Sumner, Charles.

SUGGESTED READING: Preston S. Brooks, *A Speech of the Honorable Preston*

S. Brooks: Delivered at Columbia South Carolina, August 29, 1856 (1856); David Herbert Donald, *Charles Sumner* (1996).

BROWN, JOHN (1800–1859): radical **abolitionist** chiefly known for his activities in Kansas in the 1850s and for his abortive raid on Harper's Ferry, **Virginia**, in 1859. John Brown was well over fifty years of age before the idea of freeing slaves came to dominate his thinking, even though his father, Owen Brown, had been an agent on the **Underground Railroad**. John Brown was born in Torrington, Connecticut. He received a scanty education, but grew up well spoken and well versed in the Bible. Although he dabbled in land speculation and the raising of sheep, he seems to have considered himself a tanner by trade. In 1820 he married his first wife, who bore him seven children. After her death in 1831, Brown married Mary Day, a robust girl of sixteen who was twenty years his junior and bore him thirteen more children.

Beginning in 1825 Brown moved ten times before coming to notoriety in Kansas Territory. His most interesting move was to North Elba, New York, a newly founded community of **free blacks** set up with money donated by Gerrit Smith. Nonetheless, it became painfully clear that Brown could not provide for his large family there. After two years he moved to Ohio, where he organized the League of Gileadites among the escaped slaves and freemen to help them protect themselves from "slave catchers" and anti-black whites.

In 1855 he and five of his sons went to Kansas to help win the territory for the anti-slavery forces. Arriving in a wagon filled with guns and ammunition, Brown was immediately elected the captain of the local **militia** on the Osawatomie Creek. Anti-slavery forces, thinly disguised as the Massachusetts Emigrant Aid Society, sent hundreds of anti-slavery settlers to Kansas with thousands of dollars for the **free state** crusade. Firearms were sent to the territory disguised as crates of bibles and religious tracts. James Redpath, Brown's first biographer, observed that the anti-slavery men in Kansas "trusted alone for victory to their Sharpe's rifles [*sic*] and the God of battles."

Concurrently, pro-slavery forces spilled over the border from **Missouri** with different goals in mind. The Society of Missourians for Mutual Protection pledged to keep the abolitionists out of Kansas. In 1856 the Missouri "border ruffians" crossed into Kansas to attack and burn the free state stronghold of Lawrence. Brown, with four of his sons, reacted quickly by killing five pro-slavery men at Pottawatomie Creek. Brown probably killed no one with his own hand, but he directed the executions, asserting that he was acting as an instrument of God. In revenge, pro-slavery men destroyed the Osawatomie settlements.

Thereafter, murder, lawlessness, and violence filled the territory, and pro-slavery settlers became terrorized at the mere mention of John Brown's name. One of his sons, Frederick, was killed in the ensuing guerrilla warfare.

Ultimately federal troops were sent into Kansas Territory to restore peace, and Brown left the state for some time to gain further financial support for the fight for freedom. Those who saw him during this period observed that he had become obsessed with slavery and could not converse about anything else. When he returned to Kansas in 1857, he was disappointed by the comparative calm he found.

It was at this point that Brown formulated his plan for liberating all Southern slaves by force. As his funds were almost exhausted, he turned to Gerrit Smith and a group of abolitionists in Massachusetts for support. That they were aware of his plans cannot be doubted, and they encouraged him with promises of support, thereby taking part in a treasonable conspiracy. Coincidentally, the governor of Missouri issued warrants for Brown's arrest for a murder that he committed there in 1858. Yet when Brown made some public speeches in Ohio and New York, no one attempted to arrest him.

In the summer of 1859, Brown decided to carry out his attack on the federal arsenal at Harper's Ferry, Virginia. He hoped not only to raise a slave revolt in the immediate region, but to arm the slaves from the arsenal. The attack was a tragic affair. The first man killed by Brown was a free black baggage master at the railway station. Brown quickly gained possession of the poorly guarded armory. However, the anticipated rally of black slaves did not materialize. The local militia, several of whom were killed and wounded, blocked Brown's only route of escape, and he barricaded himself with his followers in the local firehouse. During the following night a company of United States Marines under the command of Colonel **Robert E. Lee** arrived. At dawn, with Brown's refusal to surrender, the Marines assaulted and carried the building. About two dozen men were with Brown. All were taken, with about ten killed or mortally wounded, including two of Brown's sons. Brown received a minor wound.

Brown was jailed in nearby Charlestown, Virginia. One week later he was indicted for "Treason to the Commonwealth [of Virginia] and conspiring with slaves to commit treason and murder." His trial was very quick, but it was held with exemplary fairness and decorum. John Brown, to no one's surprise, was found guilty and scheduled to be hanged on December 2, 1859. Yet prior to his execution seventeen affidavits were submitted to the governor of Virginia, **Henry A. Wise**, by friends and neighbors, declaring, in so many words, that John Brown was insane and had come from a family where insanity was rampant. Although this was probably true at the time of the raid, Governor Wise refused clemency.

In his last public speech before his execution, John Brown said, "Now, if it is deemed necessary that I should forfeit my life for the furtherance of the ends of justice, and mingle my blood further with the blood of my children, and with the blood of millions in this slave country whose rights are disregarded by wicked, cruel, and unjust enactments—I submit: so let it be done."

Many among the abolitionists endorsed John Brown's attempt to foment an armed slave rebellion in Virginia, while Southerners, like **Mary Chesnut**, castigated the abolitionists for "setting John Brown to come down here and cut our throats in Christ's name." **Abraham Lincoln** probably anticipated the verdict of history when he said of John Brown: "An enthusiast broods over the oppression of a people till he fancies himself commissioned by Heaven to liberate them. He ventures the attempt, which ends in little more than his own execution." **Related Entries**: Abolition; Bleeding Kansas; Fear of Slave Revolts.

SUGGESTED READING: Elijah Avery, *The Capture and Execution of John Brown: A Tale of Martyrdom* (1906); James Redpath, *The Public Life of Captain John Brown* (1860); John Avery Scott, *John Brown of Harper's Ferry* (1988).

BROWN, WILLIAM WELLS (1812–1885): slave, author, and physician. Born in **Kentucky**, William Wells Brown was taken by his owner to **Missouri** in 1816, where he remained a slave under three successive owners. On the first day of 1834 Brown slipped away from his master's river steamer, which was docked at Cincinnati. Fearing discovery every step of the way, he made his way to Cleveland and freedom.

Brown worked in the print shop of Elijah Lovejoy (who was to become the first **abolitionist** martyr), returned to steamboating, and eventually turned to the study of medicine. His intellectual development and his literary and oratorical skills, however, made him a stellar candidate for the anti-slavery lecture circuit, where he distinguished himself. Later, he was equally eloquent for the **temperance** movement.

In 1847 his *Narrative of William Wells Brown, Fugitive Slave, Written by Himself* was published. His book was one of the most widely circulated and acclaimed of all the many **slave narratives** that appeared in this period. This work was followed by *The Anti-Slavery Harp: A Collection of Songs for Anti-slavery Meetings* (1848). Brown's play *The Escape: or, A Leap for Freedom* is acknowledged as the first by a black American writer. His most noteworthy literary effort may well be *Clotel* (1853), the first novel published by a black American.

There are four editions, and several spellings, of *Clotel*. It was first published while Brown was living in London, where he sought safety from the fugitive slave provisions of the **Compromise of 1850**. While each of the four versions differs in details, they essentially tell the same melodramatic tale of a beautiful female slave. Even though it contains a scathing rebuke of Southern racial attitudes, the novel endorses integration rather than separatism. Brown's writing was diverse; he also produced a collection of letters from his European travels and four notable works on black history.

Ultimately, Brown returned to America and was able to practice as a physician. He spent most of the last quarter century of his life practicing medicine in Boston. **Related Entries**: Black Anti-Slavery Activists; Literary Development.

SUGGESTED READING: Jay B. Hubbel, *The South in American Literature* (1954); Richard A. Long, *Black Writers and the American Civil War* (1988).

BUCHANAN, JAMES (1791–1868): secretary of state and fifteenth President of the United States (1857–1861). At the close of the **nullification** crisis of the 1830s James Buchanan had incorrectly predicted the death of **secession** as a political doctrine. Ironically, Buchanan was to be the final President of the antebellum period. His legacy as the fifteenth President of the United States was to follow, rather than to lead, the country to disunion and the brink of civil war.

In the 1856 presidential election the **Democrats** feared incurring the wrath of the Northern voters by running **Stephen A. Douglas**, whose **Kansas-Nebraska Act** seemingly sabotaged the political compromises that had characterized the previous decades of American politics. The party therefore decided to run James Buchanan against the popular **Republican** candidate, **John C. Fremont**. Buchanan, who was handsome, wealthy, and financially well-heeled, had dominated Pennsylvania politics for almost two decades and had served as secretary of state in the administration of **James K. Polk**. Moreover, he had been a minister to England during the Kansas-Nebraska debates and was therefore untainted by the bill either way. As a pro-slavery partisan, he could count on the solid support of the South.

The entry into the race of a weak **Nativist** candidate (former President **Millard Fillmore**) and the lack of a coordinated Republican effort behind Fremont ensured Buchanan's victory in the election. Having received only a minority of the popular votes—although he handily won the electoral college—Buchanan entered office knowing that he was unpopular with most of America at a time when the nation was threatening to split along sectional lines. Almost immediately his tenure in office was marked by portentous events. The **Dred Scott** decision was handed down a mere two days after his inauguration. This decision effectively reversed the **Missouri Compromise**, disabled the doctrine of **popular sovereignty**, and extended the reach of the **Fugitive Slave Law** in a single stroke. The South rejoiced at the news, but the opposite reaction in the North was equally intense. Although imbued with the considerable powers of the presidency, Buchanan was seemingly unwilling or powerless to control the excesses of the radicals in either the North or the South. His own cabinet was rife with similar sectional dissension.

Buchanan may have had an honest desire for peace; but he had positioned himself as a pro-Southern unionist and as such was amenable to making concessions to the South to maintain at least the semblance of national unity. Initially, he sent a new pro-slavery governor to the turmoil-torn Kansas Territory and supported the pro-slavery Lecompton Constitution for the proposed new state. In 1857 the national economy suffered a severe **panic**, and in the 1858 midterm elections Buchanan's followers suffered utter defeat in the North. Nevertheless, pro-Southern forces thought his policies too harsh, while Northerners found him weak and pusillanimous.

At the same time, Stephen A. Douglas, supported by the Northern wing of the Democratic Party, was winning fame in a series of debates with **Abraham Lincoln**, almost ensuring his nomination as the Democratic presidential candidate in 1860. Buchanan's supporters in the Southern wing of the party—notably **Jefferson Davis** and **William Yancey**—demanded a clear statement from Douglas repudiating popular sovereignty and pledging protection for **slavery** in the territories. Absent these assurances, and in light of **John Brown**'s raid at Harper's Ferry, **Virginia**, the Southern Democrats broke from the party and nominated Buchanan's Vice President, **John C. Breckinridge**, for President. Buchanan willingly threw Breckinridge his support, ostensibly not realizing that the introduction of a third party candidate (and later a fourth, **John Bell** of the Constitutional Union Party) would guarantee victory for the Republican aspirant, Abraham Lincoln.

On the afternoon of December 20, 1860, the South Carolina Convention passed an Ordinance of Secession, largely in response to the election of Lincoln as President. Five additional Southern states quickly followed **South Carolina**'s example: **Mississippi, Florida, Alabama, Georgia**, and **Louisiana**. In February, **Texas** joined its sister states. Concurrent with the decision to dissolve the Union, the seven seceding states began to occupy federal installations, administrative buildings, and fortifications. Buchanan's timidity ran true to course at this point, and he failed to take decisive steps either to forestall these activities or to amend them, choosing instead to leave the matter in the hands of his successor, who would not be installed in office until the spring.

Buchanan's vacillating policies during his administration had done little but engender both social and political turmoil; and as time passed and disunion became more likely, he seemed more and more willing to vacate the office of President. Buchanan thereafter was crowded from the stage of history by the momentous events of the Civil War. **Related Entries**: Democratic Party; Douglas, Stephen A.; Lincoln, Abraham; Popular Sovereignty; Secession.

SUGGESTED READING: Frederick Moore Binder, *James Buchanan and the American Empire* (1994); Philip S. Klein, *President James Buchanan: A Biography* (1995).

BUYING AND SELLING SLAVES: The importation of slaves into the United States was outlawed in 1808, but the ownership and selling of slaves within the confines of the country was continued. **Virginia** became a major supplier of slaves to other areas of the South. In 1860 the estimated value of all the slave property in the Old Dominion alone was more than $300 million. Virginians found that they could make more profit by selling slaves

This period poster chillingly illustrates the status of Negro slaves, listing them for sale amid ox teams, foxhounds and sundry farm goods. (From the authors' collection.)

than by using them as laborers. In the three decades before the war, more than a quarter million slaves were "sold south" from Virginia alone. Historians disagree as to whether slaves were purposely bred for sale. Nonetheless, the **abolitionists** taunted Virginia for selling children in the slave shambles.

Slave markets and slave brokers existed throughout the South. Many planters professed an aversion to breaking up slave families because the practice increased unrest among the blacks; but the extravagant lifestyle of the planters, coupled with the regularity of foreclosures on mortgages and demands for the repayment of loans, caused most slaves to see the auction block at least once in their lives. Slaves could be bought or sold, rented out, gambled away, or left in a will as an inheritance to almost anyone.

The law did not provide for the continuity of the slave family as a unit. Investigators in occupied **New Orleans** during the federal occupation recorded more than 500 marriages that had taken place while the couples involved had been slaves. Of these, fewer than 100 had remained unbroken. While some unions were able to last from 20 to 40 years, the average length of a slave marriage was a mere 5.6 years. Records indicate that 70% of these marriages ended due to death or personal choice, and 30 percent of the slave unions were broken up by the planters. **Related Entry**: Value of Slaves.

SUGGESTED READING: David Brion Davis, *Slavery in the Colonial Chesapeake* (1994); Ervin L. Jordan, Jr., *Black Confederates and Afro-Yankees in Civil War Virginia* (1995); Kenneth M. Stampp, *The Peculiar Institution* (1956); Jenny B. Wahl, *The Bondsman's Burden: An Economic Analysis of the Common Law of Southern Slavery* (1998).

CALHOUN, JOHN C. (1782–1850): statesman, politician, Vice President of the United States. Honored in 1957 as one of the five greatest senators of all time, John C. Calhoun figured prominently in national politics throughout the antebellum period. His formulation of the theory of state **nullification** was the first to systematize the doctrine, and he made important contributions to the world of political philosophy in his writing.

Calhoun was educated at Yale, graduating in 1804. He then studied law in Connecticut and **South Carolina**. His early republican attitudes were doubtless influenced by his close contact with Federalists in Connecticut. In 1807 he began a successful law practice in **Charleston, South Carolina**. He was first elected to state office in 1808, and moved on to Congress in 1810. He married Floride Bouneau, a widow, in 1811, and added her sizable fortune and property to his own.

As a member of the Twelfth Congress, Calhoun was one of the two dozen most outspoken proponents of war with Britain who made up the **War Hawks**. As long as the **War of 1812** continued Calhoun fought for more troops, more money, better supplies, and any measure he thought conducive to military success. In 1816, with the war over, he continued to press for an improved navy, steam frigates, and an adequate standing army. He also saw the need for a great system of permanent **roads** for national defense, a form of internal taxation (which would not be at the mercy of shrinking maritime activity in time of war, as were **tariffs**), and a national bank.

Before the end of his third term in Congress, Calhoun had become the most elegant speaker in the House. Yet this talent seems to have come from a deliberate effort. President **James Monroe** appointed him secretary of state in 1816. He held this office for more than seven years, and, once again, his concern for military matters was conspicuous. Calhoun was often at odds with other members of the cabinet.

Mourners stand by the tomb of John C. Calhoun in St. Philips churchyard in Charleston, South Carolina. (From *Harper's Weekly* IV, no. 204, November 24, 1860.)

There is no doubt that Calhoun wished to be President. In 1824 and 1828, however, he was elected Vice President, first under **John Quincy Adams** and then under **Andrew Jackson**. Calhoun's tenure with Adams was uneventful, as both men were generally in accord. His dealings with Jackson, however, proved quarrelsome. A dramatic rift in the cabinet was caused by Floride Calhoun when she refused to receive **Peggy Eaton**, the wife of the secretary of war. Jackson's intransigence in defending the Eatons led to disaffection among many of the members of his cabinet. The President's relationship with his Vice President steadily deteriorated during this period until it became an irreparable and public breach.

Moreover, Calhoun was dedicated to the destruction of the secretary of state, **Martin Van Buren**, whom Jackson viewed as a possible running mate for 1832 and whom Calhoun viewed as a rival. Jackson took up his Vice President's challenge. Having driven Calhoun's friends from the cabinet, Jackson was able to shut him out of the **Democratic** vice presidential nomination.

A serious confrontation between the men began with the tariff crisis of 1828 and the issue of state nullification which arose from it in South Carolina. Initially Calhoun, who was a late convert to the concept, wanted simply to preserve the Union and intended to use the threat of nullification to force the federal government to reduce the high tariff rates. But in 1830, the **Webster-Hayne debate** in Congress helped to make nullification a national issue, and the proposition of an equally unacceptable protective tariff in 1832 further aggravated the controversy.

As President Jackson was in favor of the 1832 tariff and had made it clear that he considered nullification a grievous political sin, Calhoun, finding that he could not support the administration, resigned as Vice President to take the Senate seat of **Robert Y. Hayne** representing South Carolina. Thereafter, Calhoun actively crusaded for the assembly of a nullification convention in the name of **states' rights**. In August 1832, Calhoun published a letter to South Carolina governor **James A. Hamilton** containing the final embodiment of the nullification doctrine. Nonetheless, Calhoun hastened to Charleston in 1833 to urge the acceptance of a compromise to end the crisis.

These events increased Calhoun's prestige in the South. He came to be regarded as the main source of Southern political inspiration, providing organization to the defense of the Southern way of life. Among the strategies Calhoun initiated were a portrayal of **slavery** as a positive good; the suppression of anti-slavery agitation; the promotion and expansion of Southern industry; the **annexation of Texas;** the formation of an alliance with the Western states; and the promotion of a single Southern voice in government.

Calhoun served briefly as secretary of state under **John Tyler**. In the spring of 1844, he concluded a treaty with the Republic of Texas to enter the Union. Although Calhoun thought the moment propitious, Northern forces in Congress were successful in portraying the annexation as a slaveowners' plot. The treaty was soundly rejected, with the votes breaking down along sectional lines. Calhoun was not offered a place in the cabinet of **James K. Polk**.

The final years of his life were given over to recording and fine-tuning his theories of states' rights and sovereignty. His writings influenced many European nationalists of the nineteenth century. In his writing Calhoun foresaw the abolition of slavery, the resistance of the South, the enfranchisement of blacks, and the subordination of the South to the North. His prophecies were virtually a picture of the nation during the period of reconstruction following the Civil War. Calhoun's health failed during this period. His final public speech was read to the Senate in 1850 while its author sat voiceless in a chair nearby. He lingered for less than a month thereafter. His final words were said to be "The South, the poor South." **Related Entries**: Jackson, Andrew; Nullification; States' Rights.

SUGGESTED READING: Irving H. Barlett, *Calhoun: A Biography* (1993); Christopher Hollis, *The American Heresy* (1930); Gerald W. Johnson, *America's Silver Age: The Statecraft of Clay—Webster—Calhoun* (1939).

CANALS. *See* Internal Improvements at Federal Expense.

CARRIAGES AND COACHES. *See* Transportation.

CATHOLICS: Many of the new immigrants to America, particularly the Irish, were Catholic. In the 1830s the Roman Catholic Church was possibly the only Christian denomination in America not divided over doctrine. The Catholic Church was intolerant of criticism, unapologetically authoritarian, resolute, and unalterable in its structure. It was the oldest religion in the Western world, and it demanded the unquestioned obedience of its members to the will of the Pope. It was the Catholic Church in America that grew fastest because of the mass **immigration** of the 1840s and 1850s.

The Catholics were prospering. They were able to begin an educational system, which still exists; and they established colleges and seminaries that provided some of the best higher **education** available in the country at the time. In 1831 **Alexis de Tocqueville** said of the Catholic colleges in **Maryland**, "There is perhaps no young man in Maryland who has received a good education who has not been brought up by Catholics."

A "Protestant Crusade" to stem the growing influence of the Catholics in America began in the 1820s and grew in proportion to the increase in Catholic immigration. This movement, truly reactionary and discriminatory, was rooted in a traditional abhorrence of Roman papism and was aimed at the recent Catholic immigrant. Americans feared the power of the Catholic Church. Anti-papist rhetoric portrayed Catholics, and especially the Catholic immigrants, as crime-ridden and intemperate, a drag on the economy, and a danger to the fabric of society. The American Party, or **Nativists**, viewed the acceptance of Catholics by the **Democratic Party** as insincere and self-serving. Even in the South, where concern over immigration and papal absolutism was marginal, due in large part to a significant minority population of French and Spanish ancestry, the authoritarian structure of the Catholic Church was viewed as incompatible with American principles and capable of marshaling Catholic immigrants against traditional American institutions. **Related Entries**: Protestantism; Religion and Religious Revivalism.

SUGGESTED READING: Albert J. Nevins, *Our American Catholic Heritage* (1972); Andrew M. Greeley, *An Ugly Little Secret: Anti-Catholicism in North America* (1977); Jon L. Wakelyn and Randall M. Miller, *Catholics in the Old South: Essays on Church and Culture* (1983).

CHARITIES: The majority of philanthropic movements initiated prior to the Civil War were essentially benevolent and focused almost solely on the visibly degraded elements of society, which were seen as unnatural in a bountiful America.

Traditional Southern culture exhibited a broader acceptance of the poor than the industrialized and urbanized sections of America. A well-ordered society was viewed by Southerners as being hierarchical, with each social level enjoying its own special privileges and obligations, and with slaves residing on the bottom rung of society. Unfortunately, this conception made the poor a permanent fixture of the social order. The place of the laborer or the artisan in Southern society was part of the natural order, not a demeaning or disparaging imposition from which one sought to escape. The leadership of society was equally well established in the leading families of the South as a natural consequence of God's will. The position of the poor was seen from the same perspective. Of course, the needy were much less conspicuous and more sparsely concentrated in the largely rural areas of the South than they were in Northern cities, where immigration from abroad had stressed the social structure to the limit.

The **planter aristocracy** were remarkably intolerant of social reform and disdainful of activism. The task of providing for the poor fell, therefore, on the **kinship** network to provide aid. As in colonial times, Southerners adopted a calm and complacent attitude toward poverty. Disinclined to design large programs to relieve poverty, and reticent in laying blame upon the poor for their condition, they quickly and without tedious investigation simply provided support for the destitute. This support often took the form of financial aid, **food**, firewood, or clothing brought to the home of the needy. If the recipients were disabled or suffering from extreme age, public support, raised by subscription from among the upper classes, was funneled through the churches or the households of relatives and friends.

Much of the resistance to philanthropy was based in a natural social inertia, but some of it was caused by the inability of the activists to articulate the scope and righteousness of their agenda to the public. Reformers demanded that the government supplement intellectual persuasion with taxation and legal coercion in many areas. The shift from moderate and sometimes symbolic goals to conclusive ones, carved into the legal fabric of the nation, was typical of many of the **reform movements** of the nineteenth century and was the basis of much of the South's coolness toward large-scale public philanthropy.

In the North the poor, regardless of the individuality of their plight, would receive public aid only while confined within the almshouse. Once inside, they would be taught order, discipline, and responsibility. The emphasis on rehabilitation and personal reformation, initially a primary goal of the anti-poverty reformers, quickly became irrelevant as the most heart-rending members of the poor community were hidden behind brick walls. The general conditions found in such institutions had often degenerated into a cruel and punitive system of custodial care. **Related Entry**: Reform Movements.

SUGGESTED READING: Alexander Johnson, *The Almshouse: Construction and Management* (1911); Roy M. Brown, *Public Poor Relief in North Carolina* (1928); Ronald G. Walters and Eric Foner, *American Reformers, 1815–1860* (1997).

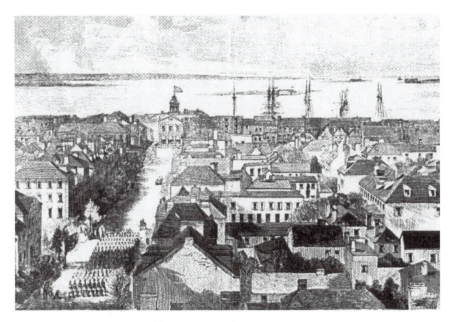

Charleston, South Carolina, as it appeared in *Harper's Weekly* in 1861. (From *Harper's Weekly* V, no. 213, January 26, 1861.)

CHARLESTON, SOUTH CAROLINA: As a great Southern city Charleston stood second only to **New Orleans**, yet it was graced by the choicest portion of society in the Old South. The streets of Charleston were laid out neatly in checkerboard squares free of the cramped tangle of filthy byways that was so common in cities that had grown spontaneously. The city owed its development to the **South Carolina** planters who left the low country to avoid malaria in the warm months and returned in the winter to enjoy the balls, private parties, and congenial company that gathered there from all over the South. The cultural and social diversions available to Charlestonians included literature, theater, opera, gentlemen's clubs, and **fashion** shows brought from Europe. Equally important were the shops of merchants, tradesmen, and artisans that developed in the commercial section of the city.

Charlestonians' natural proclivities had been reinforced in the first decade of the nineteenth century by the infusion of refugee planters from the slave revolts of the West Indies. These newcomers had amazingly sophisticated tastes. The oldest museum, the oldest surviving theater, and the oldest public library in the nation could be found in Charleston in 1860. Although the city had strict Sabbath laws, few hesitated to break them by following their church services with a visit to the cock-pits or the racing ground. Among the variations of legitimate theater were the "tableaux vivants," with actors and actresses striking attitudes from famous sculptures or paintings as through great picture frames, amateur musicals, and the tunes of Negro fiddlers in the avenues.

The most striking characteristic of Charleston was its domestic **architecture**. With the semitropical climate in mind, the fine homes of the city exhibited a subtle adaptation of English style with two or three stories of fairly open rooms and balconies that caught the breezes. Fenced gardens with wrought iron gateways contained flowers, fragrant vegetation, and shade trees among which Charlestonians could amble or relax in dignified luxury.

More remotely located were the port and the great slave market with its auction block and slave pens. Although the slave was an accepted part of the Southern environment, in the city streets only well-dressed and reserved coachmen and house slaves could be seen scurrying about their chores. Part of the uneasiness felt by Southerners over the awkward reality of the slave market in Charleston was the gangs of Negroes marching along the byways in chains. Another was their general dislike for those whites that dealt in slaves, "brutified by their employment, [and] little better than the Negroes they managed" (Sullivan, 1995). The planter and his lady, although slave-owners, attempted to preserve this sense of superiority over the low-born traders and artisans of the city by maintaining their physical distance from them. **Mary Chesnut**, a fine Southern woman, rejected the idea that Southerners were "so degraded as to defend and like to live with such degraded creatures around us" (Woodward, 1981). **Related Entries**: Nullification; Secession; Vesey, Denmark.

SUGGESTED READING: Editors of Time-Life Books, *Charleston* (1997); Walter Sullivan, *The War the Women Lived: Female Voices from the Confederate South* (1995); C. Vann Woodward, *Mary Chesnut's Civil War* (1981).

CHESNUT, MARY BOYKIN (1823–1886): diarist. At the age of seventeen, Mary Boykin, daughter of a former senator and governor of **South Carolina**, married a young lawyer of high social standing and wealth named James Chesnut. Under normal circumstances Mary Boykin Chesnut would have remained a footnote to her husband's career as a U.S. senator, a delegate to the Secession Congress, and a Confederate general. However, her ability to record the social life and circumstances surrounding the major events that took place during the Civil War has made her one of the most insightful and thorough witnesses of the war.

Mary's astounding diary, a daily journal begun in the antebellum period and meticulously continued during the war years, totaled in excess of 400,000 words. Published in 1876, the work provides a generally balanced picture of the North and the South from the frame of reference of a socially well-placed Southern woman. In her journal, Mary Chesnut supports **slav-**

ery but also expresses sympathy for the plight of the Negro. In 1981 a fuller and more complete edition of her work was published, and it is considered one of the best primary sources on Southern civilian life in the Confederacy.

SUGGESTED READING: C. Vann Woodward, *Mary Chesnut's Civil War* (1981).

CHILDREN BORN AS SLAVES: Slave children did not belong to their parents but generally were considered the property of the mother's master. The father and the father's master, should he be a different person, were denied any standing in regard to the offspring of slave unions. The offspring of a free man with a slave woman was, thereby, a slave; yet the offspring of a slave with a free woman was considered to be free born even if the woman were black. Even the children of a white master by a slave mother were born slaves. In the case of a dispute in this regard, with very few exceptions, whenever a slave's human rights came into conflict with a master's property rights, the courts invariably decided in favor of the master. The first activity of many refugee slaves during the Civil War was to begin a search for their missing mates or children. **Related Entries**: Buying and Selling Slaves; Miscegenation.

SUGGESTED READING: John W. Blassingame, *Black New Orleans* (1973); David Brion Davis, *Slavery in the Colonial Chesapeake* (1994); Kenneth M. Stampp, *The Peculiar Institution* (1956).

CHRISTMAS. *See* Holiday Celebrations.

CHURCHES. *See* Religion and Religious Revivalism.

CITIES. *See* Urbanization.

CLAY, CASSIUS M. (1810–1903): abolitionist, governor of **Kentucky**, and soldier. The career of Cassius Marcellus Clay was filled with political turbulence and physical violence. In 1841 he fought a pistol duel; and, in a separate incident, he was indicted for cutting up a man with a Bowie knife. In 1850 he stabbed a man to death, and in his old age, without forethought or provocation, he shot and killed a Negro, thereafter being adjudged a lunatic. The facts of his life suggest that he was somewhat unbalanced mentally throughout his career.

As the son of a slaveholding plantation owner in Kentucky, Clay received a fine **education** ending with a degree from Yale University. Here he heard **William Lloyd Garrison** speak and formed an implacable hatred of all slaveowners. His sudden conversion to **abolition** was reinforced by a resolve to rid Kentucky of **slavery** by any means. Wealth, education, and ambition combined to aid Clay's political career, and he was elected to the Kentucky state legislature in both 1835 and 1837. Clay became a favorite abolitionist speaker, and subscriptions to his lectures were often quickly sold out. However, his bitter hatred of all slaveowners ultimately forced him from local politics.

In 1845 he set up an abolitionist **newspaper** called the *True American.* Correctly fearing the local pro-slavery faction in Lexington, Kentucky, Clay fortified his office with two cannon, rifles, lances, and a keg of powder to be set off against any attackers, and on his tours he carried two pistols and a Bowie knife. Ironically, during his absence on a lecture tour, sixty prominent citizens broke into his newspaper establishment, boxed his belongings, and sent them to Cincinnati, Ohio. Clay doggedly followed his equipment, moved on to Louisville, Kentucky, and set up a new paper, the *Examiner.*

Politically, Clay was a strong supporter of his distant kinsman, **Henry Clay**, but the men broke over the issue of abolition during the 1844 election. In 1849 Cassius Clay won the governorship of Kentucky. One of the first members of the **Republican Party**, he supported **John C. Fremont** in 1856 and **Abraham Lincoln** in 1860. At the 1860 party convention he had a considerable following for the vice presidency, but was overlooked as being too extreme. As a close friend of Lincoln, Clay expected to be made secretary of war, and he was sorely embarrassed when he did not receive the appointment. In order to avoid a break with the administration, Clay accepted a diplomatic appointment to Russia.

In 1846 Clay had volunteered to fight in the **Mexican War** even though he opposed the **annexation of Texas** on the grounds that it might spread the practice of slavery. He fought with bravery and was, for a time, a prisoner of war. These wartime experiences brought about his appointment in 1862 as a major general when he returned from Russia. But Clay refused to fight until the government abolished slavery in all of the seceded states—a position that went beyond the war aims of the administration at the time. Lincoln therefore packed him off once again to Russia, from which he did not return until 1869. Upon his return he fell out with President Ulysses Grant and seems to have badly misread the temper of the Republican Party thereafter. **Related Entry**: Abolition.

SUGGESTED READING: Cassius Marcellus Clay, *Life of Cassius Marcellus Clay: Memoirs, Writings and Speeches* (1886); H. Edward Richardson, *Cassius Marcellus Clay: Firebrand of Freedom* (1996). The files of the *True American* are preserved in the Lexington Public Library in Kentucky.

CLAY, HENRY (1777–1852): senator, Speaker of the House, and presidential candidate. Henry Clay was born in **Virginia**, but found that the western frontier of **Kentucky** beckoned and welcomed him. By 1805 he had established a flourishing law practice there, married, and was reputed to be growing rich. Clay took an almost immediate interest in politics, urg-

Daniel Webster, Henry Clay, and John C. Calhoun. These men were the giants of the Republic in the antebellum period. (From the authors' collection.)

ing democratization of the state's constitution and the gradual **emancipation** of its slaves. As a member of the state legislature, he opposed the Alien and Sedition Acts and championed the Kentucky Resolutions.

Initially, Clay came to national prominence for the successful defense of Aaron Burr before a Kentucky grand jury in 1806. He was then chosen to go to the U.S. Senate to fill a series of unexpired terms. During these periods he stood for protectionism, expansion, and the dissolution of the national bank. These positions made him very popular with the land speculators and state banking interests in Kentucky, and he was elected to the U.S. Congress in his own right. In 1811 he was chosen Speaker of the House, and he used the office to increase its power and to establish his own political prominence. As one of the **War Hawks** he played a prominent role in bringing about the **War of 1812**. Following the war, Clay proceeded to develop his **American System**.

Clay's political ambitions were aided by his eloquence but hampered by his impetuosity. Clay was viewed as an Indian hater and an agent of land-hungry speculators. He censured **Andrew Jackson** for his conduct in the **Florida** campaign of 1818 and sharply criticized **James Monroe**'s policies. Clay's belief in protectionism put him at odds with most of the South. His newly found support of the national bank was unpopular with the electorate and exposed him to charges of vacillation and power mongering. His efforts to broaden U.S. influence in the Western Hemisphere led to participation in the ill-fated Panama Congress in 1826 and caused him some political embarrassment.

Nonetheless, Clay's shortcomings and limitations were greatly offset by his brilliant handling of the **Missouri Compromise of 1820**, and he is generally credited with ending the **nullification** crisis in **South Carolina**. These achievements added to his reputation as an arbiter of sectional issues; but it was the formidable effort that he put into the passage of the **Compromise of 1850** that brought him the sobriquet "The Great Compromiser." He was thereby instrumental in forestalling the outbreak of civil war for a decade.

Clay's public career was almost always allied with conservative interests, and his policies and rhetoric appealed largely to the upper middle class. As a Kentucky slaveowner Clay rejected radical abolitionism as a divisive force which threatened civil war and disunion. Nonetheless, he had a genuine dislike for **slavery**. In 1817 he helped to form the American Colonization Society to encourage **free blacks** to return to Africa, and he freed all of his own slaves before his death in 1852.

Clay diligently sought the presidency throughout his career. He actively pursued the office in 1824, but, as no candidate had a majority of electoral votes, Clay bargained his influence in the House to John Quincy Adams, thereby depriving Jackson of the presidency. Charges of corruption and quid pro quo were made and widely believed following Adams' election, and the selection of Clay as his secretary of state seemed to verify the "Corrupt Bargain." Clay was ultimately forced into a duel with **John Randolph** in an effort to demonstrate the purity of his motives. Clay went on to lead a revitalized Jeffersonian party draped in the mantle of conservative Federalism. As Clay became more closely identified with the nation's upper economic class, his political ambitions became further frustrated.

Clay failed to be elected to the presidency in 1832, and in 1844 he ran a spirited campaign as a **Whig** against **James K. Polk**. In 1852 an aging Clay expressed a preference for **Millard Fillmore** as the Whig candidate and died shortly thereafter. Clay's inability to achieve the presidency was largely due to his failure to maintain a sympathetic rapport with the rising force of an expanding electorate and a widening interest among the people in all things political. **Related Entries**: Compromise of 1850; Jackson, Andrew; Missouri Compromise; Nullification.

SUGGESTED READING: Clement Eaton, *Henry Clay and the Art of American Politics* (1957); Robert V. Remini, *Henry Clay: Statesman for the Union* (1991).

CLOTHING. *See* Fashion; Slave Clothing.

COBB, HOWELL (1815–1868): congressman, Speaker of the House, secretary of the treasury, governor of **Georgia**, and soldier. As a representative from Georgia from 1842 to 1851, Howell Cobb rose in prominence from floor leader to Speaker of the House, lending support to the **annexation of Texas**, the **Mexican War**, and the extension of the **Missouri Compromise** line to the Pacific. He left Congress when overwhelmingly elected governor of his state, and in 1857 he was named secretary of the treasury in the administration of **James Buchanan**. Cobb became an ardent secessionist with the election of **Abraham Lincoln** as President. He continually called for unity of sentiment and concerted action by the Southern states, but he came to believe that the immediate **secession** of individual states was more crucial than discussions about the form of a new confederation as the decade of the 1850s neared its end. "Announce and maintain your independence out of the union, for you will never again have equality and justice in it," exclaimed Cobb as he resigned his post in 1860 in order to return to Georgia and speed the process of disunion. Buchanan, who liked Cobb and viewed him as an ally in an otherwise hostile cabinet, was shocked by his precipitate resignation.

His defection from the cabinet came when the country was in poor financial condition. A depression occurred in 1858, and the public debt rose $20 million, almost 30 percent, in just the last two years of Cobb's tenure. Charges that Cobb had purposely eroded the treasury to cripple any federal response to secession can generally be dismissed.

When the Congress of the Southern Confederacy opened in **Montgomery, Alabama**, to form a new government, Cobb was made the permanent chairman and presided from the rostrum of the State House throughout the deliberations. He was strongly considered for the presidency of the Confederacy and seems to have coveted the position; but he had a number of political enemies among the delegates of the six seceded states that were present. The more conservative **Jefferson Davis** of **Mississippi** was chosen instead. Undaunted in his devotion to secession, Cobb formed the 16th Georgia Regiment and served with distinction, becoming a major general by 1863. **Related Entries**: Montgomery, Alabama; Secession.

SUGGESTED READING: Horace Montgomery, *Howell Cobb: A Confederate Career* (1959).

COLONIZATION. *See* African Colonization.

COMPROMISE OF 1850: The fundamental point of contention in the political dispute over **slavery** was the unwillingness of the North to allow slavery to spread into areas in which it did not already exist. The South, for its part, believed that slavery was absolutely protected under the Constitution wherever the flag flew. The crux of the slavery issue was whether the United States had been founded as a free republic that allowed slavery or as a slaveholding republic with pockets of freedom. Most Americans believed slavery to be a political problem, and by mid-century a number of political solutions had been tried, the most successful of which had been the **Missouri Compromise of 1820**. However, anti-slavery forces were quickly changing the political debate into a moral and ethical question, and a simple extension of the 36°30' line of the Missouri Compromise was no longer acceptable.

At mid-century the nation was suddenly faced with the disposition of the vast territories accumulated during the administration of **James K. Polk**. Although **Texas** had been annexed as a slave state in 1845, Oregon had been organized as a territory without slavery in 1848. No decision had been made with respect to the vast southwestern lands acquired from Mexico. By 1849 California, New Mexico, and Utah were preparing to apply for admission to the Union, and, with the encouragement of President **Zachary Taylor**, drew up constitutions. Taylor urged the admission of California as a free state and that of New Mexico and Utah without any reference to slavery.

Southern reaction to this expansion of free territory was bitter. **Robert A. Toombs** of **Georgia**, expressing the sentiment of the South, predicted disunion if Southerners were driven "from the territories of California and New Mexico, purchased by the common blood and treasure of the whole people . . . thereby attempting to fix a national degradation upon half the states." To the Taylor administration he exclaimed: "Deprive us of this right and appropriate this common property for yourselves, it is then your government, not mine. Then I am its enemy, and I will then, if I can, bring my children and my constituents to the altar of liberty and . . . would swear them to eternal hostility to your foul domination" (Thompson, 1966).

Some of the most distinguished leaders in Congress immediately stepped forward to save the Union. **John C. Calhoun, Jefferson Davis, Daniel Webster**, and **Henry Clay** all brought forth suggestions for concessions and compromise. From January to September 1850 the debates and discussions raged, expedited somewhat by the untimely death of Taylor, who was "an acid opponent" of compromise. Assisted by the new President, **Millard Fillmore**, who was more open to compromise than his predecessor, a complicated but comprehensive agreement was reached.

The Compromise of 1850 was largely the work of Henry Clay, and required the passage of five separate bills. The first sanctioned California's admission as a free state; the second created the Territory of New Mexico without the **Wilmot Proviso** and indemnified Texas for the surrender of some disputed land; the third created the Territory of Utah; the fourth strengthened the enforcement of the **Fugitive Slave Law** and brought drastic measures against those who helped escaped slaves; and, finally, the fifth abolished the slave trade in the District of Columbia without affecting the practice of slavery in **Maryland**.

The compromise was little different from the measures initially urged by Taylor except for the inclusion of the harsh and wide-ranging measures for prosecuting escaped slaves and their accomplices. Nonetheless, the agreement was acceptable to the overwhelming majority of concerned Americans. The **Whigs** accepted the compromise as a settlement of the question of slavery in principle, but they insisted on its strict enforcement. The **Democrats** pledged to abide by all of the agreed provisions, especially that of enforcing the Fugitive Slave Law. Moreover, they promised to resist all attempts at renewing the agitation over the slavery question. The compromise measures were widely viewed at the time as a final settlement of the slavery question. Yet Northern **abolitionists** remained committed to their cause and voiced their displeasure with the agreement, declaring that slavery was a sin against God, and a crime against man. **Related Entries**: Clay, Henry; Extension of Slavery into the Territories; Mexican War of 1846; Missouri Compromise.

SUGGESTED READING: Clement Eaton, *Henry Clay and the Art of American Politics* (1957); Robert V. Remini, *Henry Clay: Statesman for the Union* (1991); William Y. Thompson, *Robert Toombs of Georgia* (1966).

CONFEDERACY. *See* Confederate Government; Secession.

CONFEDERATE GOVERNMENT: The antebellum period closed with the first shots fired on Fort Sumter in April 1861. In the final months of the period the Southern states drew together to form a new government. The new Confederate Constitution was closer to the U.S. Constitution than it was to a revolutionary document. With the exception of a few omissions and changes in phraseology, the two documents are almost identical. As the purpose of disunion was to establish a government that would preserve Southern culture and society as it *was*, this is not surprising. The act of **secession** in 1860 was a conservative political uprising, and the Confederate Constitution has been described by historian Drew Faust as "a theoretical time capsule that embodies the distinctive principles of republican government." These principles tended to focus on the Anti-Federalist view of the government, which had been obscured by the development and implementation of Federalist political theory since 1789. Confederate President **Jefferson Davis** wrote, "We have changed our constituent parts, but not the system of our government" (Faust, 1988). This statement exemplifies the true nature of the Confederacy as the Southerners saw it. The new government was to be a continuation of those ideals fostered in the first American Revolution which had been altered by a fanatical and radical North. If the Confederate government did nothing else, it at least gave Southerners a sense of group identity.

The infant national government brought prominence and power to many who had been outside the upper classes of society before the war. **Alexander H. Stephens**, who was from a poor **Georgia** family, nonetheless became the Vice President of the new country. **Judah Benjamin**, outside the pale of acceptability in the North because of his Jewish ancestry, rose to be one of the most capable members of an otherwise ineffective Confederate cabinet and a respected and loyal friend of Jefferson Davis.

However, as champions of a new revolution and defenders of the Southern nation, the Confederates gave up much of what they held dear. The South embraced a centralized government as fully determined to control the reins of power as that in **Washington**. The concept of **states' rights** was sacrificed—not without the determined resistance of some state governments—for the defense of the country as a whole. Southern cities swelled in size, **urbanization** increased, factories and manufacturing took on a new importance, and men and women went to work much like the wage earners of the North. Ultimately even **slavery** changed as the Confederate Congress provided for the enlistment of black soldiers and dallied with bartering black **emancipation** for foreign recognition in the name of independence.

The **planter aristocracy** was sorely tested and, in many cases, their social and financial prominence did not meet the test. Although wealth and social position maintained their hold on the structure of Southern society, the military created new avenues to prominence. Many aristocratic families lost scions to the fates of battle, while many of the masters of plantations proved unfortunate choices as military leaders. **Related Entries**: Davis, Jefferson; Stephens, Alexander H.; Toombs, Robert A.

SUGGESTED READING: Marshall L. DeRosa, *The Confederate Constitution of 1861* (1991); Drew Gilpin Faust, *The Creation of Confederate Nationalism: Ideology and Identity in the Civil War South* (1988); Emory M. Thomas, *The Confederacy as a Revolutionary Experience* (1991).

CONFESSIONS OF NAT TURNER. See Turner, Nat.

CONGRESS. *See* Legislative Branch/Congress.

CONSTITUTION **(U.S. WARSHIP KNOWN AS "OLD IRONSIDES"):** The excellence of American ships in the first half of the nineteenth century is unquestioned. American maritime design and shipbuilding technology were the envy of the world, and American sailing ships were soon the fastest on the seas. This same excellence lent itself to the design of naval vessels. In the final decade of the eighteenth century, Congress authorized the construction of six large frigates to defend the American flag around the world. This plan was somewhat optimistic, as a navy twenty times this size would have been needed to stand eyeball to eyeball with the fleets of Europe. As an example, the British navy alone during the **War of 1812** had almost one hundred warships on station solely directed against the

American coastline. Many of these were mighty seventy-fours having three decks and seventy-four guns.

The United States was fortunate in its choice of a naval designer in 1794. Joshua Humphreys (1751–1838), the chief naval architect charged with the construction of the American frigates, was gifted with a combination of original thought, professional competence, and technological shrewdness. In 1793 he contacted Congress, proposing the construction of large frigates carrying forty-four guns. The ships were to be built with stout timbers of live oak from the swamplands of **Georgia** in order to add strength and durability to each vessel, and they were to have spar decks with stalwart protective sides allowing more guns to be mounted than was common with vessels that had well decks amidships.

That these frigates proved vastly superior to any other warship of the same class is largely due to Humphreys' attention to detail and to the talent of their officers and crew. Naval authority and novelist C. S. Forester was quick to point out that these were not "large frigates" or "extra powerful frigates" but rather "not-too-small" two-decked ships of the line. Humphreys took great care to make them outstanding in their class, but not outside the common understanding of the term "frigate."

Of the six vessels planned, the *Constitution* came to be the best known during the War of 1812 because of its many successful single-ship actions, including its defeat of the British frigates *Guerriere* and *Macedonian*. The strength of the *Constitution*'s sides in these battles was so great that many of the enemy's shot bounced off into the sea. This observation led to the frigate's nickname, "Old Ironsides." **Related Entry**: War of 1812.

SUGGESTED READING: C. S. Forester, *The Age of Fighting Sail: The Story of the Naval War of 1812* (1956); David S. Heidler and Jeanne T. Heidler, *Encyclopedia of the War of 1812* (1997).

CONSTITUTIONAL CONVENTION: The Constitutional Convention of 1787 was called to amend the Articles of Confederation. The delegates chose, instead, to write a totally new underpinning document. In so doing they left several important questions unanswered that were to plague the entire antebellum period. To provide for free and open discussion, no minutes of the deliberations were taken. Were it not for the personal notes taken by the delegates, particularly **James Madison**, nothing of the constitutional debates would be known today. The lack of explicit and indisputable records from the Convention created a problem during the antebellum political wrangling.

Free from the intensity of the **slavery** debates prevalent in the 1850s, it is clear that the primary desire of the framers was to design a government that would possess only those powers necessary to provide for the common needs of the thirteen states and relieve the obvious weaknesses in the Arti-

As discussion of a strong federal government takes place, a distrustful Patrick Henry rises at the Constitutional Convention to say, "I smell a rat." (From an illustration in a nineteenth-century children's schoolbook in the authors' collection.)

cles. There was considerable disagreement about the exact limits of the relationship between the new federal government, the older states, and the individual citizen. In this regard, the delegates invoked the concept of state sovereignty; but republicanism, social pluralism, and constitutionalism were deemed the primary characteristics for a new government by the majority. Both **Thomas Jefferson** and James Madison believed that the states would retain a right to self-government. Slavery and the possibility of future disunion were considered secondary issues.

The idea of limited federal power was much older than the slavery debates of the nineteenth century and was recognized as an unresolved issue at the time. Ironically, many strong reservations about "powers" came from the Northern states during the ratification debates. A fear existed that the Constitution might be interpreted so as to extend the powers of Congress, and proposals remarkable in their similarity to later statements of **states' rights** were submitted by Northern states. New England politicians threatened **secession** if their demands were not met. The delegates from **Virginia** required that the powers granted the national government be limited. Thomas Jefferson warned that if the federal government was allowed to define the limits of its own powers, the result would be "not short of despotism." This anxiety required the addition of a separate Bill of Rights defining the limits of power alluded to in the principal document without which it was deemed impossible to achieve the adoption of the Constitution by the delegates. **Related Entries**: Secession; States' Rights.

SUGGESTED READING: Fred Rodell, *Fifty-Five Men: The Story of the Constitution Based on the Day-by-Day Notes of James Madison* (1986); Emory M. Thomas, *The Confederacy as a Revolutionary Experience* (1991); James R. Kennedy and Walter D. Kennedy, *The South Was Right* (1995).

CONSTITUTIONAL INTERPRETATION: The terms *strict construction* and *broad construction* refer to the ways in which the Constitution might be interpreted in disputes arising from ambiguities over the ultimate authority of the federal or state governments. The customary premise of those who believed in strict construction was that the exact wording of the Constitution should be relied on, while those who believed in broad construction felt that reliance on literal interpretation made the Constitution a sterile and confining document.

Our present reliance on **Supreme Court** decisions as an interpretative instrument of constitutionality was not as well established in the antebellum period as it is today. The Court relied on Section 25 of the Judiciary Act of 1789 as its authority to intrude into disputes between the federal government and the states. The act allowed the federal courts to overrule a state court's decision on constitutional questions. Section 25 was a major obstacle to strict interpretation, and its repeal was actively sought in some circles.

The literal analysis of the Constitution provided a conceptual simplicity to the national government which denied powers to Congress that were not explicitly enumerated in the founding document. Broad constructionists viewed the federal government as a vital and dynamic agency which could use its creative ability to deal with problems the Founding Fathers had not foreseen. The leading items of controversy involving strict and broad construction in the antebellum period included the establishment of a national bank, the use of protective **tariffs**, the funding of a program of internal improvements, and, of course, the extension and continuation of **slavery**.

The strict constructionists had a difficult position to defend, as the Founders themselves had predicted that the Republic could not meet all the imponderable requirements of an expanding society without modification. For this reason they had provided for amendments to the federal Constitution if they were ratified by three-fourths of the states. Yet basic changes in the role of government were found to be unacceptable to many citizens, and driving such changes through the lengthy amendment process was deemed less efficient than acquiring new powers by a broad interpretation of the existing language. Broad constructionists, therefore, seized upon the "common defense" and "general welfare" clauses of the Constitution which allowed Congress to proceed with programs considered "necessary and proper" for the prosecution of the carefully enumerated powers. These were sometimes called the "elastic" clauses of the Constitution as they were used to stretch the powers of Congress. The Supreme Court agreed with the broader view in 1819 by developing the doctrine of implied powers.

Strict construction came to be associated largely with the **nullification** and **states' rights** movements; however, the idea of limited federal power was recognized as a long-standing unresolved issue and was much older than these debates. In 1788 **James Madison** noted that the task of making the proper line of partition between the authority of the federal and state governments was "arduous." The difficulty lay, as he saw it, in the complicated nature of governmental powers and responsibilities "separated by such delicate shades and minute gradations that their boundaries have eluded the most subtle investigations, and remain a pregnant source of ingenious disquisition and controversy." Over the decades attempts to discriminate and define "with sufficient certainty . . . the privileges and powers of the different legislative branches" had failed to satisfy all of the disparate political entities charged with governing (Kennedy and Kennedy, 1995).

Many believed that if Congress could expand its powers simply by claiming that its programs were related to responsibilities enumerated in the Constitution, the nation could soon devolve into a tyranny of the majority with the rights of the states sacrificed to the issues that were most popular at the moment. **Thomas Jefferson** had warned that if the federal government was allowed to define the limits of its own powers, the result would be "not short of despotism." The anxiety over the exact extent of federal authority was serious enough to require the addition of a separate Bill of Rights to the principal document guaranteeing specific rights and limiting the scope of governmental power. Proponents of strict construction pointed to the Tenth Amendment, which specified that those powers not specifically granted to the federal government were "reserved to the states or the people" as further proof that those who had ratified the Constitution had subscribed to their interpretation. **Related Entries**: Calhoun, John C.; Nullification; States' Rights.

SUGGESTED READING: James R. Kennedy and Walter D. Kennedy, *The South Was Right* (1995); Fred Rodell, *Fifty-Five Men: The Story of the Constitution Based on the Day-by-Day Notes of James Madison* (1986).

COOKING, SOUTHERN. *See* Food.

COOPER, THOMAS (1759–1839): author and speaker. This fiery Englishman immigrated to America to become an arch radical on the subject of **tariffs**, a proponent of **states' rights** and **nullification**, and an early proslavery writer. Cooper was an agitator rather than a political philosopher, and as such, he aligned himself with a number of unsuccessful causes. While he was an early opponent of the **Atlantic slave trade** in Britain, for instance, he actively supported **slavery** as an institution with much the same vigor in his later life. Moreover, his opponents often found him so belligerent in debate that they hardened their own positions to the point that compromise was often impossible. Cooper's first crusade was in Britain as an outspoken supporter of the French Revolution in the 1790s; but his position was so partisan and pro-Jacobean that it attracted a good deal of conservative British criticism. As the "Terror" developed in France, Edmund Burke attacked Cooper openly before Parliament.

Hearing of **Thomas Jefferson**'s support of democratic principles in government, Cooper became intrigued by an American form of popular government devoid of the extremes of the European bloodbath. He therefore sailed for America in 1794, and became an outspoken supporter of the Jeffersonians in their struggles with the more elitist Federalists. In this confrontation Cooper became notorious as one of the twenty-five victims of the Sedition Laws, which, inspired by the Federalists, failed to be renewed by a slim margin in Congress. Later, as a judge on the Pennsylvania bench, he was targeted by radical **Democrats** seeking judicial reform. Having been driven from politics by 1811, Cooper decided to take up an academic career. He lectured on chemistry and medicine at several colleges and universities, and finally landed a position at South Carolina College.

As president of this institution, Cooper became a leader of the **South Carolina** nullification movement, spreading states' rights dogma in countless editorials, pamphlets, and speeches. His pamphlets *Consolidation* and *On the Constitution*, written between 1824 and 1826, were characteristically controversial in tone, and his 1826 *Lectures on the Elements of Political Economy* was a pioneering American effort on the topic. Its lasting success confirmed his notable scholarship. Nonetheless, Thomas Cooper seemed at his best in controversy.

In a famous speech of 1827, Cooper noted that high protective tariffs were quietly draining Southern wealth into Northern pockets—a notion used and reused by Southern apologists thereafter. As one of the first to support disunion, he declared that the South should recalculate the value of remaining in the Union, calling it a "most unequal alliance." Cooper was one of the first to anticipate the ultimate dissolution of the Union, but he was more than a decade early in his prediction. "The Union cannot exist twenty years under a system of policy, which looks to a perpetual tampering with the great pecuniary interests of society, by laws which invade the rights and affect the distribution of property" (Malone, 1926). Until his death in 1839, Cooper remained in the forefront of those nullifiers who used Jeffersonian ideals in an effort to defend the Southern way of life. **Related Entries**: Nullification; Tariffs; Turnbull, Robert J.

By the 1830s small hand- and foot-powered cotton gins were being replaced by mule- and steam-driven models. (From the authors' collection.)

SUGGESTED READING: Dumas Malone, *The Public Life of Thomas Cooper, 1783–1839* (1926).

CORN. *See* Agricultural Products.

COTTON: The plantation **slavery** so vigorously detested by **abolitionists** was found almost solely within areas with the ability to support wide-scale, extensive agricultural operations which produced cash crops such as rice, **sugar**, or cotton. It was cotton that saved the plantation system and breathed new life into slavery. By mid-century the introduction of a superior cotton boll from Mexico, which could be more easily picked, promised increased production. Annual cotton production amounted to only 3,000 bales in 1790 but rose to 178,000 bales in 1810. This increase is generally attributed to the introduction of the **cotton gin** in 1793. Expanded agricultural investment in the new western lands of the South, coupled with the widespread utilization of the cotton gin, boosted cotton production to almost 4 million bales per annum by the Civil War. Cotton thereby accounted for two-thirds of the exports of the country and created an unprecedented demand for agricultural laborers. Profits from cotton provided a financial bulwark for slavery in the South. The archaic **plantation economy** would have faded into obscurity except for the ability of slavery to provide the labor needed to produce these crops.

Slavery's existence in a region was largely based, therefore, on the ability of the environment to support cotton plantations. The generally mountainous areas of western **Virginia** and eastern **Tennessee** had proved indifferent

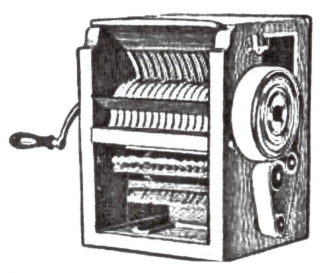

The first cotton gins, powered by a hand crank, gave new life to plantation slavery. (From an illustration in a nineteenth-century children's schoolbook in the authors' collection.)

lands for cotton production, and in these areas slavery was almost unknown. In **Texas** the only areas characterized by a plantation economy were those in East Texas, where the climate and environment were much more like those of **Louisiana** than of the American deserts. The **Sea Islands Plantations** of **South Carolina** and **Georgia** were noted for the production of luxury cotton with long, delicate, and silky fibers that could not be grown profitably anywhere else in the world. Even so, continuous experimentation to improve the quality of luxury cotton produced a superfine fiber that the world eagerly sought to make laces and fine fabrics. Even in the face of widely fluctuating prices, this cotton provided the low country gentry with a relatively stable market and virtually inexhaustible wealth. **Related Entries:** Agriculture; Cotton Gin; Plantation Economy; Sea Islands Plantations.

SUGGESTED READING: Charles Austin Beard, *A Century of Progress* (1933); Karen G. Britton, *Bale o' Cotton: The Mechanical Art of Cotton Ginning* (1992); Guion Griffis Johnson, *A Social History of the Sea Islands* (1930); Paul R. Johnson, *Farm Inventions in the Making of America* (1976).

COTTON GIN: The cotton gin (short for cotton engine) was, quite ironically, invented by a New Englander who had never even seen raw **cotton**. While teaching in Savannah, Eli Whitney became aware of the problem the South faced in supplying sufficient cotton to meet the increasing demands of England's technologically improved spinning and weaving machines.

Two varieties of cotton were being grown in the South at that time. The black-seed, long staple variety was easily cleaned but grew only near the coast. The green-seed, short staple cotton, which grew inland, proved very difficult to clean and greatly impeded production.

Whitney had become skilled in mechanics at a farm workshop as a boy. It did not take the Yale College graduate long to develop a practical machine to undertake this time-consuming task. In 1793 the first cotton gin was completed. It had two rollers and was turned by hand. The first roller had sharp metal teeth that drew the cotton fiber from the boll of the plant, leaving behind the seeds. The second roller, which turned in the opposite direction, had brushes that cleaned the lint fibers from the saw teeth of the first roller. The clean cotton was then ready for baling. The cotton gin increased the production of cotton tenfold.

Whitney patented his gin in 1794. Unfortunately, planters were generally unwilling to pay for the rights to use the machine. Many copies were made. Whitney remains famous for his invention, but most of the money he made from it was consumed by lawsuits fighting patent infringement.

By 1860 virtually every cotton plantation had a gin or, more likely, several. The small machines were pedal-operated, much like a grinder's wheel or a wood lathe, and could be piloted by even young boys. Increased production, however, required larger machines, and by the 1830s the hand- and foot-powered gins were being replaced by mule- and steam-driven gins. On the eve of the Civil War more than fifty-four manufacturers of cotton gins existed in the South. The largest gin manufacturer, an **Alabama** company, produced more than 8,000 gins between 1833 and 1860.

These larger gins were housed in separate buildings or gin houses supported by wooden pillars and raised approximately eight feet from the ground. The upper room accommodated the gin stand, or actual machinery, as well as containment areas for the harvested bolls and the cotton seed left behind. A "save room" attached to one side of the building was used to collect the ginned fiber. Beneath the upper room could be found the shaft and gears that turned the machinery. Harnessed mules, needing little more than a small child with a switch to keep them moving, were driven in a circular path to propel the gears. **Related Entries**: Cotton; Inventions; Plantation Economy.

SUGGESTED READING: Karen G. Britton, *Bale o' Cotton: The Mechanical Art of Cotton Ginning* (1992); John Michael Vlach, *Back of the Big House: The Architecture of Plantation Slavery* (1993); Caroll D. Wright, *Industrial Revolution of the United States* (1895).

COUNTY GOVERNMENT: The large plantation owners heavily influenced all levels of Southern culture, social life, and politics. Even though they ruled Southern society, they did so against a tide of small farmers of the non-slaveowning class. Although **suffrage** began to be extended to these farmers in the second quarter of the nineteenth century, not until the Civil War was the planter-dominated structure of county government broken.

The young nation had been founded by men who were essentially British, and as such they relied on English common law to fill in the gaps in governance that were not covered by the Constitution. Where written statutes were ambiguous or nonexistent, common law often provided a simple precedent for action. Although the assumptions of common law provided a generally smooth transition from British to American governance, ultimately they proved to be too narrow in scope to cope with the demands of a growing and vibrant new country. Inevitably individual localities relied on county courts to reform and revise the body of British common law to a more American form. This process gave local courts unprecedented power to shape everyday life.

Since the seventeenth century, county government had been ruled by the **planter aristocracy** in the guise of the county justices of the peace. These men, usually chosen for life and members of the upper class, wielded almost regal powers in local affairs. They selected local officeholders, adjudicated legal squabbles, and apportioned taxation by interpreting legislation. Within the county court the justice of the peace could control the most minute details of each citizen's life. Although changes in property qualifications for **office holding** and the expansion of voting to all white males in the 1830s made popular governance a good deal more widespread than previously was the case, the basic economic and social control of county government remained with the large planters. **Related Entry**: Suffrage.

SUGGESTED READING: Harvey Wish, *Society and Thought in Early America* (1955).

COURTS. *See* County Government; Supreme Court of the United States.

COURTSHIP AND MARRIAGE: The South was a structured society tied to tradition and continuity rather than progress and change. Family (and the continuation of the family name and fortune through marriage) was the most conservative and inviolable of Southern institutions. Young women passed from the domination of their fathers to the equally powerful authority of their husbands. Women had little or no legal standing in the South. Historian Victoria Bynum points out that the husband and wife were considered "one person in law . . . the very existence of the woman [being] suspended during the marriage, or at least incorporated and consolidated into that of the husband." Only for a brief period—usually between puberty and marriage—did a young woman have any control over her fate. Yet this control was very limited, residing solely in her ability to choose a husband from among a set of suitors acceptable to her family.

Couples of the antebellum period were commonly wed in their "best" attire. White gowns and veils were just beginning to come into vogue. This rare photo shows a period bride who seems to have embraced this newly emerging trend. (From the authors' collection.)

Nonetheless, as the century proceeded women gradually gained a modicum of control over the property that they brought to a marriage, and in many Northern homes, at least, the focus increasingly came to rest on the wife and children. John Tosh suggests that this evolution to a female-dominated household may help to explain the growing formalism and rigid authoritarianism Victorian husbands demanded when they were present. Many widows disdained remarriage, having found relief from the overbearing power of even the best of husbands and fathers.

Catherine Clinton has identified three significant differences between Southern and Northern courtship and marriage practices. Although these factors were most strongly entrenched among the Southern planters, they established a trend in marital custom throughout the South. For daughters of the planter class, wealth was the primary factor in arranging a marriage or choosing a husband. In order to maintain their social position, inter-marriage between cousins far enough removed to dispel charges of consanguinity was common among the **planter aristocracy**. Finally, women in the South married at a younger age—almost four years younger on average—than their Northern counterparts.

Fathers were protective of their unmarried daughters and solicitous of the welfare of their married ones, providing their sons-in-law with influence, if not money. Before a man could hope to prosecute his suit, he had to establish himself in a profession or come into his inheritance. This fact tended to drive up the age of eligible suitors and increase the disparity in age between husband and wife. Courtships could be protracted if the suitor's financial expectations took time to come to fruition. In the North the difference in age between husband and wife averaged a mere two years, while Southern couples were separated by an average of six.

A particularly attractive or well-heeled woman might have groups of suitors vying for her attentions. Such groups, calling together upon a young woman at her home, were not discouraged by parents, as the practice prevented gossip. Under such circumstances young men had little opportunity of measuring the woman's attitude toward their individual suit. Most gentlemen therefore resorted to a go-between in the early stages of any serious courting to gauge whether or not their more formal attentions would be rebuffed. The woman's brothers or male cousins often served in this capacity. All but the most eligible men met with a series of mild rebuffs, as young women were discouraged by their parents from taking too many prospective fiancés into their social circle before selecting one from a small group of two or three as a husband.

Unmarried couples—even those who were formally engaged—might easily offend the community if their behavior was perceived to be sexual in any context. The betrothed might never have touched, and certainly should never have shared a romantic kiss. As women were not permitted to correspond with men who were not relations, many young women had no knowledge of men who were not their blood kin. For this reason they favored cousin marriages where they were at least familiar with their prospective partner. Courting couples were never left alone, and chaperones (sometimes in the form of an elderly and trusted slave) were always present. Nonetheless, anxious parents frequently married off their daughters at fifteen or sixteen, fearing that they might become involved in some sexual impropriety that would cause them to be shunned by prospective suitors. Overt sexuality at any stage in a woman's life before marriage would certainly meet with social ostracism and might actually result in criminal indictment for fornication in some jurisdictions. **Related Entries**: Kinship; Planter Aristocracy; Slave Courtship and Marriage.

SUGGESTED READING: Victoria E. Bynum, *Unruly Women: The Politics of So-*

cial and Sexual Control in the Old South (1992); Catherine Clinton, *The Plantation Mistress: Woman's World in the Old South* (1982); John Tosh, "New Men? The Bourgeois Cult of Home," *History Today* 46 (December 1996); Dorothy Denneen Volo and James M. Volo, *Daily Life in Civil War America* (1998).

CREOLE: The term "Creole" comes from the Spanish and was properly applied to any native of **Louisiana**. In practice the term was applied only to whites of French or Spanish ancestry in the antebellum period. When Louisiana was first purchased from France an intense animosity was formed between the Creole population and the American newcomers. American women were initially snubbed by the Creole ladies of **New Orleans** and excluded from the social life of the city. Inevitably nearness, business, and intermarriage brought the two groups together. The common defense of the city against the British at the **Battle of New Orleans** in the **War of 1812**, however, did much to create a rapprochement. **Related Entries:** Battle of New Orleans; New Orleans.

SUGGESTED READING: James H. Dorman, *Creoles of Color in the Gulf South* (1996).

CRIME. *See* Gambling; Prostitution.

CROCKETT, DAVID "DAVY" (1786–1836): Indian fighter and congressman. Probably best known as the legendary character found in books and Walt Disney movies, Davy Crockett was a real person who was born in **Tennessee**. His father, a tavern keeper, was an Irish immigrant who fought in the Revolutionary War and married a girl from **Maryland**. In all likelihood the Crocketts moved west to Tennessee from **North Carolina** some years before Davy's birth. Davy remained at home until he was thirteen, at which point he ran away for several years and may have spent some time in Baltimore. Returning before his eighteenth birthday, Davy spent only six months in school and prided himself on his lack of formal **education**.

As a young man he married Polly Findlay and took up life as a tenant farmer with a horse, two cows, and fifteen dollars. Within a few years he moved his wife and two children west to the Tennessee-Alabama line, west again in 1816, and, several years later, west a third time to the banks of the **Mississippi River**. Although a poor farmer, Davy was an excellent frontiersman and hunter. As such Davy Crockett was the epitome of the **poor white** Southern farmer: shiftless, indolent, and living on the edge of poverty.

In the Creek War of 1813, Crockett served as a scout under the command of General **Andrew Jackson**. After his wife's untimely death, he remarried in order to provide care for his children. In 1816 he was informally made a local magistrate and later became a justice of the peace. He was also made the colonel of the local **militia** regiment, and was fond of referring to himself as "Colonel" Crockett thereafter. As a public and popular figure, Davy was elected to the state legislature in 1821, and again, in a different locality, in 1823.

His obvious popularity caused him to campaign seriously for the House of Representatives in 1827. He served as a congressman from 1827 to 1831 and again from 1833 to 1835. Never one to diminish his own reputation, he toured a number of Northern cities in 1834, emphasizing his career as a frontiersman and Indian fighter. Crockett generally opposed President Andrew Jackson throughout his tenure in Congress. He came into irreparable conflict with his former commander over the issue of **Indian removal**, and Jackson successfully targeted Crockett for removal in the 1835 election.

Disheartened by this reverse, Crockett chose to leave Tennessee for **Texas**, where he thought the revolution against Mexican authority might provide an opportunity for him to become a "founding father" in the new republic. He arrived at the **Alamo** in 1836 with about two dozen followers, took part in its heroic defense, and was probably executed by the Mexicans after the defenders were overpowered.

Several books were attributed to Crockett in this period, but his lack of education casts doubt on their authorship. The supposed author was Augustin S. Clayton, who published a number of manuscripts under Crockett's name. **Related Entries**: Alamo; Indian Removal; Texas, Annexation of.

SUGGESTED READING: David Crockett and Augustin S. Clayton, *A Narrative of the Life of David Crockett . . . Written by Himself* (1834); William C. Davis, *Three Roads to the Alamo: The Lives of David Crockett, James Bowie, and William Barret Travis* (1998).

DAVIS, JEFFERSON (1808–1889): politician, senator, secretary of war, and President of the Confederate States of America. Raised from a very young age by his elder brother Emory, who was a very successful planter in **Mississippi**, Jefferson Davis grew up as a sensitive and imaginative member of the **planter aristocracy**. Guided by his brother, he became a dedicated reader of history and politics. He studied at several schools in **Kentucky** and at Transylvania University, but he was most influenced by his time at the U.S. Military Academy at West Point, New York. Throughout his life he kept a deep-seated love of the army and of **military education**, and considered himself the equal of any general as a strategist and tactician.

After his graduation from West Point in 1828, Davis initially served as a lieutenant on the frontiers of Illinois and Wisconsin. In his last post (1833–1835) he served under future President **Zachary Taylor**, who was then a colonel. Unfortunately, Davis fell madly in love with Taylor's daughter, Sarah, and married her against her father's wishes. He was also forced by this circumstance to resign from the army. Three months later, with his wife's sudden death, Davis returned to the life of a planter in Mississippi. He was gentle and patriarchal in his relations with his slaves, and was a hard-working planter who took an intense interest in his plantation.

In 1845, after his marriage to Varina Howell—the daughter of an aristocratic planter family—he was elected to Congress as a **Democrat**, but he quickly resigned in order to accept the command of a volunteer regiment in the **Mexican War**. At the Battle of Buena Vista his regiment made a gallant stand which probably turned the tide of battle. This experience gave Davis a great deal of personal satisfaction, as he was serving under his former father-in-law, but he was criticized by his detractors for his egotism and vanity about military matters in later years.

In 1847 he was elected to the U.S. Senate. Here he supported President

James K. Polk's policies, argued for **states' rights**, and opposed the organization of **Oregon Territory** without **slavery** and the admission of California to the Union. In the 1850s the Democratic Party became divided over the issue of the **extension of slavery into the territories**. The Northern branch of the party favored **popular sovereignty**, while the Southern branch preferred an unequivocal assertion that the Constitution absolutely protected the practice of slavery. **Stephen A. Douglas** became the leader of the Northern group, while Davis led the Southern position. When Congress voted to ease the tensions over slavery with the passage of the **Compromise of 1850**, Davis voted against every provision of the measure except that which strengthened the **Fugitive Slave Law**.

In 1851 Davis volunteered to leave the Senate to run for the governorship of Mississippi against Senator Henry S. Foote, who was running on a Unionist platform. As Davis was far from being considered a radical, the Mississippi Democrats had offered him their nomination in the hope that it would convey to the voters a retreat from the extremes of the radical **secessionists**. Defeated by Foote, Davis returned again to the life of a planter, but in 1853 he accepted the role of secretary of war in the new administration of **Franklin Pierce**. According to his own account, *The Rise and Fall of the Confederate Government* (1881), Davis found this the most satisfying and happy time of his career.

In his new role Davis frequently found himself at odds with William L. Marcy, the secretary of state and a leader of the Northern wing of the party. Nonetheless, he was able to induce Pierce and Marcy to acquire a strip of land in the Southwest known as the **Gadsden Purchase**. He also supervised the massive **railroad** surveys of the West in anticipation of a transcontinental railroad.

In 1857 he was again elected to the Senate. Internal wrangling in the Democratic Party over the **Dred Scott** decision and the growing euphoria for secession caused Davis to ascend to the leadership of the Southern wing of the party. Following the election of **Abraham Lincoln** in 1860, Davis initially sought to restore calm, but when it became clear that Lincoln was dedicated to confining slavery to those areas where it already existed, Davis applied his talents to speeding disunion. He determined to leave the Senate, to call for the Southern states to seize all federal property within their domain, and to join his state in secession.

Davis expected to be offered the post of secretary of war in the new **Confederate government**, and he was somewhat disappointed at being chosen its President. Davis' devotion as President of the Confederacy was to the South as a whole rather than to Mississippi. He embraced a theory of centralized government fully as dedicated to controlling the nation as that in **Washington**. Davis thereby sacrificed the individual sovereignty of the states for the defense of the country as a whole—but not without the determined resistance of some state governments.

An anti-Davis party formed around the concept of state sovereignty. His efforts to win European recognition proved a failure, and Davis was increasingly unable to control events. Moreover, he was not wise in choosing the men in whom he put his trust. One of his few good choices was **Judah Benjamin**, who quickly proved to be one of the ablest men in a generally ineffective group in his cabinet. Davis also created a great deal of animosity by keeping a tight hand on the operations of the military.

At the end of the war, Davis fled **Richmond**, but on May 10, 1865, he was captured by federal cavalry at Irwinville, **Georgia**. Although never brought to trial, Davis spent two years in confinement in Fortress Monroe in **Virginia**. He was at first kept in irons, but was later accorded better treatment. After his release he passed his last years sadly with his wife at Beauvoir, a Mississippi plantation. **Related Entries**: Confederate Government; Davis, Varina Howell.

SUGGESTED READING: Cass Canfield, *The Iron Will of Jefferson Davis* (1978); Jefferson Davis, *The Rise and Fall of the Confederate Government* (1881); Allen Tate, *Jefferson Davis* (1969).

DAVIS, VARINA HOWELL (1826–1906): As the first lady of the South, Varina Howell Davis helped to sustain her husband, **Jefferson Davis**, in his role as President of the Confederacy under attack by the full force of the federal government. Mrs. Davis came from an aristocratic family and had been raised on a **Mississippi** plantation; but her ancestry was in the North, and she had attended school in Philadelphia. Ironically, both she and Mary Todd Lincoln had strong ties to the other side in the war and were attacked by their detractors for not being in sympathy with their respective causes.

Varina Davis was a bright and high-spirited woman when she married Jefferson Davis in 1845. As the second wife of a respected senator and secretary of war, she gained a reputation as one of Washington's most brilliant hostesses. As the first lady of **Richmond** she became known for her wit and unflagging spirit. She appears regularly, and usually favorably, in the diaries and memoirs of the notables that resided in the Confederate capital. **Mary Boykin Chesnut** described her as being "as witty as Jefferson is wise."

When their child "Little Joe" fell from the north piazza of the Southern White House in 1864 and died, Varina's support probably kept Jefferson functioning as President. Varina also stayed by the side of her husband during the dark periods of the Confederacy and when he was under personal attack by forces within the cause. She was with him when he was captured and managed to convince federal authorities to allow her to share his imprisonment. The couple spent their last years at Beauvoir, a Mississippi plantation. After the President's death in 1889, Mrs. Davis published her own account of her husband's role in the Confederacy, moved to New York City, and continued to write for various magazines until her death. **Related Entry**: Davis, Jefferson.

SUGGESTED READING: Isabel Ross, *First Lady of the South* (1973).

DELAWARE: Highlights of a description of the state from John Hayward's *Gazetteer of the United States* (1853) read as follows:

Surface and Soil: For the most part the face of the state is quite level. In the southern and western quarters, as well as in the ranges of table lands in which the waters, which flow into the Delaware and Chesapeake, take their rise, there are extensive swamps. At the north, the soil consists of a strong clay which is not very productive. In other parts it is light and sandy but there are large tracts of rich clay-like loam, of great fertility. Agricultural products include excellent wheat and Indian corn, rye and other grains, potatoes, and the usual abundance and variety of vegetable esculents peculiar to the Middle States. Fine grazing lands afford pasturage to multitudes of meat cattle, horses, and mules; and the swampy tracts yield large quantities of timber, much of which is exported.

Rivers: The principal navigable stream is the Delaware River, flowing into the bay of that name. There are also several large creeks and mill streams, running east and west from the central table lands, and emptying into the Chesapeake and Delaware Bays.

Education: The state has provided a school fund applicable to the support of free schools; provision being made for the erection and maintenance of at least one of these seminaries within every three square miles. An equal amount is raised for educational purposes, by taxes and contributions. Delaware College, founded in 1833, is the only institution of this grade in the state.

Internal Improvements: Among these are the Chesapeake and Delaware Canal connecting Elk River with the Delaware. Between Newcastle and Frenchtown, a railroad of sixteen miles forms the line of connection between the steamboat travel on the Chesapeake and Delaware Bays. The great breakwater within Cape Henlopen is also noteworthy.

Manufacture: Wheat being the chief staple product, the most important of the home manufacture is naturally that of flour. A large amount of capital is also employed in **cotton** mills, and in the pursuit of diverse other branches of domestic industry, such as the manufacture of iron, leather, gunpowder, machinery, etc.

Population: The progress of population for the past thirty years has been exceedingly slow. From 72,674 in 1810, it has increased in 1850 to only 91,532. It is still the least populous state in the Union.

Other: There are several ships belonging to the port of Wilmington which are actively engaged in the prosecution of Pacific whale fishery.

Related Entry: Geography.

SUGGESTED READING: John Hayward, *Gazetteer of the United States* (1853); Henry Clay Reed and Marion Reed, *Delaware: A History of the First State* (1947).

DEMOCRATIC PARTY (DEMOCRATS): In the 1824 presidential election **Andrew Jackson** had the largest number of popular votes, but none of the four candidates had the required majority of electoral votes to be elected. The election would be decided by the House of Representatives between the two leading candidates, Jackson and **John Quincy Adams**. As both **Henry Clay** and Adams distrusted and disliked Jackson, Clay bargained his influence in the House to Adams in order to deprive Jackson of the presidency. Charges of corruption and quid pro quo were made and widely believed following Adams' election, and the selection of Clay as his secretary of state seemed to verify the "Corrupt Bargain." Jackson never forgave either Adams or Clay, and he began his next presidential campaign almost immediately. An initial move was the formation of the Democratic Party (Democractic Republicans) with Jackson at its head. His success in 1828 was widely viewed as the beginning of an era of the people, and the elitist elements in American society felt threatened by his popularity.

Jackson's two terms as President were followed by the administration of fellow Democrat **Martin Van Buren**. In 1840 the **Whigs** gained the White House in the person of **William Henry Harrison**, and lost control when **John Tyler** (a Southern Democrat running with Harrison to balance the ticket) became President on Harrison's death. The Whigs virtually read Tyler out of the party within a few months, and Tyler replaced many of his cabinet officials with Democrats. The Democrats, sensing the weakness in the Whig Party, began to lay plans for regaining the White House in their own right. In 1844 the Democrats elected **James K. Polk**.

After virtually controlling the **executive branch** of government for twenty years, in the 1850s the Democratic Party became divided over the issue of the **extension of slavery into the territories**. The Northern branch of the party favored **popular sovereignty**, wherein the voters decided for or against the extension of slavery within the boundaries of their state or territory, while the Southern branch preferred an unequivocal assertion that the Constitution absolutely protected the practice of **slavery. Stephen A. Douglas** became the leader of the Northern group, while **Jefferson Davis** led the Southern position. When Congress voted to ease the tensions over slavery with the passage of the **Compromise of 1850**, Davis voted against every provision of the bill except that which strengthened the **Fugitive Slave Law**. When Davis introduced legislation that would have condemned Northern interference in Southern "domestic institutions," the Douglas faction refused to support their own party.

The depth of this political realignment can be seen in the reaction to the passage of the **Kansas-Nebraska Act of 1854**. A product of the optimism of the Northern Democrats and Stephen Douglas, the Kansas-Nebraska Act seemingly sabotaged the political compromises that had characterized the previous decades of American politics. Although the measure was popular among Northern Democrats, and although the Southern Democrats gave it support, its passage ultimately caused an irreparable split in the party. Moderates in the North felt betrayed. Outraged by the act, Northern Democrats began to speak of the existence of a "slave power conspiracy." In response, the Southern wing of the party began to harden its position and seriously consider disunion.

The Northern Democrats used the symbols of progress, opportunity, and mobility to considerable effect. However, they were now in trouble, having to defend their party's historic position on slavery. The planters were portrayed by the Southern Democrats as favoring progress and opportunity also, but only for whites; and they made some movement in the Southern states toward the expansion of the vote for white males. But the Democratic Party, as a whole, was widely viewed by the electorate as part of the problem. Voters were generally disenchanted with the party's "politics as usual" agenda.

The Southern branch of the Democratic Party maintained itself by championing the resistance to outside intervention in Southern lifestyle and culture, which was inexorably linked to slavery. The events, both real and fabricated, taking place in **"Bleeding Kansas"** and the schemes of fanatical **abolitionists** like **John Brown** to forcibly liberate slaves and promote slave insurrections tended to radicalize even the most moderate politicians in the party.

Northern office seekers, with their sights set on 1860, began calling for an assault on the traditions and honor of the South with all the enthusiasm that their rhetoric could convey. Such attacks fueled Southern indignation, created a desire for vindictive satisfaction, and led Southern moderates to retrench their positions. Southern radicals began to call for disunion as the best means of protecting **sectional interests**, and this brought the Southern Democrats adherents.

In 1860 the election became a four-way race mainly because the Democratic Party split between two candidates, pro-slavery **John C. Breckinridge** and Stephen A. Douglas, a moderate, who attempted to reprise his defeat of **Abraham Lincoln** in 1858. The fourth candidate was **John Bell** of Tennessee. **Tariffs**, homesteads, **railroads, immigration**, and political corruption all figured as issues in the campaign; but slavery and the fear of disunion remained the pivotal questions. When it became obvious that Lincoln was going to win, Bell and Breckinridge proclaimed dedication to immediate disunion, but Douglas, to his credit, disavowed any ideas of **secession**. Thereafter, the Northern Democrats were powerless, and the Southern Democrats were swept up in a reckless euphoria for secession and the establishment of the Confederacy. **Related Entries**: Douglas, Stephen A.; Kansas-Nebraska Act of 1854.

SUGGESTED READING: Bernard Fay, *Bernard Fay's The Two Franklins: Fathers of American Democracy* (1933); Frank L. Dennis, *The Lincoln-Douglas Debates* (1974); Robert V. Remini, *Martin Van Buren and the Making of the Democratic Party* (1959).

DEPRESSIONS, ECONOMIC. *See* Panics.

DISEASE. *See* Epidemics.

DOUGLAS, STEPHEN A. (1813–1861): politician, senator, and presidential candidate. At age twenty Stephen A. Douglas moved west from his birthplace in Vermont to practice law in Illinois. In 1835 he was chosen as a state's attorney. Although he helped to build the **Democratic Party** in the state, he was defeated for a seat in Congress in 1837 but received a position on the state supreme court instead. In 1843 he was finally elected to Congress, where he used his remarkable oratorical skills to work for the election of **James K. Polk** as President. His active participation in the campaign brought him to national attention, and in 1847 he was appointed to the U.S. Senate. Almost immediately he was placed in charge of the Committee on Territories, where he encountered the demands of the Northern wing of his party to limit the **extension of slavery into the territories**. Southerners were equally insistent that **slavery** could not be excluded from the territories. Douglas was acutely conscious of these positions, as his wife had inherited some 150 slaves, making him a slaveowner.

In the 1850s the Northern branch of the party favored **popular sovereignty**, Douglas' own concept wherein the voters decided for or against the extension of slavery within the boundaries of their state or territory. The Southern branch preferred an unequivocal assertion that the Constitution absolutely protected the practice of slavery. Douglas became the leader of the Northern group, while **Jefferson Davis** led the Southern position. When Congress voted to ease the tensions over slavery with the passage of the **Compromise of 1850**, Davis voted against every provision of the bill except that which strengthened the **Fugitive Slave Law**. Douglas was absent when the vote was taken on the bill, but his future comments show that he approved of it.

In 1852 Douglas ran as a presidential candidate appealing to "Young America." While he was unsuccessful in attaining the White House, he was reelected to the Senate. The **Kansas-Nebraska Act of 1854** was a product of the optimism of the Northern Democrats and Stephen Douglas. The act seemingly sabotaged the political compromises that had characterized the previous decades of American politics. Nonetheless, in 1856 Douglas was again a candidate for the presidency but withdrew his name in deference to **James Buchanan**.

It was no surprise when **Abraham Lincoln** was chosen by the Republicans to face Douglas in the 1858 race for the Illinois Senate race. Lincoln began his campaign with his famous "House Divided" speech. His words were widely interpreted as a declaration of war on Southern institutions. In a highly publicized series of debates, Douglas carefully pointed out that the country had been split for quite some time on the issue of slavery and could continue to be so indefinitely if the hotheads on both sides would leave well enough alone. By espousing moderation, Douglas won the race narrowly.

Lincoln probably would not have won the presidency in 1860 had the election not become a four-way race. The Democratic Party split between two candidates, pro-slavery John C. Breckinridge and Douglas. The fourth candidate was John Bell of Tennessee. Campaign issues included **tariffs, homesteads, railroads, immigration**, and political corruption, but slavery and the fear of disunion remained the pivotal questions. When it became obvious that Lincoln was going to win, Bell and Breckinridge proclaimed dedication to immediate disunion; but Douglas, to his credit, disavowed any ideas of secession saying, "If Lincoln is elected, he must be inaugurated."

Lincoln won the election with just under 40 percent of the popular vote and 59 percent of the electoral votes. Significantly, Douglas, who beat both Breckinridge and Bell with 30 percent of the popular vote, represented the views of at least some of the electorate in all parts of the country; but he received a mere 4 percent of the electoral votes. Besides **Mississippi**, the only other state won by Douglas was New Jersey. This seemingly strange pairing effectively ended the influence of Douglas and the Northern Democrats. In the last weeks of the Buchanan administration Douglas worked for compromise, and in the first weeks of the Lincoln administration he seems to have been dedicated to rousing the people of the Northwest to the seriousness of the impending crisis. On April 25, 1861, soon after delivering a speech on this subject, he contracted typhoid fever and died. **Related Entries**: Bell, John; Breckinridge, John C.; Kansas-Nebraska Act of 1854; Lincoln, Abraham; Popular Sovereignty.

SUGGESTED READING: Jeremiah S. Black, *Observations on Senator Douglas's Views of Popular Sovereignty as Expressed in Harper's Magazine* (1859); Frank L. Dennis, *The Lincoln-Douglas Debates* (1974); Robert W. Johannsen, *Stephen A. Douglas* (1997); Jeannette C. Nolan, *The Little Giant* (1942).

DOUGLASS, FREDERICK (1817–1895): former slave, writer, and **abolitionist**. From 1841 to 1860, Douglass was the most prominent black abolitionist. His *Narrative* (1845) was filled "with noble thoughts and thrilling reflections." Douglass was a slave in Baltimore for more than twenty years, and his book, published by the American Anti-slavery Society, was replete with the physical abuses of **slavery**, including whippings, rape, unwarranted punishments, and cold-blooded murder. The work appealed to a wider audience of reformers than just those who favored **emancipation**. Proponents of **women's rights, temperance**, public **education**, and **immigration** reform all found something to stir them in Douglass' work.

Southern readers pointed with incredulity to many of Douglass' childhood memories of the whipping and murder of his fellow slaves. As he carefully omitted corroborating details from the incidents, many whites were convinced that the stories were patently false. His accounts of two slaves being murdered in unrelated incidents by individual masters on adjoining plantations within hours of one another rang false to all but the most dedicated of abolitionists. Nevertheless, between 1845 and 1850 the book sold more than 30,000 copies, and it was regarded by many in the North as a true picture of slavery in **Maryland**. The reviewer of the *New York Tribune*, himself an abolitionist, praised the book upon its publication for its simplicity, truth, coherence, and warmth.

Emancipation advocate William Lloyd Garrison declared that only the great weight of slavery had deteriorated the natural goodness and intelligence the Negro had brought from Africa. "It has a natural, an inevitable tendency to brutalize every noble faculty of man." Frederick Douglass served as a favorite symbol of the ideally regenerated freeman, and was portrayed as a victim of slavery with a "godlike nature" and "richly endowed" intellect. Douglass was showcased as a naturally eloquent "prodigy—in soul manifestly created but a little lower than the angels." He was a favorite speaker on the lecture circuit, and hundreds of abolitionists flocked to his addresses.

However, Douglas was not satisfied with the limits of such audiences. He reached out to the black community of the North to support their brethren in bondage. One of the more effective means he used in the 1850s was *Frederick Douglass' Paper*, later called *Douglass' Monthly Magazine*. Unlike other black papers, which were locally popular and short-lived, Douglass' work was circulated through eighteen states and two foreign countries. It had more than 4,000 subscribers and survived for more than thirteen years.

Once the war commenced, Douglass altered his agenda from ending slavery to having blacks accepted in white society as equals. In this regard he agitated constantly for the establishment of black regiments of federal soldiers, feeling (optimistically in light of future events) that those who fought to save the Union would find an equal place in it after the war. At first he met with stubborn resistance, but finally he was successful in creating all-black infantry units from among free black volunteers. Two of Douglass' sons volunteered for this duty and served with distinction. Ultimately, black troops were placed in combat roles, where their performance proved laudable and, at times, heroic. The best known black unit was the 54th Massachusetts Colored Infantry, with which Douglass was closely associated. **Related Entries**: Black Anti-slavery Activists; Newspapers.

SUGGESTED READING: Frederick Douglass, *Narrative of the Life of an American Slave, Written by Himself* (1845); Milton Meltzer, ed., *Frederick Douglass: In His Own Words* (1995); Philip Spencer, *Three Against Slavery: Denmark Vesey, William Lloyd Garrison, Frederick Douglass* (1972); Frederick S. Voss, *Majestic in His Wrath: A Pictorial Life of Frederick Douglass* (1995).

DUELING (DUELISTS): Nowhere in America, and possibly in the Western world, was dueling so universally practiced as in the **antebellum South**.

The possibility of being involved in a duel was a social reality for all those who considered themselves gentlemen or who dealt in politics. Even in the midst of polite conversation, gentlemen were always on guard to protect their integrity. As Southern society also favored a relaxed cordiality, the two notions often required a delicate touch. Quarrels among citizens of the upper class never ended in simple fisticuffs, and it was social suicide to strike a blow in anger. At all levels of Southern society individual liberty, manliness, and respect for social position were held in such high esteem that one put his life and personal honor on the line to protect them. Ironclad rules and traditions governed every stage of such encounters from the moment of the insult up to the hours immediately after the combatants had met on the field of honor.

In some circles the *Code Duello*, supported by an incredibly strict adherence to a sense of Southern honor, was regarded with the same reverence as a religion. For almost one hundred years before the Civil War, the specter of dueling shadowed every fashionable social function, the **theater**, the opera, anywhere, in fact, where there might be the least breach of etiquette, the slightest lapse in politeness, or the smallest hint that a business dealing was unethical, even if it was. Truth might be an admirable defense against libel or slander in a court of law, but it had no standing in affairs of honor. A word and a challenge were the purest form of the dueling code. The custom reached such heights of absurdity that a moment of awkwardness might result in a challenge that could not, with honor, be ignored. A nineteenth-century commentator, Major Ben C. Truman, noted that "the purpose of a duel was to resolve a point of honor, not simply to kill an enemy. Opponents who lost sight of this might be looked upon as murderers by purists, who saw the entire process as an exercise in character" (*Wood*, 1884).

It was in **New Orleans** that the practice of dueling reached its zenith. The golden age of dueling lasted from 1830 to 1860. Initially, only swords were used in dueling and, consequently, there were few fatalities. However, with the advent of the more lethal percussion cap pistol and its reliable ignition system, fatalities increased. No attempt has been made to determine the number of duels that were fought in the South, as the task is daunting and the records of duels were somewhat concealed by the need to evade the laws which tried unsuccessfully to prevent them. Certainly, the number of duels fought in this period figures in the thousands, and the fatalities in the hundreds.

Dueling had a long history in America. The dancing masters of the eighteenth century, who had taught the finer points of swordsmanship to their well-heeled pupils, now abandoned the dance to open fencing schools and academies of dueling dedicated to teaching the requisite skills of both sword and pistol. Well-known duelists occupied much the same position in antebellum society as sports figures do in modern times. They were followed through the streets, fawned upon by waiters in restaurants, and had their mannerisms and dueling styles copied by the young men.

In the decades before the Civil War, there was hardly a man in public life in **Louisiana** who had not faced a duel, and many had fought several. Ten duels were fought on a single day at the Oaks, a favorite field of honor. Many of these affairs grew out of political party wrangling, which was, unfortunately, lacking in restraint and sophistication in this period. Duels sometimes ran through a political party or social grouping in a series involving one individual after another, one encounter producing the next. Only the violence of the Civil War was able to overshadow this apparent lust for individual combat.

An ardent **states' rights** advocate and governor of **South Carolina, James Hamilton** was a noted duelist and was much sought after as an assistant in Southern dueling circles. President **Andrew Jackson** was not unfamiliar with dueling. As early as 1788, he had called out a lawyer who found himself facing a young Jackson after a momentary slip of verbal discretion in court. The details of the confrontation were arranged, but conciliation won the day, with the two men firing their pistols in the air to satisfy their honor and then shaking hands. However, not all of Jackson's affairs of honor ended as affably. Prior to his election as President, Jackson fought a duel and killed a man in defense of his wife's honor. This affair dogged his future political campaigns.

Although formal in its procedures and acceptable at the highest levels of society, dueling quickly lost favor in the North and came to be seen as characteristically "Southern." This view has been reinforced in modern times by numerous films and romantic novels. Nonetheless, dueling began losing favor in the South prior to the Civil War mostly because it degenerated either into contests with shotguns, axes, and clubs or into brawls between groups of lower-class men using fighting knives and repeating pistols. **Related Entries**: Hamilton, James A.; Jackson, Andrew.

SUGGESTED READING: Jack Kenny Williams, *Dueling in the Old South* (1980); Steven Randolph Wood, ed., *Duelling in America*, by Major Ben C. Truman (1884).

EATON, PEGGY (1796–1879): Formerly Margaret L. O'Neale, she met a close friend of **Andrew Jackson**, John H. Eaton, while she was still married to another man and formed a relationship that lasted for a decade. In 1828, soon after the death of her first husband (too soon to appease etiquette), she married Eaton, who was the newly appointed secretary of war in Jackson's administration. While there was no hard evidence of adultery prior to the death of Mrs. Eaton's first husband, her lack of social status—she was the daughter of a tavern keeper—and the appearance of impropriety were enough to taint the couple socially. **Washington** society was scandalized.

A dramatic rift in the cabinet was caused by Floride Calhoun, wife of Vice President **John C. Calhoun**, when she refused to receive Peggy Eaton socially. This pretension spread to the wives of other cabinet members, and Jackson's intransigence in defending the Eatons led to a disaffection among many of them that resulted in a mass resignation of cabinet officers in 1831. The President's relationship with his Vice President steadily deteriorated thereafter until it became an irreparable and public breach. **Related Entries:** Calhoun, John C.; Jackson, Andrew.

SUGGESTED READING: Peggy Eaton, *The Autobiography of Peggy Eaton* (1932).

ECONOMIC DEPRESSIONS. *See* Panics.

EDUCATION: As the second quarter of the nineteenth century progressed, the movement toward community or common schools gained momentum. On the eve of the Civil War, about 50 percent of children outside the South attended school with some regularity. The largely rural nature of the South, however, hampered the creation of an effective public school system except in more densely populated areas. Southerners preferred to send their children to private institutions or employed tutors, who, ironically, were mostly from the North. Some larger domestic complexes contained separate buildings designed to serve as schoolrooms for the family's children. Private academies offered reasonably good to superior instruction primarily in the classics, with some practical study such as surveying. Students who boarded at these institutions lived in less than lavish accommodations, often little more than cabins. Other students traveled from nearby plantations, often on foot.

A few academies were open to both boys and girls, but generally the sexes were educated at separate institutions. Girls were offered courses in music, singing, drawing, painting, and French. Some were taught mathematics and Latin, but these disciplines were not generally seen as crucial to a life devoted to caring for a husband and raising babies.

Most Southerners were opposed to public education, which had created "ragged schools" filled with pauper children in England, especially when their establishment required the use of their tax dollars. There was some belief that the **poor whites** would neither appreciate the institution of public education nor make effective use of it. Additionally, the majority of school reformers were Northerners, and since most Southerners felt that Northern school systems were at least partially responsible for the distasteful attitudes displayed by residents of this section of the country, they hesitated to embrace any institution that could produce such thinking. By 1860 only four Southern states and a few isolated communities had effective common school systems.

Conditions in common schools varied tremendously, not only from North to South but from community to community. Most provided no more than crude benches without backs, slates for writing, and a limited number of shared books. There were few, if any, standards at this time. The length of the school day and year varied as the individual community saw fit.

As no textbooks were published in the South until the Civil War, Southern **teachers** depended upon the North and Europe for their materials. As the nation moved closer to the inevitable conflict, certain Southern parents were uncomfortable with some of the selections. They even began to regret the fact that so many Northerners had been employed as teachers of Southern youth.

While basic education languished—as late as the 1830s nearly one-third of Southern adults were illiterate—colleges and universities offered opportunities comparable to those provided by their Northern counterparts. The University of Virginia, founded in 1825, was unequivocally cosmopolitan and probably ranked second in the nation at the time, surpassed only by Harvard. Even at this level, however, most of the South's colleges were supported by religious denominations. Presbyterians took the lead with Hampden-Sydney, East Tennessee, Washington (later to become Washington and Lee), and Transylvania colleges. Episcopalians already had William and Mary, and followed with St. John's College and the College of Charleston. Several of these institutions received considerable state aid, which helped them to remain solvent despite declining enrollments. Medicine and law were the studies most frequently pursued in these institutions.

There were no organized educational facilities for slaves in the **antebellum South**. In 1819 the General Assembly of **Virginia** passed a law prohibiting the teaching of Negroes, and many other states followed with similar legislation. There were, however, always masters and mistresses who ignored the statutory prohibitions and instructed those slaves with whom they had the closest relationships in some basic rudiments of education. Following the insurrection of **Nat Turner**, trepidation and therefore compliance with the law increased greatly. Many Southerners were equally troubled about educated **free blacks**. Higher education was simply not an option for blacks in the South. **Related Entries**: Teachers. Also consult entries for individual states under the heading "Education."

SUGGESTED READING: Lawrence A. Cremin, *American Education: The National Experience, 1783–1876* (1980).

EMANCIPATION: Slaveowners were free to dispose of their slaves in almost any manner short of maiming or murdering them. Since slaves were often bought on credit or used as security for loans, even a humane slaveowner could not free any of his "slave property" so encumbered without satisfying his creditors. Cash-starved plantation owners rarely could afford the luxury of freeing slaves even if they inherited them or wished to do so in their will. Moreover, many state constitutions put legal obstacles in the way of masters who wished to manumit their own slaves. These ranged from minor inconveniences in the border states to outright prohibitions of private manumission in the Deep South. In many cases the law required that freed slaves not be foisted on the community as a financial burden. In others, freed blacks were required to leave the state or even the country.

The treatment of **free blacks** even in Northern states was often brutish, and they were despised and treated with contempt in many localities. Any plan for a general **abolition** of **slavery** had to deal with the touchy problem of free blacks living in a white-dominated, racist society. This led many sympathetic whites to fear for the ultimate welfare and safety of a black population suddenly at large in an unfriendly America should they attain their emancipation. The South Carolina Court of Appeals put itself on record with regard to blacks freed by private emancipation, stating that "a free African population is a curse to any country . . . [and] a dead weight to the progress of improvement."

In some circumstances slaves could buy their own freedom. They were able to earn a small amount of cash by doing extra work, turning their talents to a particularly artful or craftsmanlike project, or receiving the equivalent of tips. One slave was said to have accumulated more than $500 in this manner. Another slave, **Denmark Vesey**, used his winnings from a lottery to buy his freedom. Free black tradesmen often bought freedom for their wives and loved ones. **Joseph P. Parker**, a foundry worker, bought his own freedom and returned to the South to act as a conductor on the **Underground Railroad**. Very elderly slaves, unable to work in their old age, were often pensioned off, being provided with a small sum of cash or given a shack and a regular issue of **food** on the plantation. Some states had laws requiring slaveowners to make such provisions so that elderly slaves did not become a burden on society. Yet none of these circumstances was of common occurrence.

The majority of free blacks lived on the margins of poverty, and were subject to detention and questioning by the authorities without cause. In the South they were continually encouraged to sell themselves back into slavery; a freeman could sell himself as an indentured servant for life, contract his conditions of employment, choose his master, and retain the cash under the laws of many jurisdictions, particularly **Virginia**. The impracticality of free blacks being integrated into the fabric of American society in the antebellum period can best be measured by the resistance to racial integration seen in the South after a costly and painful war had forced emancipation upon it. **Related Entries**: Free Blacks; Value of Slaves.

SUGGESTED READING: Eric Foner, *Nothing but Freedom: Emancipation and Its Legacy* (1983); Owen A. Sherrard, *Freedom from Fear: The Slave and His Emancipation* (1959); Kenneth M. Stampp, *The Peculiar Institution* (1956).

EMMETT, DANIEL DECATUR (1815–1904): musician, comedian, and composer. Daniel Decatur Emmett was a popular personality of the **minstrel show** genre. Emmett, or Emmit, as he was later known, was responsible for some of the most popular songs of the three decades prior to the Civil War. His 1840s hits include " 'Twill Neber Do to Gib It Up So," "Gwine ober the Mountains," and "Old Dan Tucker." In the 1850s "Root Hog or Die" and "Jordan Is a Hard Road to Trabel" were popular. In the late fifties and sixties "walk-arounds" were performed by virtually all minstrel shows, and Emmett was responsible for many popular pieces for this venue, including "Billy Patterson," "Johnny Roach What o' Dat," and "Dixie's Land." Walk-arounds were performances that were sung and danced by a few soloists backed up by six or eight men.

Emmett is best known for writing the words to "Dixie," an immediate popular success that was to become inextricably linked with the Southern Confederacy. Various arrangements and lyric changes followed as other performers latched onto it. Although Emmett received little money from it, "Dixie" was perhaps the greatest lyric success in America up to that time. **Related Entries**: Foster, Stephen Collins; Minstrel Shows.

SUGGESTED READING: John Trasker Howard, *Our American Music* (1965).

EPIDEMICS: In the antebellum period the existence of bacteria and microbes as causative agents of disease was unknown. The theory that contagious disease was spread by miasmic odors or personal contact was still in vogue. Typhoid, typhus, measles, cholera, smallpox, malaria, and yellow fever were all ascribed to exposure to "bad air" or the noxious odors emanating from swamps and marshes. Epidemics swept the cities of the nation with unfortunate regularity, and those who could afford to remove themselves from the scene of an epidemic outbreak did so. Others resorted to tying brandy-soaked kerchiefs over their nose and mouth or sat breathing in the fumes of burning sulfur or smoldering tobacco and corn husks. Although cowpox vaccine had become widely used since 1798 in controlling smallpox, the mechanism of acquired immunity was not well understood.

Malaria. The innumerable swamps and stagnant ponds of the coastal regions and many other parts of the South were thought to cause malaria. It would be decades before an association between mosquitoes and the spread of the disease would be confirmed. Malaria was a fearful disease that brought chills, fever, and sometimes death. Yet malaria was thought benign when compared to other epidemics that regularly struck the Southern population. Quinine, extracted from the bark of a tree, was known to be effective in preventing and controlling the disease.

The slaves' susceptibility to malaria was a major cause of their early death. Negroes seemed to most observers at the time to be immune to the most deadly forms of malaria, but they often succumbed to less virulent strains. As slave births rarely exceeded slave deaths, planters had to spend thousands of dollars to maintain their work force in the face of an epidemic. Moreover, whites seemed to be particularly susceptible to the deadlier strains of the disease. White **overseers** invariably contracted the disease when working in the miasmic swamps that were common to the tidewater, and frequently they died. Some skilled overseers refused such employment, leaving the field open to men who were often coarse and uncultivated, if not incompetent. A contemporary observer noted that such overseers came and went on many tidewater plantations with great regularity.

Yellow Fever. Yellow fever was chronic in the South, with epidemics hitting the coastal cities every few years. In 1832 one-sixth of the population of **New Orleans** died in a twelve-day period. In the next year, one in five succumbed. The 1853 outbreak, in which there were more than 40,000 cases of fever, was described as catastrophic. One observer noted that "the dead were piled in wagons and hauled away like cordwood."

The treatment for yellow fever was always the same, and it was not effective. The patient was kept as warm as possible, and the doors and windows of the sickroom were sealed. There followed a ruthless and senseless regimen of purging and bleeding which tended to weaken the patient. Few survived either the disease or the treatment.

The uncoffined bodies of the deceased were generally interred in large trenches dug for the purpose, and sometimes whole buildings were burned down with the bodies of the dead inside and the ashes scattered in hopes of stopping the spread of the epidemic. Nonetheless, a great number of bodies were thrown into the river with stones or bricks tied to them. Others were buried in gardens and lawns, or lay unburied for days in the buildings in which they had died. In 1832, after six weeks of yellow fever, the first cases of cholera appeared and raged for two weeks. The combined attack of these two diseases was not unusual. The indiscriminate disposal of the victims of the first disease created a welcoming environment for the second.

Cholera. No disease struck terror into the population as did cholera. The disease was thought to be contained in a "deadly air" that filled the cities. "Everyone complained of a difficulty in breathing, which he never before experienced," wrote a clergyman in 1832. "The heavens were as stagnant as the mantled pool of death." Unknown to the public at the time, cholera was largely carried in the drinking water supply, and almost everyone who relied on a public water supply or the water of urban **rivers** was exposed to it. Many persons, even those of high social standing, died in their beds unattended because of the fear of an airborne infection that did not exist.

During an epidemic tar and pitch barrels were burned on street corners and gunpowder was fired from cannon in the hope that the pestilence would be eradicated by the fumes and smoke. Stray dogs, thought to be carriers of the infection, were poisoned in the street, but the fear of contamination was so great that no one would remove the putrefying carcasses. The consumption of alcohol in the form of wine and liquor increased in direct proportion to the fear engendered by the spread of the disease. Even women and children plied themselves with alcohol to the point of intoxication. The smoke-filled and putrid environment added to the atmosphere of terror and unreality, akin to a trip to Dante's *Inferno.* **Related Entries**: Geography; Medicine; Overseers.

SUGGESTED READING: Herbert Asbury, *The French Quarter: An Informal History of New Orleans* (1938); Walter Sullivan, *The War the Women Lived: Female Voices from the Confederate South* (1995).

EROSION OF THE SOIL:

EROSION OF THE SOIL: Since the seventeenth century, **Virginia** colonists had understood that tobacco farming was very hard on their soil; but it was also a valuable cash crop. In the money-conscious nineteenth century, therefore, tobacco remained an important crop, but its large-scale cultivation had become mainly confined to **North Carolina** and **Kentucky**. The tobacco plantations of Virginia and **Maryland**, once noted for their palatial splendor, had generally succumbed in the nineteenth century to the accumulated effects of depressed prices and decades of soil depletion. Many mansions were in a state of dilapidation, fields were covered in yellow weeds and scrub pine, and the occupants evinced an atmosphere of economic depression.

A field of rice with its sluice gate in position to control the flow of water. (From a nineteenth-century schoolbook in the authors' collection.)

The prominence of the Old South as a comprehensive producer of **agricultural products** was waning in the antebellum period, being replaced by the new farms of Michigan, Iowa, Kansas, and **Missouri**. This change was ascribed at the time to the depleted and eroded soils of the older plantations. **John Randolph**, seeing fields gullied and rivers full of mud, called the farming techniques commonly used in Virginia "improvident." He warned his fellow planters, "We must either attend to . . . our lands or abandon them and run away to **Alabama**." A few concerned planters sponsored programs that trained slaves to use modern plowing methods, introduced technological improvements, and encouraged soil experiments. Planter, secessionist, and politician **Edmund Ruffin** served for many years as the head of the Virginia Agricultural Society, which fostered more modern farming methods. Yet, most planters left these areas of concern to their **overseers**, who had no genuine incentive to implement them if the owner did not actively pursue the matter.

In an era when crop rotation and commercial fertilizers other than manure and guano were unknown, intensive single-crop farming and shallow plowing quickly wore out the soil. Fertilization could help to salvage many plantations; yet thin, powdery soil remained a major problem in some places. Many coastal planters, following Randolph's advice, abandoned their land in the 1840s for new fields in **Mississippi** and Alabama that promised to be more fertile. The rich black soil of these areas promised an abundance of **cotton**, if not tobacco. Yet, in just a decade, these new lands were also showing the effects of erosion and soil worn by extensive single-crop agriculture. This circumstance found the next generation of planters moving on again, to **Texas** and **Arkansas**.

The tidewater plantations were somewhat insulated from soil exhaustion, however, by the almost inexhaustible swamp muck which was annually revitalized by flooding **rivers**. In the marshes, which did not lend themselves to cotton production, rice was king. **Robert B. Rhett**, a successful **South Carolina** rice grower, claimed to have harvested profitable rice crops on the same land for more than a decade. "Our tide swamp lands in the production of rice are the most certain in the world and the price of the commodity the least fluctuating." The large rice plantation owners initially moved from South Carolina to the Savannah River and **Georgia**, then further west when rice production became more profitable along the western rivers. Rice remained a valuable export item, and the rice plantations of tidewater South Carolina were still prosperous in the 1850s.

Nonetheless, almost all of the plantations abandoned in the decade of the 1820s were in the tidewater. Evidence would suggest that the deserted tidewater plantations may have been less products of depleted soil than victims of depleted income. When crop prices fell, the economic and human conditions surrounding tidewater **agriculture** severely limited the level of prosperity that could be achieved even by intensive efforts. While the erosion of upcountry soil—that outside the tidewater—was a serious problem, it was not as grievous as the problems encountered by the swarms of malaria-bearing mosquitoes that killed off planter, overseer, and slave alike in the tidewater areas. Moreover, upcountry land was cheaper to buy than tidewater soil, and cotton could be grown there with or without slaves. The dream of many upcountry planters was to imitate the great tidewater planters, who had hundreds of slaves, by acquiring one slave, or a few, to help work their land. **Related Entries**: Agriculture; Geography; Plantation Economy.

SUGGESTED READING: Alfred G. Smith, Jr., *Economic Readjustment of an Old Cotton State* (1958).

EXECUTIVE BRANCH/PRESIDENCY: The executive branch of government was generally controlled by the South by one means or another right up to the eve of the Civil War. A long succession of **Virginia**-born Presidents in the early decades of the nation, broken only by a single term of **John Adams** of Massachusetts, became known as the "Virginia Dynasty." **George Washington** symbolically passed the torch of presidency to his secretary of state, **Thomas Jefferson**. Thereafter, Southern-born Presidents passed the office down to their secretaries of state in succession for almost a quarter century: Jefferson to **James Madison**, Madison to **James Monroe**—each serving two terms.

Influenced by increasing sectionalism, the North and East demanded an end to Virginian rule in the Executive Mansion. By the election of 1820, the opponents of Monroe were eagerly pointing out that the South was effectively ruling the Union. Not until 1824 was a New Englander again elected; but **John Quincy Adams**, like his father, failed to gain a second term. **Andrew Jackson**'s presidency, from 1828 through 1836, broke the Southern stranglehold on the executive branch. However, although a wealthy Western slaveowner, Jackson was viewed as a President of the people rather than a representative of the anxious upper classes of the Northeast.

Jackson's desire to choose New Yorker **Martin Van Buren** as his own successor to the presidency was both encouraging and distressing. Van Buren's 1836 **Democratic Party** victory was seemingly nonpartisan, based on votes from all sections of the country, yet by this time the major parties had displaced the individual states as the institutions of political polarization. In fact, the strangely heterogeneous interest groups that made up the opposition party were essentially moneyed people who were afraid of governmental interference by an unbridled executive. The **cotton** planters who opposed protective **tariffs** were **Whigs;** the factory owners who asked for protective tariffs were Whigs; and the bankers and Southern conservatives who opposed "executive tyranny" were Whigs. Van Buren's single-term presidency was largely a victim of this hodgepodge of opposition.

For a time the voters became fond of military men as presidential candidates. This fascination with general-presidents had begun with Jackson and had continued with **William Henry Harrison** and **Zachary Taylor.** The latter two had died in office, leaving the public with the unsatisfying **John Tyler** and **Millard Fillmore. James K. Polk** of **Tennessee** had won the presidency only with the support of Jackson and because of his willingness to go to war with Mexico in 1846. In this period the names of other military men surfaced on the pond of politics. General **Winfield Scott** and General Lewis Case were both serious candidates for the presidency.

Nonetheless, although the major parties tried to ignore it, by the election of 1848 **slavery** had become a major national issue. The divisiveness of this issue can be seen in the campaign for the executive office in the 1850s. When the factions of the Democratic Party were not able to unite behind **James Buchanan**, Lewis Cass, or **Stephen A. Douglas** after forty-eight ballots, dark horse candidate **Franklin Pierce** was chosen. The Whigs were so split on the issue of slavery that the Southern wing of the party dictated the platform while the Northern wing selected Winfield Scott as the candidate. Pierce's victory in 1852 was largely a product of this in-fighting over slavery, placing a minority President in the Executive Mansion. In 1856 Buchanan had a similar experience against **John C. Fremont** and Millard Fillmore. In both 1852 and 1856, Southern **secessionists** had threatened disunion if an anti-slavery candidate won the presidency—a threat that was carried out when **Abraham Lincoln** won the election in 1860. **Related Entries**: See entries on individual Presidents.

SUGGESTED READING: John A. Crittenden, *Parties and Elections in the United States* (1982); Arthur M. Schlesinger, Jr., *History of American Presidential Elections, 1789–1984* (1986); George Sullivan, *Campaigns and Elections* (1991).

EXPANSION. *See* Manifest Destiny.

EXTENSION OF SLAVERY INTO THE TERRITORIES: One of the strategic errors made by pro-slavery apologists was to allow **abolitionists** to turn the **slavery** argument into a debate over whether or not the practice would be extended into the vast expanse of unorganized territories the nation had assembled in meeting its **manifest destiny**. Although the South vociferously demanded a share in the nation's territorial opportunity, by mid-century the question of slavery in the territories had, in fact, become nothing more than symbolic in itself. Few regions remained into which slavery could be introduced economically. **Cotton** demanded at least 200 frostless days of growth, limiting production to those areas of the South in which it was already grown. Nonetheless, the question of the extension of slavery persisted, and the debate remained a focus of sectionalism and a catalyst for discord.

In the minds of most Americans slavery was primarily a political problem. From the beginning of the century only four states west of the **Mississippi River—Louisiana, Arkansas, Missouri**, and **Texas**—had been gathered to the South from the Louisiana Territory, while in the same period eight states had been added to the "Northern" side of the political ledger from above the Missouri Compromise line. The depth of violence seen in the disputes over the possibility of simultaneously admitting both Nebraska and Kansas as **free states**—possibly the last territorial area into which slavery might be economically introduced—well documents these principles. These facts help to explain the need for the reciprocal admission of **slave states** and free states to the Union found in the **Missouri Compromise of 1820** and the **Compromise of 1850**. When the Southern states despaired of maintaining their legislative and judicial advantage, they resorted to **secession** as a remedy. **Related Entries**: Bleeding Kansas; Compromise of 1850; Kansas-Nebraska Act of 1854; Popular Sovereignty.

SUGGESTED READING: Michael A. Morrison, *Slavery and the American West: The Eclipse of Manifest Destiny and the Coming of the Civil War* (1997); Richard H. Sewell, *A House Divided: Sectionalism and the Civil War, 1848–1865* (1988); Dorothy Denneen Volo and James M. Volo, *Daily Life in Civil War America* (1998).

FARMING. *See* Agriculture.

FASHION: Southern women were enamored of fashion and savored the ability to dress in a style reflective of their position and wealth. Women in fashionable circles had to balance their desire to be stylish against the extravagance of display. From an early age, girls were taught the fine points of dress, and many were favored with an abundance of outfits by doting fathers.

The isolation of Southern plantations provided little opportunity to see the latest styles firsthand. Female correspondents implored visitors to cities to share fashion news. Letters regularly requested travelers to return with ribbons and fabrics. Women in both the North and the South turned to ladies' magazines for inspiration.

One of the greatest influences on American women's fashion during the antebellum period was *Godey's Lady's Book*, a magazine founded by Louis B. Godey in July 1830. In addition to serials, essays, poems, and craft projects, it featured engraved fashion plates based on the latest French styles. Each month the magazine depicted morning dresses, walking dresses, seaside costumes, riding habits, dinner dresses, and ball gowns. Such wardrobe depth was seldom needed for the vast majority of the magazine's readers, whose clothes could generally be divided into public or social, and domestic or work, with a few seasonal additions for summer and winter. Other magazines, such as *Leslie's Fashion Monthly*, also emerged and grew in popularity.

Most new clothes of the gentry were made by dressmakers. Styles became increasingly elaborate as the century progressed, and those of true style required considerable talent and labor to produce. Everyday clothing and undergarments were often made at home. Women also took pains to rework and to update existing clothing in an attempt to make it more fashionable.

Ladies' skirts were only moderately wide in October 1837, as this *Godey's Lady's Book* illustration shows.

Although many plantation households had slaves who did sewing, much of their labor was dedicated to household linens and mending, rather than fashion. In less affluent households, women often made their own clothing.

Many of the fabrics and dyes used at this time did not hold up to frequent laundering. Garments were often taken apart and resewn when cleaned. The *Household Encyclopedia* provided nine pages of instructions for washing various fabrics employing methods that included the use of bran, rice water, ox-gall, salt, elixir of vitriol, and egg yolk. Most women's dresses were never totally laundered but rather spot cleaned as needed.

Fabrics used for dresses and skirts included silk, linen, **wool**, and **cotton**. These were available in an almost infinite variety of weights and weaves, some of which are no longer available today. By far cotton and linen were the most common choices for everyday wear. Silk was expensive. If the average woman owned a silk dress, it would be saved for very special occasions. Linen, because of its extreme durability and ability to be produced at home, was considered frontier or laborer clothing. This was particularly true in the South, where it was in common use among the slave population. Wool continued to have its place especially because of its fire-retardant qualities. Cotton, a status symbol earlier in the century, had become readily available and affordable for even modest households by the 1830s, thanks to an

Both the outdoor dress on the left and the evening dress on the right illustrate the extremes to which hoop skirts had gone by September 1860. (From *Godey's Lady's Book*).

extremely well developed textile industry, aided by the invention of the **cotton gin**.

The color palette available at this time was basically limited to what could be achieved by natural dyes. While Southern women tended to wear lighter hues, popular colors included browns, soft blues, greens, lavenders, and grays. Yellows and deep berry-toned reds were also in use. Even though chemical dyes had been introduced by the end of the 1850s, these colors were mostly found in decorative fabrics for the home.

The silhouette of women's dresses during the antebellum period evolved from the high-waisted, slender elegance of the Empire style of the opening decades of the century into a fuller skirt, lower waist, and leg-o'-mutton or gigot sleeve in the 1820s. In the 1830s the silhouette was slightly funnel shaped, with a V-shaped bodice, finally evolving into the increasingly widening hoop skirts which have become almost a signature of the prewar era. **Related Entry**: Slave Clothing.

SUGGESTED READING: Dorothy Denneen Volo and James M. Volo, *Daily Life in Civil War America* (1998).

FEAR OF SLAVE REVOLTS: The ability of the 1808–1809 slave revolt in Haiti to paint a nightmarish picture in the Southern imagination of whites slain in their beds by Negroes bent on revenge should not be underestimated. Haitian slaves had run a successful but bloody massacre of the French inhabitants of that island, and had defeated the 25,000 seasoned French troops sent there by Napoleon to quell the revolt. White Southerners had frequent contact with the "wretched fugitives" of that revolt who had escaped to the United States and never tired of repeating the graphic details. The possibility of communication between the **Denmark Vesey** conspirators in 1822 and the blacks of Haiti sent a shudder of fear through the entire South.

The South perceived a very real physical threat in slave rebellion. There were only three important black insurrections in the South: the Gabriel Revolt in 1800, the Denmark Vesey Revolt in 1822, and the **Nat Turner** Revolt in 1831. Only the Turner Revolt had led to any deaths among whites, but these had numbered mostly women and children among the sixty or so killed. The bloody Dominican revolt against the Haitian government in 1844 added more recent images of armed blacks slaughtering one another in chaotic frenzy. Against this background Southern forces in the U.S. Congress used the threat of similar revolts to quash any discourse in the halls of government on putting an end to **slavery**, saying that such debates helped to incite slaves to murder, rape, and plunder.

During the 1856 presidential election between **John C. Fremont** and **James Buchanan** anxiety over possible slave revolts swept the South. The resulting apprehension came to be known as the Slave Insurrection Panic of 1856. All across the South white communities tightened the enforcement of **Black Codes**, severely limited the movements of **free blacks**, and took "evidence" from supposed conspirators. The threat of widespread slave uprisings, instigated by **Black Republicans** in the event that Fremont lost the election, actually caused several supposed black "leaders" to be lynched. Coupled with the knowledge that **abolitionist John Brown** had attempted to foment an armed slave rebellion in **Virginia** during his attack on Harper's Ferry in 1858, such doings were taken seriously by slaveowners. **Related Entries**: Brown, John; Turner, Nat; Vesey, Denmark.

SUGGESTED READING: Herbert Aptheker, *American Negro Slave Revolts* (1943); Timothy J. Paulson, *Days of Sorrow, Years of Glory: 1831–1850* (1994); Harvey Walsh, "The Slave Insurrection Panic of 1856," *Journal of Southern History* 5 (1939): 206–222.

FEDERAL LAWS GOVERNING SLAVERY: Slavery—which proved the most contentious of all the disputes of the antebellum period—was absolutely protected by the language of the Constitution. Southerners not only saw for themselves that the Constitution clearly recognized and protected the right of a citizen to own slaves, but that it was equally clear in prohibiting the national government from interfering with it in any way. Only by the most tortured of legal arguments could slavery have been considered illegal under the original founding document. The legislature and the courts seemed to agree. Both the **Fugitive Slave Law** of 1850 and the **Dred Scott** decision of 1857 reinforced the legal legitimacy of slavery. **Related Entry**: Black Codes.

SUGGESTED READING: Martin Siegel, *The Taney Court, 1836–1864* (1995); Kenneth M. Stampp, *The Peculiar Institution* (1956); Charles M. Wilson, *The Dred Scott Decision* (1973).

FILLMORE, MILLARD (1800–1874): congressman, Vice President, and thirteenth President of the United States (1850–1853). Millard Fillmore grew up on the New York frontier and was elected to the state legislature during the **Anti-Masonic** campaign of the 1820s. He was elected to Congress as a **Whig** in 1833 and rose to chair the Ways and Means Committee. With the support of **Henry Clay**, Fillmore won the nomination for Vice President in 1848. As the presiding officer of the Senate, he managed the **slavery** debates of 1850 with firmness and fairness. On his succession to the presidency after **Zachary Taylor**'s death, Fillmore demonstrated his partiality for moderation in politics, aligning himself with those in the Whig Party who favored compromise.

Nonetheless, he exposed himself to the intense censure of the **abolitionists** when he signed the measure strengthening the **Fugitive Slave Law** of 1850, and he was abandoned by his party in 1852 when they gave the presidential nomination to **Mexican War** hero **Winfield Scott**. Fillmore thereafter aligned himself with the America-only zealots of the **Nativist** or "Know Nothing" Party. In 1856 his third-party candidacy helped to elect **James Buchanan** as President and probably cost **Republican Party** candidate **John C. Fremont** the election. Ironically, this result forestalled disunion for four years. As a former President in retirement, Fillmore opposed **Abraham Lincoln**'s conduct of the war, supported George B. McClellan against Lincoln in 1864, and was sympathetic to the concillatory policies of Andrew Johnson. **Related Entries**: Lincoln, Abraham; Scott, Winfield; Taylor, Zachary.

SUGGESTED READING: W. L. Barre, *The Life and Public Services of Millard Fillmore* (1856; 1971); Dorothea Dix, *The Lady and the President: The Letters of Dorothea Dix and Millard Fillmore* (1975); Kevin Law, *Millard Fillmore, Thirteenth President of the United States* (1990).

FIRE-EATERS: The Southern radicals most prominent in calling for **secession** were called Fire-eaters. In the **nullification** crisis of 1832 the South found the threat of secession to be a new weapon with which to enforce its will on the national government. The threat of secession thereafter dominated the rhetoric of Southern politicians. However, many Southern leaders espoused secession only sporadically, and usually only during an election campaign. Those who did otherwise did not achieve lasting prominence.

Fire-eaters considered themselves to be a conservative political force. They tended to focus on the Anti-Federalist views of the government which had been obscured by the development and implementation of a strong Federalist political theory since 1789. Although there were numerous radicals actively pursuing disunion in all the Southern states, few found places in the **Confederate government;** yet the Confederate Constitution that resulted from their rantings reflected many of the characteristics of early republicanism.

Some Fire-eaters are worthy of separate consideration, as they were conspicuously in the forefront of the clamor for secession and effective in securing disunion. **William Barkesdale** and **John A. Quitman of Mississippi, Edmund Ruffin of Virginia, Robert B. Rhett of South Carolina**, and **William L. Yancey of Alabama** were all prominent and outspoken Fire-eaters. **Related Entries**: Barkesdale, William; Quitman, John A.; Ruffin, Edmund; Rhett, Robert B.; Yancey, William L.

SUGGESTED READING: Robert E. May, *John A. Quitman: Old South Crusader* (1995); Emory M. Thomas, *The Confederacy as a Revolutionary Experience* (1991).

FITZHUGH, GEORGE (1806–1881): secessionist writer and Southern apologist. One of the most extreme of the pro-slavery propagandists, Fitzhugh was a **Virginia** lawyer who took pen in hand in an attempt to refute the anti-slavery arguments of the **abolitionists** and attack the shortcomings of a rapidly changing Northern society. While working for the *Richmond Examiner,* he wrote a series of **newspaper** articles and two books on these themes: *Sociology for the South, or The Failure of Free Society* (1854) and *Cannibals All, or Slaves without Masters* (1857). He also made regular contributions to *DeBow's Review* starting in 1857.

Most Southern apologists for **slavery** saw it as a necessary evil and were at some pains to explain their position to the North. Fitzhugh, more than most slavery advocates, proposed that slavery, rather than being a social evil, was a positive good not only for white society but also for the slaves themselves, echoing a view that was taken up by **John C. Calhoun** in Congress.

At times, Fitzhugh stretched his argument to the point of claiming that white wage earners would be better off if they were slaves. In *Cannibals All* he wrote, "We have conclusive proof that liberty and equality have not conduced to enhance the comfort or happiness of the people." Condemning free competition, Fitzhugh found "the struggle to better one's condition, to pull others down and supplant them, [a] great organic law of free society." Exploitation by capitalists and landlords was driving the majority of white wage earners into destitution. Fitzhugh pointed to the increased crime and poverty of the Northern cities, and to the riots, trade unionism, strikes, and revolutions in Europe as evidence of widespread discontent among white workers who found that their social condition was "far worse under the new than under the old order of things."

Conversely, the Southern farm, under the conditions of the American form of domestic slavery, was a "beau ideal," with each slave provided for "in old age and in infancy, in sickness and in health, not according to his labor, but according to his wants." Fitzhugh found that there was no rivalry, no competition to get employment among slaves, as among free laborers. Nor was there a "war between master and slave" as there seemed to be between employers and wage earners elsewhere. The slaveowning South was portrayed as all "peace, quiet, plenty and contentment [with] no mobs, no trade unions, no strikes for higher wages, no armed resistance to the law [and] but little jealousy of the rich by the poor."

Finally, Fitzhugh proposed a patriarchal picture of the relationship between masters and slaves that was a favorite of pro-slavery apologists. He emphasized that slavery "naturally" protected the weaker members of society—in this case slaves—just as parents, guardians, or husbands protected their relations. The patronal economy of the Southern plantation gave the mass of Southern workers more real liberty and true security because they were the chattels of their employers, who thus had the strongest interest in preserving their health and well-being. On the eve of the Civil War Fitzhugh was still trying to convert the North to his doctrines, and he deserves credit, on the Southern side, for attempting to change the great national argument over slavery from a mere rebuttal into an aggressive economic and social argument. **Related Entries**: Calhoun, John C.; Slavery.

SUGGESTED READING: Eugene D. Genovese, *The World the Slaveholders Made* (1969); Harvey Wish, *George Fitzhugh, Propagandist of the Old South* (1943).

FLATBOATS AND KEELBOATS: River transportation was one of the first means of moving people and merchandise. Many of the **rivers** in the South were navigable by small craft for most of the year despite the riffles and snags that could prevent the passage of larger craft. Indian canoes, bateaux, flatboats, and small keelboats were all used successfully on Southern rivers. The canoe could move upstream with ease and be carried around obstacles and shallow water, while the bateaux, which were propelled with oars, were much larger and heavier.

By far the greatest use of craft, other than canoes, was made by lumbermen who would float their product downriver in the form of rafts. These rafts came in many forms. Spar rafts were made of rough logs, while timber rafts were made of squared logs. Both were lashed together. Lumber rafts were made of cut and sawn boards, while arks were lumber rafts with smooth decks, a caulked bottom, and a deck cabin.

Arks and flatboats were so similar that they were almost indistinguishable. Both generally carried other cargo besides the lumber of which they were

This period print suggests both the variety and volume of river traffic. (From the authors' collection.)

built. Grain, whiskey, coal, salt, and gypsum were all carried on rafts, but they moved only downstream. Keelboats, distinctive in having a rudder post and rudder, also had a keel that kept them from slipping sideways through the water. They could be moved upstream by the use of poles, by large oars called sweeps, or by setting a square sail. More often the crew would haul the keelboat against the current with ropes from the embankment. **Related Entries**: Geography; Rivers; Transportation.

SUGGESTED READING: Michael Allen, *Western Rivermen, 1763–1861: Ohio and Mississippi Boatmen and the Myth of the Alligator Horse* (1994); Leland D. Baldwin, *Keelboat Age on Western Rivers* (1980); John F. McDermott, *Before Mark Twain: A Sampler of Old, Old Times on the Mississippi* (1998).

FLORIDA: Highlights of a period description of the state from John Hayward's *Gazetteer of the United States* (1853) read as follows:

Surface and Soil: The land, in nearly all parts of the state, is adapted to the culture of **cotton, sugar**, corn, rice, tobacco and valuable fruits. There is much grazing land which is irrigated by numerous streams of pure water.

Rivers: On the eastern coast, the mouths of the St. John's and the St. Mary's afford good harbors. On the western coast, are numerous bays and inlets furnishing safe shelter and anchorage for coasting craft.

Education: No extensive system of common school **education** has been established. There are several academical institutions, and a number of grammar and primary schools, but no colleges in the state.

Internal improvements: Several **railroads** have been constructed and others are still contemplated. The most important are between Tallahassee and St. Mark's and another extends from St. Joseph to Iola.

Manufacture: Beyond the fabrication of articles for domestic use, but little capital is employed in manufacturing operations. The exports consist principally of **raw materials**.

Indians: The Seminoles gave much trouble to the general government and with the question of their removal with other natives, to the lands provided for them, were found to be most impracticable. They were, however, subdued, and a large portion of the tribe have retired to the "far preferable country assigned them" beyond the Mississippi.

Population: There was an increase of population, during the ten years prior to 1840 of nearly sixty percent. Nearly one half were slaves. The census of 1850 exhibited the same rate of increase, but a somewhat smaller increase of slaves.

Other: Laws for the **emancipation** of slaves, or for the prevention of their introduction are prohibited. Clergymen, bank officers and duelists are excluded from participation in the civil government.

Related Entries: Geography; Indian Removal.

SUGGESTED READING: John Hayward, *Gazetteer of the United States* (1853); Gloria Jahoda, *Florida: A History* (1984).

FOOD: The cuisine of the South, built on a foundation of English cooking, fortified by native ingredients, nurtured by the abundant produce of an agrarian economy, and metamorphosed under the management of African cooks, emerged, during the antebellum period, as a very distinct style, different from the rest of the country and from its own colonial roots.

Truly American cookbooks did not exist until the appearance in 1796 of *American Cookery,* the first cookbook actually written by an American woman. Much of early American cooking was in an English style, adapted to native ingredients. Southerners quickly recognized corn as an important staple and adapted it to produce enduring dishes such as mush, fritters, yeasted bread, and boiled and baked puddings. What truly gave Southern foods their uniqueness was their preparation. In all but the poorest of households, slaves did the bulk of the cooking. These cooks were familiar with African foods such as benne (sesame) seeds and okra. They were more accepting of non-English ingredients such as peanuts, eggplants, tomatoes, and sweet potatoes. It is interesting to note that baking continued to be the domain of the white mistress and changed very little during this time. Baking recipes of the period from both English and Southern sources show little variation, if any.

Just as the South had developed a separate culture, it evolved its own particular style of cooking. In 1824 Mary Randolph published *The Virginia House-Wife,* which is said to be the first regional American cookbook. A cousin of **Thomas Jefferson**, Mrs. Randolph represented the old **Virginia** aristocracy, while Lettice Bryan's *The Kentucky Housewife* of 1839 reflected a cooking style from an area that was much more rural. *The Carolina Housewife*, written by Sarah Rutledge in 1847, includes numerous recipes for rice breads, cakes, and pilaus. Eliza Leslie was one of the most prolific food writers of her day. *Miss Leslie's New Cookery Book*, published in 1857, was widely used throughout the South.

In the decades prior to the Civil War, wealthy Southern planters, and even some of modest households, dined on egg-thickened fricassees, savory ragouts, crusty yeast breads, myriad vegetables, and delicate custards. Less affluent families lived on what is sometimes referred to as a "hog and hominy" diet. A traveler in the 1850s commented that the more modest Southern planter lived on **bacon**, turnip greens, corn pone, coffee sweetened with molasses, and little else.

With his commitment to the cash crops of tobacco and **cotton**, the Southern planter was not inclined to set aside large portions of land for the grazing of cattle. Most farmers did keep enough cows to provide their own supply of dairy products as well as some beef. Pork was the meat most frequently eaten in the South. Foreign visitors time and again were struck by the amount of meat consumed. Pork was easily served three times a day in some households; however, it was not likely fresh pork. Salt pork and smoked pork were staples except during the harvest season. Pork was abundant mainly because pigs were relatively easy to maintain. They required little space and tolerated a wide variety of foodstuffs, including leavings from food preparation. Pigs did not have to be put to pasture and consumed less feed than cattle to add the same amount of weight. Pork could be easily preserved in a number of ways including pickling, salting, and smoking. It was a common practice among farmers' and upper-class planters' wives alike to sell their cured hams as well as surplus lard, butter, and eggs. In 1856 the mistress of a **Georgia** plantation recorded the selling of 170 pounds of ham. Lamb and mutton were also popular, particularly in **Kentucky**, where they remained a mainstay of the local diet. Game was also an important part of the Southern diet, especially for poorer families.

Vegetables were eaten fresh in season. Southern cooks seemed to have especially favored fresh greens, as they are frequently mentioned in diarists' accounts. Some slaveowners encouraged their slaves to grow vegetables for themselves to supplement the basic diet of cornmeal, salt pork, and sweet potatoes provided for them. It was observed by some that the addition of fresh vegetables seemed to lessen disease. Only in the very deep South, however, were they available during the winter. Small amounts of vegetables could be grown in hot frames which utilized the heat of manure to keep temperatures warm enough to produce year-round as far north as Virginia. The rest of the region relied on a variety of methods to preserve surplus harvests.

Milk was difficult to keep in the warm Southern climate. Additionally, it provided an inviting medium in which bacteria could grow, a very real problem in an age when unsanitary conditions abounded. A visitor to the South in 1838 reported that milk was a rarity and that she found it plentiful only in Kentucky. Cheese also suffered. The only cheeses readily available were simple cottage cheeses and cream cheeses which did not require the long curing of hard cheeses. Some hard cheeses were imported and could be found in coastal cities. **Related Entries**: Food Preservation; Slave Food; Southern Hospitality.

SUGGESTED READING: Lettice Bryant, *The Kentucky Housewife* (1991); Damon Lee Fowler, *Classical Southern Cooking: A Celebration of the Cuisine of the South* (1995); Mary Randolph, *The Virginia Housewife* (1984); Sarah Rutledge, *The Carolina Housewife, or House and Home* (1979); Waverly Root and Richard de Rochemont, *Eating in America: A History* (1976).

FOOD PRESERVATION: In the mid-nineteenth century, **food** storage, particularly in the South, was a problem for everyone, no matter what their economic status. In addition to recipes for preparing food and suggestions on maintaining the household, receipt books (early books containing recipes and suggestions for household management, care of the sick, etc.) contained suggestions on food preservation and even how to restore rancid butter. *Miss Beecher's Domestic Receipt Book* (1850) advises using chloride of lime.

Vegetables such as beets, cabbage, carrots, cauliflower, onions, parsnips, potatoes, radishes, rutabagas, sweet potatoes, turnips, and winter squash were stored in root cellars where the climate allowed. In other areas, they were packed in straw and stored in barrels. The straw acted as a barrier to prevent the spread of spoilage to the entire barrel. Carrots were often buried in sawdust-filled boxes. Other vegetables such as corn, beans, and peas were dried and used in cooking. Green corn was preserved by turning back the husk, leaving only the last, very thin layer, and then hanging it in the sun or a warm room to dry. When it was needed for cooking, it was parboiled and cut from the cob. Sweet corn was parboiled, cut from the cob, dried in the sun, and stored in a bag kept in a cool, dry place. Sweet corn was also dried on the husk and then buried in salt. String beans, squash, and okra were strung on thread and hung up to dry. String beans were strung whole, while other produce was sliced thinly and dried in strips.

Vegetables could also be preserved by making them into catsups and relishes. Mushroom and tomato catsups were popular. Catsup was the general name given to sauces made from vegetables and fruits.

Meats were pickled, salted, and smoked. These methods, of course, altered the natural taste and did not suit all kinds of meat. The earliest solution to keeping food from spoiling during warm weather was the icehouse. Ice was cut from frozen ponds in large blocks and kept in structures constructed partially below ground. The ice was then covered in sawdust to help insulate it. Ice would be gathered when it was thickest, generally late January. It could last through October if conditions were favorable. By the Civil War, the icehouse had become an indispensable component of the farm. Where ice did not form naturally it was imported. The South imported thousands of tons of ice each year from the North. Meat, poultry, and perishable fruit could be kept in good condition for much longer periods in the cool of the icehouse.

The icebox gave individual homes a means of keeping food fresh. First patented by Thomas Moore in 1803, it consisted of a wooden box, inside another, insulated by charcoal or ashes, with a tin container at the top of the interior box. In 1850 *Godey's Lady's Book* called it a "necessity of life." New England eventually became so efficient in its commercial production and shipping of ice that it even shipped ice as far as the West Indies. **New Orleans** alone consumed about 400 tons of ice in the late 1820s. In a single decade this demand increased twentyfold, and as the Civil War dawned this figure reached seventyfold. An early system for refrigeration was patented in 1834 by Jacob Perkins, but a practical system did not become common until the 1870s. **Related Entries**: Agricultural Products; Food.

SUGGESTED READING: Catherine Beecher, *Miss Beecher's Domestic Receipt Book* (1850); Mary Randolph, *The Virginia Housewife* (1984); Stuart Thorne, *The History of Food Preservation* (1986); C. Anne Wilson, *"Waste Not, Want Not": Food Preservation from Early Times to the Present Day* (1992).

FORCE BILL: The administration of **Andrew Jackson** reacted to the **nullification** crisis in **South Carolina** with the passage of a Force Bill in 1833 authorizing the President to send troops to South Carolina if the state persisted in its refusal to allow the collection of the **tariff** and in its marshalling of an armed force in the form of a state **militia**. The bill was hotly contested on the floor of the Senate. A number of its opponents suggested that the root of the argument lay in **John C. Calhoun**'s thwarted presidential ambitions. The bill passed by a vote of 32 to 1, Calhoun having led his supporters from the chamber in protest. The crisis was averted by the passage of a compromise federal tariff crafted by Calhoun and acceptable to South Carolina. This was followed by a face-saving nullification of the Force Bill by South Carolina.

However, the concept of nullification had driven a wedge between Jackson and Calhoun, who had been drifting apart for some time. At a birthday party in honor of **Thomas Jefferson**, Jackson made a famous toast, addressing his words to the nullifiers: "Our Federal Union, it must be preserved." To this Calhoun replied, "The Union—next to our Liberty the most dear." The next day an indignant Jackson signed the Force Bill and the compromise tariff. The *United States Telegraph*—once a Jacksonian paper but now firmly on the side of Calhoun and his supporters—appeared with a black mourning border mistakenly announcing the imminent death of **states' rights**. The *New York Evening Post*, a firm Jackson supporter, noted that protective tariffs had now been "fully, almost fatally tried" and should in the future be avoided. **Related Entries**: Hamilton, James A.; Jackson, Andrew; Nullification; Tariffs.

SUGGESTED READING: William W. Freehling, *Prelude to Civil War: The Nullification Controversy in South Carolina, 1816–1836* (1966); William W. Freehling, *The Road to Disunion* (1990).

FOREIGN WORKERS. *See* Immigration.

FORTY BALES THEORY. *See* McDuffie, George.

FOSTER, ABBY KELLEY (1810–1887): feminist, **abolitionist**, and speaker. Like many of the female radicals of the period, Abby K. Foster was an abolitionist as well as a **women's rights** activist. Originally from a Quaker background, she began to lecture for abolition in 1837. She conducted her campaign in concert with the noted Southern reformer **Angelina Grimké**, reportedly becoming the first woman to address a mixed audience in public. For this she was denounced by the clergy, who considered her a menace to public morals. Her speeches were periodically broken up by mob violence. Her presence as a delegate to the World Anti-slavery Conference in London in 1840 caused serious disturbances, as women delegates were refused recognition. As a pioneer feminist and a leader of the radical abolitionists, she was a well-known figure in the North and a target of hatred in the South. **Related Entries**: Abolition; Women's Rights.

SUGGESTED READING: Dorothy Sterling, *Ahead of Her Time: Abby Kelley (Foster) and the Politics of Anti-slavery* (1991).

FOSTER, STEPHEN COLLINS (1826–1864): composer. Stephen Foster is considered by many to be one of the greatest melodists of American music. His greatest gift was his ability to pen melodies that were understood and embraced by people of all walks of life. Ironically, had he been a better trained musician, he might have lost this natural charm and simple, direct writing style. Foster published a little over two hundred works, many of which are still popular today. His first published song, "Open Thy Lattice, Love," was written when he was seventeen. Three years later, while working as a bookkeeper for his brother, Stephen wrote "Old Uncle Ned," "Oh! Susanna," and two other songs. These were published as *Songs of the Sable Harmonists* and were such a tremendous success that he turned to song writing as a career. Prior to 1852, with the exception of a few visits to **Kentucky**, Foster had never been south. He drew his inspiration largely from black church services and **minstrel shows**. Nonetheless, "Old Folks at

Home" and "Swanee River" seemed to capture the emotions of a truly Southern way of life.

Foster was responsible for making several contributions to the South's classical antebellum image: the contented slave, the kind-hearted master, and the white-columned plantation among them. Foster's lyrics probably did more to rehabilitate public attitudes toward the South and its "peculiar institution" than any pro-slavery lecture or treatise of the time, an ironic situation considering his pro-Northern sympathies.

Those who listened to Foster's songs were invited to escape from the materialism and aggressiveness of an increasingly industrialized society. They were reminded of such timeless states as childhood, old age, and the good old days. In Foster's music, the tender feelings of these times found popular expression. Many of his songs strike a sad note. There is a subdued longing, nostalgia, or melancholy in such pieces as "Massa's in de Cold Ground," "Old Memories Under the Willows," "She's Sleeping," and "Summer Longings."

Foster was not a businessman and failed to capitalized fully on the true commercial value of his works. Initially, he hesitated to have his name appear on his "Ethiopian songs" for fear that the prejudice against them by some would injure him as a writer of another style of music. He later reconsidered his position when he found that his songs were enjoyed by a more refined audience, owing to his avoidance of the "trashy" lyrics of other works of that genre. In the meantime, however, and in a time before common law copyright laws, Foster gave many manuscripts to performers which were then copyrighted by someone with no right to them.

Foster's popularity spread through minstrel troupes, which greatly favored his works. Some popular pieces were "My Old Kentucky Home," "Old Dog Tray," "Old Black Joe," and "De Camptown Races." For a number of years E. P. Christy had the privilege of being the first to sing many of Foster's works.

Foster's personal life was unsettled. His failed marriage went through several separations, and he later became an inveterate drinker. Living alone at the American Hotel in New York in 1864, Foster was suffering with fever and ague when he fainted across a washbasin which broke, severely cutting his neck and bruising his head. After being discovered by a chambermaid, Foster was brought to a hospital but never recovered. In 1940 Stephen Foster became the first musician elected to the Hall of Fame at New York University. **Related Entries**: Emmett, Daniel Decatur; Minstrel Shows.

SUGGESTED READING: Ken Emerson, *Doo-Dah! Stephen Foster and the Rise of American Popular Culture* (1997); Harvey B. Gaul, *The Minstrel of the Alleghenies* (1951); John T. Howard, *Stephen Foster, American Troubadour* (1939); Steven Saunders and Deane L. Roots, *The Music of Stephen C. Foster* (1990).

FREE BLACKS (FREEMEN): The treatment of blacks in Northern states was often brutish, and they were despised and treated with contempt by most whites. In the decades after American independence was achieved, towns and cities had been flooded by thousands of freed blacks, some of whom had fought in the Revolutionary army. It was widely held that free blacks were coming north to compete for scarce jobs in the cities, and an economic downturn in 1857 did not help to relieve this fear. This led many sympathetic whites to fear for the ultimate welfare and safety of a black population suddenly foisted on an unfriendly America should the abolitionists attain their goal of universal **emancipation**.

By comparison Southerners were generally ambivalent in their attitude toward free blacks, requiring considerable formality from them, but treating them with disdain or paying them no mind at all. White slaveowners were intimately involved with free blacks for almost all of their lives. In the isolation of the great plantations, it was possible that most of a white person's dealings, in human terms, were either with family members, slaves, or freemen. Although it is uncertain with how much respect these black freemen were viewed, it would be common for whites to have to deal with freemen as laborers, tradesmen, and artisans. The working white population in much of the South exhibited far less abhorrence of free blacks than did many in the upper and middle classes in the North. The impracticality of blacks being any further integrated into the fabric of American society in the antebellum period can best be measured by the resistance to racial integration seen in the South after a costly and painful war had forced emancipation upon it. The **South Carolina** Court of Appeals put itself on record with regard to free blacks, stating that "a free African population is a curse to any country . . . [and] a dead weight to the progress of improvement." **Related Entries:** Emancipation; Miscegenation.

SUGGESTED READING: Suzanne Lebsock, *The Free Women of Petersburg: Status and Culture in a Southern Town, 1784–1860* (1984); Kenneth M. Stampp, *The Peculiar Institution* (1956); Marie Tyler-McGraw, *In Bondage and Freedom: Antebellum Black Life in Richmond, Virginia* (1988).

FREE LABOR: The concept of free labor seems to have been the most fundamental element of the 1856 **Republican Party** belief system and identity. It embodied the ideals of a classless, socially mobile society held within the framework of a harmonic and expansive economic system, all deeply rooted in personal prosperity and capitalism. While others espoused many of these same principles, Republicans were more optimistic on the whole about the future of a highly industrialized America, and were certain that the new society and culture of the North would ultimately supplant that of the South to the betterment of the nation. It is ironic that in the 1856 presidential race the Republicans championed the slogan "Free Speech, Free Press, Free Soil, Free Men, Fremont and Victory," but left out "Free Labor." Nonetheless, by 1860 the Republicans and **Abraham Lincoln** stood solidly behind the concept. **Related Entries**: Lincoln, Abraham; Republican Party.

SUGGESTED READING: Don E. Fehrenbacher, *Abraham Lincoln: Speeches and Writings, 1859–1865* (1989).

FREE STATES: The following information about free states and territories is taken from data available for 1853 in John Hayward's *Gazetteer of the United States*:

Free States	Whites	Colored	Slaves	Total
Maine	581,813	1,356	—	583,169
New Hampshire	317,456	520	—	317,976
Massachusetts	985,704	8,795	—	994,499
Rhode Island	143,875	3,669	—	147,544
Connecticut	363,305	7,486	—	370,791
Vermont	313,402	718	—	314,120
New York	3,049,457	47,937	—	3,097,394
New Jersey	465,523	23,807	225	489,555
Pennsylvania	2,258,463	53,323	—	2,311,786
Ohio	1,956,108	24,300	—	1,980,408
Indiana	977,628	10,788	—	988,416
Illinois	846,104	5,366	—	851,470
Michigan	395,097	2,557	—	397,654
Iowa	191,879	335	—	192,214
Wisconsin	304,565	626	—	305,191
California	91,632	965	—	92,597
Oregon Terr.	13,087	206	—	13,293
Minnesota Terr.	6,038	39	—	6,077
New Mexico Terr.	61,530	17	—	61,547
Utah Terr.	11,330	24	26	11,380
Total	13,333,996	192,834	251	13,527,081

Related Entry: Slave States.

SUGGESTED READING: John Hayward, *Gazetteer of the United States* (1853).

FREMONT, JOHN CHARLES (1813–1890): explorer, soldier, and politician. John Charles Fremont was raised in **Charleston, South Carolina**, and, through the influence of the prominent Unionist **Joel Poinsett**, he initially received an instructorship in the navy. He quickly resigned his naval commission, however, to become an army second lieutenant in the U.S. Topographical Corps. Here during 1837 and 1838 Fremont gained much practical experience in working with astronomy, map making, and navigation.

Through this work Fremont met **Thomas Hart Benton**, the influential senator from **Missouri** who sparked Fremont's interest in exploring the American West. Fremont was married to Jessie Benton, and in 1841 Senator Benton, now his father-in-law, helped him to outfit his first expedition to examine the Oregon Trail. In all Fremont was to make five major expeditions to the West, becoming known as "The Pathfinder."

During one of these treks of exploration in 1846, Fremont helped to foment a revolt of Californians against the rule of Mexico. With his armed support, the "California Battalion" was able to capture the city of Los Angeles in 1847. Fremont—now officially a lieutenant colonel in the U.S. Army—optimistically informed Stephen Watts Kearny, the U.S. military commander sent to California, that the region had been pacified. Kearny was therefore somewhat shocked to find that he needed to fight a series of small battles against armed groups of Californians—some supported by light artillery. Kearny's command suffered several casualties and had to overcome a number of obstacles created by Fremont's theatrical heroics and unwarranted optimism.

This circumstance did not endear Kearny to Fremont, who was as pompous, reckless, and insubordinate as he was flamboyant and visionary. A bitter and involved quarrel developed between the two men. In the end, Kearny set out for **Washington, DC**, with Fremont in tow and under arrest for mutiny. In a sensational trial Fremont was found guilty as charged. President **James K. Polk** upheld the findings of the court-martial, but suspended any punishment. In response Fremont resigned his commission and set forth to find a passage to California along the Rio Grande.

There is no doubt that Fremont harbored political ambitions. In 1850 he was elected senator from California, and in 1856 he was the first presidential candidate ever put forward by the new **Republican Party**. His defeat by **James Buchanan** in that year seems to have blunted his political ambition.

Fremont's first Civil War appointment was as a major general commanding the department of the West in Missouri. Here he was justly blamed for the federal losses at the battles of Wilson's Creek and Lexington. Moreover, he rashly began to confiscate the property of Southern sympathizers and declared their slaves to be free. This early proclamation of **emancipation** was an embarrassment for the Lincoln administration, which was trying to keep the border states in line. When Fremont was superseded by General John Pope, he resigned. His popularity declined thereafter. Only his wife's writing—mostly about her husband's explorations—kept Fremont solvent; yet his reputation as an explorer is justified. In this area, at least, he was a great man. **Related Entries**: Benton, Thomas Hart; Republican Party.

SUGGESTED READING: Glenn D. Bradley, *Winning the Southwest: A Story of Conquest* (1912); Pamela Herr, *Jessie Benton Fremont: A Biography* (1987).

FUGITIVE SLAVE LAW OF 1850: Even in colonial times there had been fugitive slave laws embodied in the **Black Codes**. The first federal Fugitive Slave Act was passed in 1793 under the authority of Article IV, Section 2 of the Constitution. However, the Fugitive Slave Law that was a particular target of anti-slavery passion was part of the legislative package known as the **Compromise of 1850**. Proposed by **Henry Clay** as a salve for Southern pro-slavery sentiment, the law required that city and state officials assist in the capture of runaway slaves even in **free states** and territories. Legal penalties were provided against citizens who protected or aided escaping slaves. Many free states countered the Fugitive Slave Law with "personal liberty" laws forbidding officials and citizens from aiding the federal court in enforcing it. The **Dred Scott** decision of 1857 tended to strengthen the Fugitive Slave Law to the point that the possibility of "slave chasers" invading the cities of the North to herd escaped slaves back to the South became a very real fear. **Related Entries**: Compromise of 1850; Slave Escapes.

SUGGESTED READING: Timothy J. Paulson, *Days of Sorrow, Years of Glory, 1831–1850: From the Nat Turner Revolt to the Fugitive Slave Act* (1994); Jenny B. Wahl, *The Bondsman's Burden: An Economic Analysis of the Common Law of Southern Slavery* (1998).

GADSDEN PURCHASE OF 1853: At the conclusion of the **Mexican War of 1846**, the United States had almost completely filled out the familiar borders of the American Southwest. A small strip of territory south of the Gila River in Arizona and New Mexico was purchased from Mexico for $10 million because it was believed at the time that it provided an advantageous route for a railway to the Pacific. Anti-slavery forces opposed the purchase, and both Northerners and Southerners thought that it would help to spread **slavery. Related Entry**: Manifest Destiny.

SUGGESTED READING: Odie B. Faulk, *Too Far North, Too Far South* (1967).

GAG RULE: Faced with a flood of anti-slavery petitions in 1836, Southern members of the House of Representatives, led by **Henry L. Pinckney**, were able to pass a resolution limiting the discussion of such petitions. Northern members called this the "gag rule," and former President **John Quincy Adams** protested vehemently that the resolution was a direct violation of the right of free speech and the rules under which the House operated. Adams was not able to override the resolution until 1844. Southern representatives in Congress were also able to pass legislation exempting postmasters from delivering **abolitionist** mail sent to the South. Abolitionist **Angelina Grimké**'s *Appeal to the Christian Women of the South*, which urged Southern women to speak and act out against **slavery**, was confiscated and burned by postmasters in **South Carolina** under this measure, and the author was threatened with imprisonment if she returned to the state. Extremists in **Charleston, South Carolina**, intercepted much of the anti-slavery propaganda entering the city under this provision. **Related Entries**: Adams, John Quincy; Pinckney, Henry L.

SUGGESTED READING: William Lee Miller, *Arguing About Slavery: The Great Battle in the United States Congress* (1996).

Some waterfront gambling establishments were a far cry from the elegant casinos of Europe. (From the authors' collection.)

GAMBLING: The dominating vice of the Old South was gambling. Wagering was, for the **planter aristocracy**, an exciting way of spending leisure time. In the early days gambling among the gentry was essentially private. Isolated wagers would be made on a cock fight, the turn of a card, a steamboat race, or a horse race. Many of these activities were also orchestrated for public wagering, but no formal wagering authority existed. Steamboat racing was particularly popular, but the strain placed on the boats was blamed for boiler explosions and other river disasters.

Horseracing was much favored by those of the upper classes, and regular courses were maintained for its prosecution. **Andrew Jackson** won thousands of dollars on a match race between Greyhound and his own horse, Truxton. The race was the last event of the public racing season in middle **Tennessee**. Truxton sired an entire line of racehorses for Jackson's stable, and Jackson maintained his interest in racing horses throughout his presidency and into his old age.

Virtually every known game of chance was available for wagering. As cities grew in population and wealth, wily entrepreneurs began to operate games that were open to the public. Special gambling rooms were fitted up in **hotels**, clubs, and coffee houses providing gaming tables for the convenience of their customers. As these gambling houses became more numerous, they also became a focus for crime and disorder. The local authorities at first attempted to suppress these establishments, but quickly gave way to regulation and licensing, which seem to have provided a good deal of cash for the municipal pot in the form of fees, fines, and assessments.

Professional gamblers, who were considered social pariahs in this period, rarely frequented the gambling houses, and those who did were drab fellows compared to the sharp-witted and gaudy river gamblers who established riverboat gambling as a recognized institution. These sometimes reckless and spectacular players were the stuff of which legends were made on the **Mississippi River**. Few of them relied on their luck and skill at gaming. Rather, they were generally adept at palming and marking cards, dealing seconds, and using cheating devices such as holdouts, poker rings, and stripped decks. They were often in league with unscrupulous bartenders, waiters, or other professional gamblers traveling the river.

Some of the favorite antebellum card games were poker, faro, twenty-one, and old sledge. Sleight-of-hand affairs such as three card monte and shell games were saved for the traveling sucker and not the serious gambler. Roulette wheels and dice (craps or hazard) tables were commonly provided. There were no betting limits in the gambling houses of this period, and sometimes the stakes were very high, especially in the private rooms to which the gentry retired. Tens of thousands of dollars were won and lost in a single evening; plantations and crops were wagered; and slaves or anything of value was accepted in forming a wager.

Natchez-under-the-Hill became a well known, if somewhat infamous, stop for gamblers along the Mississippi River. A good deal of **romanticism** surrounds the contrast between the group of shabby and unpretentious gambling houses along the riverbank—each fitted with a roulette wheel and a few tables—and the elegant brothels and gambling houses on the bluff above. Gamblers unwise enough to risk their luck in either locale would probably be cheated of their money or robbed of their winnings.

The true home of elegant gambling was **New Orleans**. When gambling was legalized in 1832, the city was invaded by sumptuously appointed casinos. Orleans Street, Bourbon Street, Chartres Street, and Canal Street all became famous for their gambling establishments. At the outbreak of the Civil War, many Mississippi River gamblers initially sought refuge in New Orleans. When the city fell to the Federals in May 1862, the occupying forces left the gambling institutions unmolested upon the payment of a fee, and the gambling houses prospered for about two years on Northern money. However, in 1864 all the gambling establishments were closed under strict military scrutiny and remained closed until 1869. **Related Entries:** Horseracing; Riverboats.

SUGGESTED READING: Herbert Asbury, *The French Quarter: An Informal History of New Orleans with Particular Reference to its Colorful Iniquities* (1938); Kenneth S. Greenberg, *Honor and Slavery: Lies, Duels . . . and Gambling in the Old South* (1996).

GARNET, HENRY HIGHLAND (1815–1882): Black anti-slavery activist. A former **Maryland** slave, Henry Highland Garnet escaped to New York with his family when he was nine. When he was twenty, Garnet enrolled at the integrated Noyes Academy in New Hampshire. Not long thereafter a mob of whites opposed to integration dragged the school building from its foundation and into a swamp with the aid of ninety oxen. Fearing for his personal safety, Garnet left and pursued his studies at Oneida Theological Institute near Utica, New York, and became the minister of a black Presbyterian congregation. While he was still a student, one of his speeches, said to have drawn "tears from almost every eye," was printed in the *Anti-Slavery Standard*.

In 1843 Garnet addressed the National Negro Convention, where he delivered an emotional call for armed resistance as the only response to **slavery**. His position was denigrated by **Frederick Douglass**, who found it dangerously impractical. Garnet's remarks were only a single vote short of being adopted as a resolution by the convention. Four years later a similar resolution passed unanimously.

Garnet became involved with the short-lived Liberty Party and was the most ardent of its black supporters. He remained active in politics following the Civil War, working with the Freedmen's Bureau and later acting as a U.S. minister to Liberia. **Related Entry**: Black Anti-Slavery Activists.

SUGGESTED READING: Editors of Time-Life Books, *Perseverance: Voices of Triumph* (1993), pp. 60–70; Benjamin Quarles, *Black Abolitionists* (1969).

GARRISON, WILLIAM LLOYD (1805–1879): abolitionist, author, and publisher. William Lloyd Garrison was a radical abolitionist and publisher of the *Liberator*, possibly the best known anti-slavery publication of the antebellum years. Garrison's views seemed to justify slave revolts, social chaos, and the complete impoverishment of the South. Southerners were particularly sensitive to his rhetoric and reacted to his fanaticism by holding it forth as an example of the radical nature of the anti-slavery movement as a whole. The South was particularly enraged by Garrison's support of the activities of **Nat Turner** and **John Brown**.

Garrison was also prone to involving himself in factional disputes within the anti-slavery movement. His refusal to endorse a political solution to **slavery** based on compromise, his attacks on the religious institutions of the nation as supporters of slavery in the 1840s, and his continued characterization of the South as an aggressive enemy of all American institutions left him outside the mainstream of anti-slavery sentiment. He attacked the Constitution as a "guilty and bloodstained instrument," called for the **secession** of the New England states from the Union, disrupted religious services at "pro-slavery" churches, and castigated the clergy and the anti-slavery moderates as conspiring with Southern "slave power." Many anti-slavery activists in the North were embarrassed by his fanaticism, and his detractors recommended his arrest or confinement in an asylum. These positions caused a split in the abolition movement in 1840. Nonetheless, Garrison remains a central figure in the controversy that led to the Civil War simply because the South took him seriously and believed that he had a much greater following than reality justified. **Related Entries**: Abolition; Fear of Slave Revolts.

SUGGESTED READING: Jules Archer, *Angry Abolitionist: William Lloyd Garrison* (1969); Walter M. Merrill, *Against Wind and Tide: A Biography of William Lloyd Garrison* (1963); Henry Mayer, *William Lloyd Garrison and the Abolition of Slavery* (1998); Philip Spencer, *Three Against Slavery: Denmark Vesey, William Lloyd Garrison, Frederick Douglass* (1972).

GEOGRAPHY: The romantic view of Southern geography is filled with cypress groves, live oak, magnolia blossoms, and hanging Spanish moss. For anyone who sees the South for the first time, the variety in the landscape is impressive. As a traveler proceeds further south, the landscape and the foliage become more exotic, with areas of **Florida** sporting palm trees and semitropical plants.

Even in the antebellum period a division between the Old South of the tidewater and a New South was recognized. Many Southern states had been part of the original English colonies, including the immediate coastal areas around Savannah, **Georgia**. These made up the Old South, while **Kentucky, Tennessee,** Florida, **Alabama, Mississippi, Louisiana, Arkansas, Missouri,** and **Texas** were the New South. This division was largely based on the existence of established **cotton** plantations in the older section, while the new were entertaining an expansion of agricultural activity onto virgin soil. The fertile limestone basin of the Alabama and Mississippi "Black Belt" stood in stark contrast to the thin and sandy soils of the coastal regions, while the fertile soils and thick forests of southeastern Texas belied the semiarid prairies west of the 98th meridian. The generally mountainous areas of western Virginia and eastern Tennessee, indifferent lands for cotton production, were associated with neither.

The Shoreline. Below the shores of the Chesapeake Bay, the Southern coast was largely a ridge of sand occasionally broken by the mouths of **rivers** which discharged sediment into bays and inlets that could afford a safe haven for ships. This constantly shifting silt was incorporated into a natural series of banks, shoals, and sandbars, making the area unfriendly to deepwater shipping. As a consequence there were few harbors in the South not subject to continually shifting navigational obstructions, and few large ports capable of receiving oceangoing vessels had developed—a circumstance that affected both the economy of the **antebellum South** and the history of the Southern Confederacy.

Ports. Two of the best ports available to the South were Norfolk, Virginia, and **New Orleans**, Louisiana. Norfolk gave access to **Richmond** by way of the James River, and New Orleans ranked first among Southern ports in terms of wealth, volume of trade, and the number of alternate entrances to its harbor for oceangoing vessels. The few good ports along the coast were Baltimore, Wilmington, North Carolina, **Charleston**, Savannah, Mobile, and Galveston. Each of these was connected by rail to the inland South by mid-century with the exception of Galveston, as the **Mississippi River** had not yet been bridged.

Topography. The topography of the South can be broken down using less than a half dozen terms. Among these are the tidewater, coastal plain, piedmont, Fall Line, and Appalachian Plateau. The coastal plain was particularly important, as it ran from the marshy tidewater along Chesapeake Bay into a wide band that flowed and expanded south and west across all the seashore states that would become the Confederacy. The plain was 250 miles wide in the Carolinas, covered almost all of Florida, and swept along the Gulf coast into East Texas. The dark virgin soil of the Gulf states invited the cultivation of both **cotton** and tobacco.

The Old South's geography was divided into eastern and western regions by the Blue Ridge Mountains, which rise at Harper's Ferry in Virginia and proceed southwesterly, petering out as a small line of hills in Georgia. These divide the coastal regions from the inland regions. With the exception of several lines of hills pretentiously called mountains, the area is relatively flat. The inland areas are characterized by their yellow-red claylike soil. To the east of the mountains are two discernible areas, the tidewater and the piedmont.

The tidewater is on the coastal plain that borders the Chesapeake Bay and the inlets along the Atlantic coast; and it was from here south to Savannah that most of the large-scale cotton and tobacco plantations were located along with their population of **free blacks** and slaves. This area was cut by numerous runs, streams, and creeks which flowed generally from the Appalachian Plateau (the southern reaches of the Appalachians, the Blue Ridge, the Great Smokies, and the Cumberland Plateau) to the coast.

Rivers. The Mississippi River is the most important waterway in the South. Its course forms part of the political boundaries of Kentucky, Tennessee, Missouri, Mississippi, Arkansas, and Louisiana. The great rivers of the Old South and their tributaries wore gaps in the ranges of small eastern hills to flow to the coast. The Shenandoah River is one of the few Southern rivers that flows to the northeast. The other major rivers and tributaries that flow through the piedmont to the tidewater include the Potomac, the Rappahannock, the James, and the York in Virginia; the Roanoke and the Cape Fear in North Carolina; the Pee Dee and the Santee in South Carolina; and the Oconee, the Ocmulgee, the Altamaha, and the Savannah River in Georgia. Along the Gulf coast the Coosa and Alabama Rivers flow to Mobile, and the Tombigbee reaches into Mississippi. These had served as connections to the interior in the early years of the Republic and were navigable up to the Fall Line.

The division between the piedmont and the coastal plain was known as the Fall Line. It was along this line that the swiftly flowing streams needed to turn the waterwheels of mills and factories became deep, lazy rivers that allowed inland navigation from the coast. Here also was where many important cities developed, and it was said that two-thirds of all the markets in the South were within five miles of a navigable stream. Richmond, Raleigh, Columbia, Augusta, and Montgomery are all situated along the fall line, and a smooth curve connecting these cities precisely locates it on a modern map. **Related Entries**: Agricultural Products; Agriculture. Also see individual entries on each of the Southern states.

SUGGESTED READING: Emmie F. Farrar, *The Piedmont* (1975); Paul Wilstach, *Tidewater Virginia* (1929); S. Augustus Mitchell, *An Easy Introduction to the Study of Geography* (1852); William Warntz, *Geography Now and Then* (1964).

GEORGIA: Highlights of a period description of the state from John Hayward's *Gazetteer of the United States* (1853) read as follows:

Surface and Soil: Along the coast a rich soil is favorable to the cultivation of **cotton** and rice. Into the interior and beyond the mountains, a stronger, richer soil produces abundant wheat, corn and other grains; tobacco, cotton and a great variety of fruits and fine timber.

Rivers: Many of the rivers are of great length such as the Savannah, the Altamaha and the Chattahoochee. These are generally navigable for steamers and large boats through a considerable portion of their extent.

Education: Common **education** is but partially provided for as may be inferred from the fact that in 1840 there were upwards of **30,000** white persons above the age of 20 who could neither read nor write. There is a literary institution at Athens, called the University of Georgia.

Internal Improvements. Those consist of several important canals and **railroads** completed or still in progress.

Manufacture: A number of cotton mills and some woolen factories have been erected. Manufacturers of cast iron and other hardware, machinery, leather, carriages, furniture, soap, candles, brick, iron, and lime are carried on to some extent principally for home consumption. There are numerous flouring mills, distilleries and breweries, portions of the products of which are exported.

Minerals: On the borders of the Chattahoochee River considerable quantities of gold have been found; and numerous smelting houses, employing some hundreds of persons, are established, although the business of mining has not been very regularly pursued.

Indians: Some parts are still in the occupancy of the Creek Indians. The Cherokees also inhabit a large tract at the northwest boundary.

Population: About one third of the inhabitants are of African descent.

Related Entries: Geography; Indian Removal.

SUGGESTED READING: John Hayward, *Gazetteer of the United States* (1853); Harold H. Martin, *Georgia: A History* (1977).

GRADUAL EMANCIPATION (GRADUALISM). *See* Abolition.

GRIMKÉ, ANGELINA (1805–1879) AND SARAH (1792–1873):
feminists and **abolitionists**. The Grimké sisters were members of a slave-owning family in **South Carolina**. Together with their less notable brother, Thomas Smith Grimké, who devoted himself to educational reform, the two sisters were the most notable of Southern abolitionists who had been slave-owners. Moreover, they were described as the "only females" to combine speaking, writing, and practical skills with a wide range of eminent friends. Upon their father's death, Sarah and her younger sister were able to persuade their mother to apportion the family slaves to them as a share of the family estate, upon which they freed them at once. Originally members of the Episcopal Church, the sisters were initially attracted to the Quaker sect by friends who lived in Philadelphia, but found that they lacked the self-restraint to curb their unequivocal hatred of slaveowners.

Sarah and Angelina began their careers by addressing small groups of women on both feminist and anti-slavery topics, and ultimately they entered the lecture circuit. So great was the opposition to women speaking in public that the sisters found that they were spending as much time defending their feminism as preaching their anti-slavery ideals. John Greenleaf Whittier came to their defense, referring to them as "Carolina's high souled daughters" in his writings; but, at the same time, he privately suggested that they limit their efforts to the cause of **emancipation**.

In 1836 Angelina wrote *Appeal to the Christian Women of the South*, which urged Southern women to speak and act out against **slavery**. Angelina followed this work in 1837 with *Appeal to the Women of the Nominally Free States*, in which she strongly insisted that the women residing in **free states** were equally guilty for allowing the national shame of continued slavery. She made a "triumphant appearance" before the Massachusetts legislature to plead the cause of abolition and gave the closing speech at the 1837 anti-slavery convention held in Philadelphia, in an age that did not accept the propriety of women speaking in public.

The efforts of the sisters were important in the development of both the feminist and abolitionist causes, and it is difficult to determine to which cause they were most dedicated. Angelina confirmed her position in the anti-slavery community when she married abolition activist and author Theodore D. Weld in 1838. As a youth, Sarah Grimké found that it was impossible for her to study law because she was a woman. From this situation flowed her natural devotion to the cause of **women's rights**. Sarah wrote *Letters* *on the Equality of the Sexes and the Condition of Women* in the year of her sister's marriage, and her correspondence with her brother-in-law is a source of information about the cause of abolition in this period. As Southern advocates of radical abolition and feminism, the Grimké sisters were particularly detested by traditionally minded Southern women, who took pains to target them in their journals and letters. **Related Entries**: Abolition: Women's Rights.

SUGGESTED READING: Edward D.C. Campbell, Jr., and Kym S. Rice, *A Woman's War: Southern Women, Civil War and the Confederate Legacy* (1996); Sarah Grimké, *Letters on the Equality of the Sexes and the Condition of Women*, edited by Elizabeth Ann Bartlett (1838; 1988); Ellen H. Todras, *Angelina Grimké: Speaking Up for Human Rights* (1998).

HAMILTON, JAMES A. (1786–1857): congressman and governor of **South Carolina**. In 1820 James A. Hamilton was elected to the lower house of the South Carolina legislature and began a political career that brought him to the state's executive mansion and the halls of the U.S. Congress. Hamilton's fortunes were fixed when, as intendant of **Charleston** in 1822, he figured prominently in crushing the slave revolt threatened by the **Denmark Vesey** conspiracy. Almost immediately thereafter he formed the **South Carolina Association**, thereby leaving possibly his most lasting imprint on the antebellum period. His political career was helped again by the resignation of **William Lowndes** from Congress in the same year. Hamilton was chosen to take his place, and immediately assumed a role as a vigorous and able debater. Within a very few years, he was recognized as a leader of the Jacksonian opposition to the administration of **John Quincy Adams**, of the forces opposed to **tariffs** in Congress, and of **slavery** proponents in general.

Always an intense Southern nationalist, Hamilton became a devotee of **states' rights** and agitated almost fanatically on the subject. His devotion ultimately helped to bring **John C. Calhoun** to a similar dedication. Introduced to the **Virginia and Kentucky Resolutions** by his friend **John Randolph**, Hamilton became thoroughly imbued with the basic political principles contained therein, and he tried to implement them in his state. In 1828, in reaction to the Tariff of Abominations (Tariff of 1828), it was he who outlined the theory of state **nullification** that was to evolve into the doctrine of states' rights so ably described by Calhoun. In 1830 Hamilton was elected governor of South Carolina, and he was able to convince the politicians in his state to call the **Nullification Convention of 1832** in opposition to the federal tariff. Ironically, Hamilton was elected president of the convention and found himself in a face-to-face confrontation over the implementation of the **Force Bill** with President **Andrew Jackson**, whom he had formerly defended. His sincerity in espousing nullification was questioned by his most extreme supporters in 1832 when he agreed to a compromise tariff arranged by Calhoun to end the stalemated controversy without resorting to armed conflict.

States' rights advocates thereafter resented his conservatism, and the Federalists never forgave him for his past activities. His national political career had been sacrificed on the altar of compromise and Hamilton turned his mind and body to other interests. He profitably operated five rice plantations, a rice mill, two **cotton** plantations, and a brickyard. He was a railroad director and was instrumental in organizing the Bank of Charleston, of which he was president.

He was a famed **duelist** and was widely sought after as a second in affairs of honor. He served in this capacity for John Randolph in a famous duel with **Henry Clay**, and served, among other notables, Oliver Perry and Stephen Decatur in the same capacity. Called the "Bayard of the South" by his closest friends, Hamilton was a polished example of the Southern aristocracy both in the drawing room and on the dueling ground. In fourteen confrontations, Hamilton wounded as many men, but never killed anyone.

Hamilton took an extraordinary interest in the struggle for the independence of **Texas** but believed that the **annexation of Texas** would harm the South. In 1835 he was made a perpetual citizen of the Republic of Texas and was offered the command of its armies. As an American diplomatic envoy to the major courts of Europe, Hamilton was able to secure the recognition of the Texas Republic in 1839 and to conclude a renewal of the treaty for the suppression of the **Atlantic slave trade** with Britain. Extraordinarily, Hamilton used his wealth to help finance Texas, a debt (more than $200,000 in gold) that went largely unrepaid.

In 1844 Hamilton came to support President **James K. Polk**'s expansionist theories, and he became reconciled with Jackson. Concurrently he became an advocate of annexation. His motives seem to have gone unquestioned in this regard, but in 1855 he was given a huge land grant in Texas, and moved there. During a sea passage from **New Orleans** to Galveston in 1857, his ship having been damaged in a collision in the Gulf of Mexico, Hamilton relinquished his life preserver to a woman and her child and, in the best chivalric tradition of a Southern gentleman, drowned. With his history of compromise and vacillation, only the wildest speculation could predict what part Hamilton would otherwise have played in the coming Civil War. **Related Entries**: Calhoun, John C.; Dueling; Nullification; Texas, Annexation of.

SUGGESTED READING: William W. Freehling, *Prelude to Civil War: The Nullification Controversy in South Carolina, 1816–1836* (1966); James A. Hamilton, Jr. Papers, University of North Carolina Library Collection, Chapel Hill.

HAMMOND, JAMES H. (1807–1864): U.S. senator and governor of **South Carolina**. James H. Hammond was educated at South Carolina College and read law in Columbia, SC. Entering the bar in 1828, Hammond built up a lucrative practice in that city. Entering politics at an early age, he was an ardent opponent of protectionism. His **newspaper**, the *Southern Times* (begun in 1830), supported **nullification** and the **Nullification Convention of 1832**.

Although his fiery editorials and speeches caught the attention of the **states' rights** forces, Hammond failed to be elected as a delegate to the convention. Instead he threw himself into the task of securing volunteers for the state **militia** being raised by the new governor, **Robert Y. Hayne**, who proposed to confront the federal troops being raised by President **Andrew Jackson** under the **Force Bill**. Not surprisingly, Hammond was elected colonel of his regiment; and, even after a compromise had quieted the immediate crisis, he outspokenly urged continued military preparations.

From this point Hammond must be considered one of the leading proponents of Southern nationalism. For the next twenty years, he persistently sought a united stance by the South and the withdrawal from the Union of all the Southern states. In 1834 he was elected to Congress, where he expounded the most radical Southern positions. He advocated the death penalty for **abolitionists** found inciting Negroes to rebellion and considered **emancipation** not only undesirable, but impossible. **Secession** seemed inevitable for Hammond during this period, and he believed that it was worth the very cost of their lives for Southerners to defend **slavery**.

In 1836 Hammond's health failed, requiring his resignation from Congress. Nonetheless, by 1839 he had recovered sufficiently to run for governor of South Carolina. Although he failed to gain the office, his continued dedication to armed resistance caused him to be chosen as a general in the state militia. In the next election, held in 1842, he obtained the governorship and served for two terms. During this period he oversaw the transformation of the Columbia Arsenal and the Charleston Citadel-Magazine into military schools.

For more than a decade his extreme political views seem to have kept him from office. After returning to private life in 1846, Hammond was frustrated in his attempt to gain a seat in the Senate. Many Southern leaders espoused secession only sporadically, and usually only during an election campaign. Those who did otherwise, like Hammond, did not achieve lasting prominence.

Having acquired a substantial fortune from his law practice, Hammond purchased several thousand acres, was a successful **cotton** planter, and obtained at least 300 slaves. As one of the founders of the South Carolina Agricultural Society, his plantation was superbly managed and run in a "scientific" manner.

In 1857 he finally gained a Senate seat (which he would resign in 1860 upon the election of **Abraham Lincoln**). During his stay in the Senate, Hammond began to question his own beliefs about secession. He was outraged by the Southern disregard for Northern opinions about slavery, and he felt that the radicals among the secessionists—among which he had long been numbered—were supplying the abolitionists with ammunition for their campaigns. The majority of Southerners seemed to prefer to stay in the Union as long as their rights were guaranteed, and Hammond came to believe that the South could, by judicious handling, come to control the nation. Coming to the conclusion that the New England mill owners and manufacturers were dependent on Southern cotton, he gave over all of his attention to the application of economic pressure on the North. "You dare to make war on cotton," he declared in 1858. "No power on earth dares to make war upon it. Cotton is king!"

Nonetheless, with secession accomplished in 1861, Hammond went to **Richmond** to urge that cotton be held as the basis of Confederate credit. Until his sudden death in 1864, he was extremely supportive of the Confederacy but was bitterly critical of the actions of **Jefferson Davis** and the Confederate cabinet. **Related Entries**: Nullification; Nullification Convention of 1832; Tariffs.

SUGGESTED READING: Carol K. Bleser, ed., *Secret and Sacred: The Diaries of James Henry Hammond, a Southern Slaveholder* (1998); Drew Gilpin Faust, *James Henry Hammond and the Old South: A Design for Mastery* (1982); the Hammond Papers in the Library of Congress, Washington, DC.

HAMPTON, WADE (1818–1902): plantation owner, soldier, U.S. senator, and governor of **South Carolina**. Wade Hampton was the third in his family to bear the name. His grandfather served as an officer in the American Revolution, and his father spent a lifetime creating a fortune almost totally represented by agricultural interests. Although Hampton's holdings were spread across the South, he considered himself to be a South Carolinian. He was born in **Charleston** in 1818, attended school in Columbia, and studied law at South Carolina College. Evidence suggests, however, that Wade had little intention of actually practicing law; and after the death of his father in 1835, his interests seem to have been devoted to the life of a planter. He successfully expanded and developed his legacy so that on the eve of the Civil War he was easily the richest man in the South.

Hampton had no military experience or training, but was fond of riding and hunting, and he seems to have had some training and skill in swordsmanship. In 1852 he was elected as a state representative for the Richland district and later won reelection. In 1856 Hampton became a state senator, but he espoused decidedly different views from many in South Carolina. As head of a wealthy Southern family, and one of the largest slaveowners in the South, Hampton pleaded for peace and compromise. He was rigidly opposed to **secession**, doubted the expediency of such an action, and cautioned against it without sufficient provocation.

Although he was able to resist the "bloody minded euphoria of secession" that was sweeping his state in 1861, Hampton nonetheless supported the Confederacy from the outset, but had a mysterious personal dispute with **Jefferson Davis** which neither man ever put into words. Governor Francis W. Pickens of South Carolina, highly valuing Hampton's social and political leadership, secured a colonel's commission for him. The forty-four-year-old Hampton was described by a contemporary as "the idealized statue of a mounted warrior." By 1862 he was a brigadier general of cavalry. With J.E.B. Stuart's death at Yellow Tavern in 1864, Major General Wade Hampton served as the commander of the cavalry corps of the Army of Northern Virginia until the end of the war.

Although said to have owned 3,000 slaves on his various plantations in **Mississippi, Louisiana**, and South Carolina, Hampton had always espoused moderation on the question of **slavery**. He disliked slavery's abuses, wanted to limit its scope, and hoped that eventually all Negroes would be free.

In 1876 he received the **Democratic** nomination for governor of his state. Hampton, always a Unionist, was victorious largely because enough black voters recognized his message of toleration and political equality to give him a small margin of victory. Hampton acknowledged these blacks voters as his "fellow citizens," and while he remained in public office blacks in South Carolina kept the franchise. Hampton probably accomplished more for both races than any other leader North or South in the postwar era. **Related Entry**: Plantation Economy.

SUGGESTED READING: Richard F. Snow, "Wade Hampton," *American Heritage Magazine* (March 1979); Manly Wade Wellman, *Giant in Gray: A Biography of Wade Hampton of South Carolina* (1988).

HARPER'S FERRY, VIRGINIA. *See* Brown, John.

HARRISON, WILLIAM HENRY (1773–1841): soldier, congressman, senator, and ninth President of the United States (1841). For a time antebellum voters became fond of military men as presidential candidates. This fascination had begun with **Andrew Jackson** and continued with William Henry Harrison. In 1791 Harrison took the first step along this road toward the Executive Mansion when he accepted a commission as an ensign in the 1st Infantry. Serving in the Northwest Territory under General "Mad" Anthony Wayne, he rose to the rank of lieutenant fighting against the Indians. After the restoration of peace, he remained on garrison duty for three years and was later appointed territorial secretary.

In 1799 he was elected to Congress, but quickly accepted an appointment as the governor of the newly organized Indiana Territory. During his term,

William Henry Harrison's historic confrontation with Tecumseh in 1809 over the acquisition of Native American land. (From a nineteenth-century history textbook in the authors' collection.)

he acquired the rights to millions of acres of Indian land for the government from willing tribes, but the increased pressure of white settlement quickly raised native resentment. Harrison was thereby thrown into a confrontation with the most famous native leader of his day, Tecumseh. Their face-to-face confrontation during a treaty negotiation in 1809 would become the stuff of high drama and political propaganda in later years.

In 1811 Harrison was camped at Tippecanoe Creek with about 1,000 men when he was attacked by the Shawnee, who were under the provocation of British agents. Although he fended off the attack and claimed a victory over the Indians, his losses were very heavy, and he became convinced of the need for a general war against the Indians. However, the battle at Tippecanoe proved to be the first conflict of the **War of 1812**, inflaming all the Indians of the West and sending the **War Hawks** in Congress crying for blood.

During the War of 1812, Harrison was made a brigadier general and commander of the Army of the Northwest. He campaigned against both the British and the Indians. In 1813 he was able to defeat the British at Thames River, and they quickly thereafter abandoned the war in that quarter. In the battle Tecumseh was killed, although the native leader's body was never identified or recovered. The Indian threat largely collapsed. Harrison was able to claim during his political campaigns that he had subdued the Indians in the Northwest.

From 1816 to 1819 Harrison served in the House of Representatives, and from 1825 to 1828 he was in the Senate. In neither case was he an outstanding figure. He served a short period as a minister to Colombia, but for some years thereafter he was on the outskirts of the political process. Suddenly in 1836, with his political star rising, he was nominated in several states by the local caucuses of the **Whig Party** for President. The nomination of three separate Whig candidates in 1836 caused Harrison to lose to **Martin Van Buren**.

In the election of 1840 he had better success, however. The Whigs drew up no platform, relying instead on Harrison's military reputation, "frontier" character, and good showing in the previous election. At Whig rallies hard cider flowed freely from barrels set among representations of the log cabin in which Harrison was supposedly (but not actually) born. Detractors claimed that the Whigs floated to victory on a river of alcohol. Using the slogan "Tippecanoe, and Tyler too," Harrison was elected by a landslide electoral vote. The campaign was, according to a contemporary observer, "one of unexampled excitement, characterized by immense popular gatherings, political songs, the use of symbols, and the participation of both sexes to a degree hitherto unknown in America."

Harrison was inaugurated on a cold and blustery day in 1841 amid great enthusiasm, but he became sick and died of pneumonia within the month. William Henry Harrison's sole contribution to the office of the presidency was to catapult **John Tyler** into the Executive Mansion. **Related Entry**: Tyler, John.

SUGGESTED READING: Douglas E. Clanin and Ruth Dorrel, eds., *The Papers of William Henry Harrison* (forthcoming); Freeman Cleaves, *Old Tippecanoe: William Henry Harrison and His Times* (1939; 1990).

HAYNE, ROBERT Y. (1791–1839): politician, senator, and Southern apologist. Robert Y. Hayne served in the **South Carolina** state legislature from 1814 to 1818 and was the state attorney general until he was elected to the U.S. Senate in 1822. He was reelected in 1828 and was a leading advocate of the strict construction of the Constitution and of the propriety of state **nullification** as an instrument of government. His most historic moment came in a forensic tour de force with **Daniel Webster** in 1830.

Hayne moved on from the Senate to become governor of South Carolina. Here he remained a staunch nullifier and raised a force of state **militia** during the nullification crisis of 1832 to oppose the threat of armed invasion by federal forces. Hayne continued to preach dedication to state, rather than federal, allegiance. "This is our own—our native land," declared Hayne. "It is the soil of Carolina . . . [to] which we are bound, by every tie divine and human. . . . Let others desert her, if they can, let them revile her, if they will—let them give aid and countenance to her enemies, if they may—but for us, we will stand or fall with Carolina." The end of **slavery**, a side issue in Hayne's view, would condemn **free blacks** to an existence that was "poor, wretched, vile and loathsome" (Jervey, 1970). **Related Entries**: Nullification; Webster-Hayne Debate.

SUGGESTED READING: Theodore D. Jervey, *Robert Y. Hayne and His Times* (1970).

HELPER, HINTON ROWAN (1829–1909): anti-slavery author. Hinton Rowan Helper was born and educated in **North Carolina**. In 1850 he was attracted to the gold fields of California, where he remained for three years. Here his observations led him to a firm belief in the value of **free labor**. In 1855 he wrote a book about his California experiences, *The Land of Gold*, initially muting his strong criticisms of **slavery** because of the fears of his publishers for their personal safety. In the following year, he moved to New York and wrote *The Impending Crisis*, an economic discourse in behalf of the non-slaveowning whites of the South.

The Impending Crisis contrasted the economic condition of the **slave states** and the **free states**, and attributed the backwardness of the South and the impoverishment of Southern white labor to the competition of raced-based slavery. While he showed no consideration for the plight of the Negro, Helper attacked the large slaveowners, using the threat of a slave uprising to destroy the slave labor system from within. "Would you be instrumental in bringing upon yourselves, your wives, and our children, a fate too horrible to contemplate?" Helper's eleven-step program to abolish slavery formalized a growing feeling that Southern economic and social welfare was being sacrificed on the altar of continued plantation slavery.

The Impending Crisis created a greater sensation than *Uncle Tom's Cabin*, and it has been described as a contributing cause of the Civil War. Men were hanged for merely possessing a copy of the book in some areas of the South. The book was furiously attacked in the South, and a good deal of effort and propaganda were put into casting doubts on Helper's integrity. In the North, it was a great success. One hundred thousand copies were printed for the **Republican** campaign of 1860. An appreciative **Abraham Lincoln** appointed Helper the American consul in Buenos Aires in 1861, a position he kept until 1866. **Related Entries**: Plantation Economy; Poor Whites; Yeoman Tradition.

SUGGESTED READING: Hinton Rowan Helper, *The Impending Crisis* (1857; 1976); Richard Hildreth, *Despotism in America: An Inquiry into the Nature, Results, and Legal Basis of the Slave-Holding System* (1854).

HEMINGS, SALLY: As the female slave of **Thomas Jefferson**, the possibility of Sally Hemings also being his mistress proved a never-ending em-

barrassment to the President, his party, and his policies. The rumor of
Jefferson's paternity of at least one of Sally Hemings' children began in 1802
and was recently (1998) confirmed by a DNA test. The practice of **miscegenation** among elite Southern gentlemen was common enough, but Jefferson seems to have been reluctant to admit the liaison.

Sally, although a mulatto slave, was also the half-sister of Jefferson's deceased wife and twenty-eight years his junior. She accompanied him to
France when he served as minister there, and was the social hostess of his
household until his legitimate daughter became old enough to take up the
task. Sally made no claims on the Jefferson estate, and Jefferson never recognized any of Hemings' offspring as his own during his life and neglected
to do so in his will. It was a common practice among gentlemen in these
situations to posthumously recognize their mixed-race offspring and provide
for them. The white children of such gentlemen often went to great lengths
to undo those parts of their father's will favorable to their biracial siblings.
Related Entries: Jefferson, Thomas; Miscegenation.

SUGGESTED READING: Jerome D. Wright, *Sally Hemings and Thomas Jefferson*
(1991).

HOLIDAY CELEBRATIONS: Unburdened by the prohibitions of a Pu-
ritanical past, unlike New England, the South celebrated Christmas with a
passion dating well back to the eighteenth century. The holiday itself retained its religious significance and was observed by church attendance. Festivities in plantation households included presents, parties, teas, and feasts.
Holly, evergreen boughs, and fir branches were placed over and around
doors, mantels, pictures, and mirrors. Charles Minnegerode, a German immigrant, introduced the Christmas tree to the **Virginia** aristocracy in 1842.
Shortly thereafter, Queen Victoria's family was depicted around their tree
in the *London Illustrated News*, and the tradition was embraced by all.
Southerners quickly adopted the custom, dressing the tree with **cotton** balls,
gilded nuts, berries, and ribbons.

Holiday guests on the remote plantations came for the entire week. One
plantation mistress noted that some of her neighbors had "30 and some
40 in the house all the holiday." Every morning started with great glasses
of eggnog, and a fiddler would stroll about the mansion and grounds singing and playing. Preparations for such extravaganzas commenced weeks in
advance, anticipating the extended household, stockpiling puddings and
fruitcakes, and readying sufficient attire to satisfy the social scene.

Christmas Eve day featured a hunt for pheasant or blue-winged teal. That
night the yule log was brought in and sprigs of holly were thrown in the
fire to rid the house of evil spirits. Cinnamon-soaked apples were hung from
a string from which children were to try to secure a hands-free bite. Successful youngsters were rewarded with the whole apple. Finally children

Music for celebrations, such as this New Year's Eve in the country, was often supplied by an accomplished servant. (From *Harper's Weekly* V, no. 210, January 5, 1861.)

hung their stockings from the mantel hoping to find them filled with surprises the next morning. Even **Andrew Jackson** is said to have hung his stocking up in the White House.

Slaves were given rice, **sugar**, coffee, tobacco, and other treats. They, in return, presented the mistress with items such as chickens and eggs (which they had raised), handmade baskets, and carved candlesticks. Some bartered with members of the household for castoff clothing so that they might be well attired for the evenings of singing and dancing. The planter generally supplied an ox and other provisions to the slaves for their festivities. Slaves decorated the tables, doors, and windows of their quarters using such natural materials as greenery, gourds, shells, and persimmons. Slave children hung their stockings too. During the Christmas holiday celebrations slaves enjoyed evenings of music and dance and the children were entertained by storytelling. The burning of the yule log was a common barometer for the length of the celebration. The slaves responsible for bringing in the log were known to take particular care in selecting a particularly large one. While the period given to slaves varied, even harsh masters were known to allow a three-day holiday.

New Year's Day was also a day of feasting. For many slaves, however, it brought considerable heartbreak, as slaves who were to be hired out had to leave for their new positions. In some cases slaves were transferred to settle debts being cleared for the new year. The Christmas season closed with

Twelfth Night, which was marked in plantation society by feasting and a ball.

Carnival celebrations may be rooted in ancient bacchanalian rituals but are said to have originated in Mobile, **Alabama**, on New Year's Eve in 1832 when a group of inebriated young men created considerable ado parading up and down the streets ringing cowbells. Since New Year's Eve was already cause for celebration, the event was moved to Twelfth Night and eventually to Shrove Tuesday. A visitor to **New Orleans** in 1846 described the festivity, saying that "all wore masks" and that revelers perched on balconies armed with bags of flour to shower upon anyone who looked too pleased with their appearance. The "blending of Negroes, quadroons and mulattos" added to the exotic mystique of the night. It was customary, especially in the country, for those of French extraction to keep open house.

Easter was mainly a religious observance marked by church attendance. Many masters recognized Easter Monday as a day off for the slaves if the work schedule permitted.

The Fourth of July was another cause for celebration. Many Southern states were extremely proud of the many contributions their forefathers made in the American Revolution and marked the nation's birthday with speeches by prominent citizens and parades of local military units. By the 1820s it was difficult to find a town where the holiday was not celebrated, and even women were gradually being included. By the 1850s fireworks and barbecues became standard fare as the holiday became more family-oriented. Firing old muskets replaced fireworks in rural areas, and pigs' bladders were blown up and thrown into the fire to provide additional noise. Servants cooked fish and roasted pigs while the young people danced to fiddle music. City folks came to enjoy excursions on this day. The citizens of Norfolk, **Virginia**, took to boats to enjoy the fireworks at Old Port Comfort.

Thanksgiving feasting goes back to colonial times, but there was no specified date for its celebration. It was not until 1846 that Sarah Joseph Hale, editor of *Godey's Lady's Book*, succeeded with the concept of having Thanksgiving celebrated on the same day across the nation. One by one states began adopting the measure until the Civil War interrupted the process. Those masters who celebrated Thanksgiving gave their slaves a holiday too. **Related Entry**: Southern Hospitality.

SUGGESTED READING: Catherine Clinton, *The Plantation Mistress* (1982); Emyl Jenkins, ed., *The Book of American Traditions* (1996); Anne Sinker Whaley LeClercq, *An Antebellum Plantation Household* (1996).

HORSERACING: Horseracing was much favored by those of the upper classes, and regular courses were maintained for its prosecution. Races were held locally throughout the South, and match races between well-bred horses were often widely advertised and drew large crowds at raceways and

Southern men embraced horseracing with unbridled passion. (From the authors' collection.)

fairgrounds. All thoroughbreds have a lineage traced back to one of three original stallions: the Byerly Turk, the Darley Arabian, or the Godolphin Arabian. Because of their importance these horses are called the "Foundation Sires" of British thoroughbred racing. The great-great-grandson of the Darley Arabian was Eclipse, the sole ancestor of all American racing thoroughbreds. The line of Lexington, another fine American thoroughbred of the period, unfortunately was allowed to run out, and no descendants of this commendable **Kentucky** stallion are known to exist.

The exclusivity of horse breeding appealed to the class conscious planters of the South. The raising and racing of thoroughbred horses became a passion in the antebellum period. President **Andrew Jackson** won thousands of dollars racing his own horse, Truxton, who sired an entire line of racehorses for his stable. Jackson maintained his interest in racing horses throughout his presidency and into his old age. Many householders, otherwise financially unable to be involved directly, prominently displayed lithographs and paintings of fine racehorses on the walls of their homes amid the images of their own ancestors and children. The great popularity of horseracing can be further gauged by the widespread public mourning seen at the death of a famous racehorse named Diomed.

Sundays and court days were favorite times for races, which often ended in near riots when the outcome was in dispute. The greatest sensation of the period was the match race between Henry and Eclipse (not the English sire but a descendant referred to as the "American" Eclipse) held in New

York in front of 40,000 spectators and followed with great attention by the whole nation. **Related Entries**: Gambling; Livestock.

SUGGESTED READING: Kent Hollingsworth, *The Kentucky Thoroughbred* (1985).

HORSES. *See* Livestock.

HOSPITALITY. *See* Southern Hospitality.

HOTELS: Americans invented the hotel, even though they borrowed the word "hotel" from the French. In Europe the term meant a grand house or city hall. In America it came to be a genteel place where travelers could both sleep and eat. Unlike the old colonial inns, taverns, or "ordinaries," which were rarely more sophisticated than a large private home, the American hotel was often the biggest and most imposing building in a community. Porticoes, columns, and domes graced many hotels, and the accompanying lobbies, courtyards, and public ballrooms allowed large numbers of people to congregate.

One reason so many early political conventions were held in Baltimore was the existence of the Barnum's City Hotel, an elegant six-story edifice with rooms for 200 people and dining facilities for many more. The United States Hotel at Saratoga Springs, New York, was one of America's most popular luxury hotels and a favorite destination of many wealthy Southern families. The St. Charles Hotel in **New Orleans** attracted rich merchants from that city as well as wealthy planters from **Arkansas, Alabama**, and **Tennessee**, and the more haughty and polished landowners from far away **Georgia**, the Carolinas, and **Virginia**. The nation's capital was graced by the Willard Hotel, which became a magnet for politicians, military officers, and purveyors of military goods in the coming conflict. **Related Entry**: Travel and Vacations.

SUGGESTED READING: Janice Devine and Leslie Dorsey, *Fare Thee Well: A Backward Look at Two Centuries of Historic American Hostelries* (1964); Irvin Haas, *America's Historic Inns and Taverns* (1985).

"HOUSE DIVIDED" SPEECH. *See* Lincoln, Abraham.

HOUSEHOLD FURNISHINGS: The rooms in individual dwellings could be divided into three classifications. There were public rooms such as the hall, parlor, dining room, and library. Bed chambers were considered private rooms and were almost exclusively located on the second floor to take advantage of evening breezes on warm nights. Finally, there were workrooms including the kitchen, pantry, laundry, scullery, and cellar.

It was important that the front hall be decorated in a fashion appropriate to the social standing of the family. It was likely to be furnished with a pair of chairs for visitors, a mirror for checking one's appearance, and a table to receive calling cards. Upscale homes often had massive pieces of furniture that combined several of these features. Floors were commonly tiled for the practical purpose of accommodating the traffic.

The parlor was the most public room in the house. Parlors were common to both the North and the South and to the upper and lower, middle classes. Some more affluent homes had a front parlor solely dedicated to formal visitations and a back parlor for family use. The parlor was the place where visitors would be received, and therefore where the first impressions of a family were formed. Decorating decisions were made in a very calculated manner to project the image a family wished to portray. The parlor contained a family's "best" in every way. It would have the highest ceilings, the largest fireplace, and the most elaborate furnishings. Here the family would gather to write, read, converse, play games, or engage in needlework.

Other furnishings might include an upholstered sofa, armchairs, and a pair of easy chairs, all done in matching fabric. It was not unusual for sofa ensembles to contain a large gentleman's armchair and a smaller chair with half arms for the lady. This accommodated the ever widening skirts of the period and kept the lady's posture properly erect. The placement of chairs around the room allowed social groupings to change as activities varied. A person might move from the solitary activity of reading quietly to join a game with other family members at the table. Sofas were designed with slight curves inward to encourage conversation. In summer months mirrors and ornate candelabras were covered with netting to protect them from insect damage.

Although it was common to see period house plans showing libraries and although trade catalogs displayed library furniture, only the rich could afford a library. This was truly a man's domain. It was a place to which a man could retreat and engage in the kind of activities that did not coincide with the outward picture of home life. Here a man could smoke, drink, and discuss money, politics, and war without exposing the rest of the family to such vulgarities. Libraries were usually on the ground floor but off to one side. Decorations were more subdued than in the parlor. Heavy bookshelves were often featured. Other furniture would include a desk or writing table, large gentlemen's chairs, and various tables. If a man had hobbies or interests, it would be here that he would pursue them. Specimen cases containing fossils or insects would be displayed among accompanying magnifying glasses and other optical aids.

Families of lesser means ate in the kitchen, but wealthy families had separate dining rooms. Dining room furniture tended to be massive, often of mahogany or other dark wood. A sideboard of some type commonly provided an excellent place to display oversized serving pieces and candelabras.

The kitchen was a utilitarian room. It was here that the most mundane, labor-intensive household duties were performed. The kitchen was always located on the ground floor with a door to the outside. It was not necessary for it to be adjacent to the dining room, and in certain circles distance was considered an asset, keeping odors contained. Kitchen furnishings were functional and simple. There was usually a large central work table and a cupboard for storing dishes. In many homes the kitchen was also the laundry, but large plantations had separate buildings to house such activities. Pots were stored by hanging them from racks. Other furnishings included the meat safe, a kind of screened cupboard that protected the meat from insects, pets, and vermin but did nothing to regulate temperature. By the 1850s a primitive icebox was considered a necessity. Dry goods such as flour, **sugar**, and cornmeal were stored in crockery or wooden containers. Rural kitchens, and those of families of lesser means, were also likely to be more family-oriented, and may have been used for sewing or helping children with studies, in which case they would contain additional furnishings to suit their multiuse needs.

Beds were hung with bed curtains in winter months and with netting in the summer. Clothing was stored in chests of drawers and wardrobes. Beside the bed might be found a small table upon which to rest the chamber stick used to guide one to the bedroom upon retiring. Cribs and cradles were frequently found close to the parents' bed to facilitate breastfeeding and as a precaution should the child take ill during the night. Older children in lower economic situations might also sleep in the same room. Children of wealthy families would sleep in the nursery with their nanny.

Full-fledged baths, taken in the bedchamber, were labor-intensive events that involved bringing up heated water from the kitchen so that a compact metal tub could be filled. This relegated total-immersion baths to special occasions. Sponge baths were the more common occurrence. Outhouses were not convenient at night, so most bedrooms contained a covered chamber pot. Some chamber pots were hidden in various pieces of furniture, mostly chairs and stools, but some were merely stored beneath the bed until they were emptied into the slop jar in the morning.

Families who could afford it had a nursery for the children. Modest households had a single nursery room, often found on an upper floor. Affluent households could afford both day and night nurseries. These rooms were designed to withstand the abuse children can sometimes inflict on furnishings. Walls were often whitewashed. There would be a table with several chairs, perhaps simple pine furniture bought for the purpose or cast-off furniture from other rooms. There were shelves and cupboards for books and toys and perhaps an armchair or two. Nurseries often doubled as schoolrooms and would also contain globes, maps, and perhaps a blackboard as needed for instruction. Some plantations had separate buildings to house the schoolroom. **Related Entry**: Architecture.

SUGGESTED READING: Dorothy Denneen Volo and James M. Volo, *Daily Life in Civil War America* (1998).

HOUSTON, SAMUEL (1793–1863): soldier, politician, governor of **Tennessee**, and President of the Republic of **Texas**. Sam Houston's early life, although lacking in formal **education**, prepared him well for the life he was to lead. In 1813 he received a commission as an ensign in the war with Britain. His first active service was under **Andrew Jackson** in his campaign against the Creeks. In a decisive battle at Horseshoe Bend, Houston was noted for his bravery, receiving wounds that would bother him for the rest of his life.

His army record, taken together with his physical size and equally impressive ability as a stump speaker, prepared him for a political career on the Tennessee frontier. In 1823 he was elected to Congress without opposition and did much to organize a new political movement around his old commander, Jackson. With Jackson as his benefactor in the White House, Houston was able to take his own undiminished popularity to the governor's mansion of Tennessee by stressing a need for **internal improvements** and development of the West.

Houston's star seemed to be ascending still further when he announced his engagement in 1829 to Eliza Allen, the daughter of a wealthy and influential family. Ironically, the subsequent marriage proved Houston's undoing in Tennessee. Hardly had the marriage begun when Eliza retreated to her father's home with no intention of returning to her husband's side. Although Houston later received a divorce on the grounds of abandonment, his initial reaction to his wife's departure was extreme. Houston, who was standing for reelection, resigned his office and told his constituents that he "was going to the Indian Territories, and they could go to Hell."

Taking up a career as an Indian trader, Houston demonstrated an ability to act as a go-between and peacemaker among the tribes. Although his interest was in the financial opportunities of the Indian country, Houston's honesty allowed him to be adopted by the Cherokees. In later years, he was able to live among the dangerous and unpredictable Comanche near San Antonio in Texas. His innate political sense brought him to Texas just as the 1833 convention sent Stephen Austin to the government to ask for statehood in Mexico.

Although the relationship between Mexico and Texas was initially symbiotic, the need for an armed struggle between the two quickly became clear. Although rumors suggested that Houston was an agent of the United States charged with provoking a revolution, there is no documentary evidence to uphold such an accusation. Nonetheless, because of his commanding presence and ability to persuade, Houston was quickly selected as a commander of volunteers, and finally as commander-in-chief of the armies of Texas.

After learning of the fall of the **Alamo** and the massacre of 400 volunteers at Goliad, Houston retreated with the army of Texas before General Santa Anna's victorious Mexicans. In one of the finest military maneuvers in history, Houston allowed Santa Anna to become overconfident, drawing him forward for several weeks. At the San Jacinto River, he engaged the Mexicans by a surprise attack. Almost the entire Mexican force was killed or captured in the fifteen-minute battle. Only six Texans were killed, with Houston among the worst of the twenty-five wounded.

The capture of Santa Anna almost guaranteed Houston's election in 1836 as President of the Republic of Texas, an office he filled with comparative ease. In 1841 he was again elected, but under more trying circumstances. Mexico was showing signs of renewing the war, and calls for the **annexation of Texas** were being heard from the United States. He retired from office in 1844 and supported the annexation in 1846.

Not satisfied with a glorious and unexpectedly successful role in Texas history, Houston went on to serve for fourteen years as the U.S. senator from the new state. In this position he found himself largely insulated from the politics of his fellow senators from the South. He opposed the repeal of the **Missouri Compromise** and voted for the anti-slavery provisions of the organization of the **Oregon Territory**. His constituents in Texas quietly displaced him when he became an advocate for the **Nativist Party**, but inexplicably elected him governor two years later.

As a strong Unionist, Houston did not believe that the election of an anti-slavery **Republican** in 1860 would justify **secession**. He hoped at first to arrange some compromise, but his ideas were generally disregarded in the euphoria for disunion. Houston refused to acknowledge the authority of the secession convention of 1861 or of the **Confederate government**, regarding Texan secession as a return to the status of an independent republic. These positions were unfortunate for Houston politically. He was deposed as governor in March 1861, quietly left office, and retired to his farm, where he lived happily with his second wife and family. In 1863 he died in prayer, seeking the happiness and safety of the people of Texas. **Related Entries**: Alamo; Jackson, Andrew; Texas, Annexation of.

SUGGESTED READING: Donald Day and Harry H. Ullom, *The Autobiography of Sam Houston* (1954); Marquis James, *The Raven: A Biography of Sam Houston* (1997); John Hoyt Williams, *Sam Houston: A Biography of the Father of Texas* (1992).

IMMIGRATION: Antebellum immigration from abroad, reaching its peak between 1845 and 1855, had an incalculable effect on the nature of American society. More than 3 million immigrants, ten times as many as had come since the founding of the Republic, entered the country in this decade alone. There were three major countries of origin for the immigrants that entered America: Ireland, Germany, and Great Britain. Together, they provided about 85 percent of all immigrants to the United States up to the beginning of the Civil War. Most congregated in the cities of the North.

The influx of other Europeans would not become significant until late in the century. Yet very small communities of Jews had existed since colonial times, and even smaller groups of Italians, skilled masons and plasterers, were able to maintain themselves by applying their talents to the construction of ornate plantation houses and public structures. **Free blacks** and other "people of color" from around the world generally avoided immigration to slaveowning America. Nonetheless, a considerable number of middle-class blacks, fleeing the bloodbath of Haitian slave revolts and nascent Dominican republicanism on the island of Hispaniola, entered the country through Southern ports in 1804 and again in 1844. Finally, more than 13,000 Chinese immigrated to the west coast of the United States in 1854, beginning a constant prewar flow of oriental immigration.

Immigrants from Great Britain merged fairly well with the surroundings of America, which were dominated by an upper class that had strong English origins, but the Irish had an unfortunate history which followed them to this country. The Irish were the first truly urban immigrants in American history, banding together in inner-city neighborhoods that quickly took on all of the outward appearances of slums. One had only to walk through an Irish slum to discover the overwhelming atmosphere of social decay and moral degeneration. The Irish seemed to tolerate—if not frequent—taverns, dance halls, **gambling** establishments, and houses of ill repute with an amazing disregard for traditional American standards of conduct. They were also accused of voting illegally, of selling their votes to unscrupulous politicians, and of engendering crime and immorality. Many observers saw this development only in prejudicial terms and blamed the slumlike conditions on the Irish themselves, ignoring the anti-Irish bigotry of employers and landlords.

The Germans tended to separate themselves from traditional America by moving away from the cities into more rural agricultural areas in Pennsylvania and the upper Midwest. By this means they avoided being the targets of overwhelming prejudice and achieved far greater social solidarity than any other group of immigrants up to that time. Nonetheless, as they generally followed a European Sabbath tradition, Germans hurried home from their religious observances to a convivial afternoon in music halls and beer gardens that violated the more sober American concept of proper conduct on the Lord's Day. In this way they became the particular target of Sabbatarian and **temperance** crusaders.

Jews made up such a small proportion of the American population that their presence was mathematically insignificant. Nonetheless, Sephardic Jews, those whose ancestry lay in the Iberian Peninsula, had been part of the city of New York since the time of the Dutch occupation. A half dozen Sephardic families had added to the commercial importance of **Charleston, South Carolina**, and a small community could be found in **New Orleans, Louisiana**. However, in 1845 an economic depression caused many European Jews to immigrate to North America. German Jews made up the largest portion of this wave of immigration, with the majority clustering in the urban centers of America. The infrequency of intermarriage between the German-speaking newcomers and the more established Spanish and Portuguese Jews tended to keep the communities apart. Between 1850 and 1860, the number of American Jews tripled to 150,000—a significant number, but still less than one-half of 1 percent of a population of 32 million Americans. **Related Entries**: Benjamin, Judah P.; Fear of Slave Revolts; Religion and Religious Revivalism; Urbanization.

SUGGESTED READING: William L. Burton, *Melting Pot Soldiers: The Union's Ethnic Regiments* (1988); Alfred N. Hunt, *Haiti's Influence on Antebellum America: Slumbering Volcano in the Caribbean* (1988); Dorothy Denneen Volo and James M. Volo, *Daily Life in Civil War America* (1998).

INDIAN RELATIONS WITH SLAVES: The Seminole Indians broke away from the Creek Nation in 1750, taking refuge in **Florida**. They commonly found themselves caught between Britain and the United States in territorial disputes and, in a kind of retaliation to American onslaughts, they provided shelter to escaped slaves. The slaves were readily accepted. They dressed in Seminole attire and married into Seminole families. The Seminoles welcomed the knowledge of farming and husbandry the slaves brought with them. The slaves also possessed an understanding of how to deal with whites which the Indians felt could be useful.

The United States became increasingly determined to eliminate the Seminole lands as a haven for runaways, to recapture escaped slaves, and to compel the Seminole to emigrate to reservations in **Arkansas** and the Indian Territory. In 1817 and again in 1842 the United States waged war against the Seminole during which the blacks fought alongside their Indian allies. By 1843 the cause was lost. Seminoles, both native and mixed-race, were forced to move west, as had the Chickasaw, Cherokee, Choctaw, and Creek who preceded them.

On the journey, mixed-race Seminoles of black ancestry became the targets of white and Creek slave hunters. The Creeks, like other Southern tribes, were slaveholders, and they made a practice of capturing runaways and returning them for the rewards that were offered. In 1848 a declaration was made by the attorney general of the United States that blacks held in Indian Territory were free; however, U.S. military power would not be used to protect them from raiders. This prompted hundreds of Seminoles still in Florida to flee to Mexico. **Related Entry**: Indian Removal.

SUGGESTED READING: Jesse Burt and Robert B. Ferguson, *Indians of the Southeast: Then and Now* (1973).

INDIAN REMOVAL: The heart of the South, the area that would become the states of **Georgia, Alabama, Mississippi**, and parts of **Louisiana** and **Tennessee**, was occupied by tens of thousands of native Americans at the birth of the nation. Since its inception, treaties between the U.S. government and the Indian tribes were conveniently broken whenever coveting settlers became numerous or aggressive enough to work their collective will upon the federal law. The efforts of the native population to thwart white incursions into their lands brought the federal government to intervene repeatedly—but always on the side of the local whites, and usually with devastating military force.

General **Andrew Jackson** gained a large part of his reputation crushing the Creek Nation at the Battle of Horseshoe Bend in Alabama and battering the Seminoles in **Florida**. Ultimately, like his predecessors, **John Adams** and **James Monroe**, President Jackson came to believe that the government should institute a policy of removal, relocating the southern Indian tribes in an area west of the **Mississippi River**. Congressional debate questioned what was best for the Indians, but neither side suggested that the Indians retain or reestablish their former aboriginal lifestyle. Realistically, the raids and hunting associated with tribal existence could no longer be accommodated within the boundaries of the previously mentioned states.

The issue of removal was complicated by two facts. First, the Five Civilized Nations of the South—the Choctaw, Chickasaw, Creek, Cherokee, and Seminole—were settled in villages in this region and were using agricultural techniques that made them greatly more advanced than the western tribes. The Cherokee and the Creek mounted a particularly strong opposition to removal for this reason. Second, there had been intermarriage between the native peoples and both whites and blacks, producing many mixed-race persons. The lifestyle adopted by these "half-breeds" very closely resembled that of neighboring white farmers: dressing in the same style, following Christianity, and even owning slaves. Full-blooded natives tended to retain their tribal dress and customs. The full-blooded native population and the "half-breeds" generally held each other in mutual contempt.

In 1830 the Indian Removal Act—empowering the states, if they so chose, to expel any of the native residents of a region—was signed into law. The act provided for the compensation of any tribe relocated west of the Mississippi River, but Congress provided only half a million dollars for this purpose. Alabama and Mississippi followed Georgia in passing laws requiring the Indians to comply. Georgia further stipulated that Indians and their descendants residing in the Creek or Cherokee Nations would no longer have standing in any state court, effectively limiting any legal response by those tribes. With the discovery of gold in Georgia on Cherokee land, further laws were passed that forbade any meeting of a Cherokee council, but the tribe remained steadfast in its opposition to relocation.

The Cherokee retained William Wirt to take their case before the **Supreme Court**. The state of Georgia refused to appear on the grounds that the court had no jurisdiction over a sovereign state. Nonetheless, Chief Justice **John Marshall** rejected Wirt's argument that the Cherokee had the same status as a sovereign nation. Georgia continued to pressure the Indians and their supporters by passing other laws, such as a law ordering all whites to leave Cherokee lands or to obtain a license from the state while swearing an oath of allegiance to Georgia. This law was particularly aimed at the missionaries who served the Indian population. The Cherokee withstood threats, bribes, confiscation of property, severed supplies, barbarous treatment at the hands of the rabble, and other harassments to remain on their tribal lands. Finally, in 1838, with an escort of armed troops under the supervision of **Winfield Scott**, the trek westward was begun. Over a quarter of the Indians died on this journey, which came to be known as the "Trail of Tears."

The Creek in Alabama had a multitude of legitimate grievances against the state when they met with the secretary of war, Lewis Cass. More than 10,000 whites began moving into the Indian lands in anticipation of their removal, burning native homes and confiscating livestock. It was reported that many whites were willing to lynch federal soldiers if they attempted to protect the natives. Conversely, the residents of Georgia and Alabama feared retaliation on the part of the Indians and sent a memorial to Congress seeking further help. Ultimately the Creek were gathered together and marched off, many in manacles, to the western lands.

The Seminole had begun to accept the removal treaty upon the advice of their leaders until they discovered that any of them who had black ancestry would not be allowed to leave and might be sold into **slavery**. This led the Seminole to begin an armed and violent resistance. They fled into the swamps of Florida, and a war was on. **Zachary Taylor** was given command of 1,100 men to fight the Seminole. He was made a brigadier general after winning the Battle of Lake Okeechobee but failed during the next three years to eradicate the Indian problem. Beginning in 1834 troops entered the swamps to meet with defeat and sometimes disaster. Seven generals in as many years tried, desperately in some cases, to bring the Seminole to heel without success. Ultimately, the government resorted to treachery. Osceola, one of the great Seminole leaders, was encouraged to come to a peace conference, but was assaulted and bundled off to jail in **Charleston, South Carolina**, where he died in 1838. Thereafter, the government abandoned its attempt to exterminate the Seminole, and some of the tribal leaders agreed to removal to Oklahoma. Others stubbornly refused to leave their refuge and simply stayed out of sight. By the late 1840s, with a few small exceptions, the Indian removal problem had ended. **Related Entry**: Indian Relations with Slaves.

SUGGESTED READING: Jane F. Lancaster, *Removal Aftershock: The Seminoles' Struggles to Survive in the West, 1836–1866* (1994); Page Smith, *The Nation Comes of Age*, Vol. 5 (1981).

INTERNAL IMPROVEMENTS AT FEDERAL EXPENSE: Sectional differences over political questions other than **slavery** were able to hold the public attention quite as well as any **abolitionist** rhetoric during the antebellum period. One of the major political questions in the early decades of the century was the financing of internal improvements at national expense. For the West, where farm profits were expended in transporting crops to market and where manufactured goods were rare and expensive, the development of roads and canals was viewed as a necessity. Many ardent Westerners pledged their votes to political candidates solely on this issue and were rewarded with **roads** and canals, and later **railroads**, which allowed them to ship directly to Eastern markets. This development generally displaced the Southern ports as points of transfer for Western produce from river barges to coasting vessels and weakened the natural political alliance of the West and the South in the U.S. Congress.

In the East the issue of internal improvements was not a vital one. The existing roads were, for the most part, well engineered and numerous, and the population centers more closely placed than in any other section of the country. Many canals had been built in the early decades of the century, the

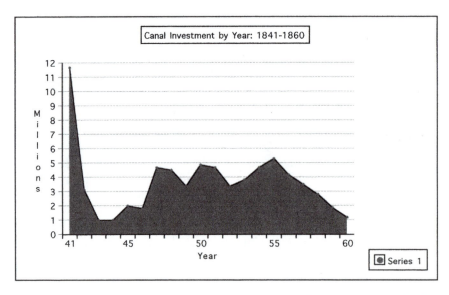

As the antebellum period wore on, canals came into fashion especially for the movement of merchandise. The phenomenal success of the Erie Canal in New York attracted imitation and investment, and in the second and third decades of the century capital placed in canals far outstripped investments in any other projects reaching a peak in 1840. Thereafter, interest became focused on railroads. Canals, though long lasting once they were built, could compete with railroad freight rates as little energy was needed to move freight, but not compete with their speed of transportation. (*Source:* U.S. Hist. Stats., Vol. II, p. 9766.)

Erie Canal (1825) across New York State serving as the prime example. Most feasible canal routes had already been developed by private syndicates, and Eastern investment capital had generally been transferred from canals to railroad building by 1840. Thereafter a flourishing railway network existed to transport manufactured goods from the East to more remote markets. The railroad building mania that swept the country and continued unabated through the war years made the construction of additional canals in the East largely a moot question.

For the South, with its system of inland **rivers** which moved agricultural produce at little expense, the building of roads and canals in other parts of the country was a sore point. Nonetheless, in 1796 Congress authorized the construction of **Zane's Trace**, a road from western **Virginia** to **Kentucky** that became a major westward route for settlers in the upper South. While the **Mississippi River** was the most profoundly important waterway in the South, many other major rivers flowed through the Old South to the tidewater. These had served as connections to the interior in the early years of the Republic and were navigable up to the Fall Line, sometimes providing

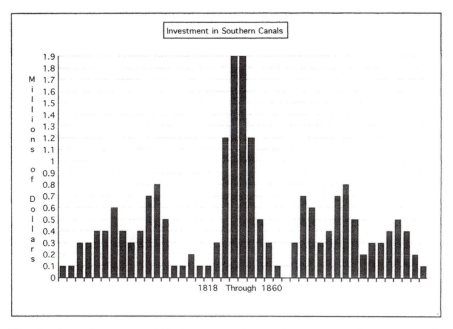

The South made an appreciable investment in canal construction both to provide transportation and to drain swamps and marshes.

transportation for more than 100 miles inland. **Flatboats and keelboats** used these rivers to float cargoes from the interior to the Gulf or the Atlantic. Modern steamers further complemented the efficiency of the system. Few plantations lacked river landings, and such natural waterways continued to have traffic on them into the railroad era. Southern farmers and planters therefore had no need for extensive canals and highway systems and saw no reason to pay taxes to aid Western farmers, who were their natural competitors. **Related Entries**: Riverboats; Rivers; Transportation.

SUGGESTED READING: Horace Bushnell, *The Day of Roads: A Sermon* (1846); Alice M. Fleming, *Highways into History* (1971); Ronald E. Shaw, *Canals for a Nation: The Canal Era in the United States, 1790–1860* (1990); Peter Way, *Common Labour: Workers and the Digging of North American Canals, 1780–1860* (1993).

INVENTIONS: American inventors showed great ingenuity in the antebellum period. American industry and **agriculture** were the beneficiaries of the new processes, simplified methods, and genuine mechanical insight that characterized this period of invention. The greatest change in employment and manufacturing from the colonial period to the Civil War was the transition from hand labor to increased mechanization in almost every task.

In 1794 Eli Whitney saw the need to mechanize the removal of **cotton** seeds from raw cotton. His invention of the **cotton gin** made cotton fiber a more thoroughly marketable material and stimulated the growth of cotton agriculture in the South. Cotton mills in Massachusetts began producing cloth with water-powered machinery in 1823, and by 1851 some were using steam power. In 1834 Cyrus McCormick patented the mechanical reaper, which further increased agricultural efficiency.

By 1860 there were more people involved in shoemaking than in any other industry in the nation save agriculture. The continuous-stitch sewing machine, first patented by Isaac Singer in 1851 for use with cloth, had quickly been modified to sew leather. Women set to work sewing the leather uppers of shoes in factories, while shoemakers (cobblers, really, as they needed less skill than true shoemakers) fitted the finished product with soles and heels. By 1858 Lyman Blake had patented a sewing machine that attached the soles to the uppers, greatly facilitating the shoemaking process. This made shoes, especially work shoes, much more affordable. For the first time, the public could buy shoes in standard sizes, and slaveowners could provide cheaply made shoes to slaves by the barrel.

By 1840 charcoal had been replaced by more efficient coal in blast furnaces. The decreasing price of ferric materials spurred a spate of technological advancement. In 1848 cast iron was used for the first time to build a five-story structure, and the height of taller buildings moved Elisha Otis to invent the safety elevator for passengers in 1853. Higher quality iron and steel, taken together with a theoretical revolution in steam technology, allowed George Corliss to patent a more efficient four-valve steam engine in 1849, which in turn spurred the introduction of horse-drawn steam fire engines.

More than 350 patents for improved steam engines and **railroad** equipment were issued by the U.S. Patent Office in the decade of the 1850s alone following the publication of William Rankine's *The Steam Engine and Other Prime Movers* (1848) in Great Britain. Almost 1,000 of the 6,600 patents issued in 1857–1858 were for agricultural and farm machinery, many of them variations on Cyrus McCormick's patent for the mechanical reaper granted in 1834.

Eli Whitney first pioneered the use of machine tools to make interchangeable parts for machinery. The Federal Armory at Springfield, Massachusetts, had used this concept since the 1840s to make its weapons, and in 1855 the government had adopted the highly efficient conical minié ball as a standard bullet for its firearms. Other inventors, spurred by the success of Samuel Colt's invention of the revolving pistol in 1835, were improving firearms. In 1854 Horace Smith and Daniel Wesson invented the first practical cartridge revolver, and Christian Sharps produced an efficient breech-loading rifle based on his own 1848 patent.

A fundamental improvement in communications was begun in 1838 when Samuel F.B. Morse introduced the Morse Code and sent the first telegraph message from Baltimore to Washington in 1844. His ability to send a message by electric current over wires many miles apart was built on the development of the wet-cell battery by the Italian Alessandro Volta in 1800 and the electromagnetic studies of Joseph Henry at Princeton in 1836. By 1861 telegraph wires crisscrossed the East and a transcontinental telegraph connected New York to California. Moreover, Cyrus Field's transatlantic telegraph cable stretched from Canada to Europe.

In 1839, when Louis Daguerre invented the daguerreotype, the first successful form of **photography**, he had little idea that it would be an American, Mathew Brady, who would become the best known photographer of the period, establishing studios in New York and **Washington, DC**, before the war and gaining lasting fame for his visual record of the Civil War.

In 1825 the first American patent for tin **food** containers was filed by Ezra Daggett. By 1849 a machine was developed that limited the amount of hand labor needed to produce tin cans, further stimulating the processing of food as a commercial endeavor. Lobster and salmon were the first foods to be commercially canned. These were rapidly followed by the canning of corn, tomatoes, peas, and additional varieties of fish. By 1860, 5 million cans were being produced annually.

Less momentous developments of the period include the successful shipping of ice from New England to the West Indies in insulated containers in 1805; the invention of the icebox by Thomas Moore in 1803; the patenting of an early system for refrigeration in 1834 by Jacob Perkins; the acceptance of ether as an anesthetic in 1847; the invention of safety matches in 1852; the patenting by Gail Borden of a process for making canned condensed milk in 1856; and the patenting of the attached pencil eraser by H. L. Lipman in the same year. **Related Entries**: Cotton Gin; Food Preservation.

SUGGESTED READING: Charles Austin Beard, *A Century of Progress* (1933; 1977); Paul R. Johnson, *Farm Inventions in the Making of America* (1976).

JACKSON, ANDREW (1767–1845): soldier, congressman, senator, and seventh President of the United States (1829–1837). Andrew Jackson was possibly the most prominent historical character of the early antebellum period. He was alternately pictured by his supporters and detractors as a man of the people and an absolute tyrant; a frontiersman, although he was actually a wealthy plantation owner; a man deeply loyal to his friends, and an unforgiving man dedicated to getting even with his enemies. Certainly there was no more flamboyant and colorful figure in the period.

Jackson was a self-made man. He studied law and helped to write the state constitution of **Tennessee**. He represented his state as a congressman and senator, and was appointed a justice of the state supreme court. In 1804, at the early age of thirty-seven, he "retired to private life." Not unfamiliar with **dueling**, he gained notoriety when he fought a duel to defend the honor of his wife, **Rachel Donelson Jackson**. Her divorce from Lewis Robards had not produced a clean break, and she had eloped with Jackson before her divorce was final. Although the legalities had been ironed out by 1806, Charles Dickinson nonetheless made an allusion to Rachel's matrimonial history to which Jackson took exception. With appropriate formality a duel was arranged that dogged all of Jackson's future political campaigns.

Given the command to fire, the confident Dickinson fired almost instantly, raising a flap of material from Jackson's coat and causing him to clutch at his breast. For a moment both men thought that Jackson might fall. But Jackson took command of himself, raised his pistol, and with great deliberation shot his opponent through the bowels. Dickinson died in agony later that evening. Jackson's loose overhanging coat, draped over a slender figure, had caused his opponent to misjudge the structure of the man from that of the clothing by a small enough margin to keep him alive.

By the end of the first decade of the century Jackson had established

Andrew Jackson at the Battle of New Orleans.
(From the authors' collection.)

himself as an Indian fighter, and in 1814 he destroyed the power of the Creek Indians at the Battle of Horseshoe Bend, **Alabama**. A masterful tactician but a strict disciplinarian, Jackson had six militiamen shot during the **War of 1812** for desertion. This decision was also used against him in his election campaigns, but it was largely overshadowed by his defeat of a regular British army at the **Battle of New Orleans**. In 1818 he invaded **Florida** to punish the Seminole. Here he executed two British citizens who were purportedly dealing in arms with the Indians. He was made military governor of Florida in 1821. When he chose to enter national politics in 1824, the **newspapers** that sprang to the his side—and they were too numerous to be counted—became organs of his political party and an effective tool for convincing the voters of his universal appeal as a candidate.

By the end of the second term of President **James Monroe** in 1824, there was only a single viable political party, the Jeffersonian Republicans. A series of presidential candidates had come forth, each with his own minority of sectional backers, so that the party failed to unite behind a single person. Nonetheless, one-third of the members were able to compromise on William

H. Crawford of **Georgia**. Additional candidates were nominated at local party meetings and through state legislatures for a total of four. Among these were Jackson, **Henry Clay**, and **John Quincy Adams** of Massachusetts.

In the election Jackson had the largest number of popular votes and 90 electoral votes; Adams had 84 electoral votes from New England and New York; Crawford carried most of the South with 41; and Clay came in last with 37, mostly from the old Northwest. No one had the required majority to be elected, and the election would be decided by the House of Representatives between the two leading candidates. As both Clay and Adams distrusted and disliked Jackson, Clay used his influence in the House to deprive Jackson of the presidency. Charges of corruption and quid pro quo were made and widely believed following Adams' election, and the selection of Clay as his secretary of state seemed to verify the "Corrupt Bargain." Jackson never forgave either Adams or Clay, and he began his presidential campaign for 1828 almost immediately.

In 1828 the **Democratic Party** (Democratic Republicans) was formed with Jackson at its head. Jackson was widely viewed as a man of the people, and the elitist elements in American society felt threatened by his popularity. Jackson's newspaper cohorts bitterly assailed the administration of John Quincy Adams. The largely intemperate campaign that followed was almost devoid of restraint and vastly changed the nature of the American political process by expanding the role of popular participation. Jackson won easily. A few weeks before his inauguration, his wife died, some say from the harsh attacks made on her character during the campaign. Jackson never lost his great love for his wife, Rachel.

Upon taking office, President Jackson immediately shook up the government, removing many older officeholders and replacing them with his loyal supporters. This was called the **spoils system**, and it caused a great deal of consternation among career bureaucrats. Moreover, a dramatic rift in Jackson's cabinet was caused by his vigorous defense of **Peggy Eaton**, the socially unpopular wife of the secretary of war. Jackson's intransigence in defending the Eatons led to a disaffection among the members of his cabinet. He thereafter focused on a few of his closest advisers, who became known as the Kitchen Cabinet.

The President's relationship with his Vice President, **John C. Calhoun**, steadily deteriorated during this period. Calhoun's wife had been at the center of the Eaton dispute. Calhoun himself was dedicated to the destruction of the secretary of state, **Martin Van Buren**, whom Jackson viewed as a possible running mate in 1832 and whom Calhoun viewed as a rival. Jackson took up his Vice President's challenge. Having driven Calhoun's friends from the cabinet, Jackson was able to shut him out of the Democratic vice presidential nomination in 1832.

A major question in the Jacksonian years revolved around the **Bank of** the United States, or National Bank. Jackson had opposed the bank in 1817 on the grounds that it was unconstitutional, yet his political ambitions had controlled his outspoken antipathy for almost a decade. During the political campaign of 1828, Jackson had returned to his earlier position, and his tone had become very hostile. By the election of 1832, Jackson's refusal to recharter the bank had become a primary political issue. After his over-whelming reelection as President, which he viewed as a mandate, Jackson removed all government funds from the bank, virtually killing the institu-tion. For this action he was later censured by his enemies who controlled the Senate.

In 1833, in the disputes between **South Carolina** and the federal gov-ernment over **tariffs**, Jackson's relations with his Vice President deteriorated even further. Calhoun not only opposed Jackson, but he openly promoted **nullification** as a moderate alternative to **secession**. Jackson saw that the logical conclusion of Calhoun's plan would be to render the federal gov-ernment impotent. Congress agreed, adopting the **Force Bill**, which al-lowed Jackson to use force against the nullifiers. The President looked to provide arms to a group of South Carolinians friendly to the federal cause and willing to enforce federal law. To this end he sent 5,000 muskets to **Joel Poinsett**, a noted Unionist. Notwithstanding this support, Poinsett was reluctant to see any form of federal intervention, and the crisis was averted by compromise.

In 1835 an unsuccessful attempt was made to assassinate Jackson—the first such attempt in American history. Richard Lawrence, who was later committed to a lunatic asylum, fired two pistols at Jackson at point-blank range. Only the priming caps ignited, although both weapons were loaded with fine dueling powder and ball. When recapped after the incident the pistols fired perfectly. The odds of two successive misfires taking place in this manner were 125,000 to 1. Partisans hinted that the assassination at-tempt was politically motivated by Jackson's enemies, which afforded him some sympathy as the target of a conspiracy.

Land speculation in this period was so widespread that it almost became a national hobby. Wildly inflating currency during these years caused spec-ulators to borrow paper money. In 1836 Jackson published a Specie Circular requiring payments in **specie** (gold or silver rather than paper money) for all federal land purchases. This essentially put a halt to the speculative buying and selling. Unfortunately, the specie requirement also initiated a vast eco-nomic depression in the following year. Martin Van Buren, Jackson's chosen successor, opened his administration with the **Panic** of 1837.

Once out of office, Jackson took up the life of a genteel plantation owner at the Hermitage in Tennessee, became increasingly involved in **horseracing** (where he won thousands of dollars on a match race), and maintained an outsider's interest in politics into his old age. He devoted himself to the family of his adopted son, Andrew. In June 1845, on the eve of the war with Mexico, Andrew Jackson died at his plantation. Everywhere there were solemn services and observations. The nation grieved in a manner that would not again be observed until the death of **Abraham Lincoln. Related Entries**: Adams, John Quincy; Bank of the United States; Calhoun, John C.; Eaton, Peggy; Force Bill; Indian Removal; New Orleans, Battle of; Nullification.

SUGGESTED READING: Donald B. Cole, *The Presidency of Andrew Jackson* (1993); Daniel Feller, *The Jacksonian Promise: America, 1815–1840* (1995); John F. Marszalek, *The Petticoat Affair* (1997); Arthur M. Schlesinger, *The Age of Jackson* (1953; 1988); Robert V. Remini, *The Life of Andrew Jackson* (1988).

JACKSON, RACHEL DONELSON (1767–1828): wife of **Andrew Jackson**. Born in **Virginia**, the daughter of Colonel John Donelson, Rachel entered into a very unhappy marriage with Captain Lewis Robards of **Kentucky**, a man of jealous disposition and unforgiving temper. In 1788 they separated. An attempt at reconciliation failed. In the winter of 1790–1791, having received information that Robards had been granted a divorce by the Virginia legislature, she married Andrew Jackson. Three years later, Jackson learned that the previous information about the divorce had been erroneous. Not only had the divorce not been granted in Virginia, it had not actually taken place until after the date of their marriage. Jackson immediately procured a new license, and the couple was remarried in January 1794.

Rachel was devoted to Jackson. Although she could barely read and write, she was an admirable housekeeper. She was a firm but fair mistress to the plantation's many slaves, and she proved a generous neighbor and good hostess. Having no offspring of their own, the Jacksons adopted one of Rachel's nephews; he was formally named Andrew Jackson and made his heir.

During a vicious political campaign, the details of Rachel's double marriage were brought to light. She was desolate over this defamation, and her already poor health failed rapidly. A few days after Jackson won the presidency, Rachel overheard some particularly vicious gossip about her marriage, took to her bed, and died shortly thereafter. **Related Entry**: Jackson, Andrew.

SUGGESTED READING: John F. Marszalek, *The Petticoat Affair* (1997).

JEFFERSON, THOMAS (1743–1826): revolutionary philosopher, statesman, and third President of the United States (1801–1809). At the time of the First Continental Congress in 1774, Thomas Jefferson, a delegate of the colony of **Virginia**, championed some of the most revolutionary political views of his day. In an essay entitled *A Summary View of the Rights of British America* he questioned both the power of Parliament and the authority of the King to rule the American colonies. With ideas based largely on the work of John Locke, a British philosopher of the seventeenth century, Jefferson was able to explain in clear and eloquent language the conceptual basis of the American Revolution. These ideas were best represented in the Declaration of Independence, a document written by Jefferson and, with only minor changes and omissions, representing his views of limited government.

Jefferson's feelings about **slavery** are often tied to the phrase he included in the Declaration: "all men are created equal." But it should be noted that Jefferson was a slaveowner, had kept **Sally Hemings**, a black slave, as a mistress, and had also written that "blacks . . . are inferior to the whites in the endowments both of body and mind" (Thomas, 1991). Recent research has shown that he did indeed father at least one mixed-race child, whom he refused to acknowledge even in his will. Notwithstanding this enigma in his personality, Jefferson's Bill for Establishing Religious Freedom (1786) is rightly regarded as one of his greatest contributions to the whole of humanity.

In 1798 he joined with **James Madison** in drawing up the Virginia and Kentucky Resolutions in answer to the Alien and Sedition Acts. The **states' rights** doctrine expressed in the Resolutions gained a great deal of traction with those who were proponents of **nullification** and as a matter of some controversy in the **sectional disputes** that preceded the Civil War. By the beginning of the antebellum period, Jefferson had already done most of that for which he is best known. He left office in 1809 and during the remaining years of his life he never ventured far from his home at Monticello. He maintained a voluminous correspondence during these years and devoted much time to the problems of popular **education**, the advancement of science and technology, and tireless promotion of the University of Virginia. In the final years of his life, Jefferson resolved his political differences with John Adams, and they began a lively and lengthy correspondence. Ironically, on July 4, 1826—exactly fifty years after they signed the Declaration of Independence—Adams (age ninety) and Jefferson (age eighty-three) died within hours of one another. **Related Entries**: Constitutional Convention; Constitutional Interpretation; Hemings, Sally.

SUGGESTED READING: Henry Steele Commager, *Jefferson, Nationalism, and the Enlightenment* (1975); Willard Sterne Randall, *Thomas Jefferson: A Life* (1993); Emory M. Thomas, *The Confederacy as a Revolutionary Experience* (1991); Leonard Wibberley, *Time of Harvest: Thomas Jefferson, the Years 1801–1826* (1966).

JUDICIAL BRANCH OF THE FEDERAL GOVERNMENT. *See* Supreme Court of the United States.

KANSAS-NEBRASKA ACT OF 1854: In 1853 the House of Representatives decided to designate a large portion of the unorganized land in the Midwest as the territory of Nebraska. While Americans were eager to enter the area, **slavery** there was ostensibly forbidden by the 36°30' provision of the **Missouri Compromise of 1820**. The Kansas-Nebraska Act of 1854 revised the division of the unorganized territory into two parts, Kansas and Nebraska; repealed the provisions regarding slavery from the Missouri Compromise; and replaced them with the doctrine of **popular sovereignty**, which allowed the settlers of each area to decide the question of slavery by majority vote.

Although the brainchild of the astute **Democratic** politician **Stephen A. Douglas**, it is difficult to see what advantage there was in the Kansas-Nebraska Act for him, his party, or the nation. That Nebraska would be a free territory was never in doubt. However, Kansas—possibly the last territorial area into which slavery might have been economically introduced—faced a more uncertain future. Certainly no one—especially Douglas—expected that the area bordered by **Missouri**, one of the **slave states**, would soon come to be known as "**Bleeding Kansas.**" A serious misreading of the temper of the nation had taken place.

Upon passage of the bill, anti-slavery and religious organizations immediately recruited and financed settlers to claim the region. Equally intense pro-slavery Missourians crossed over the border in the hope of expanding their plantations into the new area. What ensued can best be characterized as a civil war, with Missouri border ruffians and "jayhawkers" and anti-slavery "red legs" and bushwackers spreading terror, bloodshed, and murder throughout the territory. The anti-slavery settlers were reinforced by arms—including state-of-the-art Sharps breechloading rifles—sent to them by **abolitionists** in New England. Nonetheless, at the height of the troubles the anti-slavery city of Lawrence, Kansas, was burned by a pro-slavery mob from Missouri. Three days later, a small band of ultra abolitionists led by **John Brown** and his four sons murdered five unarmed and innocent pro-slavery settlers at Pottawatomie Creek in retribution. Nonetheless, the slavery forces prevailed when the abolitionists abandoned the effort to adopt an anti-slavery state constitution, and the federal government accepted the legitimacy of the pro-slavery Lecompton Constitution.

As a product of the optimism of the Northern Democrats and Stephen Douglas, the Kansas-Nebraska Act was a political failure. It seemingly sabotaged the political compromises that had characterized the previous three decades of American politics. Three months of bitter and contentious debate was needed to pass the bill. Although the measure was popular among Northern Democrats, and the Southern Democrats gave it support, its passage ultimately caused an irrevocable split in the party. A coalition of Northern moderates felt betrayed and bolted from the party, vowing to adhere to the Missouri Compromise. Outraged by the act, Northern voters began to speak of the existence of a "slave power conspiracy." In response, moderates in the South began to harden their position and seriously consider disunion. So disastrous were these consequences that the Democratic Party chose to overlook Stephen Douglas as a presidential candidate in 1856, giving the nod to **James Buchanan**, who had been a minister to England during the Kansas-Nebraska debates and was therefore untainted by the bill either way.

While the Democrats were hurt by the response to the act, the old **Whig Party** was devastated by it. The Southern wing of the Whig Party, sympathetic to compromise on the slavery issue, bolted from the party, thereafter aligning themselves with the Southern Democrats; the remainder of the Whig Party, already weak after years of deterioration, was left in disarray.

Yet the Kansas-Nebraska Act was a godsend for the nascent **Republican Party**. They used the passage of the act, and the decision of the courts in the **Dred Scott** case, which closely followed, as symbols verifying the existence of the slave power conspiracy. Not only was such a conspiracy dangerous in itself, but the events taking place in Kansas were clear evidence that the old powers wished to spread slavery to every corner of the land. As a new party the Republicans benefited greatly from the ongoing tide of sectional resentment and were in the unique position of being able to stand as the defenders of an idealized Northern culture, untainted, as were the Democrats, by former associations with the slavery of the South. **Related Entries**: Brown, John; Democratic Party; Douglas, Stephen A.; Popular Sovereignty.

SUGGESTED READING: Thomas Goodrich, *War to the Knife: Bleeding Kansas* (1998); James C. Malin, *The Nebraska Question, 1852–1854* (1953).

KEELBOATS. *See* Flatboats and Keelboats.

KEMBLE, FANNY (1809–1893): diarist. Married in 1834 to Pierce Butler, who owned a large and prosperous plantation in **Georgia**, Fanny Kemble was wealthy enough to reside in Philadelphia. Here Fanny, who had first
appeared on the social scene as an actress on the New York stage, was considered a great adornment to the social life of the city, exhibiting magnificent
beauty and a very gracious and unaffected style. During the initial years of
her marriage, Fanny was insulated from plantation life by distance. However,
after several years she set off with her husband and family to visit the plantation. Here she found the breeding and manners of Southerners generally
praiseworthy. Nonetheless, she expressed a horror of the institution of **slavery** which made her more and more miserable each day. Her stay proved a
difficult trial for a Northern woman unfamiliar with such Southern ways.

Fanny kept a journal of her time on the plantation which was later published as *Journal of a Residence on a Georgia Plantation.* The work was
notable for its penetrating and compassionate accounts of the survival of
plantation life in the Old South, and it was particularly revealing of the life
of female slaves. Her written accounts show an amazing combination of
sympathy for the condition of black slaves and an overriding disdain for the
black race in general and for black men in particular, whom she found shiftless and inconceivably stupid. These attitudes—concurrently contemptuous
of slavery as an institution and ambivalent toward blacks as a race—may
have been typical of Northern observers of plantation slavery. **Related Entries**: Plantation Economy; Slavery.

SUGGESTED READING: Frances A. Kemble, *Journal of a Residence on a Georgia
Plantation, 1838–1839* (1863; 1984).

KENTUCKY: Highlights of a period description of the state from John
Hayward's *Gazetteer of the United States* (1853) read as follows:

Surface and Soil: The soil throughout the state is generally of excellent quality,
producing hemp, tobacco, wheat, corn, and numerous fruits in great abundance.
Grapes of fine quality abound. Large quantities of salt are annually exported.

Rivers: The largest rivers are the Cumberland and the Tennessee. There are numerous others, all of which are extensively navigable.

Education: Nearly one half of children between five and sixteen attended the district schools connected with the public system.

Internal Improvements: The Louisville and Portland Canal is a work of extraordinary magnitude and importance. There are several **railroad** projects under way.

Manufacture: A large amount of capital is invested in the manufacture of hemp,
cotton, wool, iron, tobacco, leather and other staple commodities. The fabrication
of almost every article of domestic use is also carried on throughout the state.

Minerals: The most abundant mineral products are iron, coal, lime, and salt. Large
quantities of the latter are annually exported.

Indians: Few or none of the descendants of the aboriginal possessors of the soil
now remain within the limits of the state.

Population: By the 1850 census, the population reached over 1,000,000—more than one fifth of which are slaves.

Related Entry: Geography.

SUGGESTED READING: Steven A. Channing, *Kentucky, a History* (1977); John Hayward, *Gazetteer of the United States* (1853); Clark McMeekin, *Old Kentucky Country* (1957).

KENTUCKY RESOLUTIONS. *See* Virginia and Kentucky Resolutions.

KINSHIP: It went without saying that Southern gentlemen came from good stock. Their parentage and pedigree were considered to be aristocratic, at least. In order to maintain their high social position and authority, it was important for Southerners to have a strong sense of obligation to their blood relatives. A number of words and phrases have come down to us expressing this obligation: kinfolk, blood kin, blood ties, and kissing cousins are among a few.

Family was the most conservative and inviolable of Southern institutions. Many families had resided in the same section of the country for hundreds of years. By the time of the Civil War, there was hardly a family of note that did not occupy at least the same social position that it had at the time of the founding of the colonies. In order to maintain this position, intermarriage between second and third cousins was common. Periodically, the family would gather, and cousins, aunts, and grandparents would trace the family tree from long before the Revolution.

With kinship came advantage and obligation. Birth into one of the leading families of the South was essential to making a political career. Prominence, and the presumption of ability—whether it was present or not—were inherited from one's father or uncle in much the same way that land and slaves were inherited. So pervasive was this assumption that kin were given positions as sheriffs, justices of the peace, **militia** captains, or county lieutenants by influential relatives without the slightest charge of favoritism being made by anyone in the system.

Fathers were protective of their daughters, providing their sons-in-law with influence, if not money. Unmarried daughters were often given the position of companion to their fathers. Granddaughters were treated in much the same way, especially in the absence of their father. Men were similarly solicitous of their nieces, daughters-in-law, and all their children.

Siblings were treated in a hierarchical manner, with all the male offspring being given a superior position over their sisters. The inferior position of females implied an obligation placed upon brothers to defend their honor. A brother could intervene in the affairs of his sisters and their circle of friends with or without their permission. At times these brothers could take on a very combative stance when dealing with a sister's reputation. Female cousins came under the same type of protection. As women were not permitted to correspond with men who were not relations, many young women had no acquaintance with men who were not their blood kin until after their marriage. Even then their social relationships with males were limited to the friends and acquaintances of their husbands. Southern men also felt obliged to counsel, support, and defend not only their own families, but all females and minor children placed under their protection. **Related Entries**: Courtship and Marriage; Plantation Aristocracy.

SUGGESTED READING: Anne C. Rose, *Victorian America and the Civil War* (1992).

KNOW-NOTHINGS. *See* Nativists.

LAFAYETTE, MARQUIS de: Marie Joseph Paul Yve Roch Gilbert Du Motier, Marquis de Lafayette (1757–1834), soldier and statesman. In 1824 President **James Monroe** invited this French hero of the American Revolution to visit the United States. Lafayette was quickly approaching seventy years of age, but his 1824–1825 visit became a triumphal tour through all parts of the country. Wild enthusiasm greeted him in all sections of the country, and many towns were renamed in his honor. Though an aristocrat, Lafayette had survived the terror of the French Revolution, and his appearance in America was particularly symbolic to Southerners who most closely identified with the ideals of the American Revolution. Expressions of revolutionary ideals were freely used by Southern apologists during his tour and throughout the first half of the nineteenth century. **Related Entry**: Constitutional Convention.

SUGGESTED READING: Stanley J. Idzerda, *Lafayette, Hero of Two Worlds: The Art and Pageantry of His Farewell Tour of America* (1989).

LAND SPECULATION: In 1794 the legislature in **Georgia** decided to sell 35 million acres of land to four land speculating companies for one and a half cents an acre. The land, known as the Yazoo Strip, stretched from Spanish **Florida** to **Tennessee**, comprising most of present-day **Alabama** and **Mississippi**. The obvious collusion between the legislators and the land companies in this affair caused a political scandal in Georgia that lasted two decades and led to the **Supreme Court**. With the original enabling bill rescinded by the succeeding state legislature in Georgia, the court of Chief Justice **John Marshall** created a new legal precedent by overturning a state law for the first time. Unfortunately, this was the Rescinding Act. Nonetheless, the federal government interceded by buying the land and indemnifying the stockholders in the land companies. Thereafter the government found itself in the land business.

Between 1834 and 1836 the federal government sold more than 40 million acres of public land at little more than one dollar per acre to land speculators. The proceeds were sufficient to pay for all the expenses of government during those years. Speculators bought up choice sites in the West and sold them for a profit to others. It was not unusual for a prime parcel to pass through ten different owners before coming into the possession of an actual settler. In the wilderness the bounds of towns and cities were staked in the virgin soil, and imagination provided the turnpikes, canals, and railways that would link them to Southern and Eastern markets.

Land speculation was so widespread among the public that it almost became a hobby. Although widely seen as a windfall for those who had the cash to invest, a wildly inflating currency during these years made such investments a necessity for maintaining one's wealth. Southerners were increasingly unable to participate in these investments, as their cash was tied up in plantations and slaves. Some began to borrow money to make investments in land, thereby fueling further inflation and placing themselves at the mercy of money lenders and produce buyers.

The process was also basically unfair to the settlers, who paid much higher prices for their land than if they had purchased it directly from the government. Land speculation soon became a political issue, closely intertwined with the debates raging over banking and "hard" currency. President **Andrew Jackson** essentially put a halt to the speculative buying and selling by requiring payments in **specie**—gold or silver rather than paper money—for all federal land purchases. **Related Entry**: Specie.

SUGGESTED READING: Coy F. Cross, *Go West, Young Man: Horace Greeley's Vision for America* (1995); John R. Stilgoe, *Common Landscape of America, 1580–1845* (1982).

LAWS GOVERNING SLAVERY. *See* Black Codes; Federal Laws Governing Slavery.

LECOMPTON CONSTITUTION. *See* Bleeding Kansas.

LEE, ROBERT E. (1807–1870): soldier and Confederate general. Robert E. Lee was the son of "Light Horse Harry" Lee, a famous military leader of the American Revolution. Lee knew little of his father other than his reputation as a warrior. Harry Lee left his family when Robert was five, and died in Barbados—having fled his creditors—when the boy was eleven. Robert's mother did her best to maintain the family and instill in her children responsibility and righteousness, but she suffered from poor health. Lee learned to discipline himself, and as the son of an American hero, he passed through the United States Military Academy at West Point, New York, without a single demerit, graduating second in his class in 1829.

Lee was assigned as an engineering officer to several intimidating construction projects that occupied almost two decades of his military career. His first and most frustrating engineering challenge was the building of a massive fort on Cockspur Island, located in the Savannah River in **Georgia**. This work proved to be seasonal, and Lee returned annually to **Washington, DC**, in the summer. He also laid the groundwork for the outworks of Fortress Monroe, a giant project at the confluence of the York and James Rivers in **Virginia** which proved critical to federal military plans in the Civil War. In 1837 he was assigned to superintend the dredging and stabilization of the river channel at St. Louis, **Missouri**.

In 1831, while working at Fortress Monroe, Lee married Mary Custis, daughter of George Washington Parke Custis (Martha Washington's grandson), whom he had courted during his seasonal leaves. This should have been an advantageous marriage for the almost destitute young army lieutenant. George Custis had inherited a good deal of wealth from the Washingtons, and Mary was his only child. However, Custis was a poor businessman and a worse planter. He gave other men his best land and lived off the money sent to him by his tenants. His finest asset was the plantation at Arlington, Virginia, where he lived. Ultimately Lee came to reside with his father-in-law, and upon Custis' death Lee found that he was responsible for reconciling his father-in-law's debts and carrying out the provisions of his will.

The will called for the freeing of all the Custis slaves, and Lee was slow to accomplish this last task. In 1829, at his mother's death, Lee had inherited several slaves. He had chosen at that time, together with his brothers Henry and Carter, to sell the male slaves and invest his share of the proceeds. However, he also chose to hire out (rent) the female slaves that he owned as a result of the bequest. In 1857 there were more than ninety slaves at Arlington, as well as almost two dozen **freemen**. Lee pledged to free all the Custis slaves in five years, but he was accused of withholding their freedom for his own benefit when he hired out a half dozen men. In fact the Custis estate was bequeathed to Mary Lee encumbered with an overwhelming debt which her husband was trying to retire. During this period Northern **abolitionists** were detected trying to persuade the Arlington slaves to escape.

Lee was never comfortable in the role of a slaveowner. He disliked **slavery** in the abstract but accepted it as a source of labor and a means to maintain wealth and social position. He wrote of slavery as a great moral and political evil, but he also wrote that "blacks are measurably better off here [in the United States] than in Africa, morally, socially, and physically. The painful discipline they are undergoing is necessary for their instruction as a race, and I hope will prepare and lead them to better things" (Emory, 1995). Nonetheless, Lee considered slavery a greater evil for white society than for blacks, and he believed that the final abolition of human slavery was on the horizon. While his stated abhorrence of slavery set him apart from most Southern slaveowners, his belief that blacks were better off as slaves than as poor freemen, fending for themselves in a racially biased society, closely echoed similar statements made by many Southern apologists.

Like many military leaders of the Civil War, Lee gained his battlefield experience during the **Mexican War of 1846**. He learned from his initial experiences with actual combat, but mostly he gained an increased confidence in his capacity as a soldier. A competent engineer, Lee was surprised to find that he was also an excellent field officer. His work at reconnaissance throughout the campaign gained him the praise of his commanding officers, and he seemed to be able to judge the fitness of the ground for military operations at a glance. He learned useful lessons in Mexico, such as the value of maneuver and the ability of a small army to defeat a larger opponent—especially a second-class one like the Mexicans. Nonetheless, he also became convinced, as did many of his contemporaries, that offensive tactics could overcome static defenses. This was unfortunate, and such beliefs are largely credited with causing the unusually high number of casualties in the Civil War.

Lee returned from the Mexican War as one of the premier officers of the Army of the United States. In 1852 he was appointed superintendent of West Point, an assignment he considered a "snake pit" of professional politics. Unfortunately, both his oldest son, George, and his nephew. Fitzhugh, were cadets at the academy at the time, placing Lee in the position of appearing either too harsh or too lenient in his treatment of them. Fitzhugh was particularly troublesome, although he later became one of Lee's finest subordinate commanders. Nonetheless, during Lee's tenure, which ended in 1855, he made several unique changes in the curriculum and in the organization of the academy.

In 1855 Lee was assigned to active duty on the Western frontier with the 2nd Cavalry. He lived a simple and happy existence on the plains of **Texas** chasing marauding bands of Comanche and Kiowa, and moving from frontier post to frontier post. He was called back east by the death of his father-in-law in 1857. At this point Lee could have become a planter (his wife having inherited the bulk of the Custis estate), but he decided to stay in the army and took a two-year leave to settle the Custis will.

In 1859 Lee was placed in charge of the troops that captured the radical abolitionist **John Brown** at Harper's Ferry, Virginia, and he was present at Brown's execution. He then returned to assignment in Texas. In February 1861 Lee was again recalled to the War Office in Washington. Here, in April, he was offered the field command of the Union Army in the coming war. He refused.

With the **secession** of Virginia, Lee resigned his commission. Within days he was serving as a military consultant to Confederate President **Jefferson**

Davis. Not until June 1862 did Lee receive command of the Army of Northern Virginia, and at no time during the war did he command all the Confederate forces. However, as Virginia was the primary theater of the war, Lee's victories and failures over the next thirty-four months were widely viewed as a barometer of Confederate success. His surrender at Appomattox Court House in April 1865 was the practical, if not the actual, end of the conflict.

Lee's place in Southern history was that of a great soldier. Even Northerners considered him the finest general of the war. In 1865 he accepted the presidency of Washington University (later Washington and Lee). Here he rebuilt the college and quietly dedicated himself to restoring the economic, cultural, and political life of the South. In retirement and after his death he was idolized by Southerners who surrounded him with a mythical legacy that was to become the center of the South's "Lost Cause" tradition.

SUGGESTED READING: Thomas L. Connelly, *The Marble Man: Robert E. Lee and His Image in American Society* (1977); Emory M. Thomas, *Robert E. Lee: A Biography* (1995).

LEGISLATIVE BRANCH/CONGRESS: One of the reasons for the durability of the **slavery** question lies with the manner in which Southerners controlled the government at the federal level. The **Supreme Court**, often top-heavy with Southern justices, had generally sided with the South on questions of slavery, and an overwhelming number of Presidents came from the South or exhibited pro-Southern attitudes in office. Southerners prevented many changes in law or amendments to the Constitution by holding a precarious balance in the Senate maintained through a series of coalitions with other sections of the country. The farmers of the Midwest were particularly supportive of the South as long as they were dependent on shipping their produce down the **Mississippi River** to Southern ports; but as midcentury approached, Western support of the Southern agenda softened.

With an all but stagnant population base, the South perceived a threat to the legislative balance in the burgeoning populations of Northern cities. In 1820 the North had a population 20 percent larger than that of the South, which translated in the House as 123 representatives for the **free states** and 89 for the **slave states**. As representation was proportional to population, the North would experience a growing advantage in the House of Representatives as its population grew, and every four years a similar advantage in the electoral college that actually elected the President. This inequity had been the foundation of the Southern rationale for insisting during the Constitutional debates of 1787 that each slave be counted as three-fifths of a person for the purpose of determining representation.

Conversely, representation in the Senate was set by the Constitution to two senators per state without regard to population. These senators were selected by the state legislatures rather than through popular election. Southern planters generally controlled senatorial selections. In 1820 there were eleven slave and eleven free states, with twenty-two senators representing each side. Southern leverage in the Senate could be lost if a large number of free states were added to the Union without a counterbalancing number of new slave states. Moreover, since the Senate approved all appointments to the Supreme Court, practical control of the Senate meant the continuation of a Court friendly to its agenda, a circumstance the South saw as an effective remedy to growing anti-slavery hysteria in the North. **Related Entry**: Executive Branch/Presidency.

SUGGESTED READING: William Lee Miller, *Arguing About Slavery: The Great Battle in the United States Congress* (1996).

LEMMON CASE: In 1852 Jonathan and Juliet Lemmon decided to move from **Virginia** to **Texas** and take the eight slaves that belonged to Mrs. Lemmon with them. Although the details of the trip are confused and unimportant, it was decided to take a side trip by steamer to New York City and then book a luxury passage from there to **New Orleans**. The slaves were thereby brought into New York harbor while New York was a **free state**. Mr. Lemmon, conscious of a possible problem, made plans to transfer the slaves to a southbound steamer without actually landing them in New York. He feared that the **abolitionists** would make an effort to rescue them. But his plans failed, and as soon as they touched land the owners and the slaves were arrested and brought before the New York state courts.

The state argued that Lemmon was a slave trader and that these blacks were confined and held against their will. The attorneys for the Lemmons argued that they had the right under federal law to transport their "property" anywhere in the country. Moreover, it was argued that the slaves had never touched free soil except for the purpose of "passage and transit." Justice Elijah Paine granted the state of New York's writ, citing the anti-slavery statutes of the state as his authority. He ordered the eight slaves freed. Paine's decision was greeted with approbation by the New York press, **free blacks**, and abolitionists everywhere. Nevertheless, a group of New York businessmen raised funds to compensate the Lemmons for their loss. The Lemmons received $5,200 in indemnification and returned to Virginia, while the former slaves were secretly whisked off to Canada to ensure their future safety. **Related Entry**: Scott, Dred.

SUGGESTED READING: Ervin L. Jordan, Jr., *Black Confederates and Afro-Yankees in Civil War Virginia* (1995).

LIBERATOR, THE. See Garrison, William Lloyd.

LINCOLN, ABRAHAM (1809–1865): lawyer, politician, and sixteenth President of the United States from 1861 to 1865. The rising star of national politics in the 1850s was a young former **Whig** politician from Illinois. Abraham Lincoln had not rushed to join the first groups that formed the **Republican Party;** but in 1854, in a speech in Peoria, he began to speak out against the **Kansas-Nebraska Act**. The deep crusading tenor of this speech was closely linked to Lincoln's ambition for office. Instead of casting his fortunes with the Republicans, who were expounding on the issue of the **extension of slavery into the territories**, he mistakenly continued to identify himself with the nearly defunct Whig Party. Viewed as an old party candidate, he lost the 1854 Senate seat in a close race.

Immediately thereafter, he transferred his allegiance to the Republicans and helped to organize the party in Illinois. It was no surprise when Lincoln was chosen by the Republicans to face **Stephen A. Douglas** in the 1858 race for the Senate. Lincoln began his campaign with his famous "House Divided" speech. In this address Lincoln called for the country to become all free or all slave. It was the most radical speech on the subject of **slavery** of his political career. The Republicans seemed especially absorbed by the concept of the immediate **abolition** of slavery and the granting of full civil rights to blacks. They saw no compromise position in these matters. By aligning himself with the radical wing of the party in order to gain their substantial influence, Lincoln came to be despised in the South. During the debates with Douglas in 1858, Lincoln backed away from his initial radicalism, supporting gradualism and **African colonization** to attract moderates in the North and expressing a belief in an inherent inequality among the races to appease Southern liberals. While supporting an end to slavery, he disclaimed any hopes for "social and political equality of the white and black races," and disavowed any plan to make "voters or jurors of Negroes, [or] of qualifying them to hold office, [or] to intermarry with white people." Most important, he pledged his support for colonization of freed slaves, saying, "[T]here is a physical difference between the white and black races which I believe will forever forbid the two races living together on terms of social and political equality" (Steers, 1996).

Never again did Lincoln express such radical views. Despite his attempts at moderation, his words were widely interpreted as a declaration of war on Southern institutions. Douglas carefully pointed out that the country had been split for quite some time on the issue of slavery and could continue to be so indefinitely if the hotheads on both sides would leave well enough alone. By espousing moderation Douglas won the race narrowly, but Lincoln's stance had catapulted the young lawyer into a position of leadership in the Republican Party.

Lincoln went on to engineer the Republican Party's nominating convention in 1860 and received the party's presidential nod instead of **William H. Seward**, who was more moderate on the slavery issue. While Lincoln had used the radicals to gain the nomination, he immediately began to modify his radical image to make himself more acceptable to other factions of the party. He focused on preserving the Union rather than on eradicating slavery. By failing to center himself within the party spectrum, Lincoln essentially drove the moderates in the party toward the radical position. Certainly this was the light in which the South viewed the Republicans and Lincoln during the election, and they began to preach of **Black Republicanism** as a counterpoint to the charges of a "slave power conspiracy."

Lincoln probably would not have won the presidency in 1860 had the election not become a four-way race. The **Democratic Party** failed to unite behind a single candidate, the Northern branch choosing Stephen Douglas, a moderate Unionist, and the Southern branch uniting behind pro-slavery secessionist **John C. Breckinridge**, a former Vice President of the United States. The fourth candidate, of the new Constitutional Union Party, composed of former Whigs and **Nativists**, was **John Bell** of **Tennessee**, a Southern Unionist. **Tariffs**, homesteads, **railroads, immigration**, and political corruption all figured in the campaign, but slavery and the fear of disunion remained the pivotal questions. When it became obvious to the candidates, based on the results of two gubernatorial elections in Pennsylvania and Indiana, that Lincoln was going to win, Bell and Breckinridge proclaimed dedication to immediate disunion; but Douglas, to his credit, disavowed any ideas of **secession**, saying, "If Lincoln is elected, he must be inaugurated."

Lincoln won the election with just under 40 percent of the popular vote and 59 percent of the electoral votes. He carried eighteen states, yet, with the exception of coastal California, not one of them was below the **Mason-Dixon Line**. This result reinforced his position as a sectional leader rather than a national one and almost ensured secession. Significantly, Douglas, who beat both Breckinridge and Bell with 30 percent of the popular vote, represented the views of at least some of the electorate in all parts of the country; but he received a mere 4 percent of the electoral votes. Besides **Mississippi**, the only other state won by Douglas was New Jersey. This seemingly strange pairing effectively ended the influence of Douglas and the Northern Democrats. Breckinridge, with 18 percent of the popular vote, carried every state that would come to be in the Confederacy except Mississippi and **Virginia**. The former Vice President also carried **Maryland** and **Delaware**. Bell captured the states of **Kentucky**, Tennessee, and Virginia and received 13 percent of the popular vote. Notwithstanding this result, 70 percent of the voters had shown support for at least a moderate stand against slavery, but they almost all resided in the North.

The state of **South Carolina** had threatened to secede in 1852 and again in 1856. It renewed the call in 1859 by inviting its sister slaveholding states to consider a course of concerted action. Nonetheless, a positive decision was deferred pending the outcome of the 1860 election. It is not clear what result a Lincoln defeat or a Breckinridge, Douglas, or Bell victory would

Jenny Lind's performances drew huge crowds, as depicted in this period print from the authors' collection.

have meant to the secession movement. But in its declaration the South Carolina convention listed as one of the reasons for its secession "the election of a man to the high office of President of the United States whose opinions and purposes are hostile to slavery." Certainly, the Lincoln victory had been a signal for action. **Related Entries**: Bell, John; Breckinridge, John C.; Douglas, Stephen A.; Republican Party; Secession.

SUGGESTED READING: Frank L. Dennis, *The Lincoln-Douglas Debates* (1974); Carl Sandburg, *Abraham Lincoln: The Prairie Years and the War Years* (1939; 1974); Edward Steers, Jr., ed., *The Quotable Lincoln* (1996).

LIND, JENNY (1820–1887): singer known as the "Swedish Nightingale." This singer's grand tour of the United States (1850–1852) was widely promoted by the great showman and huckster P. T. Barnum, who offered a prize of $200 for the best song written specifically for her. Barnum combined her performances with lectures on **temperance** given by himself. His daughter, Carolina C. Barnum, went along on the tour as a companion for Lind. Carolina kept a journal for part of the year 1851 in which she describes the tour.

Lind was particularly popular, and **theater** owners demanded and received as much as $225 for a seat at her performances. She added to her own popularity by reportedly contributing half of her salary to various **charities**. At one point in her Southern tour it was suggested that she had made a donation to an **abolition** group in Boston—a rumor P. T. Barnum emphatically denied.

Jenny Lind, who had established her reputation in Europe, was known as a young woman of "very great musical taste" with a brilliant and precise voice. She was greeted by a crowd of over 40,000 admirers when her ship docked in New York City in 1850. Besides performances in Northern cities such as New York, Boston, Philadelphia, Baltimore, and Cincinnati, Lind also toured many of the major cities of the South. In **Richmond, Virginia**, she sang at the Marshall Theater. She spent ten days entertaining the social elite of **Charleston, South Carolina**, and about a week in Wilmington, **North Carolina**, before sailing to Havana, Cuba. Returning to the United States through the port of **New Orleans, Louisiana**, she gave twelve sold-out performances at the St. Charles Theater in that city. Thereafter Barnum chartered the steamer *Magnolia* to sail up the **Mississippi River** with stops at Natchez, **Mississippi;** Memphis, **Tennessee;** St. Louis, **Missouri;** Louisville, **Kentucky;** and Nashville, Tennessee. In total Lind gave more than ninety performances.

However, it was her performances in **Washington, DC**, in 1851 that had the most lasting effect on the American public. Her rendition of "Home, Sweet Home" at the New National Hall before President **Millard Fillmore** was so moving that there was no applause at its completion. The solemn respect for Lind's ability was overshadowed only by the tears and sentiment that swept the hall. President Fillmore declared that the performance was the most exciting thing that had happened to him since entering the White House. Ironically, only a few weeks later the New National Hall suffered the collapse of a section of its walls while it was unoccupied, sparing many of the lives that might have been lost had the collapse taken place in the packed house attending her performances.

In 1852 Lind fell out with P. T. Barnum, who threatened to sue her for more than $70,000 if she did not finish the tour. "I hired her. She didn't hire me!" (Shultz, 1962). Shortly thereafter she married her music director, Otto Goldschmidt, a German American immigrant. After living briefly in the United States while giving a tour of her own, she returned to Europe to live in semi-retirement, teaching music at the Royal College of Music in London. Jenny Lind's grand tour of the United States created one of the first great "manias." Unfortunately, it sometimes seemed violent and uncontrolled, with as many as 20,000 fans crowding the streets around the theaters in which she appeared. **Related Entries**: Amusements and Diversions; Theater.

SUGGESTED READING: Joan Bulman, *Jenny Lind, a Biography* (1956); Frances Cavanah, *Jenny Lind's America* (1969); Gladys Denny Shultz, *Jenny Lind: The Swedish Nightingale* (1962).

LIQUOR. *See* Temperance.

LITERACY. *See* Reading.

LITERARY DEVELOPMENT: The literary development of the **ante-bellum South** was stunted by a social structure whose **slavery** and feudalistic ideals weighed it down in a time when native literature sought a loftier spirit. Southern **romanticism** focused on the heroic and objective elements of history, while Northern romanticism was dominated by the transcendentalists who contemplated its philosophical and metaphysical meaning. As the issues of **slave states** and **free states** brewed, many Southern writers became mired in answering the charges of the Northern **abolitionists** and assumed defensive postures or romanticized slavery. The largely rural nature of the South and its weak educational system inhibited the opportunity for the exchange of ideas and the intellectual stimulation that abounded in larger population centers. The absence of effective Southern publishing houses left the Southern writer at the mercy of the tastes of Northern editors.

As a Southern consciousness emerged, so did magazines written by and for a Southern audience. Periodicals such as *Niles' Weekly Register* (1811), the *Southern Literary Messenger* (1824), the *Review* (1828), and *Literary Gazette* (1834) rose to defend the aristocratic sentiments, chivalric loyalties, and feudal virtues most Southerners held so dear. Most of these were outgrowths of the few literary communities that did emerge. One center was in Lexington, sometimes referred to as "the Athens of the West." Another cadre crystallized around **William Gilmore Simms** of **Charleston**. These circles were mainly composed of lawyers who met to discuss political and literary matters. As the antebellum period moved forward, the political rather than aesthetic perspective of these works gained increasing prominence.

Unfortunately, professional writers were held in low esteem in the South. Literary pursuits were deemed a gentleman's avocation. Southern magazines, which had to struggle to survive, paid little to contributors. Many Southerners failed to patronize the work of their own sons, whether in books or periodicals.

The one writer to emerge from the South who attained lasting national recognition was **Edgar Allan Poe**. Although born in Boston, Poe referred to himself as a Virginian, and in fact spent most of his life in **Richmond**. Although he defended the South's institutions and traditions, his writings seldom challenged social issues. One of Poe's greatest contributions to Southern literature was his tenure as editor of the *Southern Literary Messenger*. He encouraged the work of Southern writers, and under his hand the magazine emerged as one of the most important periodicals of its time.

William Gilmore Simms was perhaps the only other Southern writer of significance during the antebellum period. Simms is more typical of the mind-set of the region, and his political beliefs paralleled the South's evolution of thought. His historical romances were typical of the Southern romanticism which evolved out of Sir Walter Scott and James Fenimore Cooper and touched on both national and sectional themes.

The first examples of writing in the formal genres by blacks are seen in the 1820s. Some appeared as poetry, but certainly the **slave narratives**, which began to appear in the 1830s, had the greatest effect. While the influence of an anti-slavery editor is clearly visible in some, others are clearly the work of the avowed author. **Frederick Douglass'** 1845 *Narrative* has perhaps garnered the most fame. Other significant works were penned by **William Wells Brown**—America's first black novelist—Josiah Henson, and Henry "Box" Brown. Slave narratives sold very well, supplying sensationalism and sentimentality to an audience who relished both.

While Southern women were frequent writers of letters and diaries, writing as a profession was not one to which the Southern woman aspired. Eliza Wilkinson's *Letters* detailing the British invasion of Charleston in 1779 were published in 1839, but even periodicals of the day contained few female contributions. One notable exception was Caroline Howard Gilman. Although born in Boston, Gilman spent her adult life in Charleston, where she wrote numerous stories, poems, and novels. Her 1837 *Recollections of a Southern Matron*, like other women's fiction in the North, is highly sentimental. It tells the story of a plantation girl as she grows into womanhood and is noteworthy as the first Southern work on that theme. Additionally, Gilman founded a children's magazine, *Rose Bud*, in 1832.

Some urban areas supported **theater** groups, although few Southern playwrights basked in any literary or financial success. George Washington Parke Custis wrote numerous plays on historic themes. *Pocahontas, or The Settlers of Virginia* was extremely well received when it played at the National Theater in **Washington**. Most Southern theaters emphasized performance rather than unique writing. **Minstrel shows** were actually more important to the long-range development of Southern literature, as they fixed the stereotype of plantation tradition and stimulated interest in African American culture that would emerge decades later. The minstrel show is thought by some to actually be the earliest development of a truly indigenous American drama and the birth of American comedy.

Ironically, though little poetry of value was produced below the **Mason-Dixon Line** at this time, Southern life served as the inspiration for some of the most original and endearing of American lyrics. Francis Scott Key's "The Star Spangled Banner" is undoubtedly the most famous. The earliest Southern poet considered to be of any merit is William Crafts (1787–1826), who celebrated the sporting passion of his native Charleston in "The Raciad" and later penned "Sullivan's Island." William Grayson (1788–1863) authored several volumes, but only "The Hireling and the Slave" (1856), which showed the superior condition of the unpaid slave to the paid hireling, gained notice. **Related Entries**: Antebellum South; Brown, William Wells;

The yeoman farmer relied on his own energy and that of his livestock to supply his needs. (From the authors' collection.)

Minstrel Shows; Poe, Edgar Allan, Romanticism; Simms, William Gilmore; Theater.

SUGGESTED READING: Edward L. Ayers and Bradley C. Mittendorf, *The Oxford Book of the American South: Testimony, Memory, and Fiction* (1997); Jay B. Hubbel, *The South in American Literature* (1954); Elizabeth Moss, *Domestic Novelists: Defenders of Southern Culture* (1992).

LIVERY. *See* Transportation.

LIVESTOCK: A sizable and determined effort at scientific animal husbandry was found to exist among Southern farmers in the antebellum period. Planter, **secessionist**, and politician **Edmund Ruffin** served for many years as the head of the Virginia Agricultural Society, and from 1833 to 1842 he was the editor of the *Farmer's Register*. Other Southern states had similar organizations and newsletters. Even modest farms, however, might be stocked with beef cattle, dairy cows, oxen, sheep, mules or horses, hogs, chicken or other fowl, and a dog or two. Plantations could be presumed to house most, or all, of these animals on their grounds. George Washington Parke Custis (grandson of Martha Washington) had, according to a description of his estate at Arlington, **Virginia**, at the time of his death in 1857,

28 mules, 1 jenny (a female donkey), 3 horses, 28 oxen, 66 cattle, 73 sheep, and 101 hogs.

Cows were needed to provide milk, butter, and cheese. Chickens required little space and turned available reserves of corn and meal into meat; but chicken meat was both difficult to preserve and prone to spoil. Like other domesticated fowl, chicken was generally eaten fresh. Chickens had the additional appeal of being egg producers. Sheep were used almost exclusively for their **wool** as Americans had not developed a taste for mutton. Yet lamb was popular, particularly in **Kentucky**, where it remained a mainstay of the local diet. Pork was very important because of its ability to withstand spoilage when cured, and breeders were producing tastier pork and fatter hogs. Razorback hogs, running free in the brush and allowed to forage for themselves, provided even the poorest Southern families with nourishing, if stringy, meat, as they had since colonial times.

Southerners loved their horses, but they relied almost entirely on breeds from Europe. The first draft horses, imported to America in 1800, were heavy work animals used to pull wagons and plows, known as Shires. Although the Shire was immensely powerful, it was not immediately accepted as a draft breed among American farmers. A wider acceptance was gained by the first Percherons imported by Edward Harris of New Jersey in 1839. Other European draft breeds did not make inroads in North America until the 1880s.

However, America produced its own unique breed of utility work horse. Justin Morgan developed the breed of compact work horse named for him from a single unusual stallion in the last quarter of the eighteenth century. The breed not only provided pulling power, but was a fine riding animal with a respectable turn of speed. The noteworthy qualities of the Morgan breed were incorporated into a large number of otherwise indistinguishable animals. American saddle horses of this period were rarely taller at the withers than fifteen hands, while thoroughbreds were one or two hands taller (one hand is four inches). The yeoman farmer might have one or two riding horses, but many were scrubby backwoods horses and ponies that also served to pull a light cart or wagon.

The exclusivity of thoroughbred breeding appealed to the class-conscious planters of the South. The raising of thoroughbred horses became a passion in the antebellum period. Southerners could not be made to dispense with their horses even under the most trying conditions. During the **nullification** crisis there was no lack of volunteers for the mounted **militia**. Many among the **South Carolina** gentry, who should have provided officers for the state infantry companies, were more willing to serve in the mounted arm, even if that meant serving as privates. Their mounts were often of the best-bred horseflesh.

In the absence of draft horses most farmers and plantation owners chose to use mules or oxen for farm work. Moreover, they often provided their servants with four-footed transportation in the form of an ancient mule or jenny. There were, without doubt, endless arguments about the comparative qualities of mules and oxen, and these same debates carried over onto the many emigrant trails to the West. Mules were faster, but oxen could pull more weight through the mud. Mules could be ridden like horses, but oxen were more tractable. Oxen were more likely to get sore feet and usually needed to be trained to work in pairs, but mules tended to run away and often behaved peevishly. Neither animal was capable of reproducing itself. Mules were the offspring of a donkey and a horse, while an ox was a bull neutered as an adolescent.

In 1843 Peter H. Burnett, an ox fancier, wrote, "The ox is a most noble animal, patient, thrifty, durable, gentle, and easily driven." Altogether, Burnett, who was later governor of California, found oxen to be "greatly superior to mules" (James, 1992). In 1849 James Stewart, a mule proponent, expressed the following sentiment: "It is a noble sight to see those small, tough, earnest, honest Spanish mules, every nerve strained to the utmost, examples of obedience, and of duty performed under trying circumstances" (Johnson, 1975). As both animals were used, sometimes within the same establishment, the deciding factor was quite often price. Mules were relatively expensive animals. A period price list shows that a pair of oxen could be had for $50, while a single mule cost $75. **Related Entries**: Horseracing; Transportation.

SUGGESTED READING: Terry James, *In Praise of Oxen* (1992); Paul C. Johnson, *Farm Animals in the Making of America* (1975).

LOUISIANA: Highlights of a period description of the state taken from John Hayward's *Gazetteer of the United States* (1853) read as follows:

History and Early Settlement: The first settlements were made at about the commencement of the 18th century by French adventurers; and in 1731, the proprietors relinquished their jurisdiction to the king, who ceded it to Spain, in 1762. It was conveyed to France in 1800. The state became a member of the Federal Union in the year 1803. The province embraced all the country west of the **Mississippi River**, reaching to the **Texas** boundaries. It was admitted as a[n] independent state in 1812.

Surface and Soil: Nearly the whole surface of the state consists of level prairies, many of them [of] immense extent. **Sugar, cotton** and rice are the most important staples; and these are cultivated extensively and profitably. Among the other valuable products of the soil are corn and other grains, potatoes, tobacco, hay, etc. Large numbers of horses, cattle, sheep and swine are raised in the central and northern parts of the state.

Rivers: The magnificent Mississippi traverses the entire length of the state, partially forming the eastern boundary.

Education: The state has a fund, the interest from which is applied to the maintenance of free schools.

Internal Improvements: There are sundry **railroads** connecting the capital with different places in the vicinity, none of which, however, are of any length. There are several canals of considerable magnitude connected with the navigation of the Mississippi.

Manufacture: These include a few cotton factories, producing articles only for home consumption; several furnaces, forges, and tanneries; a number of sugar refineries, distilleries and mills of various sorts.

Minerals: But little attention has been given to the mineral resources of Louisiana.

Indians: Of the numerous tribes which once peopled the region, scarcely a vestige remains.

Population: The people of Louisiana are composed of both native Americans and of the descendent[s] of emigrants from many foreign nations. The inhabitants of the northern settlements were chiefly from Canada, those in the center are mostly German and those at the south comprise large numbers of French and Spanish **Creoles**, descended from the original settlers. The population, which in 1810 was 76,556, more than doubled itself in the next ten years. In 1850 it increased to 517,739. Nearly one half of the population are slaves.

Related Entries: Creole; Geography; New Orleans.

SUGGESTED READING: Thomas R. Beard, *The Louisiana Economy* (1969); John Hayward, *Gazetteer of the United States* (1853); Joe Gray Taylor, *Louisiana: A History* (1976).

LOUISIANA PURCHASE: In 1803 all of the Louisiana Territory (an area the size of the United States at that time) was transferred from Spain to France. The French quickly showed America that they meant to control access to the **Mississippi River** and that they could extract whatever price they pleased for the freedom to pass through **New Orleans** to the rest of the world.

When President **Thomas Jefferson** heard that Napoleon was taking control of the mouth of the river, he understood that it was a matter of great importance to those who lived along the river and its tributaries. He sent **James Monroe** as his special envoy to France to purchase either New Orleans and all the lands on the east bank of the river (called West **Florida**), or some form of guaranteed right of passage. Congress approved between $2 and $10 million for the project. When Monroe and Robert Livingston, the U.S. minister to Paris, offered to buy the small piece of land around New Orleans, the French shocked them by offering the entire region for $15 million. Using their own judgment, Monroe and Livingston agreed to the purchase.

The Constitution said nothing about the power of the government to buy land from a foreign nation. Still, Jefferson went before Congress to ask for the additional $5 million in 1803. After a long and bitter debate, in which Jefferson's enemies tried to make the most of his dilemma, Congress voted the money and the Senate ratified the treaty with France. Within a year an American governor was sitting in New Orleans, which had become, by its acquisition, the largest non–English-speaking city in the United States. By 1804 Meriwether Lewis and William Clark, with forty men, started west from the mouth of the Missouri River on a great expedition of discovery to map the region, make a record of its flora and fauna, and impress the almost 1 million Native Americans living there that they were now ruled by a new government in **Washington**. Subsequently, the Lewis and Clark Expedition extended the American claims beyond the bounds of the purchase.

The Louisiana Purchase doubled the land area of the United States, and it made continued westward expansion possible. The problem of exactly what was to be done with an area so large suddenly became a matter of public policy and political dispute. Some people in the Eastern states feared that too many new states, carved out of the expanse of Louisiana, might rob the Northeast of its power, diminish the importance of America as a seacoast power, and bolster **slavery**. Ultimately all or part of more than a dozen states were established within the Mississippi–Missouri River valleys east of the Rocky Mountains from the Louisiana Purchase. **Related Entry**: Extension of Slavery into the Territories.

SUGGESTED READING: James K. Hosmer, *The History of the Louisiana Purchase* (1992); John Keats, *Eminent Domain: The Louisiana Purchase and the Making of America* (1973); Marshall Sprague, *So Vast So Beautiful a Land: Louisiana and the Purchase* (1974; 1991); Amos Stoddard, *Sketches, Historical and Descriptive, of Louisiana* (1812; 1973).

LOWNDES, WILLIAM (1782–1822): As a congressman from **South Carolina**, William Lowndes was one of four **War Hawks** from that state— **John C. Calhoun**, David R. Williams, and Langdon Cheves being the others—who forced President **James Madison** to declare war on Britain in 1812. An ardent nationalist, Lowndes joined with Calhoun in advocating a strong national defense. As chairman of the Ways and Means Committee in 1815, William Lowndes supported the protective **Tariff** of 1816, but only because it strengthened the national defense. In light of the traditional misgivings found among South Carolina planters about anything that limited free trade, Lowndes' support of the tariff provides a striking illustration of his ardent nationalism in the period following the **War of 1812**. However, most South Carolina planters strongly approved of the Calhoun-Lowndes style of nationalism as long as it could ward off foreign enemies without endangering Southern interests.

Lowndes' objectivity and fairness quickly led him to a position of leadership in Congress. He was active in the creation of the second **Bank of the United States** and was the author of the "Sinking Fund" Act under which the national debt was retired in just fourteen years. The debate on the **Missouri Compromise** was the last important legislative work in which Lowndes was involved. Lowndes was noted for his calm and dispassionate speech even in the most closely argued debates. His calm and studied speeches in support of the compromise before a Congress churned by partisan **sectional disputes** won him the respect of both parties. His continued poor health limited his activities to the point that he declined the nomination of his party for the presidency in 1821, and he was forced to entrust the passage of the Missouri Compromise to **Henry Clay**, who described Lowndes as "the wisest man I ever knew." **Related Entries**: Calhoun, John C.; Missouri Compromise of 1820.

SUGGESTED READING: Hans Norman and Harold Runblom, *William Lowndes and the Transition of Southern Politics, 1782–1822* (1989).

MADISON, DOLLEY PAYNE (1768–1849): wife of **James Madison**, the fourth President of the United States (1809–1817). Dolley Madison was born in **North Carolina** and raised in **Virginia**, where she married a lawyer, John Todd, Jr., and was widowed in 1793. In the next year she married one of the most influential framers of the Constitution, James Madison. Dolley Madison became socially prominent when her husband became the secretary of state in the administration of President **Thomas Jefferson** in 1801. Her natural charm and social grace allowed her to assume the position of hostess in the Executive Mansion for Jefferson, who was a widower. Her friendliness and tact proved a great advantage to her husband when he assumed the presidency. She was one of the most dynamic first ladies to occupy the White House for many decades. From Madison's retirement until his death in 1836, Dolley remained the hospitable mistress of their typical Southern plantation at Montpelier in Virginia. In 1837 she returned to the federal capital and resumed a career as an honored and respected figure in **Washington** society. **Related Entry**: Madison, James.

SUGGESTED READING: Betty Boyd Caroli, *First Ladies* (1987).

MADISON, JAMES (1750–1836): framer of the Constitution and fourth President of the United States (1809–1817). As **Thomas Jefferson**'s chosen successor, James Madison had little trouble securing the presidency in 1808. In 1810 he oversaw the peaceful acquisition of West Florida from Spain, but he was to experience eight difficult and troubled years in office. During his tenure American shipping was savaged in an undeclared naval war with France, and American sailors were impressed at sea to serve on British vessels. Accepting the assurances of the French that they would change their ways, Madison turned against the more intransigent British, sending a special message to Congress asking that they declare war. The Federalists were generally against the war, and the Republicans, especially the **War Hawks**, were for it, seeing an opportunity to bring Canada into the United States.

The 1812 presidential election was widely seen as a referendum on the war. A vote for Madison was seen as a vote for war, and a vote for his opponent, DeWitt Clinton, governor of New York, was seen as a vote for peace. Politically, the South had seemingly ruled the nation during its first two decades of the Republic, with four of the first six Presidents coming from **Virginia**, yet the 1812 election was the first to exhibit a truly sectional result. Every state south and west of **Delaware** voted for Madison, and he was reelected. The **War of 1812** was woefully mishandled, and history has dismissed the dismal failure of American arms in "Mr. Madison's War" by concentrating on some of the less bitter illusions of victory: "Old Ironsides," "The Star Spangled Banner," and the **Battle of New Orleans** among them. With the armistice in December 1814, Madison found that not a single American war aim had been attained. No territory had been won, no concessions had been made by the British, and no national prestige had been gained. From Madison's retirement until his death in 1836, he and his wife, Dolley, remained the hospitable residents of their typical Southern plantation at Montpelier in Virginia.

Notwithstanding his tenure as President, James Madison's major contribution to the antebellum period was in the areas of governance, political doctrine, and constitutional principles. As a diligent student of history and government, Madison had been active in the political struggle that freed America from British rule. He helped to frame the Constitution and Declaration of Rights of the Virginia convention of 1776, being chiefly responsible (with Thomas Jefferson) for the declaration of the right to free exercise of religion.

The revolutionary founders of the American Republic produced a loose-knit union of sovereign states under the Articles of Confederation which embodied a dedication to the historic concepts of personal, political, and property rights. The limitations of the Articles became almost immediately apparent, however, and the **Constitutional Convention** of 1787 was called to amend them. The delegates to the convention chose, instead, to write a totally new underpinning document.

To provide for free and open discussion, no minutes of the deliberations were taken. Were it not for the personal notes taken by Madison, almost nothing of the constitutional debates would be known today. The lack of explicit and indisputable records from the convention created a problem during the antebellum political wrangling, as advocates of one position or another tended to use self-serving and selective excerpts from the writings of the Founding Fathers. Madison's *Journal of the Federal Convention* (by far the most complete record of the proceedings), published in 1840 after his death, clearly shows his influence in disestablishing the Anglican Church, blocking the adoption of paper money as legal tender, and creating the **Three-fifths Compromise**. His suggestions for the new Constitution were embodied in the Virginia Plan of 1787. Their adoption won him the so-briquet "Father of the Constitution."

In cooperation with Alexander Hamilton and John Jay, Madison helped to write a series of essays that appeared in several New York **newspapers** and were collected into *The Federalist* (1788). Herein he argued that an unrestrained majority could be just as despotic as an unrestrained monarchy. He stressed the idea that the separate branches of government must be interrelated in such a way that they provided for checks and balances on one another. Moreover, although the majority might agree on a position, it did not necessarily mean that they were right. "There is no maxim, in my opinion, which is more liable to be misapplied," wrote Madison. No form of government could guard against an abuse of power unless it provided security to the minority against the formation of oppressive majorities.

In 1798 he joined again with Jefferson in drawing up the Virginia and Kentucky Resolutions. The **states' rights** doctrine expressed in the Resolutions gained a great deal of traction with **nullification** advocates and was a matter of some controversy in the **sectional disputes** that preceded the Civil War. Madison clearly considered the application of these doctrines by nullifiers and **secessionists** a misrepresentation of his opinions. He and Jefferson had proposed no more than cooperation among the several states in securing the repeal of laws or the amendment of the Constitution. **Related Entries**: Constitutional Convention; Madison, Dolley Payne; Nullification; Three-fifths Compromise; War of 1812.

SUGGESTED READING: Drew R. McCoy, *The Last of the Fathers: James Madison and the Republican Legacy* (1989); Clinton Rossiter, *The Federalist Papers* (1961); Robert A. Rutland, *James Madison and the American Nation, 1751–1836: An Encyclopedia* (1994).

MAGAZINES. *See* Literary Development.

MALARIA. *See* Epidemics.

MAMMY: Prominent among the traditions associated with the Old South is the stereotypical character of Mammy. Plantation records acknowledge the presence of female slaves who held a position equivalent to that of a head housekeeper and care giver to the master's children. Yet their appearance in the antebellum record is incidental, and not until after the war were there a significant number of black women in such circumstances. The secure place of the Mammy in the mythology of the plantation has been created by a combination of historic revisionism and romantic imagination.

The character of Mammy (and her male counterpart, as in "Uncle" Tom) seems at first to have been a projection of the slaveowners' own delusions that their household slaves were devoted to them on a personal level—a repeated allusion found in contemporary Southern diaries, especially those of young women. Besides being characterized as benign and maternal, Mammy exhibits wisdom and "folksy" common sense. She represents a social relationship between blacks and whites that transcends the auction block, fetters, injustices, and punishments of the **overseer**. Mammy interacts directly with the white slaveowning family without offending the traditional hierarchy of a stratified and race-conscious society.

No historian or revisionist cemented the image of Mammy more firmly in the mythology of Southern culture than the film makers of Hollywood. When Margaret Mitchell published her novel *Gone with the Wind* (1936), she incorporated into it a large number of Southern stereotypes including the mythological Mammy. The character of Mammy in the resulting 1939 film, ably portrayed by Hattie McDaniel, exhibits all of the characteristics of "Mammy-ism." She chides the debutante Scarlett in a motherly way, is concerned in family complications, weeps during its tragedy, and is aware of the most private interpersonal feelings of the family members. While McDaniel's performance as Mammy provided moving, warm moments (garnering her an Academy Award), there is no hard historical evidence that such women existed as anything other than a balm for guilty Southern consciences. **Related Entry**: Race Relations.

SUGGESTED READING: John M. Cassidy, *Civil War Cinema: A Pictorial History of Hollywood and the War Between the States* (1986); Catherine Clinton, *The Plantation Mistress: Woman's World in the Old South* (1982); Susan Jean Tracey, *In the Master's Eye: Representations of Women, Blacks, and Poor Whites in Antebellum Southern Literature* (1996).

MANIFEST DESTINY: This catchphrase for the entire expansive movement to the West was provided by a New York newspaperman, John L. O'Sullivan, who wrote in July 1845 in the *United States Magazine and Democratic Review* that it was the nation's "manifest destiny to overspread and to possess the whole continent which Providence has given for the development of the great experiment of liberty and federated self-government entrusted to us." More importantly, "manifest destiny" was more than a mere slogan. It embodied a number of ideas that Americans had about the nation.

Although the specific purpose of his article was to support the annexation of **Texas**, it was clear that O'Sullivan was challenging his fellow Americans to accomplish a grandiose objective limited only by the bounds of **geography**, but the challenge was couched in very careful terms. His was a divinely inspired challenge. "Providence" had ordained a new chosen people to bring "Liberty" to the continent. But this was the liberty of the European masses, not the liberty sought by the opponents of **slavery**. One of the strategic errors made by pro-slavery apologists was to allow manifest destiny to become a debate over whether or not slavery would be extended into the vast expanse of unorganized western territory. Yet the South sought the added weight of new **slave states** to preserve a balance between the different sections of the country. Northerners, for their part, genuinely feared that slavery would take root in the new Southwest if barriers were not raised to prevent it. **Related Entries**: Extension of Slavery into the Territories; Mexican War of 1846.

SUGGESTED READING: Conrad Cherry, ed., *God's New Israel: Religious Interpretations of American Destiny* (1971); Winthrop S. Hudson, *Nationalism and Religion in America: Concepts of American Identity and Mission* (1970); Mary Ellen Jones, *The American Frontier: Opposing Viewpoints* (1994); Michael A. Morrison, *Slavery in the American West: The Eclipse of Manifest Destiny and the Coming of the Civil War* (1997).

MANUMISSION. *See* Slavery.

MARRIAGE. *See* Courtship and Marriage.

MARSHALL, JOHN (1755–1835): Chief Justice of the **Supreme Court** (1801–1835). John Marshall was a tall Virginian who had been raised in a frontier cabin and fought in the Revolution. As secretary of state in the administration of John Adams, Marshall was sent to deal with the new French government known as the Directory and its foreign minister, Talleyrand. When it became known that Talleyrand had required a bribe from the American ministers to France in order to receive them, Marshall refused, saying, "Millions for defense, but not one cent for tribute!" Marshall was widely praised for this statement, and was appointed to the Supreme Court by Adams while concurrently holding a post in the cabinet. In the last moments of the Adams presidency, Congress rushed through a Judiciary Act that created jobs for twenty-one new federal judges. The President appointed only members of his own Federalist Party to these positions, and Marshall signed their commissions on the eve of **Thomas Jefferson**'s inauguration. With the appointment of the "Midnight Judges," Marshall took the first steps toward making the Supreme Court a Federalist fortress, and began to build a legal bastion around the federal union.

The Court of Chief Justice John Marshall created several new legal precedents, including that of judicial review, by overturning a **Georgia** state law. It also strengthened the power of the federal government to tax in the *McCulloch v. Maryland* decision. The Court thereby strengthened the power of the federal government over the states while simultaneously raising personal property rights above those of the state governments. Most important, it established the power of judicial review by the Court in *Marbury v. Mad-*

ison. In this case Marshall chided Secretary of State **James Madison** for refusing to deliver a commission as justice of the peace to William Marbury. These decisions were very important to the development of the federal government. **Related Entries**: Scott, Dred; Supreme Court of the United States; Taney, Roger B.

SUGGESTED READING: David G. Loth, *Chief Justice John Marshall and the Growth of the Republic* (1949; 1970); Adrienne Siegel, *The Marshall Court, 1801–1835* (1995); Jean Edward Smith, *John Marshall: Definer of a Nation* (1996).

MARYLAND: Highlights of a period description of the state from John Hayward's *Gazetteer of the United States* (1853) read as follows:

Surface and Soil: The Eastern Shore presents a low and flat surface, with frequent marshy tracts and stagnant ponds. The soil of this region, though not remarkably fertile, produces wheat of peculiar whiteness and excellence; also Indian corn, tobacco, sweet potatoes, and most of the ordinary descriptions of vegetables. The land in the valleys of the western section is of superior quality. The staple products are tobacco and wheat; but **cotton**, hemp, and flax are also raised in large quantities. Fruits of the finest kinds are abundant, particularly apples, pears, and the choicest stone fruit. The woodlands contain much valuable timber.

Rivers: The Potomac, the Susquehanna, and the Patapsco, and Patuxent, both navigable and affording good water power, are among the principal streams immediately connected with the trade and commerce of Maryland.

Education: The common school system, so deeply cherished in the Northern and Eastern States, has not yet attained a very great measure of public favor in Maryland. The schools throughout the state, supported at public cost, do not in aggregate, contain so large a number of pupils as are contained in the common schools of the single city of Boston. There are numerous private institutions of learning, some of great merit, and generally well sustained. Among them are several Catholic colleges.

Indians: There are no organized tribes of the red races now extant.

Population: During the last sixty years the average increase of population does not seem to have exceeded one percent per annum. Nearly one fifth of the inhabitants are slaves.

Internal Improvements: Among the most important public works in the country are two which owe their origin to Maryland viz., the Chesapeake and Ohio Canal, and the Baltimore and Ohio Railroad. They were both commenced in 1828; and by their aid the markets of the world may readily be supplied with the treasures of the immense coal regions of the west.

Manufacture: **Wool**, cotton, hemp, and iron are manufactured in many parts of the state. There are also numerous tanneries, chandleries, breweries, distilleries, potteries, paper mills, [and] powder mills. A very large amount of capital is invested in the business of manufacture of wheat flour.

Minerals: Iron ore abounds in various localities; and bog ore obtained in the southern quarter of the Eastern Shore is wrought to much advantage. By far the most valuable mineral product is the bituminous coal, of which there are exhaustless beds in the mountainous region near the western border.

Other: No gift or devise of property to clergymen is valid without consent of the legislature, excepting land for a church or cemetery, not to exceed two acres. All civil officers must declare their belief in the Christian religion.

Related Entry: Geography.

SUGGESTED READING: Carl Bode, *Maryland, a History* (1978); John Hayward, *Gazetteer of the United States* (1853); Richard Walsh and William Lloyd Fox, *Maryland: A History, 1632–1974* (1974).

MASON-DIXON LINE: The popular name for the boundary between **Maryland** and Pennsylvania is derived from the two British astronomers, Charles Mason and Jeremiah Dixon, who surveyed and marked it between 1763 and 1768. The undertaking was commissioned by the sixth Lord Baltimore and Thomas and Richard Penn to settle an eighty-year-old dispute about the boundary between the two colonies. It was drawn at a point 234 miles west of **Delaware** and extended "233 miles, 17 chains and 48 links." Part of the boundary was surveyed again in 1849–1850. During the debates over the **Missouri Compromise**, the Mason-Dixon Line was commonly referred to as the partition between the **slave states** and **free states**. When used in this context, it meant not only the old disputed boundary, but also the line of the Ohio River from the Pennsylvania boundary to its mouth, the line of the east, north, and west boundaries of **Missouri**, and from that point west, the parallel of 36° 30'. **Related Entries**: Geography; Missouri Compromise of 1820.

SUGGESTED READING: Judith St. George, *Mason and Dixon's Line of Fire* (1991).

MCCORD, LOUISA SUSAN CHEVES (1810–1879): writer and observer of Southern life. The daughter of Langdon Cheves and the second wife of David J. McCord, Louisa was an outspoken defender of **slavery** in her native city of **Charleston**. In a period when women were reluctant to take strong political positions in the press, Louisa became a major contributor to the **newspapers** of her day. Her well-written and persuasive essays flaunted a very conservative pro-slavery position. **Related Entry**: Literary Development.

SUGGESTED READING: Richard C. Lounsbury, ed., *Louisa S. McCord: Poems, Drama, Biography, Letters* (1996).

MCDUFFIE, GEORGE (1790–1851): politician and Southern apologist who explained exactly why the protective **tariffs** were detrimental to the Southern economy. The genius of his "Forty Bales of Cotton Theory" was that it stated in disarmingly simple terms how the tariff duties were being directly paid by all Southerners.

George McDuffie was a **cotton** planter and partisan politician from **South**

Carolina. He was such an impassioned nationalist that he almost lost his life to the issue while **dueling**. Left partially paralyzed by the experience, he evolved, nonetheless, into a turbulent and intense proponent of **nullification**, stomping about on the House floor as he spoke in a bawling manner. As chairman of the Ways and Means Committee in 1830, he introduced a bill to repeal both the 1824 and 1828 tariff rates. Acceptance of this moderate proposal would have lowered the rates appreciably without removing the tariff itself. The House of Representatives rejected his overture by such a wide margin that McDuffie became enraged. When a bill for the reform of tariff collection procedures was proposed by the opposition, McDuffie rose to the floor of the House and proceeded to harangue the protectionists for more than two hours. Congress had no intention of making any disposition on the tariff. Nonetheless, in reacting to McDuffie's tour de force, a vigorous debate ensued over the issue, giving national publicity to what had been largely a matter of concern between South Carolina and the federal government.

In his Forty Bales speech, McDuffie equated the tariff duty to a loss of forty out of one hundred bales of exported **cotton**. The intervention of merchants and shippers in the process simply obscured the process. One hundred bales exported to Europe came back to the South as a value equivalent to only sixty. In McDuffie's view, the missing forty bales were being deposited directly in the hands of the North in the form of increased profits and wages. **Related Entry**: Tariffs.

SUGGESTED READING: Edwin L. Green, *George McDuffie* (1936).

MEDICINE: The medical profession in the antebellum period thought of itself as knowledgeable and humanitarian, but its practitioners were neither selective in their methods nor well regulated by their fellows. Local remedies were often chosen over unknown pharmaceuticals. The medicines that doctors prescribed were just as likely to kill as cure the patient because they were very often ineffective, allowing sicknesses to progress too far before alternative procedures were initiated. The state of care had made some headway in large cities such as New York, Philadelphia, and Chicago, but in rural areas little had changed in more than a century.

Physicians still believed in the medieval concept that a balance of four primary fluids, or "humors," in the body maintained its health. Blood, phlegm, urine, and bile were all associated with some bodily condition. As late as 1799 George Washington was bled, purged to nausea, blistered to rawness, and bled again in an attempt to save him from pneumonia. Fevers, in particular, were associated with an accumulation of bad blood in the system. Hence, the "bleeding" of the ill was widely practiced. The opening of veins, "cupping," and the use of leeches were common methods found in the physician's bag of tricks. Ironically, the loss of blood actually helped to produce new blood cells—both the oxygen-carrying red cells and the disease-fighting white cells.

The existence of germs and microbes was unknown. Operations were primitive and wholly unsanitary. The theory that contagious disease was spread by miasmic odors or personal contact was still in vogue. Typhoid, typhus, measles, mumps, smallpox, malaria, and yellow fever were all ascribed to exposure to "bad air" or the noxious odors emanating from swamps and marshes. Although cowpox vaccine had become widely used since 1798 in controlling smallpox, the mechanism of acquired immunity was not well understood.

The mentally ill and intellectually challenged were generally treated like criminals or stigmatized as insane. They were feared, imprisoned, and suffered unbearable tortures which were prescribed as cures or treatments. In 1843 Dorothea Dix, a young Boston school teacher, submitted a report to the Massachusetts legislature wherein she stated that the mentally ill were confined "in cages, closets, stalls and pens! Chained, naked, beaten with rods, and lashed into obedience." Dix began her own crusade to end such treatment, and she toured the nation and Europe pleading that the mentally ill be treated with compassion and given proper medical attention.

Civilian nursing, especially by women, was in its infancy. During the Civil War, the Nursing Service, directed by Dix and staffed by women, was established to care for the wounded and sick in the numerous soldiers' rests and regimental hospitals; but the recruitment of nurses was hobbled by the strict "moral" requirements Dix placed on potential candidates. Women were required to be no less than thirty years of age, plain looking, and unadorned. There was no requirement that they be efficient or capable.

However, **Catholic** nuns proved to be expert medical and surgical nurses, as they had experienced service in asylums and hospitals during their long novitiates. The Sisters served as nurses in the hospitals of Boston, New York, Philadelphia, Baltimore, **Washington, DC**, and other cities with large Catholic communities. Sisters of Charity, Sisters of Mercy, and Sisters of Saint Vincent de Paul were all the more conspicuous in their unique religious habits in the hospitals of **Richmond, Charleston**, Nashville, and **New Orleans**. The hospitals of the South were often overwhelmed by the task before them, and the sick were often shipped home to recuperate under the care of their families. **Related Entry**: Epidemics.

SUGGESTED READING: William F. Byrum, *Science and the Practice of Medicine in the Nineteenth Century* (1994).

MERCER, CHARLES FENTON (1778–1858): congressman and Southern **abolitionist**. While representing **Virginia** in **Washington, DC**, for two decades (1817 to 1839). Mercer led efforts to found a new national bank, to promote the colonization of Negroes to Africa, and to build roads and canals with federal support. As a freshman congressman he offered a bill, which passed in the House but was defeated in the Senate, to establish a complete system of public **education** from common school to university. In these things he was atypical of most Southern representatives.

Although a strong Unionist, Mercer had left the Federalist Party to become a **Whig** because he was alarmed at the increasing power of the President. Mercer was an open critic of President **Andrew Jackson**, whom he disliked personally. He used his considerable oratorical ability to assail Jackson at every opportunity, especially concerning his activities in the Seminole War and his control of federal patronage.

After leaving Congress, Mercer was active in helping to foster banking in **Florida** and in promoting the settlement of colonists in **Texas**. In 1847 he built a home in **Kentucky**, but disposed of his property there after just five years. Thereafter he traveled in Europe working for the abolition of the slave trade. This activity made him one of the many high-profile Southerners who openly supported the end of **slavery. Related Entry**: Abolition.

SUGGESTED READING: Douglas R. Ederton, *Charles Fenton Mercer and the Trial of National Conservatism* (1989).

MEXICAN WAR OF 1846: Mexico considered the **annexation of Texas** and the demand that its southern border with the United States be fixed at the Rio Grande an act of war. Rumblings of discontent with Mexican rule coming from Americans in California, similar to those voiced by the residents of **Texas** in 1836, caused feelings against the United States to run high in Mexico. President **James K. Polk** aggressively sent General **Zachary Taylor** with 2,000 troops to the Rio Grande to enforce the boundary. In April 1846, a party of American soldiers pressing forward into the disputed territory was ambushed, and several were killed or wounded. Polk, anticipating the result of Taylor's excursion, introduced a previously drafted message to Congress asking for a declaration of war as soon as he heard of the attack. Although Northern forces in Congress feared an **extension of slavery** into any lands acquired in such a war, patriotic passions prevailed.

American settlers under the leadership of **John C. Fremont** set up a short-lived republic of California in June 1846, and General Stephen Watts Kearny marched across the Southwest to raise the American flag over New Mexico. Victories during the next year and a half by General Taylor and General **Winfield Scott** at Monterrey, Buena Vista, and Mexico City forced the hapless Mexicans to give up.

The **Treaty of Guadalupe Hidalgo** recognized all American claims to Texas, established the Rio Grande border, and ceded to the United States California, New Mexico, and most of the present states of Utah, Nevada, Arizona, and Colorado. In return the United States paid $15 million to Mexico and assumed an additional $3 million of Mexican debt.

The highly vaunted successes of Southern warriors during the Mexican War greatly enhanced the prestige of a military life in the South. Among these were many minor officers, such as **Robert E. Lee**, James Longstreet, Jubal Early, and Thomas J. "Stonewall" Jackson, who were to lead the armies of the Confederacy a dozen years later. The military legacy of a largely volunteer force successfully opposing a regular army—whether martial mythology or historical reality—had far-reaching effects in the initial organization of the Infant Confederate army along the lines of local and state **militias. Related Entries**: Scott, Winfield; Taylor, Zachary; Treaty of Guadalupe Hildalgo.

SUGGESTED READING: John S.D. Eisenhower, *So Far from God: The U.S. War with Mexico, 1846–1848* (1989).

MILITARY EDUCATION: As early as the first decade of the nineteenth century an interest in military **education** had been clearly manifest in the South, and by the final antebellum decade the movement toward military education and the establishment of schools dedicated specifically to the martial arts had gained marked momentum. A military career became increasingly acceptable for the sons of the **planter aristocracy**, who reveled in a military mythology that traced their descent from the Cavallers of the English Civil Wars who had ridden at Naseby. The success of Southern warriors during the Revolution and the **Mexican War of 1846** also greatly enhanced the prestige of a military life.

Nonetheless, a wider usefulness was recognized in having a cadre of military personnel that could quickly respond to slave uprisings in the South. In 1854 a Charlestonian noted that the very nature of domestic **slavery** required that the South "cherish a military spirit" and "diffuse a military science" among its young men so that they might "defy the world in arms."

North Carolina was among the earliest of the Southern states to initiate the study of the martial arts as a regular part of the course of study. By the 1840s a generation of young men had been trained in light infantry tactics, broad sword exercises, and cavalry evolutions on "the plan of the West Point Seminary." Nonetheless, the period **newspaper** *Citizen Soldier* found the U.S. Military Academy at West Point "monopolizing, aristocratic, unconstitutional, and worse than useless." Notwithstanding the negative comments, the "aristocratic" character of military education certainly appealed to Southerners. So highly prized was the quality of this military and academy preparation that more than one-third of the student body at West Point had Southern roots, although public sentiment increasingly frowned upon a military education at a Northern school.

Schools in **South Carolina, Mississippi**, and **Alabama** showed some interest in military education by the second quarter of the century, but military schools required financial support. Most initiatives simply added to the ordinary branches of academic studies the study of camps and tactics—a modification that was found "agreeable" to the youth of the country. Nowhere did Southerners better understand this problem than in **Virginia** and South Carolina. In 1836 Virginians decided to substitute a military school for the company of state guards by diverting the financial resources of the state from the Lexington Arsenal to the Virginia Military Institute in its stead. Virginians pointed to the development of VMI as "thoroughly and exclusively Virginian" and pointed with pride to the state patriotism engendered therein. South Carolinians attempted to combine the "enterprise and decision of a military character" with the acquisition of a scholastic education by converting the Arsenal, at Columbia, and the Citadel and Magazine, at **Charleston**, into military schools.

Nowhere else in the South were there any developments remotely approaching the success of VMI and the Citadel. The remainder of the decade of the 1840s saw various activities—riding, military drill and tactics—incorporated into the academic curriculum of many schools in the Southern states. Companies of uniformed cadets were established in many places. Most prospered only briefly, to be abandoned when the novelty wore off. State support was generally limited to providing the school with tax exemptions and "as many arms as shall be sufficient for its purposes."

A third major Southern school, the Georgia Military Institute, was opened in 1851. As the war approached, town after town in the South boasted a new "military academy." An important factor in the growth of these military schools was the zeal of those who graduated. The graduates of Southern military schools, especially those of VMI, devotedly promoted military education throughout the South and went on to serve as instructors in new institutions. When the war came, it was not surprising that two-thirds of the highest ranking officers in the Confederate army were from Virginia.

Military schools enjoyed excellent public relations in the South, engaging in activities designed to excite the interest of the populace. Cadets made frequent off-campus visits to communities to display their skills at drill and their attractive, if rather gaudy, uniforms by parading in the town square or on the county fairgrounds. An unbridled martial spirit was abroad by the 1850s, and most Southerners regarded their military schools as among their most valuable regional assets. Some of these institutions received increasing public support as the **sectional disputes** tearing at the nation proceeded toward war. A visitor to VMI exclaimed, "God grant that our State may never need their services . . . but . . . should the terrible cry, 'To Arms!' be ever heard from her, the graduates and cadets of her military school will be the main element of her defense" (Franklin, 1956; 1968). **Related Entries:** Militia; Planter Aristocracy.

SUGGESTED READING: John Hope Franklin, *The Militant South, 1800–1861* (1956; 1968).

MILITIA: During the **Constitutional Convention** the Founding Fathers exhibited a strong aversion to the concept of a standing army. The roots of this hostility may be linked to a history of distrust for and contempt of professional soldiers that began during the last of the colonial wars in which American provincial forces fought alongside British regulars. As late as 1841, there appeared a weekly newspaper "devoted to the interests of the militia, to military science and national defense in general" called *Citizen Soldier*. The paper, published by Sweet and Jackman of Windsor, Vermont, printed plans for the improved organization and drill of the militia; "synopses" of the militia laws of the several states; and dissertations on tactics and military campaigns. Not surprisingly, the editors found the U.S. Military Academy at West Point an institution formed by "Executive usurpation without even the shadow of law to sustain the act. . . . It is astonishing to witness the passiveness with which American citizens have suffered the usurpations of the military Academy, and the stupidity and indifference they manifest towards its growing evils." These comments reflected the long-held discomfort that Americans had for professional military officers and standing armies.

As early as 1792 Congress chose to provide for the defense of the nation by relying on a militia. Every able-bodied white male between the ages of eighteen and forty-five was to be enrolled in a local militia company and to provide himself with a good musket or rifle, two spare flints, powder and ball, and other accouterments. These men were also required to appear for drill periodically and to turn out for service when called. By 1808 the law authorized the several state governors to control the militia, appoint volunteer officers, and amass stores. The federal government retained the authority to choose general officers as long as they were appropriately apportioned among the states.

The military leaders of the American Revolution were held in awe in the South. The signal victories of the war over the British forces, and the ultimate victory at Yorktown, were perceived to have been Southern victories, and the outcome of the Revolution to have been decided south of the **Mason-Dixon Line**. Many Southerners were of the opinion that they were thereby the natural guardians of Revolutionary ideals. Besides George Washington, a litany of Southern battlefield heroes was commonly called forth to support the myth. The value of the militia system was magnified by a signal victory over the British at the **Battle of New Orleans** in 1815.

The usefulness of militia was immeasurably enhanced by the successful war in Mexico in 1846. The legacy of a militia successfully opposing a regular army—whether martial mythology or historical reality—had far-reaching effects in the initial organization of the infant Confederate army along the lines of local and state-controlled militia.

During the **nullification** crisis of 1832, Governor **Robert Y. Hayne** of **South Carolina** found that he had no lack of volunteers for a mounted minuteman militia. Unfortunately, many among the gentry, who should

Stephen Foster wrote "Old Folks at Home" in 1851. This is the cover of an arrangement done for the Christy Minstrels in 1866. (From the authors' collection.)

have provided officers for the state infantry companies, were more willing to serve in the mounted arm, even if that meant serving as privates. An observer of Southern cavalry organization noted, "[O]ur people, even down to little boys, are expert riders. . . . We should want all our men [to] fight in the saddle who could not or would not march in the infantry" (Miers, 1958). Nonetheless, a love of riding and the understanding of horsemanship that came with long experience gave a distinct advantage to the Confederate mounted arm in the Civil War. **Related Entries**: Military Education; South Carolina Association.

SUGGESTED READING: Jean M. Flynn, *The Militia in Antebellum South Carolina Society* (1991); John Hope Franklin, *The Militant South* (1956; 1968); Earl S. Miers, ed., *A Rebel War Clerk's Diary* (1958).

MINSTREL SHOWS: The theatrical impersonation of blacks in action and song by white men began in the 1820s, and although it degenerated following the Civil War, the practice continued, in some form, for much of the century. "Blackface" acts, as they were sometimes called, affected two stereotypes—one in ragged clothes, modeled after the Southern plantation slave, and the other, dressed as a dandy, mocking the false sophistication of Northern blacks. These shows fixed images of blacks key to the plantation tradition. They also demonstrated the allure that black culture had for whites.

Minstrel shows were part of theatrical performances that featured a variety of short dramas and farces, dances, and songs, all on a single program. The "Ethiopian Delineator," as the playbill was likely to herald them, was popularized by such men as Thomas Dartmouth (Daddy) Rice, who is credited with starting the idea, Bob Farrel, and George Washington Dixon. In between the songs and dance steps there was always time for gibes about political issues of the time.

In the 1830s solo performances by banjoists and dancers in blackface became popular. Joe Sweeny and Billy Whitlock were famous as banjoists. John Diamond gained fame as a dancer. The dances were already common among frontiersmen and river boatmen and had Irish and Scottish roots. The blackface dancer mixed jumps and heel-and-toe moves with gestures mimicking plantation blacks. These evolved, in the 1840s, into small ensembles that included banjoists, fiddlers, singers, and dancers in various combinations.

There were also short plays billed as "Ethiopian Operas," which featured a larger cast and were an outgrowth of the English ballad-opera. They included spoken dialogue and songs which featured choral refrains, duets, and dances. Female roles were played by men who specialized in playing "Negro wenches."

The Virginia Minstrels, the first successful minstrel band, appeared in 1843. Led by "Old Dan Emmit" (**Daniel Decatur Emmett**), the composer of "Dixie," who played the fiddle, the group included Billy Whitlock on the banjo, Frank Brower on the bones, a kind of castanet, and Dick Pelham on the tambourine. The banjo, fiddle, and bones were popular slave instruments. The tambourine in combination with the fiddle had been popular with river boatmen, who also served as inspiration for the minstrels, who sat in a semicircle. The ensemble's program included songs, choral refrains, banjo solos, dances, jokes, and comic banter. Throughout the next decade the size of minstrel bands increased, numbering as many as a dozen members.

Initially, the songs of these minstrels were borrowed heavily from British folk music and Italian operas, and then the lyrics were adapted to slave dialect and inflections. In time, the works became more original, although it is often difficult to trace a particular tune to any specific author. The most prominent minstrel song composers of the 1850s and 1860s were **Stephen Foster** and Dan Emmett. Foster's works, designed for soloists, were performed during the first part of the minstrel show, which was less "black" in content, while plantation life dominated the second portion. Emmett composed the pieces for the entire company, which were given at the end of the performance. Some minstrel songs are still popular today, including

"Old Dan Tucker," "Oh! Susanna," and "Camptown Races." **Related Entries**: Emmett, Daniel Decatur; Foster, Stephen Collins.

SUGGESTED READING: Eric Lott, *Love and Theft: Blackface Minstrelsy and the American Working Class* (1993); Robert C. Toll, *Blacking Up: The Minstrel Show in Nineteenth-Century America* (1974).

MISCEGENATION: One of the unique features of **slavery** in this period was the pervasiveness of miscegenation, or interracial sexual activity. The desire of white men to have sexual contact with black females was seemingly so common in the South that there was no social stigma attached to it. An antebellum **abolitionist** confidently reported that half the slave population of the South was mixed with white blood. However, statistical analysis suggests that fewer than 10 percent of the slaves in the South were of mixed ancestry; and only a small percentage of the children born to slaves in a given year were fathered by white men (Blassingame, 1973).

The extent of miscegenation is somewhat obscured by the methods used by nineteenth-century investigators to quantify the mixed-race population of the South as mulattos (half black), quadroons (one-quarter black), and octoroons (one-eighth black) by the criteria of the outward appearance of the skin and the absence or presence of certain "defining" racial features. A large population of mixed-race persons "passing for white" may also have obscured any meaningful estimates at the time.

Evidence suggests that female slaves were often bribed, cajoled, or simply seduced by their masters, but any romantic notions involving the practices of miscegenation are best avoided as romantic sentiment rather than as an unbiased assessment of the abusive situation in which these women were placed. Notwithstanding this reservation, some white Southerners demonstrated a long commitment to their black mistresses, recognized their mixed-race offspring, and attempted to provide for their upkeep and well-being. Often this took the form of a public admission after death, and many interracial alliances were recognized in a planter's will. The white children of such men often went to great lengths to undo those parts of their father's will favorable to their biracial siblings. Rarely did the courts uphold a will favorable to mixed-race children in the face of a concerted effort by their white relations.

The question of how common sexual affairs between slaves and masters actually were, as opposed to how often they appear as titillating tidbits of gossip in journals and letters, is undecided. Southerners went to great lengths to structure laws and cultural norms that would prohibit such interaction. Many slaveholding states passed anti-miscegenation measures providing severe social penalties for white men who openly bedded black women, as well as massive physical retaliation upon any black men who had relations with white women.

The concept of white women sleeping with black men was a proposition too explosive for the delicate egos of white males. White women were expected to respond to blacks as they would to any animate property, like pets, ignoring the indelicacy of even naked adult males. Young women were expected to steel themselves into viewing the naked slave as a dehumanized object, no more indelicate than **livestock** in the barnyard. Documented cases of the daughters of wealthy plantation owners bearing mixed-race children are rare, and, when found, are accompanied by tales of social rebuff, revulsion, and personal disaster. **Related Entries**: Children Born as Slaves; Plantation Mistress; Prostitution.

SUGGESTED READING: John W. Blassingame, *Black New Orleans* (1973); Catherine Clinton, *The Plantation Mistress: Woman's World in the Old South* (1982); Eugene D. Genovese, *Roll, Jordan Roll: The World the Slaves Made* (1976); Dorothy Denneen Volo and James M. Volo, *Daily Life in Civil War America* (1998).

MISSISSIPPI: Highlights of a period description of the state from John Hayward's *Gazetteer of the United States* (1853) read as follows:

Surface and Soil: The soil throughout is naturally very fertile, especially the alluvial lands on river banks, which are not liable to inundation. The staple product is **cotton**, which is raised in great abundance. The soil yields profusely Indian corn, rice, wheat, rye, and other grains, sweet potatoes, indigo, **tobacco**, melons, grapes, figs, apples, plums, peaches, lemons, oranges &c.

Rivers: Besides the Mississippi, the Yazoo is the most considerable stream which flows wholly within the state. There is a sea coast of 70 miles but no harbors sufficient for the admission of large vessels.

Education: There are several colleges in the state. Academies aand literary institutions are numerous. Common schools are also established throughout the state.

Internal Improvements: Several **railroads** have been completed or partially finished. The most extensive work of this kind commences at Vicksburg, and proceeds in an easterly direction.

Manufacture: There are a number of cotton factories on a small scale, several mills of considerable importance for the manufacture of flour and numerous other establishments producing articles for domestic consumption.

Minerals: Clay of good quality, suited to the manufacture of pottery and bricks, abounds in various localities.

Indians: Large portions of the northern and eastern sections of the state are still held by the Choctaw and Chickasaw Indians. These tracts include some of the best lands in the state, abounding in broad and fertile prairies which are well cultivated by their owners, who also possess large numbers of cattle, horses, swine and sheep. The Indians are intelligent and industrious, many of them being good mechanics. The females are expert at spinning and weaving.

Population: Between 1820 and 1830 the population increased 80 percent; by 1840 the increase was 175 percent. Of a population of 175,000, upwards of one half were slaves. The population of 1850 was 606,555.

Related Entry: Geography.

SUGGESTED READING: John Knox Bettersworth, *Mississippi: A History* (1959); John Hayward, *Gazetteer of the United States* (1853); Frederick Law Olmsted, *The Cotton Kingdom: A Traveler's Observations on Cotton and Slavery* (1861; 1996); John Ray Skates, *Mississippi, a History* (1979).

MISSISSIPPI RIVER: The Mississippi River system and the enormous region it drains in the center of the American continent served as an artery of exploration, settlement, and commerce for the nation. As more Americans settled in the old Northwest Territory and in the area between the Appalachian Mountains and the river, they came to rely on their ability to float their crops down its major tributaries, to the Gulf of Mexico, and out to the world.

When the United States purchased all of **Louisiana** from the French in 1803 it received all the land drained by these tributaries. These **rivers** included the Wisconsin, the Illinois, the Missouri, the Kansas, the Kaskaskia, the Wabash, the Miami, the Ohio, the Cumberland, the Tennessee, the Arkansas, the Red, and the Yazoo, among others. A simple reading of this list evokes the images of settlement and pioneering spirit that characterize American history. The Mississippi River system was the highway that made possible the life of the Western farmer, and, prior to the establishment of the **railroads,** tied the West to the **sectional disputes** of the South. **Related Entries**: Geography; Riverboats; Sectional Disputes.

SUGGESTED READING: Michael Allen, *Western Rivermen, 1763–1861: Ohio and Mississippi Boatmen and the Myth of the Alligator Horse* (1994); Leland D. Baldwin, *Keelboat Age on Western Rivers* (1980); John F. McDermott, *Before Mark Twain: A Sampler of Old, Old Times on the Mississippi* (1998).

MISSOURI: Highlights of a period description of the state from John Hayward's *Gazetteer of the United States* (1853) read as follows:

Surface and Soil: The surface and soil are much varied throughout the state. The uplands are very productive, consisting both of prairies and woodlands. The lowlands are extremely rich. Indian corn and other grains, hemp, flax, tobacco and sweet potatoes are among the products of the field. **Cotton** is raised in the southern section of the state. Grapes are found in profusion in the underwood of the forests; and most fruits common to the latitude are successfully cultivated.

Rivers: The state is watered by numerous large streams besides the great rivers Mississippi and Missouri.

Education: Several colleges flourish in different quarters of the state, most of them under the special auspices of some religious denomination. A good number of academies and literary institutions have also been established. The common and primary schools are tolerably numerous.

Internal Improvements: Missouri is favored with extraordinary facilities for internal intercourse, especially by water communication. St. Louis and all the great commercial marts of the South are joined by means of steamboats and other craft which navigate the principal rivers for hundreds and even thousands of miles.

Manufacture: Iron, lead and lumber are among the chief articles manufactured. There are also large numbers of grist mills, distilleries, potteries, brick, stone and marble yards, salt works, breweries, carriage and machine factories and other establishments for the production [of] commodities requisite to home use.

Minerals: Missouri is remarkably rich in mineral treasures especially in the value of its lead mines. These are known to occupy an area of over 3000 square miles. Iron ore of excellent quality also abounds.

Indians: There are no distinct bands of Indians permanently settled within the state, most of the tribes having withdrawn to their allotted country beyond the western boundary for the state.

Population: In 1810 the population was less than 20,000. During the following ten years it had increased to upwards of 66,000. In 1830 it numbered 140,000; and in 1840, 383,000 including 58,000 slaves. The population in 1850 numbered 684, 132.

Related Entry: Geography.

SUGGESTED READING: John Hayward, *Gazetteer of the United States* (1853); Paul C. Nagel, *Missouri: A History* (1988).

MISSOURI COMPROMISE OF 1820: As the second decade of the nineteenth century began, eleven **slave states** and eleven **free states** constituted the Union. As the country prepared to expand into the trans-Mississippi West, both the North and the South viewed the process with some trepidation. The North feared that the vast lands beyond the great river, acquired in the 1803 **Louisiana Purchase**, might become slaveholding territory, destroying the political balance in the national government.

When the Constitution had been ratified, the population of the Southern states—counting each slave as three-fifths of a person for the purpose of representation—had been about equal to that of the North. The South had been favored by a number of Southern Presidents and supported by a **Supreme Court** that was generally in agreement with its positions on the issues of the day. The South had maintained a precarious balance in Congress by forming mutually beneficial coalitions with other states.

When **Missouri** asked for permission to draw up a constitution and be admitted to the Union, the proposal created a great deal of agitation all over the country. Congressman James Tallmadge of New York immediately introduced a bill to forbid **slavery** in any state carved from the Louisiana Territory. The South, fearing a further strengthening of the political position of the North in Congress, unanimously protested the Tallmadge bill and was able to defeat it in the Senate.

When Congress next visited the matter, the possibility of a compromise was seen in the application of Maine for statehood. Maine could be admitted as a free state while Missouri entered as a slave state without disturbing the

North-South balance in the Senate. Moreover, in the hope of forestalling similar disputes in the future, a provision was added to the Missouri Enabling Act, better known as the Missouri Compromise, guaranteeing that all of the Louisiana Territory north of the 36°30' line of latitude would remain free.

The compromise was widely supported by the whole country and seemed to herald an era of political harmony. Taken together with flourishing business prospects and seemingly unbounded prosperity, an "Era of Good Feeling" was initiated in America that was not shattered until the 1837 economic **panic**. As a result of the Missouri Compromise four states west of the **Mississippi River** were gathered to the South—**Louisiana, Arkansas, Missouri**, and **Texas;** while eight states were added to the Northern side of the political ledger—a net gain for the North.

The Missouri Compromise itself came under attack in the form of **popular sovereignty**, which was first proposed in 1844 and which was closely associated with the **Kansas-Nebraska Act of 1854**. The Missouri Compromise was finally repealed by the Supreme Court in its **Dred Scott** decision in 1856. **Related Entries**: Extension of Slavery into the Territories; Kansas-Nebraska Act of 1854; Popular Sovereignty.

SUGGESTED READING: Richard H. Sewell, *A House Divided: Sectionalism and the Civil War, 1848–1865* (1988).

MODERNIZATION: Cultural and social changes were sweeping the country in the 1840s and 1850s. Industry and **urbanization** had moved the North toward a more modern society, while the South had essentially lagged behind in the traditions of the eighteenth century. The differences between the "folk culture" of the South and the "modern culture" of the North fueled the broad-based **reform movements** of mid-century and may have ignited the turmoil over state sovereignty and **slavery**.

The most obvious modern element of society was the rapid growth of urban centers as more and more people flocked to the cities to find work in the factories. Although the class structure was still dominated by the old social elite, a new middle class was striving to become socially acceptable. Unfortunately, the urban lower classes continued to be characterized by sharp contrasts in wealth, ethnic origin, and religion. One of the ironic characteristics of the new modernism in Northern society was the simultaneous existence of anti-slavery sentiment and widespread ethnic prejudice.

The South was a structured society tied to a romanticized version of an older aristocratic order remarkably intolerant of social reform and disdainful of activism. Yet Southerners thought of themselves as well mannered, chivalrous to women and children, religious, and protective of all that was still fundamentally good in America. At all levels of Southern society individual liberty, manliness, and respect for authority or position were held in such high esteem that one put his life and personal honor on the line to protect them.

As the century progressed men in Northern cities increasingly worked in the special atmosphere of business premises such as factories or offices. Fathers commonly left the home to work for ten to fourteen hours, and their children rarely saw them during daylight hours. A father's work and workplace became foreign to his children. This tendency to go to work, rather than to work at home, led to the virtual removal of men from the home environment, leaving it the sole province of the female. The modern nineteenth-century home increasingly came to focus almost solely on the wife and children.

With the general availability of the pocket watch, men increasingly lived their lives by the clock. Factory workers were expected to work in shifts dictated by the public clocks that came to be prominently displayed on towers, in the streets, and on the factory walls. The idea of being "on time" represented a significant change in the lifestyle of most city dwellers; and since the North was the most urbanized section of the country, the need to be on time became characteristic of Northern life.

The vast majority of Southern citizens remained small farmers and planned their lives around rural activities and seasonal chores. Free white laborers and artisans rarely worked by the clock. Tradition provided continuity in the work relationship between employer and employee, and it was not unusual for one family to be employed by another in the same capacity for several generations in an idyllic, if not a mechanically efficient, simplicity. Southerners, who had no need to work by the clock, were often mistakenly viewed as shiftless and lazy.

Southern laborers feared the development of the "work for wage" economy of the cities, and they saw Northern wage earners as degraded and enslaved persons. Many in the laboring class believed that the North was determined to enslave them to the factory system or counting house. The expansion of a "work for wage" system was dreaded by Southerners almost as much as **abolitionists** dreaded the expansion of slavery. Southern whites were clearly anxious to maintain their status as freemen, even if this required that they be very poor freemen.

The most modern element in American life in the first half of the century was a vigorous interest in politics. Politics became a great national pastime, almost a hobby, shared by both the North and the South. This interest crossed many of the old social and economic lines to engage devotees from many classes, with sharp debates resulting on an almost daily basis. Unfortunately, restraint was conspicuously absent from the political process. Failing to acknowledge the good in Southern society because it was tied to slavery, Northerners made no attempt to hide their disapproval of all things

Southern and were widely viewed as interventionists, fanatics, anarchists, or worse by the Southern population. **Related Entries**: Immigration; Sectional Disputes.

SUGGESTED READING: Richard H. Sewell, *A House Divided: Sectionalism and the Civil War, 1848–1865* (1988); John Tosh, "New Men? The Bourgeois Cult of Home," *History Today* vol. 46 (December 1996): 9–15.

MONROE, JAMES (1758–1831): statesman, governor of **Virginia** (1799–1802), and fifth President of the United States (1817–1825). James Monroe entered the American revolutionary army at the age of nineteen and rose to the rank of major. He was wounded at the Battle of Trenton, and left to study law with his fellow Virginian **Thomas Jefferson**. The two men formed a close relationship that lasted until Jefferson's death in 1826.

Monroe began his political career as a strong Anti-Federalist, fearing a strong central government. He was a delegate to the Virginia Convention of 1788, which voted to ratify the Constitution. As a U.S. senator (1790–1794), Monroe moved even closer to Jefferson, and he severely criticized the federal government. He opposed the **Bank of the United States** and led the fight to investigate the financial dealings of Alexander Hamilton. In 1794 he left the Senate to take a position as a minister to France; however, he became a conspicuous Anglophile, and this interfered with his effectiveness with the French.

Upon his recall he ran for and won election as governor of Virginia. He returned to France in 1803 and helped to negotiate the **Louisiana Purchase** with Robert Livingston. He then spent some time working in Spain and Britain. While these were important posts, Monroe was acutely unsuccessful in moving his agenda. In 1808 he ran unsuccessfully for President against **James Madison**, and won another term as governor of Virginia in 1811. Notwithstanding this result, Madison offered him a post as secretary of state in 1811, which Monroe accepted.

Throughout the **War of 1812**, Monroe exhibited strong ambitions for the Executive Mansion. He accepted the post of secretary of war in 1814, and held the two cabinet posts of state and war simultaneously. American victories at Plattsburg and **New Orleans** served to enhance his personal prestige even though the war was being poorly handled. In 1816, with Madison's support, he was elected President. He was the fourth in a long succession of Virginia-born Presidents which came to be known as the "Virginia Dynasty." His sympathies over the next eight years were with the South. He held a middle-of-the-road view of **internal improvements at federal expense** and reluctantly signed the **Missouri Compromise of 1820**.

Monroe's tenure in the **executive branch** is best remembered for the Rush-Bagot agreement for limitation of armed vessels on the Great Lakes;

the mediation of the Canadian fisheries disputes in Labrador; and the peaceful acquisition of **West Florida** in 1819. The slow recognition of the independence of Spain's former colonies in the Western Hemisphere led to Monroe's famous message known as the Monroe Doctrine, which essentially warned the European powers to stay out of the politics of the Western Hemisphere. Although he did not shine in the presidency the way Jefferson or Madison had, the Monroe Doctrine has caused his name to be inextricably linked with a major tenet of American foreign policy for generations. **Related Entries**: Louisiana Purchase; War of 1812.

SUGGESTED READING: Harry Ammon, *James Monroe: The Quest for National Identity* (1971); Charles Wetzel, *James Monroe* (1989).

MONTGOMERY, ALABAMA: Until supplanted by **Richmond, Virginia**, Montgomery was the first capital of the Confederacy. When the Congress of the Southern Confederacy opened in Montgomery, **Howell Cobb**, presiding officer of the convention, took his position at the rostrum of the State House to oversee the constitutional deliberations among the six states that had seceded to that time. The new Confederate Constitution was closer to the U.S. Constitution than it was to a revolutionary document. With the exception of a few omissions and some changes in phraseology, the two documents were almost identical. The new constitution embodied a set of the distinctive principles which tended to focus on a view of government long obscured by the development and implementation of Federalist political theory since 1789. The new government was to have a President, who would serve a single six-year term, a Vice President, and a cabinet.

Howell Cobb, an ardent **secessionist**, was strongly considered for the presidency of the Confederacy along with disunion fanatics **Robert A. Toombs, Robert B. Rhett**, and **William L. Yancey**. However, the more conservative **Jefferson Davis** was chosen instead, and **Alexander H. Stephens** was made Vice President. Ironically, Stephens, who had survived a train wreck on the way to the convention, had not sought the position, and Davis, now the President, had been more interested in becoming the Confederate secretary of war. **Related Entries**: Cobb, Howell; Confederate Government; Davis, Jefferson.

SUGGESTED READING: Marshall L. DeRosa, *The Confederate Constitution of 1861* (1991).

MORMONS. *See* Young, Brigham.

MUSIC. *See* Minstrel Shows.

NATCHEZ TRACE: Also known as the Old Chickasaw Trail, the Natchez Trace was an Indian path that led from **New Orleans, Louisiana**, to Natchez, **Mississippi**, and thence to Nashville, **Tennessee**. Except in the vicinity of Natchez and Nashville it was little more than a track used by pedestrians and those on horseback. The Trace had been used by Native Americans for centuries as part of a network of well-worn trails that connected the pre-Columbian inhabitants of the continent and became many of the earliest **roads** "discovered" by while explorers.

In the antebellum period it was used by the bargemen who floated rafts, **flatboats, and keelboats** down the interior **rivers** to the mouth of the **Mississippi River** and who, lacking the propulsion of the great steamboats, were forced to walk back up the river. Runaway slaves often chose the Trace as a route to freedom in the North. The Trace offered little danger to travelers from unfriendly Indians once **Andrew Jackson** had crushed the Creek at the Battle of Horseshoe Bend; but unscrupulous white outlaws continued to terrorize small groups of travelers. These grim criminals were among the most inhuman highwaymen in history, lacking any shred of gallantry or **romanticism. Related Entries**: Rivers; Transportation; Westward Movement.

SUGGESTED READING: Jonathan Daniels, *The Devil's Backbone: The Story of the Natchez Trace* (1998).

NATIONAL BANK. *See* Bank of the United States.

NATIVE AMERICANS. *See* Indian Removal; Westward Movement.

NATIVISTS: In the wake of the disaster visited upon the old political establishment following the passage of the **Kansas-Nebraska Act of 1854**, several new parties moved in to fill the void. A growing disenchantment with politics as usual, and with politicians out of touch with the pulse of the people, and dedicated only to entrenched interests, led to the founding of new parties with intriguing agendas designed to ensure the defeat of the old party candidates. With interest in politics increasingly popular, the Nativist, or American Party, rose very rapidly, gaining seats in several Northern states, but falling to carry its message of pure Americanism and anti-Catholicism to an accepting national audience. Nativism appeared intermittently and under the guises of several "All American" movements that targeted immigrants, the best known being the Know-Nothing Party.

Nativist propaganda was widely promulgated throughout the nation, and even those who disagreed with Nativist positions were well aware of them. For support Nativists tapped into the growing fear and resentment that paralleled the rapid changes taking place in American society. Nativist rhetoric portrayed **Catholics**, and especially the Irish Catholic immigrants, as crime-ridden and intemperate, a drag on the economy, and a danger to the fabric of society. The Nativists were deeply immersed in the evangelical movement and the growing "Protestant Crusade." They were strongly supported by some of the finest established families of the North but had few adherents among Southerners, who were generally more tolerant of Catholicism.

Politically, the Nativists made some gains at the state level, especially in Massachusetts, only to have the movement collapse after a few years because it failed to generate enough voter support nationally. Nativists were particularly embarrassed by their inability to influence more stringent **immigration** laws. More generally, the Nativists failed because of their lack of political experience, their association with several prominent old party **Whigs**, and their violent anti-Catholic rhetoric, which bothered many politically active Protestants. The most important aspect of Nativism was that it demonstrated, in a visible way, the general disillusionment with the old party system. **Related Entries**: Catholics; Immigration; Kansas-Nebraska Act of 1854.

SUGGESTED READING: Ray A. Billington, *The Origins of Nativism in the United States* (1979); Andrew M. Greeley, *An Ugly Little Secret: Anti-Catholicism in North America* (1977).

NAVAL STORES. *See* Raw Materials.

NEGRO SEAMAN CONTROVERSY: One of the earliest confrontations over sovereignty between the states and the federal government came over the institution of the Negro Seaman Law by authorities in **Charleston, South Carolina**. Some historians view this as the first round in the **nullification** struggle. During the investigation of the **Denmark Vesey** conspiracy it became clear that the plot had gained strength through the whispered instigations of **free blacks** and **abolitionist** agitators. In an attempt to rid the streets of Charleston of free blacks, authorities passed an ordinance in 1822 that placed all free Negro seamen under arrest until their ships were to leave port.

Many free Negro seamen came from Northern vessels, but it was the Negroes from British vessels, who were considered free citizens of that country, around whom the controversy swirled. Federal treaties with Britain ensured that inhabitants of each country had the freedom of the other's ports. The Negro Seaman Law proved an embarrassment to the secretary of state, **John Quincy Adams**, who had to deal with complaints from the British government. In answer to an entreaty from Adams, the South Carolina state authorities temporarily suspended the practice, and the immediate problem seemed settled.

Nonetheless, South Carolina continued to view all blacks with increased suspicion after the Vesey conspiracy. In 1823 a group of low country planters formed the **South Carolina Association** for the purpose of more strictly enforcing the **Black Codes**. As a result the controversy flared up once more when a free Negro seaman from the British colony of Jamaica, Harry Elkinson, was detained when he left his ship. Elkinson applied to the **Supreme Court** for a writ of habeas corpus. Justice William Johnson immediately called a hearing, and found that the Seaman's Law violated the treaty and took precedence over state law. This decision created a sensation on both sides of the question of federal or state domination.

Despite the justice's opinion, South Carolina continued to detain Negro seamen, and the British protests continued to embarrass Adams. In 1824 an attempt at reconciling the two positions in the state legislature failed. Proponents of nullification rightly pointed to the Negro Seaman Law controversy as an initial attempt to nullify federal law. For all practical purposes the state was successful, and this taught the state authorities that they had a powerful weapon to be used against the federal government. **Related Entries**: Nullification; Vesey, Denmark.

SUGGESTED READING: Donald G. Morgan, *Justice William Johnson: The First Dissenter* (1954); "Justice William Johnson on the Treaty Making Power," *George Washington Law Review* (December 1953).

NEW ORLEANS: When New Orleans was first acquired by the United States as part of the **Louisiana Purchase**, it had a population of French and Spanish residents (known as **Creoles**); a large itinerant population of traders, bargemen, and clerks; and a considerable white population which had come from the United States before 1803. It was the largest non–English-speaking city in the United States, and its laws were variously based on the Spanish *Siete Partide* and the French *Code Napoleon*. The city and the immediate

View of New Orleans from a nineteenth-century reference work of the period. (From the authors' collection.)

surrounding area boasted the largest black community in the country, composed of numerous **free black** businessmen and artisans, urbanized former slaves, and slaves from the plantations. The free blacks looked with great disdain upon the slave population, and an intense animosity between the Creole population and the American newcomers took decades to overcome.

Many of our present ideas of what made up a Southern city are modeled on New Orleans. The homes were generally made of stucco, stone, or brick. Most were roofed with slate or tile. As private wells could not guarantee potable water, it was brought by cart from the **Mississippi River**, afterwards being filtered through porous stones and treated with a combination of lime, alum, and charcoal.

The city grew as planters and farmers came in from their outlying and relatively isolated holdings to take advantage of the social and cultural benefits it offered. Throughout the first decade of the nineteenth century, fashionable balls and masquerades were held in the St. Philip Theater. This fine building could accommodate over 700 people and had a permanent wood parquet floor. The St. Philip Theater was transformed into the Washington Ballroom by 1832. Creole and American **theater** goers moved on to the Theatre d'Orleans, a grand structure costing $80,000 to erect in 1815.

French and occasionally English plays were given here. A ballroom was added in the 1820s, and grand opera was introduced in 1837.

By mid-century, however, New Orleans had also developed a seamier side. The lower-class Irish immigrants who began to come to the city in the 1840s were widely blamed for this development. Criminals and ruffians could find refuge in scores of grog shops, dance halls, bordellos, cheap taverns, and coffee houses. Probably no other city in the United States had such a large ratio of unsavory places to its population. Nonetheless, New Orleans was described in a child's geography text as "remarkable for the number of ships and steamboats that crowd its levee." Most of these were busy exporting **cotton** to Europe. **Related Entries:** Amusements and Diversions; Louisiana Purchase; Prostitution.

SUGGESTED READING: Robert C. Reinders and John Duffy, *End of an Era: New Orleans, 1850–1860* (1989); Martin Siegel, *New Orleans: A Chronological and Documentary History, 1539–1970* (1975).

NEW ORLEANS, BATTLE OF: It has often been asserted that the Battle of New Orleans occupies an ambiguous position in American history because it was fought after the Treaty of Ghent, which ended the **War of 1812**, had been signed. This assertion is generally unfounded. While a treaty to end hostilities had been negotiated, it had not been endorsed by Parliament or the King, nor had it been approved by the President and the U.S. Senate. It had no binding effect, and its conditions were mere suggestions. A legitimate state of war existed between the Americans and the British throughout and after the battle.

Andrew Jackson's heterogeneous army of 5,500 consisted of **militia** units, riflemen from **Tennessee**, a few regular infantry and marines, two free Negro battalions, and several bands of buccaneers. His Kentuckians did not arrive until a critical point had been reached in the contest. Jackson had more than three dozen pieces of artillery, some transferred from the schooner *Louisiana*, and a fleet of gunboats on Lake Borgne.

The British force of over 11,000 men, commanded by Major General Sir Edward Pakenham, was composed almost entirely of British regulars—battle-tested veterans. The British had as much artillery as they could drag ashore from a fleet of almost sixty vessels and the support of a battery of Congreve rockets. These same rockets had instilled fear and disorder in the American militia at the Battle of Bladensburg outside the nation's capital the previous August.

The opening stages of the battle on Lake Borgne, outside the city of New Orleans, were a disaster for American naval policy, which had relied on gunboats for coastal defense. Swarms of British soldiers clambered aboard and captured the gunboats with little trouble. Conversely, from a military point of view, the actual defense of the city was a decisive victory for Jackson and a showcase for American combined arms, composed mostly of militia who deserve the major credit for the victory.

The climax of the battle took place on the east bank of the **Mississippi River** in front of the main American position along the old Rodriguez canal, providing a ready-made moat in front of the five-foot-high breastworks built by Jackson's men. On January 8, 1815, Pakenham launched four simultaneous assaults along the top of the river levee. The British line, advancing in perfect order, found itself before the American entrenchments with nowhere to go—helplessly trapped. No man in either army was braver than Pakenham, but he was shocked and stunned by this failure. Leading his men forward, Pakenham was wounded twice and was killed while being treated on the field. Finally the 93rd Highlanders advanced to attack the redoubt in the center of Jackson's right wing held by General William Carroll's Tennessee and **Kentucky** riflemen. Marching in closed ranks with bagpipes blaring, the Highlanders, courageous to the end, were caught in the American fire. In five minutes almost 800 of the 925 officers and men of the 93rd were struck down. Taken together with over 2,000 losses on other parts of the field, the action was essentially over.

The Battle of New Orleans was essentially a victory of small arms, especially for the American rifle. Unfortunately, American military tacticians of the Civil War did not appreciate the lesson in futility provided by these frontal assaults in the face of rifle fire. The victory of the militia was to have repercussions in the way the South viewed its military preparations in its disputes with the federal government decades later; and Southern martial mythology was enhanced by the utter extent of the triumph. Some historians see the Battle of New Orleans as a defining moment in the development of the American fighting character. More important, the defeat of the British regulars at New Orleans was to catapult Andrew Jackson to national prominence. **Related Entries**: Jackson, Andrew; Militia; South Carolina Association.

SUGGESTED READING: Dee Brown, *Andrew Jackson and the Battle of New Orleans* (1972); Tim Pickles, *New Orleans 1815: Andrew Jackson Crushes the British* (1994).

NEWSPAPERS: Newspapers gained influence steadily during the first half of the nineteenth century as **education** spread the power of **reading** across the population. **Alexis de Tocqueville** noted in 1831 that Americans had settled the continent with the Bible, the axe, and the newspaper. Southern papers were slower to develop than those in other parts of the country as they were almost completely dependent on Northern sources for type, presses, and newsprint—a weakness sorely felt during the Civil War. Nonetheless, an incredibly large number of local publications appeared as citizens came to favor the newspaper as an individualized form of communication.

Newspapers were a major source of information. Papers were often read aloud to large groups of listeners. (*Mexican News*, 1853, engraving by Alfred Jones after painting by R. C. Woodville, negative number 28545. © Collection of The New York Historical Society.)

Newspapers printed speeches in their entirety within a few days of their being given. Political arguments, essays, letters to the editor, and discussions among dedicated readers—both genuine and planted for effect—flowed in the wake of every issue. Persons read alone, or in small groups, with the leisure to reread and analyze what was printed. In the estimation of the publishers, the most important articles to be printed were the official proceedings taking place in **Washington, DC**, often with biting editorial preambles. Even routine congressional debates were reported in nauseating detail.

The power of the press to influence a wider audience than that which could be assembled at any one place and time was not to be underestimated. Some papers tried to remain neutral, but others sought out political alliances either because of the agenda of the editors, or, more commonly, to attract a lucrative trade in political advertising and public printing. Neutrality on any topic of public interest often doomed a newspaper to failure. At times the papers were so full of scandal and untruth that their publishers were prosecuted for libel; and more than once the comments made in the press led to **dueling**.

The papers that sprang to the side of **Andrew Jackson** in his 1828 presidential campaign—and they were too numerous to be counted—bitterly assailed the administration of **John Quincy Adams**. In this way they became an organ of the political party; and, in an era of slow-moving news and uncorroborated sources, they became an effective tool for convincing the party voter of the universal appeal of its candidate or position.

One of the earliest influential newspapers in the South was the *Courier*. Begun in **Charleston, South Carolina**, in 1803, it quickly became one of the most influential and popular Southern papers. Its editors refused to give in to public pressure during the tariff **nullification** and **secession** crises, reporting only the activities of the conventions without adding any editorial support for their positions.

As early as 1828 **Robert B. Rhett** used his Charleston-based newspaper, the *Mercury*, to urge resistance to the unrestrained rule of the federal government. Rhett pleaded with his readers for the Southern states to secede en masse in defense of **states' rights** and Southern culture. The *Mercury* continued to plead the case of disunion right up to the eve of the Civil War.

The *Richmond Whig* was a leader when it came to strong opposition to disunion. The *New Orleans Crescent* opposed any form of violence. The *Memphis Eagle* portrayed peaceful secession as an absurd pipe dream. Many papers, including the *Natchez Courier*, the *Nashville Banner*, and the *New Orleans Bulletin*, reminded the South of its intense reliance upon the North and warned that before any drastic measures be taken, the South had best make itself economically independent first.

Other papers foresaw and accepted the inevitable conflict. *DeBow's Review*, a monthly commercial publication located in **New Orleans**, urged the South to diversify its economy and to build **railroads**, factories, and canals, thereby freeing itself from any dependence on the North. By mid-century *DeBow's* was increasingly seen as a vehicle for secessionist propaganda. The *Hornet's Nest* of Charlotte, **North Carolina**, published a list of Northern businesses that did not support the South's position and urged other editors to print the list in their publications, counsel the *Southern Confederacy*, one of the most vehement secessionist papers, applauded.

The secession press was most intense in South Carolina and **Mississippi**. Besides the Charleston *Mercury*, several other newspapers were actively stressing Southern independence. Some, like the *Natchez Free Trader*, plainly recommended secession as the only recourse for Southern grievances. Southern nationalism was hawked by the respected *Southern Literary Messenger*, once edited by **Edgar Allan Poe;** and even the *Southern Quarterly Review* was pleading the cause of disunion.

Virginian papers tended to be less unanimous in these opinions. Yet the **Richmond** *South*, edited by Roger A. Pryor, and its sister paper, the *En-*

quirer, edited by **Henry A. Wise**, both sported prominent secessionist themes. The Richmond *Examiner* and the *Dispatch*—once neutral and conservative—threw all their powers, and their large circulation, into the cause of secession by 1860. **Related Entries**: Fire-eaters; Nullification; Reading; Secession.

SUGGESTED READING: Carl R. Osthaus, *Partisans of the Southern Press: Editorial Spokesmen of the Nineteenth Century* (1994); Donald E. Reynolds, *Editors Make War: Southern Newspapers in the Secession Crisis* (1970).

NORTH CAROLINA: Highlights of a period description of the state from John Hayward's *Gazetteer of the United States* (1853) read as follows:

History and Early Settlement: North Carolina was included in the extensive region granted to Sir Walter Raleigh under the general name of **Virginia** in 1584. In 1667 the country now forming North and **South Carolina** had been granted to Lord Clarendon and others who undertook a form of government, prepared for the grantees by John Locke. Singular features were provisions for establishing an hereditary nobility, for vesting the legislative power in a "Parliament," and the exercise of executive authority by a chief magistrate, to be styled the "Palatine." After a few years, its practical defects became palpable, and it was abandoned in 1633. In 1729 the colonies were ceded to the king and formed into two distinct colonies which now constitute the States of North and South Carolina. The people of this state during the American Revolution, were distinguished for their patriotic devotion to the cause of national independence. North Carolina was one of the thirteen original states adopting the federal constitution November, 1789.

Surface and Soil: The soil bordering the sea-coast is generally poor, producing naturally no other timber than pitch pine, from which are produced large quantities of **raw materials** such as tar, pitch, and turpentine, constituting the chief articles of export from the state. The swampy spots are well adapted to the culture of rice. Upland, and beyond the mountain ranges, the land is exceedingly fertile. Indian corn grows well in all parts of the state, and **cotton** is successfully cultivated in many places. The low country, especially on the river borders, produces plums, grapes, strawberries and other fine fruits; it is also well adapted to the growth of rice and **sugar** cane. There are within the state upwards of two million acres of swampy land, which may be reclaimed and made to produce abundant crops of rice, corn, cotton and tobacco.

Rivers: While there are several large rivers, they are all subject to obstructions by sand bars at their mouths, owing to the sluggish course through a long distance of low level country.

Education: The free school system has not yet a very near approximation to that of the New England, Middle and some of the Western States. In 1840 the common schools contained less than 15,000 scholars. There are two colleges and about 150 literary seminaries. Provisions for the establishment and maintenance of asylums for the insane, and for the deaf and dumb have recently been made by the legislature.

Internal Improvements: There are several **railroads** and canals, most of which connect with those of Virginia. The Dismal Swamp Canal, which commences in Virginia, is extended into North Carolina.

Manufacture: Coarse fabrics of cotton and **wool** are manufactured to some extent, principally for home use. There are numerous furnaces, forges and smelting houses for the conversion of native mineral ores, iron, lead and gold into marketable shape. The manufacture of flour is carried on somewhat largely; and among the remaining commodities manufactures are hats and bonnets, hardware and cutlery, soap and candles, furniture and carriages, leather and saddlery, and distilled and fermented liquors.

Minerals: The state contains gold, iron ore, and other valuable minerals: but attention is chiefly directed to the former. The region which is most prolific in gold occupies both sides of the Blue Ridge. The mines have been extensively wrought. The ore is found occasionally in veins, sometimes in small lumps, but more frequently in grains or dust. The amount annually obtained has been estimated at some $5,000,000. Only a comparatively small amount of this finds its way to the United States mint or is retained within this country, a considerable portion being transmitted to Europe.

Indians: No distinct tribes, and but a few scattered families, of the Indian race remain. At the last census, the inhabitants of Indian blood numbered only 710.

Population: During the forty years ending in 1830, the population increased very steadily. In 1850 it increased to 868,903, about one third of whom are slaves.

Other: The right of **suffrage** is denied to all persons of Negro blood.

Related Entry: Geography.

SUGGESTED READING: John Hayward, *Gazetteer of the United States* (1853); Frederick Law Olmsted, *The Cotton Kingdom: A Traveler's Observations on Cotton and Slavery in the American Slave States* (1861; 1996), pp. 110–173; William S. Powell, *North Carolina: A History* (1977).

NULLIFICATION: Nullification was a political theory formulated in part by Governor **James A. Hamilton** of **South Carolina** and made into a systematic Southern doctrine by **John C. Calhoun**. The concept, based on strict construction of the Constitution, suggested that the federal government had no right to impose its will on individual sovereign states. The logical conclusion to this thinking was that each individual state had the power and the right to nullify any federal statute with which it disagreed.

The group of men who believed in nullification were not a politically homogeneous lot. Some nullifiers, like **Thomas Cooper** and **George McDuffie**, espoused nullification as the most direct means of accomplishing Southern **secession**. Their main purpose was to force South Carolina to secede, and if other Southern states chose to join it, all the better. Another large group of nullifiers was represented by political conservatives like Calhoun and **Robert Y. Hayne** who believed that unrestrained federal power, protective **tariffs**, and the **abolition of slavery** would doom the South to become the backwater of the nation unless reined in by the states. Still others like James A. Hamilton and **Henry L. Pinckney** were accused of questionable sincerity in espousing nullification as they sought compromise in the midst of controversy rather than an appeal to armed conflict. On the farthest end of the spectrum were those, like Judge John Richardson, who believed that nullification empowered the North to do as it pleased while endangering many of the constitutional restraints the South relied on to support its positions on a wide variety of issues.

John C. Calhoun, elected Vice President in the administration of **Andrew Jackson** in 1828, promoted nullification as a moderate alternative to secession; but its logical conclusion would have rendered the federal government impotent. Calhoun, a brilliant legal mind, realized that even in a democracy 49 percent of the people could be tyrannized by the other 51 percent if the majority were well organized behind a single issue. Therefore, if the majority was to rule, the minority must be willing to assert its rights.

The most serious confrontations over the issue of nullification began with the tariff crisis of 1828. Initially Calhoun, who was a late apostle of the concept, wanted simply to preserve the Union and intended to use the threat of nullification to force the federal government to reduce the high rates proposed in the Tariff of 1828 (the "Tariff of Abominations"). But in 1830, the **Webster-Hayne debate** in Congress helped to make nullification a national issue; and the proposition of an equally unacceptable protective tariff in 1832 further aggravated the controversy.

After resigning as Vice President, Calhoun actively crusaded for the assembly of a nullification convention in the name of **states' rights**. When the South Carolina legislature convened just such a body, it adopted an Ordinance of Nullification and began to raise bodies of armed troops. The ordinance, which prohibited the collection of the tariff as well as any appeal to the **Supreme Court**, was widely condemned by the other states—even those in the South. Jackson responded to the crisis, saying, "Disunion by armed force is treason." It became obvious to all concerned that the controversy was getting out of hand. The Jackson administration reacted with the simultaneous passage of a compromise tariff and a **Force Bill** authorizing the President to send troops to South Carolina if the state persisted in its activities.

Fortunately, armed conflict was averted by the acceptance of the compromise tariff by South Carolina. This was followed by the nullification of the Force Bill by the **Nullification Convention**. Disunion and violence were averted by this face-saving device. Although Calhoun and his supporters had failed to unite the Southern states behind nullification, they found a new weapon with which to enforce their will on the national government—the threat of secession. The radical politicians of the South raised the concepts of states' rights, nullification, and secession to the level of political gospel during the decade of the 1850s, and the entire scenario would be played out again in 1860 with very different results. **Related Entries**: Calhoun, John C.; Force Bill; Jackson, Andrew; Nullification Convention of 1832.

SUGGESTED READING: William W. Freehling, *Prelude to Civil War: The Nullification Controversy in South Carolina, 1816–1836* (1965; 1995).

NULLIFICATION CONVENTION OF 1832: In October 1832, a special session of the **South Carolina** legislature was held to vote on the convocation of a state convention for the purpose of nullifying the protective **tariffs**. The state's political theorists believed that a convention had to be called for this purpose, as a similar body had ratified the Constitution in the first place. If the delegates to a convention were parties to the original "social contract" of the Constitution, then only they could alter or nullify it. Of course, after fifty years, most of the original delegates were dead; but new delegates chosen in the same fashion were thought to be equally legitimate.

South Carolina conservatives, called Unionists, tried unsuccessfully to contest the vote in the legislature which established a delegate selection process; but, due in part to the overwhelming strength shown by the nullifiers in winning the decision, the Unionists did not contest the elections of the delegates themselves. The state legislature voted for the convention by a vote of 96 to 25, and the state senate agreed by a 31 to 13 margin. Some Unionist groups, mostly in the tidewater, refused to run candidates for the delegate positions; others chose to actively campaign for convention seats in the hope that they might hamper the **nullification** process. As a result, the select committee of the convention, which largely directed its activities, was almost devoid of Unionist sentiment.

The select committee, composed of extremists who viewed nullification not as an end in itself, but as a first step to **secession**, had an unopposed hand in shaping many important policy questions. The most important of these led to an unqualified declaration for secession if the federal government used any form of coercion within the state. On November 22, therefore, the convention was offered several radical proposals for the approval of the delegates: a *Report of the Select Committee of Twenty-One*, written by arch nullifier **Robert Y. Hayne;** an *Address to the People of the United States*, drafted by **John C. Calhoun** and revised by **Fire-eater George McDuffie;** an *Address to the People of South Carolina*, written by **states' rights** activist and author **Robert Turnbull;** and a Nullification Ordinance, crafted by the lot, which declared the tariffs of 1828 and 1832 unconstitutional and null and void in South Carolina.

All of these proposals met with the approbation of the delegates; but the most meaningful of them was the Nullification Ordinance. The ordinance made it unlawful to collect tariff duties in the state and, remarkably, also banned the payment of duties and the bringing of court cases to collect them. Moreover, it authorized the employment of the state **militia** in resisting federal coercion and required an oath to uphold the ordinance and all legislation needed to sustain it, called the Test Oath, to be sworn by any state official, judge, or jurist before they could take office. Unionists who refused to take the oath could not hold the offices to which they might be elected in the future. The Test Oath thereby became a weapon in the hands of the nullifiers by which they could disenfranchise the conservative elements in South Carolina politics. Although the oath was ultimately found to be unconstitutional, it effectively eliminated all conservatism from the state of South Carolina by the 1850s. **Related Entries**: Calhoun, John C.; Force Bill; Hamilton, James A.; Nullification.

SUGGESTED READING: David F. Houston, *A Critical Study of Nullification in South Carolina* (1896; 1990); Charles M. Wiltse, *The New Nation, 1800–1845* (1961; 1982).

OFFICE HOLDING: A love of democracy had been instilled in most Americans from the time of the Revolution, but during the first two decades of the nineteenth century popular participation in governance was limited largely to males with social status. The political campaigns of **Andrew Jackson** and his election as President vastly changed the nature of the American political process. Thereafter, politicians were pressed by their political base to reform the requirements for office holding and enfranchisement. By mid-century most state and local offices had been made elective instead of appointive. This allowed the electorate to replace officials with whom they became displeased, and had the effect of further democratizing the process.

Although changes in property qualifications for office holding and voting often masked attempts to protect those with entrenched power or to limit the influence of the rising middle class, popular governance became a good deal more widespread than previously was the case. Rotation in office came to be viewed as a leading principle of a republican form of government and was seen as a means of enlarging the ranks of public servants to include those outside the sphere of the landed gentry or the socially elite.

As the control of politics gradually shifted, it came to reside, in many cases, in unexpected hands. Political neophytes and petty politicians were suddenly given unexpected opportunities in municipal government. Day-to-day politics became the domain of the men who had a hand on the pulse of local opinion, including storekeepers, tavern owners, and lawyers. By mid-century candidates for public office were increasingly chosen for their popular appeal, physical appearance, and oratorical ability. While the procedure brought many fine statesmen into government, the caliber of many other officeholders was unfortunate. Genius, dedication to the commonwealth, and talent often lay neglected as offices were increasingly filled by the am-

Office holding became much more widespread in the antebellum period. Prospective candidates often tried to "get out the vote" by personally canvassing the electorate. (Detail from *Canvassing for a Vote* by G. C. Bingham. Reproduced by permission of The Saint Louis Art Museum.)

bitious, the reprobate, the dishonest, or those who could barely read and write.

When **Alexis de Tocqueville** visited America in the 1830s he found the men who were elected to the House of Representatives coarse and boisterous. Conversely, he found the senators well bred and statesmanlike. This finding may have reflected Tocqueville's own bias. He frowned on popular democracy with its widely divergent representation and favored the more republican form of government by which only two senators were designated by each state legislature. **Related Entries**: Planter Aristocracy; Suffrage.

SUGGESTED READING: Oscar and Lilian Handlin, *Liberty and Expansion, 1760–1850* (1989).

OLMSTED, FREDERICK LAW (1822–1903): architect and journalist. Although he is probably best known as the designer and developer of New York's Central Park, Frederick Law Olmsted began a series of travels in the 1850s that were to bring out his literary talent and leave one of the most accurate pictures of conditions in the South prior to the Civil War. Beginning in 1852, Olmsted was commissioned by the *New York Times* to write an unbiased impression of the institution of **slavery** and the overall condition of the Southern **plantation economy**. His letters to the editor were very successful and were published as a book, *A Journey in the Seaboard Slave States* (1856). A second tour on horseback took him through **Texas, New Orleans**, and **Richmond**. His reports on this trip appeared in two books: *A Journey Through Texas* (1857) and *A Journey Through the Back Country* (1860).

The three works, written on the eve of the Civil War, were very popular and were condensed and reissued in both America and England in 1861 under the titles *The Cotton Kingdom* and *Journeys and Explorations in the Cotton Kingdom*. The works were heralded by anti-slavery proponents for their thoughtfulness, their calm examination of fact, and the fairness of the scenes they presented of Southern life. Notwithstanding their apparent impartiality, as a personal acquaintance of **William Lloyd Garrison**, the noted **abolitionist**, Olmsted's objectivity must be questioned, and his text does seem to record a less sophisticated view of Southern life than was warranted at the time. Also, as a Northern traveler possibly thought to be unfriendly to slavery, Olmsted was turned away from many of the well-to-do plantations in his travels, a fact that needs to be remembered when reading his work.

During the Civil War Olmsted became the general secretary of the U.S. Sanitary Commission, which monitored the hygiene needs of the federal army and the needs of both soldiers and displaced civilians, but his labors at the front and in the camps seriously affected his health. He was forced to resign in 1863. Olmsted was thereafter noted for his contributions to landscape **architecture**. His design for Central Park in New York City may be his finest work. **Related Entry**: Cotton.

SUGGESTED READING: Broadus Mitchell, *Frederick Law Olmsted, a Critic of the Old South* (1924; 1991); John E. Todd, *Frederick Law Olmsted* (1982).

OREGON TERRITORY: Although the Spanish had reported some of the incidental features of the Oregon coast in the seventeenth century, it was not until 1792 that Robert Gray, an American sea captain in search of Pacific sea otter furs, entered the Columbia River. In 1804 Meriwether Lewis and William Clark brought their exploratory party to the mouth of this same river, and in 1811 American fur traders established a post at nearby Fort Astoria. Nonetheless, by 1819 the American fur trading post had been sold to the Canadian North West Company, and by 1821 the British Hudson's Bay Company had established itself therein as a commercial outpost of the British Empire. Ultimately these assorted occupations led to a number of conflicting claims between the British and Americans to Oregon north to the 54°40' parallel.

American interest in Oregon initially grew slowly, and for a time the British and U.S. governments agreed to a joint occupation of the area. In 1834 Jason and Daniel Lee, Methodist missionaries, traveled to the Willamette Valley where they established a small pioneer community. Over the next decade American settlers began to quietly penetrate the region. In 1843, in anticipation of an influx of settlers from the United States, a provisional government was established by the American residents. They were bolstered by the arrival of more than 1,200 new settlers—the first wave in what was to become a great migration on the Oregon Trail. In 1846 the Oregon boundary was set at the 49th parallel by agreement between the British and the administration of President **James K. Polk**. Within two years the region had received its status as the Oregon Territory. Although the discovery of gold in California diverted some of the migration to the region, Oregon continued to attract settlers seeking fertile farmlands rather than sudden wealth. As the introduction of widespread **slavery** in the Northwest was impractical, Oregon acted as a counterpoint to the **extension of slavery** in other areas of the country. Although reduced in size by about half with the organization of Washington Territory in 1853, a free state of Oregon was admitted as the thirty-third state in 1859. **Related Entries**: Extension of Slavery into the Territories; Polk, James K.

SUGGESTED READING: Dorothy O. Johansen and Charles M. Gates, *Empire of the Columbia: A History of the Northwest* (1957; 1967); Francis Parkman, *The Oregon Trail* (1849; 1996).

OSTEND MANIFESTO: In 1852 the **Democratic Party** was successful in winning the presidency by running **Franklin Pierce** on a platform that advocated sectional harmony. His election showed that the nation was tired of never-ending **sectional disputes** and political bickering. He was the only candidate to be elected to the presidency between 1840 and 1864 to win a popular majority. Pierce's administration was marred in 1854 when a dispatch, the Ostend Manifesto, was sent by the American ministers to the courts of Great Britain, Spain, and France suggesting that an offer of $120 million be made to Spain to acquire the island of Cuba. Furthermore, the ministers declared that if Spain refused to sell, the island should be seized by force to prevent it from becoming "Africanized," like Haiti. There was a great deal of fear, especially among the slaveowners of the South, that the example of slaves revolting, killing their masters, and setting up their own government would spread to the slaves in the American South. The suggestions expressed in the Ostend Manifesto met with disapprobation in the United States and were strongly condemned by the public at large. **Related Entries**: Fear of Slave Revolts; Pierce, Franklin.

SUGGESTED READING: Roy F. Nichols, *Franklin Pierce, Young Hickory of the Granite Hills* (1958; 1993).

OVERSEERS (SLAVE DRIVERS): Southerners were generally ambivalent in their attitude toward Negroes, requiring considerable formality from them, but treating them either with disdain and cruelty, or paying them no mind at all. Slaveowners rarely dealt directly with their field hands and avoided punishing their bondsmen personally. This was left to the overseer who controlled and directed the labor of the slaves on the plantation, usually under the direction of the planter. Much of the physical abuse distributed to slaves came from these often coarse and uncultivated men. Overseers came and went on individual plantations, and some, considered to be too severe and brutish by their employers, were deemed little better than the slaves they managed. These white men were aided by slave drivers, who, although black slaves themselves, could apply the lash with pitiless regularity and were used to chase down fugitives. Some blacks, like the slave drivers, were devoted to the master and his family and alienated from the general slave community. They were viewed by other slaves with disgust, as it was feared that they might curry favor with the master at the expense of other slaves by betraying them. **Related Entries**: Punishment of Slaves; Race Relations.

SUGGESTED READING: John W. Blassingame, *Black New Orleans* (1973); Edward D.C. Campbell, Jr., with Kym S. Rice, *Before Freedom Came: African-American Life in the Antebellum South* (1991); Kenneth M. Stampp, *The Peculiar Institution* (1956).

PAINTERS: Portraiture abounded in the **antebellum South**, as it did in the North. Artists painted likenesses from head size to full length, but the head and bust size seems to have been the most favored. One of the most sought-after portraitists of the time was Thomas Sully who, after starting out in the South, moved to Philadelphia. Sully never lost his Southern patronage and was a mentor for a number of noteworthy Southern artists. Sully's style included rich, soft colors and a very effective use of light that greatly flattered his subjects. Southern painters influenced by him include Oliver Frazer, John Henry Bush, Alfred J. Miller, James Reid Lambdin, and Lewis M. Morgan. While each man had his own particular style, they all had the same fluidity, highlighting and, most of all, the proclivity to idealize as did their mentor. The myth of the **planter aristocracy** was reinforced and perpetuated in the works of these men.

One of the few known black American painters prior to the Civil War was A. Joshua Johnson. From 1796 to 1824 Baltimore directories list him as a portrait painter or limner. *Limner* is an archaic term used in relation to the illumination of manuscripts. By the nineteenth century, it was generally used to describe artists whose skill was more dependent on line than shadings of color. The fact that he worked for white patrons in **Maryland** and **Virginia** indicates an acceptance of this skilled craftsman in a slaveholding society. It also speaks well of the ability of a man who once described himself as self-taught.

The majority of portraits done during the prewar years were in this simple, linear, hard-edged style rather than in the romantic manner of Sully and his students. Many were done by itinerant painters like P. Henry Davenport and C. R. Parker, who traveled widely across the South. Many itinerants even did posthumous portraits. John Wood Dodge painted *Posthumous Likeness of Felix Grundy Eakins, Aged Three Years* and included such death imagery as wilted flowers and a broken toy with tools cast aside to symbolize the unfinished life. Many Americans of this period were more interested in acquiring copies of old masters' paintings than becoming patrons of American artists, so painters wishing to make a living had to comply with paying clients' requests.

Despite the picturesque scenery that abounded in the South and the popularity of bedecking walls with handsome landscapes, no major group of native artists of this genre emerged until after the Civil War. The works of John Gadsby Chapman, Henry Joseph Jackson, and S. Bernard captured the Southern landscape but never the attention of their Northern contemporaries. Just as American painters traveled to Europe to broaden their knowledge and to gain inspiration, European artists journeyed to America seeking similar adventure and stimulation. The **Mississippi River** proved to be rife with both. Many of the landscapes and scenes of the antebellum South are the product of non-natives. Detailed scenes of plantation life, such as *The Slave Market in Richmond, Virginia* and *Plantation Burial*, have come to us through the works of two English artists, Eyre Crowe and John Antrobus.

Perhaps one of the most celebrated works of a Southern painter was the historical piece *General Marion Inviting a British Officer to Dinner* by John Blake White. The exaltation of the Revolutionary War soldier's virtue and native heroism later earned this work a place on the ten dollar banknote issued by **South Carolina** during 1861. Marion also provided inspiration to another Southerner, William D. Washington, who aspired to use historic themes to advance the values of the nation.

Virginian David Hunter Strother was one of *Harper's* best known writer-illustrators of the antebellum period. He is particularly known for his scenes of country folk and the Southern mountains. William Henry Brown was one of the last great silhouette artists of the period. The Charlestonian snipped silhouettes of such distinguished personages as **Andrew Jackson, Henry Clay, John C. Calhoun**, and **Abraham Lincoln**. Brown did more comprehensive pieces that captured entire families, military and fire companies and their equipment, sporting scenes, marine views, and scenes portraying plantation life. **Related Entry**: Newspapers.

SUGGESTED READING: Jessie Poesch, *The Art of the Old South* (1983).

PANICS (ECONOMIC DEPRESSIONS): In both 1794 and 1819 deep economic depressions hit the nation. In response manufacturers in the industrialized Northeast called for high protective **tariffs** to shield their domestic markets from foreign competition. These would raise the price of almost everything that Southerners could not grow on their plantations or manufacture for themselves with their own inadequate factory system. The Panic of 1819, particularly, opened the eyes of many Southerners to the dangers inherent in losing control of the Senate. Whoever controlled that body could also regulate government policy on a wide range of critical issues including the national bank, tariffs, federal expenditures for highways and canals, and **slavery**.

A wheat failure in 1835 required that Americans import grain from abroad for the first time. The lack of confidence engendered by this unexpected circumstance caused European exporters to refuse credit to American importers and to demand hard money payments. American businessmen also began to demand gold and silver for merchandise. This placed a heavy burden on almost all the financial institutions in the country. Worse yet, the **Bank of the United States**, recently under attack as the evil creation of greedy Northerners, had been denied its recharter in 1836. The economic paralysis that followed resulted in the worst economic downturn of the antebellum period, the Panic of 1837.

There was no escape from the depression into which the nation passed. By 1839 the surplus in the Treasury, on which many states had counted to complete projects creating new **roads** and canals, had disappeared. Northern factory workers lost their jobs as manufacturers closed their businesses for lack of credit. Western farmers lost important markets in Europe as mills and factories—especially those in England dependent on Southern **cotton**— were unable to collect on American debts and went into bankruptcy. For half a decade thereafter the South suffered from the resulting crash in demand for cotton. Finally, many slaves found that they faced the auction block for the first time, and slave families faced permanent separation as even the most humane slaveowners were forced to sell slaves to raise cash.

Slowly the nation recovered, regaining much of its prosperity in the 1840s, and expanding in the 1850s under the influence of the giant gold strike in California. Although the country was to experience minor economic downturns in 1854 and 1858, the Panic of 1837 remained the worst economic disaster experienced by the nation until a similar panic hit in 1873. **Related Entries**: Plantation Economy; Value of Slaves.

SUGGESTED READING: Jonathan R.T. Hughes, *American Economic History* (1998).

PAPISM. *See* Catholics.

PARKER, JOSEPH P. (1827–1900): conductor on the **Underground Railroad**. The son of a black woman and a white man, Joseph P. Parker was born into **slavery** in Norfolk, **Virginia**. At eight years of age he was sold and marched in chains to Mobile, **Alabama**, where he was purchased by a kindly doctor. Befriended by the doctor's two boys, Joseph was taught to read. On a journey north, Quaker **abolitionists** attempted to free Joseph. When he related these events to the doctor, their travel plans were changed, and they returned home. The doctor explained to Joseph that he was not suited as a house man and posed two options, field work or apprenticeship. Knowing the latter to be the better choice, the doctor arranged for Joseph to be apprenticed to a plasterer. Unfortunately, the man was a brutal drunkard, and following a series of unpleasant events, Joseph ran away to **New Orleans**. Upon his capture and return, Joseph convinced a widow to buy him from the man, promising he would pay her back by working in a local foundry. In 1845 Parker became a free man.

Parker married and settled in Ripley, Ohio, a flourishing abolitionist community, and became involved in rescuing fugitive slaves. For fifteen years he worked as an iron molder by day and led slaves to freedom across the Ohio River by night. Parker's fearlessness girded him as he smuggled a few hundred slaves into the service of the Union Army.

Parker also distinguished himself as a businessman. He purchased a foundry, machine shop, and blacksmith shop as well as a coal yard. Parker also patented a number of **inventions**. Toward the end of the century, Parker experienced a number of business setbacks but survived. It is likely that these misfortunes led him to forbid his children to carry on with the family business following his death. Fulfilling their father's wish, all five of his progeny graduated from college and became respected community members. **Related Entry**: Underground Railroad.

SUGGESTED READING: Stuart Seely Sprauge, ed., *His Promised Land: The Autobiography of Joseph P. Parker, Former Slave and Conductor on the Underground Railroad* (1996).

PETIGRU, JAMES L. (1789–1863): politician, Southern Unionist, and opponent of **nullification**. A thorough nationalist and an intense opponent of nullification, James L. Petigru was the leader of the Unionist Party in **South Carolina** during the **Nullification Convention of 1832**. In several addresses to the people of South Carolina, Petigru claimed that he could find no justification in law, logic, or morality for nullification. He naturally opposed the Test Oath required of state officials by the convention, and he led a successful campaign in the courts to have the oath declared unconstitutional. During the 1832 crisis he cooperated with **James A. Hamilton** in suppressing violence by using compromise.

Petigru's position in the nullification controversy proved detrimental to his political career, and he held no important political post prior to the Civil War. In this period he opposed **secession** with the greatest vigor but could not stop the movement. He referred to the Secession Convention of 1860 as "a lunatic asylum," and he denounced the delegates who passed the Secession Ordinance as "one hundred and sixty-four maniacs [who] have this day set a blazing torch to the temple of constitutional liberty" (*Harper's*, December 1860). While his heart was with the South, Petigru opposed the **Confederate government** at every turn. Nonetheless, he was no **abolition-**

ist, owning slaves himself and approving of domestic **slavery** as an institution. He maintained his position as a Southern Unionist throughout the war even though his nationalism doomed his political career.

Petigru retained the respect, if not the support, of his opponents. An admirer justly called him the greatest private citizen that South Carolina had ever produced. His reputation was known and admired all over the country, and **Abraham Lincoln** seriously considered nominating him to the **Supreme Court**. Only his advanced age kept Petigru from receiving the nomination. **Related Entries**: Force Bill; Nullification; Nullification Convention of 1832.

SUGGESTED READING: J.P. Carson, *The Life, Letters, and Speeches of James Louis Petigru* (1920); William H. Pease and Jane H. Pease, *James Louis Petigru: Southern Conservative, Southern Dissenter* (1995).

PHOTOGRAPHY: The nineteenth century produced, for the first time, widespread photographic documentation that was representative of the people. Louis Daguerre invented the daguerreotype in 1839. This was the first clear and long-lasting form of the photograph, a one-of-a-kind image deposited on thin metal plates without a negative. An immediate technical innovation was the use of cameras with several lenses, creating as many images in a single exposure. With the development of the ability to print photographs on albumen paper from a single glass plate negative, multiple prints became popular. Photographic portraits were affordable even to those of middle income. Prints were distributed to friends and family. Mounted on heavy card stock and known as *cartes de visite*, they became very popular, and large collections of them were made. Fortunately, they have survived in great numbers and provide tremendous insight into the **fashion** of the period.

Great care must be taken in drawing overly broad conclusions from these period photographs, however. With the exception of costly "views" of places like Paris or London, most were studio portraits, and as such do not provide the informal insight of the twentieth-century candid snapshot, showing a variety of attire or common settings. The wet plate process used in taking these photographs was very slow, precluding any action shots, and catching accidental motion as blurs or ghostlike images. The subjects of photographic portraits had to stay perfectly still to prevent blurring. Only original prints were available, and enlargement equipment was as yet in a formative stage of development. Prints were almost always made by placing the glass plate negative in contact with the photosensitive paper and exposing it to the sun. This resulted in a "contact print" the same size as the glass plate negative.

Mathew Brady is possibly the best known photographer of the period, and people flocked to his studios to have photographic portraits taken in their best clothes. Southern photographers were also able practitioners of their art, but their work was generally limited to portraiture. The technology of reproducing photographs for the print media was almost nonexistent, requiring that an artist redraw the image and make a woodcut or engraving. This process neutralized most of the advantages of photography for the **newspapers**, and the public was forced to be content with rough woodcuts and engravings of rural landscapes, public gatherings, and momentous events. **Related Entry**: Fashion.

SUGGESTED READING: Beaumont Newhall, *The Daguerreotype in America* (1968); Floyd Rinehart, *The American Daguerreotype* (1981); Dorothy Denneen Volo and James M. Volo, *Daily Life in Civil War America* (1998).

PICKENS, FRANCIS W. (1805–1869): congressman and Southern apologist. While still in college Francis W. Pickens began writing letters to the **Charleston** *Mercury* and the Edgefield *Carolinian* supporting the doctrines of **states' rights** and **nullification**. At the tender age of twenty-five, Pickens was elected to the state legislature of **South Carolina** largely because he was so dedicated to these principles. Here he gained a reputation as a man of both words and actions. Not only did he castigate the **Force Bill**, but he also raised more than two thousand armed volunteers to defend the state should federal forces be dispatched to put down the **Nullification Convention of 1832**.

In 1834 Pickens succeeded firebrand **George McDuffie** in the U.S. Congress and served there for almost a decade. His speeches on foreign affairs and treasury reform were surpassed only by his defense of states' rights and **slavery**. Returning to the state senate in 1844, he blasted the **abolitionists** as overzealous meddlers, anarchists, and worse; and he quickly became a leader of the growing **secession** movement. In the 1850s, feeling the overwhelming pressure of a growing Northern majority, he declared for immediate Southern secession. As this movement failed to bring about immediate disunion, he quite unexpectedly became more politically conservative.

In 1856 he helped to elect **James Buchanan** to the presidency but was defeated in the race for his own Senate seat. Buchanan salved Pickens' wounds with a diplomatic position in Russia, but he quickly returned to South Carolina when imminent disunion appeared on the horizon. In 1860 conservatives in the state legislature engineered his election as governor. As such, on January 9, 1860, he was responsible for the firing of the first shots of the Civil War on the ship *Star of the West*, which had been sent to the relief of Fort Sumter—a rash action on his part. Pickens played no active part in firing on Fort Sumter. At the end of his term in 1862, Pickens retired from public life at age fifty-seven, reappearing only once, in 1865, to urge his state to cooperate with President Andrew Johnson's reconstruction plans. He died, deeply in debt, in 1869, but his Edgewood estate survived to become a center of lavish Southern hospitality in the second half of the century. **Related Entry**: Secession.

SUGGESTED READING: John B. Edmunds, *Francis W. Pickens and the Politics of Destruction* (1977; 1986).

PIEDMONT. *See* Geography.

PIERCE, FRANKLIN (1804–1869): lawyer, congressman, senator, and fourteenth President of the United States (1853–1857). As a youth Franklin Pierce was particularly fond of military matters, and as an adult he was a strong nationalist. Beginning in 1833, he was elected to the House of Representatives and to two terms in the Senate by the state of New Hampshire. In the Senate he made only a few speeches and was a loyal Jacksonian **Democrat** who followed the party line with little resistance. Although from New England, he consistently respected Southern rights and voiced an ardent dislike for **abolitionists**, whom he considered a danger to the Union. In 1842 he resumed his legal career, but he kept a firm hand on local Democratic campaigns, enforcing strict party discipline.

In 1846 President **James K. Polk** invited Pierce to join the cabinet as attorney general, but he declined the appointment to serve in the **Mexican War**. By 1847 Pierce had been made a brigadier general, but illness prevented him from participating in any actual conflict. As soon as the war was over, Pierce resigned his commission and returned to local politics. In 1850 he took the lead in defending the great compromise to his Northern constituents, and he firmly corrected at least one party member for speaking out against the **Fugitive Slave Law**. This attitude did not endear him to Northern abolitionists.

In 1852 Pierce's supporters and friends advanced his name as a potential presidential candidate. Pierce seems to have had some reservations about the prospect. Nonetheless, after many abortive attempts to find a candidate acceptable to both the Northern and Southern wings of the Democratic Party, both finally agreed on Pierce.

Pierce took a strict view of constitutional construction and ran on a party platform that promised nothing to the voters except to abide by the **Compromise of 1850**. He made no speeches and few public appearances, seemingly putting very little effort into his own election bid. But his opponents ran equally lackluster campaigns, and Pierce carried all but four states, although with a very small popular majority. On his way to the inaugural he was in a severe railway accident in which he saw his eleven-year-old son killed. The event completely unnerved both Pierce and his wife, and he began his term in office in a state of nervous exhaustion.

Unfortunately, the Democratic Party was rife with sectional factionalism at this time. Although the policies of his administration were generally orthodox, his attempt to include both anti-slavery Democrats and Free Soilers in his cabinet convinced Southerners in the Senate that he might revive the **slavery** issue. The anti-slavery forces nevertheless attacked him as being in a conspiracy with the slaveowners. In the 1852 campaign they had published *The Abolitionist Attack! Abolitionists Against General Pierce*, a scathing attack on Pierce's lackluster anti-slavery record. His support of the **Kansas-Nebraska Act of 1854** ultimately destroyed any credibility he may have had in the North. The act seemingly sabotaged the political compromises that had characterized the previous decades of American politics. Its passage ultimately caused a split in the party that Pierce was not able to repair.

During the second half of his single term as President, Congress paid no heed to Pierce's recommendations. Nonetheless, he was determined to fairly apply the concept of **popular sovereignty** to the Kansas and Nebraska territories. He therefore appointed an anti-slavery governor in Nebraska and a pro-slavery man in Kansas. Unwittingly Pierce had sprung a trap on himself, and he would be forced to oversee the events in **"Bleeding Kansas"** and along the **Missouri** border during the remainder of his presidency. Ultimately he sent troops to the territories to maintain comparative peace.

Replaced by **James Buchanan** in the 1856 election, Pierce retired from the responsibilities of office. In 1860 he reproached the **Republicans** for their destruction of personal and property rights, seemingly failing to recognize the depth and sincerity of anti-South feeling in the North. Pierce was a failure as a national political leader, and he died in social and political obscurity. **Related Entries**: Bleeding Kansas; Compromise of 1850; Kansas-Nebraska Act of 1854.

SUGGESTED READING: Roy F. Nichols, *Franklin Pierce, Young Hickory of the Granite Hills* (1958; 1993).

PINCKNEY, HENRY L. (1794–1863): editor, congressman, and politician. As the editor of the **Charleston** *Mercury* and as a state and national politician, Henry L. Pinckney was a proponent of **states' rights** and a defender of **nullification**. In 1816 he secured a seat in the **South Carolina** legislature, where he served as the chairman of the Ways and Means Committee and as Speaker. During the height of the nullification crisis, the *Mercury* probably had the largest circulation of any **newspaper** in the state; and, as proprietor and editor, Pinckney had a good deal of influence and power. When he sold the paper to **Robert B. Rhett** in 1832, it was one of the most uncompromising champions of states' rights in the South, having just completed a successful agitation in opposition to the **tariffs** of 1828 and 1832.

After serving as intendant of Charleston, Pinckney was elected to two successive terms in the U.S. Congress (1833–1837). Throughout his first term he was in complete accord with **John C. Calhoun**'s states' rights faction, and defended nullification at every opportunity. Nonetheless, early in the next Congress he broke with the Calhounites by securing the passage of a resolution, called the **gag rule** by its Northern opponents, which tabled all petitions for the **abolition** of **slavery** without discussion. Calhoun's forces wished instead for the opportunity to defeat each of these proposals in detail. Pinckney was unjustly denounced as a traitor to the South, and the suggestion was made that he had sold out to the Unionists for a highly influential position in the federal navy yard. Largely on this account, Pinckney lost much of his former influence on the national scene. Reelected as intendant, he accomplished much in the way of civic improvements in Charleston from 1837 to 1839, the most notable being the conversion of the College of Charleston into the first municipal college in the United States. Thereafter, he filled only undistinguished public offices until the end of his life in 1863. **Related Entries**: Gag Rule; Newspapers; Nullification.

SUGGESTED READING: W. L. King, *The Newspaper Press of Charleston, S.C.* (1872; 1978); Carl R. Osthaus, *Partisans of the Southern Press: Editorial Spokesmen of the Nineteenth Century* (1994).

PLANTATION ECONOMY: Although slaves could be found in almost every state of the Union before the middle of the nineteenth century, the plantation **slavery** so vigorously detested by **abolitionists** was found almost solely within areas with the ability to support widescale, extensive agricultural operations that produced cash crops. Such operations required land that would support crops of rice, **sugar**, or **cotton**. Rice and sugar production required semitropical environments, which were all but nonexistent in the territories, and sugar production required substantial amounts of investment capital for machinery. It was cotton, therefore, that saved the plantation system and breathed new life into slavery.

By mid-century cotton accounted for two-thirds of the exports of the country and created an unprecedented demand for agricultural laborers. Seventy-five percent of the world's supply of cotton fiber came from the American South. Profits from cotton provided a financial bulwark for slavery, yet the limited capital available to Southerners also made them dependent on the good will and good credit of cotton buyers and brokers. The archaic plantation system, periodically suffering from cash starvation, would have faded into obscurity were it not for the ability of slavery to provide the labor needed to produce these crops.

Slavery's existence in a region was largely based, therefore, on the ability of the environment to support cotton plantations. Cotton was grown in all the states that were to become the Confederacy. The generally mountainous areas of western **Virginia** and eastern **Tennessee** had proved indifferent lands for cotton production, and in these areas slavery was almost unknown. In **Texas** the only areas characterized by a plantation economy were in East Texas, where the climate and environment was much more like that of **Louisiana** and **Arkansas** than of the American deserts. Similarly, the vast arid territorial expanses west of the 98th meridian could not have supported an extension of slavery. Moreover, the climate and topography of Oregon and much of California were thought at the time to be unsuited to the health and longevity of blacks and unsuitable for the crops that supported the Southern way of life. One of the greatest tactical errors made by the South in its disputes over slavery was in allowing the abolitionists to define the argument in terms of its expansion into areas that would probably have proved unsuitable to the plantation system in any case. **Related Entries**: Cotton; Sectional Disputes; Slavery—Task Labor.

SUGGESTED READING: Joyce E. Chaplin, *An Anxious Pursuit: Agricultural Innovation and Modernity in the Lower South, 1730–1815* (1993); James L. Michie, *Richmond Hill Plantation, 1810–1868: The Discovery of Antebellum Life on a Waccamaw Rice Plantation* (1989); John S. Otto, *The Southern Frontier, 1607–1860: The Agricultural Evolution of the Colonial and Antebellum South* (1989).

PLANTATION MISTRESS: Contrary to popular image, the daily life of the plantation mistress was one of seemingly endless work and worry. Just like her Northern counterpart or her less affluent neighbors, she was charged with managing the entire household. This meant that she was accountable for the **food**, clothing, and medical needs of family and servants alike. It was not unusual for the matron of the household to rise shortly after dawn and commence her extensive duties by overseeing the preparation of breakfast. As the keeper of all the keys of the household, she would then spend some time carefully tending to the storeroom. The remainder of her day was spent in such seasonally appropriate activities as gardening, preserving fruits and vegetables, processing pork and other meats, tending the dairy operation, and making such household essentials as candles, soap, and other seasonal necessities. Even when entertaining, the mistress could not join her guests after dinner until all the silver was secured and the slaves fed.

The plantation mistress managed the household budget, dealt with merchants to acquire products the plantation could not produce, and supervised the stock kept for food as well as attending to her duties as mother and wife.

While it might seem that having a number of household servants at her disposal would lessen the mistress' workload, caring for these slaves presented additional strain. A Philadelphia woman who became a plantation mistress upon her marriage remarked that the large number of servants in the house created "great confusion." The mistress of the plantation was responsible for distributing the foodstuffs to slaves, including field hands. She had to prepare medicines for any slaves who fell ill. This was a fiscal as well as a humanitarian concern. The mistress was also responsible for the overwhelming task of overseeing the semiannual clothing distribution to the entire plantation population. Additionally, some mistresses doubted the competency of slaves to perform certain tasks such as candle making and would often assume responsibility for these undertakings themselves, using the slaves only in a supplementary manner.

While the mistress did not engage in mundane daily routines such as laundering, dishwashing, sweeping, and so forth, she did coordinate and oversee spring cleaning and the routine care of more prized possessions.

What time there was for pleasure was often spent in horseback riding, visiting, **reading**, corresponding, and playing music.

The mistress or matron of the plantation was commonly the wife of the planter, but in some cases was his unmarried or widowed sister. More than one male diarist complained that young women of the South were not prepared to assume the many and varied duties that they would face as household mistress. Female academies emphasized intellectual and artistic endeavors. What sewing instruction young women received was likely to be in ornamental work rather than of practical application. It was not unusual, therefore, for the female relatives of a young plantation mistress to visit at various times to assist with such annual events as hog butchering or "scalding" to prevent bedbugs. **Related Entries**: Slave Clothing; Slave Religion; Southern Hospitality.

SUGGESTED READING: Catherine Clinton, *The Plantation Mistress* (1982); Elizabeth Fox-Genovese, *Within the Plantation Household: Black and White Women of the Old South* (1988); Anne Sinker Whaley LeClercq, *An Antebellum Plantation Household* (1996).

PLANTATIONS: For the day-to-day operations of the plantation, *see* Cotton Gin; Overseers; Plantation Economy; Plantation Mistress; Sea Islands Plantations; Slavery; Slaves—Gang Labor; Slaves—Hired Out; Slaves—Task Labor.

PLANTER ARISTOCRACY: Wealthy antebellum planters saw themselves and their class as the natural leaders of their communities and as a social elite whose wants were rightly supplied by the labor of the rest of society. Historically, the South had been neither democratic nor purely aristocratic. Instead, Southern politics had reached a balance much closer to the classical Roman concept of the republic, a public order in which the power rested with an elite group of people who ruled for the good of all. The planters saw the institution of **slavery** as a tool that had elevated the character of the slaveowners, making them independent, generous, affectionate, brave, and eloquent. Slaves and servants not only made their master's wealth evident, but they helped to sustain it with their labor.

Few in the Southern planter class actually had aristocratic roots. For the gentry, the need to maintain a large body of servants was greatly intensified by the lack of blood ties to some form of royalty. **Abolitionists**, by their constant attacks on slavery, indirectly threatened the Southern social structure and the hierarchy that helped the planters to define themselves in historically acceptable terms.

The planters invented a social mythology in which the blood of their class was deemed noble or at least tinted blue. Most upper-class Southerners incorrectly traced their ancestry to the royalty of Europe—a royalty that still ruled due to its blood ties to past kings. Planters with an English heritage might claim descent from the Cavaliers of the English Civil Wars of the 1640s. No mere followers of the Stuart kings, planter ancestry might be derived from dukes, earls, knights, and loyal squires who had ridden at Naseby. Those with Scotch-Irish blood, who could not trace themselves back to the Bruce or Brian Boru, easily found ancestors among the Celtic chieftains of their clan. There were enough Southern families that had legitimate family trees of this sort—the Lees, the Fairfaxes and the Randolphs, for instance—to maintain the "truth" of the fiction.

Although half of the white population of the South had come to the colonies as indentured servants, generations of close and sometimes carefully planned intermarriage spread the royal connections so thin that all families of position and power in the South could claim rule by some form of "divine right." Marriage into an influential family was also a distinct advantage in politics. **Thomas Jefferson**'s father had substantially improved his social standing by marrying a daughter of the well-placed Randolph family, and **John Marshall**'s marriage into the powerful Ambler family brought him influential connections and led to a seat on the **Supreme Court**. Whether through birth, marriage, or myth, support of the Southern gentry was indispensable for the man who would rise in politics.

The upshot of all this ancestral mythology was that the planters themselves came to believe it. They behaved in a haughty manner reminiscent of the old nobility of Europe; taught their sons an aristocratic code of social behavior; married their daughters as if sealing treaties between feudal estates; and demanded positions of authority and command in their communities. "Civilization would cease but for the universal desire of white men to become aristocrats," wrote **George Fitzhugh** in *Cannibals All, or Slaves Without Masters* (1857). Strangely, this proved a self-fulfilling delusion, as the planter aristocracy generally responded to the deference of the white underclasses and to the submission of their black slaves with benevolence and chivalric obligation. The Southern elite voluntarily assumed the role of benefactor and knight errant to all other levels of their society. Like knights on a quest, Southern men felt obliged to counsel and defend, not only their own families, but all females and minor children placed under their protection. This obligation was extended to their slaves in an ambiguous, but serious, way. Many planters were genuinely concerned for the physical and moral welfare of their slaves, but only in terms of continued racial separation and subjugation.

The planter class thought of themselves as well mannered, religious, and protective of all that was still fundamentally good in America. They lionized the stratified but benevolent social order portrayed in the nineteenth-century romance novel, and always strove to maintain a romanticized version of the old aristocratic order as it was before the American Revolution. At all levels of Southern society individual liberty, manliness, and respect for authority and position were held in such high esteem that one put his life and personal honor on the line to protect them—a fact attested to by the continued prevalence of **dueling**.

As the decades wore on toward the war, the Northern opposition to slavery came to criticize the aristocratic pretensions of the South, and Southerners found some necessity to explain themselves. George Fitzhugh recorded a defense of the Southern way of life that was used over and over during the antebellum years. "Pride of pedigree . . . ancestral position . . . [and] respectable connexion . . . will, ere long, cease to be under the ban of public opinion. Every man in America desires to be an aristocrat, for every man desires wealth, and wealth confers power and distinction, and makes its owner an unmistakable aristocrat. What vile hypocrisy, what malicious envy and jealousy, to censure and vilify in others, that which every man of us is trying with might and main to attain. . . . [the] desire to found a family and make aristocrats of their posterity" (*Cannibals All, or Slaves Without Masters*, 1857).

The planter aristocracy successfully dominated Southern society for almost two centuries by applying their wealth and political influence to the wheels of government. Their numbers were so small that no more than 50,000 persons—men, women, and children—in a population of several million qualified as part of this class. As long as the planters could support themselves with the products of their own plantations, they were relatively insulated from economic depression and spiraling consumer prices. This economic security, once the hallmark of the great plantations, which stood like isolated agricultural city-states across the South, gradually became less certain as the war approached. **Related Entries**: Fitzhugh, George; Kinship.

SUGGESTED READING: James L. Michie, *Richmond Hill Plantation, 1810–1868: The Discovery of Antebellum Life on a Waccamaw Rice Plantation* (1989); James Oakes, *The Ruling Race: A History of American Slaveholders* (1982); Anne C. Rose, *Victorian America and the Civil War* (1992).

POE, EDGAR ALLAN (1809–1849): author and editor. Orphaned in Boston at age three, Edgar Allan Poe was adopted by a **Richmond** merchant, John Allan, and educated in private schools in **Virginia**. Although he made several moves back and forth over the **Mason-Dixon Line**, Poe always thought of himself as a Southerner.

Poe was the most renowned poet and short story writer from the South and the only Southern antebellum writer to make a lasting national impression. What made Poe different from his regional contemporaries was that he was not a Southern apologist. Politically Poe was a Southern **Whig**, but he rarely let his politics interfere with his writing.

Today, Poe is best known for his poetry and short stories. In his own time, however, his criticism attracted a great deal of attention. Poe was committed to raising American literary standards by introducing an objective method of reviewing books rather than employing solely a moral one. He employed rhetorical methods to evaluate the language and meter of poetry and demanded tight plots, functional details, and limited length in other works. The *Southern Literary Messenger*, the only periodical from the South to attract significant Northern subscriptions and contributors, flourished during Poe's tenure as editor.

Poe's personal life was filled with great frustration and sorrow. He had little patience with editors who were intimidated by his aggressive journalistic style and refused to work with those who did not share his vision. Financially, this translated into only four years of regular income out of an eighteen-year career. Poe found that some of his inferior work commanded greater fees than what he considered to be his best work, a frustrating fact of life for any writer. Poe's lapses from sobriety caused additional problems throughout his career. When his young wife, Virginia Clemm Poe, died, Poe was devastated and had to be nursed back from total collapse by friends. He longed to publish his own magazine, but his *Broadway Journal* lasted only two months. In fact, Poe was on his way north to pursue backing for another magazine when he fell ill and died in Baltimore. **Related Entry**: Literary Development.

SUGGESTED READING: Wolf Mankowitz, *The Extraordinary Mr. Poe: A Biography of Edgar Allan Poe* (1978); Kenneth Silverman, *Edgar A. Poe: Mournful and Never Ending Remembrance* (1991); George Edward Woodberry, *Edgar Allan Poe* (1980).

POINSETT, JOEL R. (1779–1851): diplomat, politician, and Southern Unionist. Although best known to Americans today for the poinsettia, the winter holiday plant named after him, Joel R. Poinsett was an important player in both the national history of the United States and the **nullification** crisis of 1832. After years as the minister to Mexico (where he cataloged the poinsettia), Poinsett returned to his native **South Carolina** to become a leader of the conservative Unionist Party that opposed the **Nullification Convention of 1832**, the Nullification Ordinance, and the Test Oath. His opposition during this period has been described as ambivalent; however this may be due to the natural sluggishness seen in most conservatives when they are compared to the intense, dynamic personalities of a group of self-inspired radicals.

There is no doubt that Poinsett helped to coordinate the Unionists' marches through **Charleston** that characterized the weeks before the election of the legislature that would assemble the Nullification Convention. More than 800 Unionists with white armbands and clubs marched through the streets, and it was only through the offices of other leaders such as Unionist **James L. Petigru** and nullifier **James A. Hamilton** that violence was avoided.

Poinsett worked hard to recruit these volunteers, and helped to set up "Washington Societies" to counteract the success of Hamilton's **South Carolina Association**, which was recruiting followers to the cause of nullification. Moreover, it was Poinsett's volunteers to whom President **Andrew Jackson** looked to provide a group of armed South Carolinians friendly to the federal cause and willing to enforce federal law as a *posse comitatus*. To this end Jackson sent 5,000 muskets to Poinsett so that "the Union [might] be preserved and traitors punished" (Freehling, 1965). Notwithstanding this support, Poinsett was reluctant to see any form of federal intervention—even by his own hand—and begged Jackson "to do nothing to irritate" the nullifiers or the convention and thereby bolster a movement toward secession. **Related Entry**: Nullification.

SUGGESTED READING: J. Fred Rippy, *Joel R. Poinsett, Versatile American* (1935); William W. Freehling, *Prelude to Civil War: The Nullification Controversy in South Carolina, 1816–1836* (1965); David F. Houston, *A Critical Study of Nullification in South Carolina* (1896; 1990).

POLK, JAMES K. (1795–1849): congressman and eleventh President of the United States (1845–1849). Although born and educated in **North Carolina**, James Knox Polk was most closely associated with **Tennessee** during his life. Polk had a keen interest in politics, and after his graduation from the University of North Carolina he returned to Tennessee to practice law and serve in the state legislature.

Polk entered Congress in 1825 as a loyal Jacksonian **Democrat**. He was fiercely opposed to the policies of **John Quincy Adams**, and became a bitter political enemy of **John C. Calhoun**. He took a leading role in defending **Andrew Jackson** and his policies in Congress, and was charged with being the "abject slave" of the President by his detractors. Polk was made the head of the Ways and Means Committee in 1832, where he did all within his power to help Jackson kill the national bank. In 1834 Polk ran for Speaker of the House against fellow Tennessean **John Bell**. Bell won the position by soliciting anti-administration votes, and Polk was widely considered a martyr who had suffered because of his loyalty to the President. In the next Congress he defeated Bell but was the object of more heckling and abuse as Speaker than had ever before been witnessed.

In 1839 Polk served an uneventful tenure as the governor of Tennessee.

In 1840 the **Whigs** gained the White House in the person of **William Henry Harrison**, but lost control when a maverick Vice President, **John Tyler**, became President on Harrison's death. The Democrats, sensing weakness, began to lay plans for regaining the Executive Mansion. Because former President **Martin Van Buren**, the leading candidate for the 1844 nomination, had committed political suicide in opposing the **annexation of Texas**, Polk's name was brought forward as a dark horse candidate. He proved an adept politician and ran on a platform that stressed the need to admit both **Texas** and the **Oregon Territory** to the Union simultaneously. His opponent, **Henry Clay**, opposed annexation, and this cost the Whigs the election. Although Polk had won election by a slim margin, Tyler declared the result a popular mandate for the acquisition of Texas and rushed a resolution to this effect through both houses of Congress in February 1845, admitting Texas even before Polk had taken office.

Mexico, predictably, considered the annexation of Texas an act of war. Polk aggressively sent General **Zachary Taylor** with 2,000 troops to the Rio Grande to enforce the new boundary of the United States. In April 1846, a party of American dragoons pressing forward into the disputed territory was ambushed, and several were killed or wounded. Polk, anticipating this result, introduced a previously drafted message to Congress asking for a declaration of war as soon as he heard of the attack.

America was swept by martial euphoria, and its forces were successful in the **Mexican War** that followed in gaining a great deal of new territory for the United States. Polk was totally dedicated to the concept of **manifest destiny**. It was his total dedication to the annexation of Texas that had spurred its acquisition. Although he had run on a slogan of "Fifty-four Forty or Fight" with respect to the specific boundary of Oregon, Polk had settled the Oregon boundary dispute with British Canada at the 49th parallel. Therefore, in just four years, Polk's expansionist policies added the entire Southwest, much of the Oregon Territory, and California to the nation, filling out most of the familiar outline of the modern United States. Seldom in American history had so sweeping a program of expansion been attempted.

Nonetheless, with every stroke of good fortune, the nation was rocked by additional controversies over the **extension of slavery into the territories**. By siding with neither faction in the **slavery** issue, and by being exposed to opposition from extremists on both sides, Polk failed to gain a second term. In 1849, only a few months after his retirement as President, Polk's frail health failed, causing his death at age fifty-six. **Related Entries**: Mexican War of 1846; Texas, Annexation of.

SUGGESTED READING: E. I. McCormac, *James K. Polk: A Political Biography* (1922; 1995); Charles Allan McCoy, *Polk and the Presidency* (1960); Charles Grier Sellers, *James K. Polk, Jacksonian* (1957).

POOR WHITES: It is important to differentiate the small farmers who occupied most of the South from those people known as "poor whites" and "poor white trash" in the antebellum period. Poor whites were the economic failures who dwelt in the rural slums of the South, or on the thin, unforgiving soils of the Cumberland Plateau and the sandy barrens of the coastal plains. Some estimates put their number at 1 million individuals. Living in ramshackle huts lacking floors, furniture, and cultural appointments, poor whites were looked down on by all segments of Southern society, even by slaves, as slothful and listless persons basking in the sun of racial superiority and producing little other than future generations which would continue to live in abject poverty. Fiercely defensive of their status as free white men, they detested any type of labor that might "make them look like slaves."

Ironically, poor whites could work, but largely because of the scarcity of jobs (slaves did most of the labor in the South), farm wages were so low for white workers that it was not worth their while to take employment. When Daniel Pratt, a Northerner, offered good-paying jobs to poor white laborers in a **cotton** mill in **Montgomery, Alabama**, and when William Gregg offered similar employment in **South Carolina**, poor whites rose to the occasion. Many of them realized their potential in the pine forests of Alabama in the growing turpentine industry. Nonetheless, many slaveowners found it undesirable to have poor whites living on the fringes of plantations where the slaves might be "impaired" by contact with them.

Poor whites identified closely with the political and racial principles that led to the Civil War. They quickly recognized that their support was needed for **secession** and that their physical assistance would be required on the battlefield. They sought to trade their assistance to the **Confederate government** for social reforms that had been denied to them in former years. They responded to the flattery of army recruiters by turning out in large numbers, wore their Confederate uniforms proudly, and gave a good account of themselves on the battlefield. Nonetheless, these "crackers," "clay eaters," "rednecks," "wool hats," and "sand hillers" proved to be generally boisterous and fiercely independent soldiers who ignored military discipline and shunned pretentious officers. **Related Entries**: Planter Aristocracy; Race Relations.

SUGGESTED READING: Charles C. Bolton, *Poor Whites of the Antebellum South* (1994); Paul Buck, "The Poor Whites in the Antebellum South," *American Historical Review* 31 (1925); Susan Jean Tracey, *In the Master's Eye: Representations of Women, Blacks, and Poor Whites in Antebellum Southern Literature* (1996).

POPULAR SOVEREIGNTY: Popular sovereignty was a political doctrine—largely the brainchild of Lewis Cass of Michigan, but more closely associated with **Stephen A. Douglas** and the **Kansas-Nebraska Act of**

1854. Its major tenet was that settlers could decide for themselves whether their territory would come into the Union as a **free state** or **slave state**. A similar plan had been added to the **Democratic Party**'s election platform in 1848. Popular sovereignty effectively repealed the **Missouri Compromise of 1820**, which had prevented disunion for more than three decades. Douglas defended his proposition as a natural outgrowth of the compromise measures of 1850, which had allowed the territories of New Mexico and Utah to choose to organize with or without **slavery**.

Many in the South initially supported Douglas, but in the light of future events, popular sovereignty damaged his political career and was a major cause of the disintegration of the old political parties—both **Whigs** and Democrats. The doctrine had little practical long-term value as there remained few regions into which plantation slavery could be introduced economically. Nonetheless, in the hands of radicals from both sides of the slavery issue, the doctrine proved detrimental to the pursuit of national peace and unity. These radicals came into conflict over control of the Kansas Territory. Very quickly **"Bleeding Kansas"** came to characterize the bloodshed, murder, and terror associated with the continued expansion of slavery. **Related Entries**: Bleeding Kansas; Douglas, Stephen A.; Kansas-Nebraska Act of 1854.

SUGGESTED READING: Robert Walter Johannsen, *Stephen A. Douglas* (1997); Daniel Lessard Levin, *Representing Popular Sovereignty: The Constitution in American Political Culture* (1999).

PORK. *See* Bacon and Pork.

PRESIDENCY, U.S. *See* Executive Branch.

PROSTITUTION: The openness of prostitution in the nineteenth century scandalized the social and religious elite everywhere. Proper Southern ladies universally frowned upon any man who was too open in his lustfulness, but they could do little to enforce their displeasure on the male population at large. Upper-class unmarried men involved in relationships with prostitutes, black or white, seem to have received a special dispensation from Southern society.

The manifestation in which prostitution appeared in Southern cities was somewhat dictated by the class and means of the clientele. Some men of wealth seemingly relied on the common practice of supplying themselves with a quadroon mistress for short-term affairs. Others, too far displaced from cities to conveniently satisfy their lustful desires with a professional harlot, simply considered every slave cabin a bordello. Comely slave girls brought exaggerated prices on the auction block, with mixed-race, "light-skinned girls" bringing a premium.

The nightly trade in amorous economics was available in most large towns and cities. Most prostitutes were poor white women who worked their clientele in cheap saloons, hotels, or dance-houses. These women were of the lowest class, commonly having taken up prostitution in their teens. They moved in and out of the dance-houses and bordellos, and could be brought in from the street for as little as a dollar. They were described as "degraded beings [and] habitual drunkards" who were "remarkable for bestial habits and ferocious manners" (Asbury, 1938).

Although ordinances were passed that prohibited the renting of rooms to prostitutes, bordello owners were often protected by local politicians or the police. A madam might run a bordello in **New Orleans** by obtaining an annual license at a small cost. The law prohibited soliciting on the streets or from the doors and windows of the bordello. Indictments for prostitution, charging the keeping of a "disorderly house," usually targeted madams who engaged in interracial social activity. Within these bounds, the authorities made little attempt to halt the expansion of the trade into the residential areas of the city, forcing the more virtuous residents to abandon their homes in pure frustration.

So-called high-class places were operated with considerably more circumspection. These bordellos were housed in brick or brownstone buildings filled with mahogany woodwork, brass fixtures, and marble fireplaces—and furnished with fine carpets, pianos, furniture, art, and statuary—making them some of the most pretentious and luxurious residences in the country. Only the finest wines and champagnes were served; the ladies wore evening gowns while being entertained by musicians, dancers, and singers in the public rooms; and they changed to the finest lingerie in their boudoirs. As many as thirty women might work in a single house, each paying a fee to the madam, and receiving between five and twenty dollars for an amorous experience.

Any romantic notions involving these practices, without regard to the fine trappings that surrounded them, should best be avoided as sentiment rather than as an unbiased assessment of the situation. Any other conclusion, even from a historic perspective, would be lacking in sensitivity with regard to the effects of the sexual exploitation experienced by these young women. Poor kinless women received little protection from a patriarchal society in which "gentlemen" considered them a proving ground for their sexual prowess. For these women there was no return route to social acceptability once their female purity and innocence had been violated. **Related Entry**: Miscegenation.

SUGGESTED READING: Herbert Asbury, *The French Quarter: An Informal History of New Orleans with Particular Reference to Its Colorful Iniquities* (1938); Victoria E. Bynum, *Unruly Women: The Politics of Social and Sexual Control in the Old South* (1992); John W. Blassingame, *Black New Orleans* (1973).

PROTESTANTISM: The United States had been predominantly Protestant from its inception. Although widely Episcopal in colonial times, the Protestantism of the Founding Fathers from New England had been essentially related to the Puritanism of the Congregational churches. Quakers, considered dissenters since colonial times, congregated mainly in Pennsylvania. Presbyterians, Baptists, Methodists, and Lutherans were largely within the same religious compass as traditional American Protestants.

Unitarians, Universalists, and Disciples of Christ splintered away from established churches, while Mormons and Adventists were probably the furthest from traditional Protestantism. A "Protestant Crusade" to stem the growing influence of the **Catholics** began in the 1820s and increased in proportion to Catholic **immigration**, which grew most precipitously in the 1840s and 1850s. **Related Entries**: Catholics; Nativists; Religion and Religious Revivalism.

SUGGESTED READING: Jenny Franchot, *Roads to Rome: The Antebellum Protestant Encounter with Catholicism* (1994).

PUNISHMENT OF SLAVES: As late as 1847 the practice of exposing slaves to the ridicule of the public in a pillory was still in use as a punishment for minor offenses in several Southern states. Rotten fruit and other missiles were commonly thrown at the offender by small boys and other riffraff, but the upper classes commonly ignored those who were so exposed. The same treatment had been available for white offenders in colonial times, but such punishments for whites had been abolished in favor of fines or confinement by 1830.

Unlike white employees, slaves could be physically chastised by their employers for many forms of disobedience, for insolence involving a white person, and for petty crimes. Incredibly, masters did not have unlimited legal power over their slaves. A slave accused of a felony could not be purposely mutilated, maimed, or killed as a punishment without the intervention of a court. The jurisdiction of these courts varied from place to place; but, generally, their procedures were set down in the **Black Codes**. Of course, a slave defendant was not entitled to a jury trial. However, a hearing officer was required to determine the merits of the case and to act as a finder of fact. The county would then mete out punishment to slaves found to be guilty of serious crimes.

As the hearing officers came from the community of free white slaveholders, questions of guilt or innocence were often moot. As slaves were valuable property, masters looked down on any form of physical punishment that permanently devalued slaves. Moreover, as many slaves were bought on credit and were in themselves the security for the loan, they could not legally be maimed without the consent of the creditor. Some masters intervened in behalf of their slaves even when their guilt had been firmly established. Hamstringing, various forms of dismemberment, and death were uncommon punishments for mere disobedience or petty crime. If only for economic reasons, the master wanted to maintain a chastised but physically capable slave in his employ, not a handicapped cripple. Punishment most often took the form of an informal laying on of the ever-present lash, while a hitching up to the whipping post for a formal flogging was reserved for major offenses. **Related Entries**: Black Codes; Overseers; Race Relations.

SUGGESTED READING: Harrison Berry, *Slavery and Abolitionism, as Viewed by a Georgia Slave* (1861); David Brion Davis, *Slavery in the Colonial Chesapeake* (1994); Kenneth M. Stampp, *The Peculiar Institution* (1956); Jenny B. Wahl, *The Bondsman's Burden: An Economic Analysis of the Common Law of Southern Slavery* (1998).

PURVIS, ROBERT (1810–1898): black anti-slavery activist. Robert Purvis was a wealthy black **abolitionist** who co-founded the American Anti-Slavery Society in 1833 with James Forten, an affluent freeman and fellow Philadelphian. Purvis inherited a fortune from his father, a white **cotton** broker in **South Carolina**, when only sixteen. Using his wealth, Purvis provided great financial support and assistance to runaway slaves. The Pennsylvania Vigilance Committee, with Purvis as president, facilitated some 300 escapes per year. His home, which was nicknamed Saints' Rest by other abolitionists, contained a secret room to hide fugitive slaves. He was the only black admitted to the Pennsylvania Society for Promoting the Abolition of Slavery, serving as its president from 1845 to 1850.

Purvis married Forten's daughter, Harriet, and together they became staunch supporters of the "Free Produce" movement, which encouraged people to boycott foods and other products brought to market through the efforts of slave labor.

To no avail, Purvis protested a Pennsylvania constitutional provision that rescinded the right of blacks to vote in 1838. He was more successful against a policy that excluded black children from public schools; the school board reversed its decision in the face of Purvis' stance to withhold his substantial tax payment. **Related Entries**: Black Anti-slavery Activists; Underground Railroad.

SUGGESTED READING: Editors of Time-Life Books, *Perseverance: Voices of Triumph* (1993), pp. 60–70; Benjamin Quarles, *Black Abolitionists* (1969).

QUAKERS. *See* Religion and Religious Revivals.

QUARANTINE. *See* Epidemics.

QUARRELING: Fisticuffs and shouting matches were considered unfashionable and characteristically lower class throughout the antebellum period. Brawling was relegated to **gambling** halls, lower-class saloons, and bordellos. Gentlemen were expected to settle their differences under only the most formal of circumstances. A public surrender of one's honor to anger, as in the caning of Senator **Charles Sumner** by Representative **Preston Brooks** in the Senate chamber, was therefore particularly distasteful. Had the two men blown out one another's brains or passed three feet of steel through their opponent's bowels while **dueling**, both would have been held in much higher esteem. **Related Entry**: Dueling.

SUGGESTED READING: Jack Kenny Williams, *Dueling in the Old South* (1980).

QUININE. *See* Epidemics.

QUITMAN, JOHN A. (1798–1858): lawyer, congressman, and **secessionist**. As the premier secessionist of antebellum **Mississippi**, John A. Quitman was a fervent disciple of the **nullification** theories of **John C. Calhoun;** but his position on secession was firmly rooted in the controversies surrounding **slavery**. He served as a brigadier general of volunteers in the **Mexican War**, where he fought at Monterrey, Veracruz, and Chapultepec. He served briefly as the military governor of Mexico City.

   Quitman, a noted **Fire-eater**, was described as Mississippi's "most strident slavery imperialist," and he advocated secession mainly because he feared for the future of slavery under the federal union. As governor in 1850, he worked desperately, but to no avail, to get Mississippi to secede during the compromise debates, and he took an equally extreme position on the questions raised by the **Kansas-Nebraska Act of 1854. Related Entry**: Fire-eaters.

SUGGESTED READING: Robert E. May, *John A. Quitman: Old South Crusader* (1995); Emory M. Thomas, *The Confederacy as a Revolutionary Experience* (1991).

RACE RELATIONS: While on an intellectual level many Southerners claimed racial superiority for the white race, they nonetheless depended on the Negro to tend their animals, repair their vehicles, cook their food, and care for their children. White slaveowners were intimately involved with blacks for almost all of their lives. In the isolation of the great plantations, it was possible that most of a slaveowner's day-to-day dealings, in human terms, were either with family members or blacks. It is strange to consider that white slaveowners, who so underestimated the value of human beings as to enslave them, were also able to entrust their bondsmen with the well-being and protection of their property and families. This fact seems to say much more about the humanity and responsibility exhibited by the slaves themselves than about their masters.

Rich Southerners maintained their **planter aristocracy** largely through the exploitation of black labor. Certainly there were upper and working classes among the whites, but nowhere was the equality between white men so complete as in their ability to force Negroes to work without working themselves. Race-based **slavery** promoted a type of equality among all white Southerners regardless of their social status, and the law lent authority to whites by divesting blacks of their very humanity.

The lowliest white man could find comfort in the knowledge that he was the legal superior of even the wealthiest black freeman. Yet many slaveowners found it undesirable to have lower-class whites living on the fringes of plantations where the slaves might be contaminated by contact with **poor white** laborers. Nonetheless, slaveowners with small holdings often worked in the fields with their black slaves, and it was common for them to deal with **free blacks** as laborers, tradesmen, and artisans in town. It is uncertain with how much respect these whites viewed the freemen with whom they came in contact.

The institution of slavery had been in decline for some time before the Civil War, particularly among the small tobacco planters who had worn out their soil. Under the pressure of economic destitution, the attitude toward slavery among moderates in the South had become more "enlightened," and the idea that slavery was a great evil and should be abolished was gaining ground. By 1831 New York and Pennsylvania had abolished slavery, and similar suggestions had even been spoken of in the legislatures of **Maryland** and **Virginia**.

Although the North was generally thought to oppose slavery, many Northerners openly detested the black race. In 1834 anti-abolition riots broke out in many Northern cities, including New York and Philadelphia. Not until 1848 was slavery abolished in most of New England, and not without considerable turmoil over the incorporation of free blacks into New England society. European immigrants to Northern cities showed a particularly strong prejudice against the Negro. *Harper's History of the Great Rebellion* (1866) reported that "no class of our foreign population is more jealous of its own liberties than the Irish, and there is also none which more strongly resents every liberty accorded to the Negro race."

By comparison Southerners were generally ambivalent in their attitude toward Negroes, requiring considerable formality from them, but treating them either with disdain and cruelty, or paying them no mind at all. The working white population in much of the South exhibited far less abhorrence of blacks than did many in the working classes in the North. Many Southerners were genuinely concerned for the physical and moral welfare of their slaves, but only in the context of continued racial separation and subjugation. **Related Entry**: Planter Aristocracy.

SUGGESTED READING: Ervin L. Jordan, Jr., *Black Confederates and Afro-Yankees in Civil War Virginia* (1995); Kenneth M. Stampp, *The Peculiar Institution* (1956).

RAILROADS: A railroad building mania swept the country in the 1840s. By 1860 there were more than 30,000 miles of railway. Most of the construction was in the North above the Ohio River because investment capital was available there, whereas in the South money was largely tied up in land and slaves.

Southern railway construction was characterized by a strange regional pattern of development. The planters of **Virginia, Georgia**, and the Carolinas warmly supported the development of railways, while those of the Gulf states, who relied on easily navigable waterways to ship their produce to coastal seaports, were much less supportive. Nowhere was this difference better evidenced than in the disparity of Southern railway mileage between the two areas on the eve of the Civil War.

While the Southern states along the Atlantic had more than 5,000 miles

The train in this print is pulled by a typical 4-4-0 "American" style engine followed by its tender and a series of rather nondescript cars typical of those used in the period. (From the authors' collection.)

of track, the much larger states of **Mississippi, Alabama,** and **Louisiana** had less than 1,800, much of it represented by stray threads of track providing individual plantations with a connection to a river landing, and going nowhere else. The minimal rail mileage in **Arkansas** and **Texas** proved scattered and local. Nonetheless, the strategically placed railways of **Tennessee** and southwestern **Kentucky,** planned far in advance of any immediate need and built largely in the 1850s, totaled an amazing 1,300 miles by 1860. Even half-explored **Florida** had more than 600 miles, mostly in the northern portion of the state. Although there was no overall developmental plan, by the war the South had the outline of two major railroad systems, one complete and the other unfinished. Both routes joined the Gulf states to Virginia. **Richmond,** the eastern terminus of both networks, had only a single line directly connected to **Washington, DC**.

An obstacle to rail transport in all parts of the country was the difference in the gauges, or track widths, used on different lines. Many ingenious expedients were used to overcome this problem, including third rails, wide wheels that would accommodate both narrow and wide track, and adjustable train axles. Ironically, the construction of several short connections between competing lines, estimated at less than 200 miles of track, would have provided an uninterrupted railway system throughout the entire South.

A major limitation of Southern railways remained a lack of maintenance.

Damaged cars and worn-out engines became the victims of the South's limited industrial technology. The construction and maintenance of the roadbed involved a small army of specialized mechanics, few of whom were to be found in the South. Initially constructed through regions of the South that were expected to produce only light traffic, roadbeds soon began to fail under increased loads and growing traffic. Track bent back and forth around mountains in violent curves, and waterways and depressions were bridged with wooden trestles of the simplest kind. The lack of adequate bridging technology was an obstacle to railway construction, not only in the South, but throughout the country.

The life expectancy of wooden ties in the South was no more than five years, a problem peculiar to its hot and moist climate. Track was composed of a wide range of wrought iron rails, and many of the types that were incorporated into critical stretches of connecting track had become technically obsolete. The rails had enough durability to withstand a decade of light traffic and slow speeds, and were spiked directly to the ties without tie plates, severely limiting the speeds at which trains could travel.

The lack of efficient braking also kept speeds low, seldom exceeding twenty-five miles per hour. Derailments due to high speed were much more common than one would think. A collision with great loss of life between two trains in Rhode Island in 1853 was partially caused by the inability of the trains to stop. This had a chilling effect on high-speed railway operations and engendered a good deal of technological rethinking throughout the country.

Locomotives were commonly of a distinct "American" type known as the 4-4-0 with large funnel-shaped "balloon" smokestacks. The weight of the engine was initially distributed only over the four drive wheels. The four-wheel swivel truck helped the engine negotiate the sharp curves of American railways. Locomotives weighed between 10 and 30 tons, and with a proper arrangement of reciprocating arms and drive wheels, an appropriately heavy engine could pull a train of up to 150 tons.

Invariably, behind the engine came the tender, which held as much as 1,000 gallons of fresh water and had space for firewood. Without exception every Southern locomotive burned wood as a fuel in the antebellum period. The large smokestacks on period engines were needed to divert wood smoke and produce a draft large enough to maintain a satisfactory head of steam. Cordwood was stacked at intervals along every line, and the best and cleanest-burning firewood was reserved for passenger traffic. Depending on the engine, load, and topography, an engine averaged between fifty and sixty miles per cord of wood, requiring long delays every few hours to reload the tender.

The cars were differentiated into freight and passenger types and were innocent of any luxury. Passenger cars were designated as first and second class, and there is some evidence of separate cars for "servants." Freight cars were commonly distinguished as boxcars or flatcars. Tank cars and the caboose existed only in rudimentary form. Rolling stock had a load limit of about eight tons with a gross weight of ten tons. Freight trains were generally limited to fifteen cars due to the need for individual braking. **Related Entries**: Inventions; Transportation.

SUGGESTED READING: Francis A. Lord, "The United States Military Railroad Service: Vehicle to Victory," *Civil War Times Illustrated* (October 1962); Robert C. Black, *The Railroads of the Confederacy* (1952; 1987).

RANDOLPH, JOHN (1773–1833): congressman and senator from **Virginia**. Best known as John Randolph of Roanoke to differentiate him from his similarly named forbears, Randolph was a statesman and an incomparable orator. He incorporated into his speeches wit, literary allusions, parables, and colorful metaphors. He was educated at various institutions but disliked school and failed to finish his studies. As Randolph was noted for his restlessness and extreme imprudence, his failure to complete his **education** surprised no one. In fact, many of his colleagues in Congress were reluctant to acknowledge his leadership because of his lack of formal training. Nonetheless, as a young man he was able to speak in opposition to no less an eloquent speaker than Patrick Henry and acquit himself with credit.

From the outset Randolph was a Jeffersonian and an opponent of the Federalists. Following Thomas Jefferson's presidential victory in 1800, Randolph was appointed chairman of the powerful House Ways and Means Committee. He supported the **Louisiana Purchase** and was an indefatigable proponent of **states' rights** and strict **constitutional interpretation**.

Randolph came into opposition with the administration over the issue of the Yazoo Strip, alienating him from not only Jefferson but from **James Madison** as well. He opposed the Embargo Act, and during 1806 he controlled Congress by terrifying and silencing his opponents in a way that they found intolerable. His failure as a congressional leader to impeach Justice Samuel Chase was a bitter disappointment to him and a blow to his reputation. His opposition to the **War of 1812** caused him to lose his seat in 1813, but he returned in 1819 and served continuously until 1825. During the debates over the admission of **Missouri** to the Union he became a sectional leader, and, as such, he reached the height of his popularity.

From 1825 to 1827 Randolph served out an unexpired term in the Senate. Randolph's speeches as a senator became disordered and largely irrelevant. He ultimately came into conflict with **Henry Clay**. In a famous duel in 1826, Clay's bullet pierced the skirt of Randolph's coat, while Randolph fired purposely into the air. After **Andrew Jackson**'s victory in 1828, Randolph announced that he would no longer seek national office. However, he did serve as a delegate to the Virginia Convention of 1829–1830.

During 1831 he was literally demented, but recovered his wits in late

1832. Meanwhile he drank excessively, used opium, and was uncharacteristically harsh and abusive to his slaves. His last public activity was to condemn Jackson for his stance against **South Carolina** in the **nullification** controversy. His position on states' rights is nowhere better summarized than in a quotation attributed to him: "Asking one of the States to surrender part of her sovereignty is like asking a lady to surrender part of her chastity." In a way he marked the transition from Jeffersonian democracy to the rigid Southern orthodoxy of the antebellum period. "I am an aristocrat," he said. "I love liberty, I hate equality." John Randolph will go down in history as a champion of lost causes—pathetic, yet dauntless in spirit. **Related Entries**: Dueling; James A. Hamilton.

SUGGESTED READING: W. C. Bruce, *John Randolph of Roanoke, 1773–1833* (1922; 1992).

RAW MATERIALS: The South had the potential to produce a wide range of raw materials, including **wool**, hides, leather, feathers, beeswax, lime, guano, salt, coal, copper, gold, and iron ore. **Kentucky** led the nation in the production of saltpeter, an essential ingredient in gunpowder. Other states provided horn, bone ivory, and shell. Forest products such as lumber, paper, firewood, and charcoal made up the bulk of the raw materials produced in the South in the antebellum period.

About the turn of the nineteenth century the Southern states showed a considerable ability to produce naval stores. Hemp, the basic ingredient in cables and cordage for use on sailing ships, could be grown as a cash crop. **Virginia** and **Maryland** had more facilities for the production of naval stores than any combination of two Northern states which normally prided themselves on their production. **Georgia** and the Carolinas supplied excellent naval materials for building ships. Cedar, pine, and live oak grew in abundance. Turpentine, tar, and pine pitch could be manufactured in large quantities. However, the lack of good harbors and trained shipwrights hampered the development of the shipbuilding industry in much of the South.

Relying solely on the fertility of its soil, the South mistakenly wasted the first half of the century before turning the rest of its natural resources into wealth. Slave laborers, largely kept in ignorance by laws forbidding their **education** in all but the most menial of tasks, did not have the required knowledge of modern technology to make this happen. Meanwhile millions of European immigrants brought with them the secrets of an industrial economy, but avoided the fertile soil and untouched resources of the South largely to escape the contamination of race-based **slavery**. These men and women bypassed the South, carrying their skills instead into the western wilderness. **Related Entries**: Agriculture; *Constitution*; Plantation Economy.

SUGGESTED READING: John S. Otto, *The Southern Frontier, 1607–1860: The Agricultural Evolution of the Colonial and Antebellum South* (1989); Joyce E. Chaplin, *An Anxious Pursuit: Agricultural Innovation and Modernity in the Lower South, 1730–1815* (1993).

READING: Literacy was quite high in antebellum America. In the South at least 70 percent of the white male population could read, and in the North the ability of this segment of the population to read may have run as high as 90 percent. Nonetheless, the books on a planter's bookshelf were more often for display than for reading. Aristotle, Caesar, and Cicero were more likely to be the names of slaves laboring in the front yard than the authors of books on a planter's nightstand. Prior to 1820, English texts, less expensive and more fashionable, had almost closed the literary market to American authors and publishers. Thereafter, the emergence of a new popularity in reading and writing among the American middle class underpinned a new national interest in publishing and professional authorship.

Middle- and upper-class women were the chief consumers of the novel, a popular form of escapism. So great was the popularity of the novel that it drew criticism. As late as 1856 the State of New York officially recognized the "necessity" of excluding from all public libraries "novels, romances and other fictitious creations of the imagination." The state also expressed an "obvious" disgust for works dealing with "pirates, banditti and desperadoes of every description."

Few among the **planter aristocracy** failed to read the romantic novels of Sir Walter Scott or the adventures of James Fenimore Cooper. The power of this literature to govern the mind of the nineteenth-century reader should not be underestimated. Fictional characters possessed a remarkable ability to influence a society that read as much as nineteenth-century Americans did. Characters often seemed to become nearly as real and as influential to the reader as actual friends and relations.

The works of Charles Dickens were widely read in America, but many in the South misinterpreted his message and saw the misfortune, destitution, and disease that filled his works as characteristic of all urban life. Modern urban life was the great evil haunting the romantic domains of the Southern imagination. For these, Dickens' novels mirrored the inevitable bleak future of America if Northern concepts of progress continued to be implemented without noticeably improving society. Southerners despised such ambiguous social remedies as the poorhouses and workhouses that filled Dickens' pages. The debtor's prison of *Little Dorrit* and the orphanage of *Oliver Twist* were obviously not sufficient to solve the social ills of an urban society. Southerners were left with a portrait of cities veritably teeming with the exploited masses. Scrooge's treatment of Bob Cratchit emphasized the abuses possible in an age governed by the "work for wage" system. The personal responsibility many Southerners felt toward their neighbors, their workers, and even their slaves stood in stark contrast to the socially anonymous caretaking of unfortunates found in Dickens' works.

Southern intellectuals of the antebellum period were widely read, and they used romantic allusions freely in their writing. Sir Walter Scott's *Waverley* novels were immensely popular. Their theme of the Scottish struggle to throw off the oppression of the English served as an analogy for the position in which the South saw itself with respect to the North. His use of romantic characters, lords and ladies, knights in armor, and grand estates was particularly resonant with the Southern image of itself. So familiar was Scott's work to Southerners that in later years Mark Twain only half-jokingly listed Scott as a cause for the Civil War.

Second only to Scott in popularity were the American adventure novels of James Fenimore Cooper. His second novel, *The Spy*, published in 1822, was an outstanding success. Cooper's subsequent novels emphasized American manners and scenes as interesting and important. Still, many Americans considered novels to be "trivial, feminine, and vaguely dishonorable" because they appealed to the emotions and aroused the imagination (Taylor, 1996). Nonetheless, Cooper found that there was a great demand for adventure tales derived from the Revolution, and his writing was sufficiently manly and moral to find acceptance by a wide audience.

Like Scott, Cooper promoted a social vision of a stable and genteel society governed by its natural aristocracy, "perpetuating property, order, and liberty" as represented by a reunited American gentry (Taylor, 1996). That this view resonated with the Southern image of itself would have upset Cooper, with his very Northern attitudes. *The Pioneers*, Cooper's third book, was dedicated to the proposition that the American republic, poised on the verge of "demagoguery, deceit, hypocrisy, and turmoil," could be transformed into a stable, prosperous, and just society. Nonetheless, Cooper's novels were very popular with Southern men mainly because of their masculine adventure themes.

When **Harriet Beecher Stowe** published *Uncle Tom's Cabin* in 1852, the book sold 300,000 copies in America and Britain in one year. Stowe's work was one of total fiction, stressing the evils of **slavery** and presenting a picture of total brutality. Stowe had no personal knowledge of slavery. The factual basis for the story was found in Theodore D. Weld's radical **abolitionist** tract *Slavery as It Is: The Testimony of a Thousand Witnesses*, published in 1839. *Uncle Tom's Cabin* was immensely more effective in preaching the anti-slavery message in the form of a novel than the earlier tract had ever dreamed of being.

The South considered Stowe's work a slander and abolitionist propaganda. **Mary Boykin Chesnut**, a Southern woman, wrote that she could not read a book so filled with distortions as it was "too sickening" to think that any man would send "his little son to beat a human being tied to a

Performances of *Uncle Tom's Cabin* were incredibly popular and became quite spectacular, as this poster, heralding twenty-five people, horses, bloodhounds, and other assorted livestock, illustrates. Pictured is the escape of Eliza Harris and her child to free soil in Ohio. (From a playbill in the authors' collection.)

tree" (*Mary Chesnut's War*, 1981). She suggested that Mrs. Stowe's work portrayed as much fiction as Squeers beating Smike in Dickens' *Nicholas Nickleby* or the gouging of Gloucester's eyes in Shakespeare's *King Lear*. Nonetheless, amicably disposed Northerners found the passages describing the murderous brutality of Simon Legree indicative of the typical behavior of Southern slaveowners. **Related Entry**: Literary Development.

SUGGESTED READING: David Kaser, *Books and Libraries in Camp and Battle: The Civil War Experience* (1984); Alan Taylor, "Fenimore Cooper's America," *History Today* 46 (February 1996): 21–27.

RECREATION. *See* Amusements and Diversions.

REFORM MOVEMENTS: The **planter aristocracy** was remarkably intolerant of social reform and disdainful of activism. Southerners were particularly incensed by Northern reformers working in the South, and repeatedly expressed frustration with what they termed "isms" (abolitionism, alcoholism, feminism, republicanism, etc.). The majority of the reform movements initiated prior to the Civil War were, nonetheless, essentially benevolent. They were characterized by the activism of the haves for the have-nots rather than by a demand for reform from those who were oppressed. Personal protest would not become popular until late in the century. Philanthropic reforms focused almost solely on the visibly degraded elements of society, including paupers, drunkards, orphans, illiterates, Indians, slaves, prostitutes, and prisoners. Reform activities were characterized by a laudable "urge to remedy visible social ills, alleviate suffering and discourage behavior that was considered immoral."

The dangers of immoderate drinking, for example, were real, and alcoholism could end in disaster. Strong drink was often cited as the cause for eternal damnation and earthly licentiousness, as well as spouse abuse and rape. In fact, the **temperance** movement was very closely allied with **women's rights** issues such as **suffrage** and abandonment. This may have mirrored a rising tide of female discontent with their place in the social order. Women took up the temperance struggle by forming prayer groups and railing against saloons with their bottles, mirrors, and portraits of reclining nudes.

The temperance movement was set back for a time by the defection of activists to the cause of **abolition**. Yet the temperance reformers increased the stakes of their game and insisted on total abstinence from alcohol in any quantity or strength and supplemented their demands with calls for its legal prohibition. This shift from moderate and sometimes symbolic goals to conclusive ones, carved into the legal fabric of the nation, was typical of many of the reform movements of the nineteenth century.

Besides their well-known intolerance for abolitionists, social conservatives in the South particularly deplored the development of free public schools which admitted children from many class, ethnic, and family backgrounds, and inculcated in them a set of novel values that stressed social equality. Southerners worked to rid their communities of the destitute Indian population, not by providing aid and **education**, but rather by removing them to the western wilderness. Moreover, they exhibited a remarkable toleration of **prostitution**—at least in private. Southern anti-poverty reforms emphasized a faith in the efficacy of the **kinship** system (a responsibility they took quite seriously), preferring to succor the abandoned members of society in their homes rather than to consign them to some anonymous agency. Of course, the needy were much less conspicuous and more sparsely concentrated in the largely rural areas of the South than they were in Northern cities.

Much of the resistance to reform was based in a natural social inertia, but some of it was caused by the inability of the activists to articulate the scope and righteousness of their agenda to the public. The activists proved most controversial in their insistence on immediate and total reform, and in their unwillingness to compromise. This was particularly true of the radical abolitionists. Moreover, reformers demanded that the government supplement intellectual persuasion with legal coercion in many areas.

The dimensions of the schemes put forth by the reformers of the early nineteenth century were outweighed only by the depth of their failure. This may have been due to their adoption of an overly confrontational style and their inability to admit to any good in the Southern way of life because of its association with **slavery**. Despite the incongruity between their utopian ideals and the consequences of reality, mindless social tinkering and disgraceful forms of public altruism persisted and proliferated until well after the Civil War. Nonetheless, the majority of social reformers worked through a genuine sense of moral obligation and national pride. **Related Entries**: Abolition; Charities; Education; Kinship; Temperance.

SUGGESTED READING: Lawrence A. Cremin, *American Education: The National Experience, 1783–1876* (1980); Ronald G. Walters and Eric Foner, *American Reformers: 1815–1860* (1997).

RELIGION AND RELIGIOUS REVIVALISM: The United States had been predominantly Protestant from its inception. Although widely Episcopal in colonial times, the **Protestantism** of the Founding Fathers from New England had been essentially related to Puritanism of the Congregational churches. Quakers, considered dissenters since colonial times, congregated mainly in Pennsylvania, and the Episcopal Church remained strong in the South.

In the colonial period the country digested a wide variety of newcomers: Germans, Scandinavians, Swiss, Welsh, French Huguenots, and Jews. The Scotch-Irish immigrants added an element of Presbyterianism to American religion, and later the Baptist Church became popular among the Welsh and Germans. Both the Presbyterians and the Baptists played a major role on the colonial frontier but were largely within the same religious compass as traditional American Protestantism. Lutherans—largely Germans and Scandinavians—were the first to introduce a new element to the religious mix. Nonetheless, their churches were essentially Protestant, and they were assimilated with little fuss into the American social fabric.

Jews made up only a small proportion of the population. Sephardic Jews, those whose ancestry lay in the Iberian Peninsula, had significant communities in both New York and **Louisiana**. In 1845 an economic depression caused many European Jews, especially Germans, to immigrate to America. They brought Reform Judaism with them. In their synagogues, they innovated the ritual, used both German and English, and allowed men and women to be seated together. Nonetheless, most still observed the traditional laws in their homes. The lack of intermarriage between the German-speaking newcomers and the more established Sephardic Jews tended to keep the communities apart. Apparently, Jews experienced little overt anti-Semitism, and a significant number of individuals played important roles in the coming war.

It was the Christian religious revival at the beginning of the century, the second Great Awakening, that most affected American society. It drew its vitality from the Southern and Western frontiers. Evangelism, with its strong emotional appeal, was particularly influential among nineteenth-century Americans. Beginning on the banks of the Cumberland River in **Kentucky** and **Tennessee**, the spark of faith was reignited. Methodist and Baptist preachers reaped a rich harvest of souls. By the 1830s Methodism had become one of the two largest religions in the country. Under the influence of the evangelical spirit most American Protestants came to believe that the path to salvation lay in placing themselves in a position to receive God's grace if they were worthy. This belief was to have a profound effect on Civil War soldiers who strove to be worthy of God's protection by exhibiting courage and steadiness under fire.

The Great Awakening with its vast camp meetings spread like a wildfire, especially in the Southwest. Campbellites, Shakers, Rappites, Fourierists, and other minor sects popular in the North espoused theories of associative communism and utopian socialism by making provisions for the correction of inequalities of temporal possessions among their members. Unitarians (the followers of which were largely devoted **abolitionists**), Universalists, and Disciples of Christ splintered away from established churches, while Mormons and Adventists sprang from the soil of America itself. Non-revivalist churches, especially in the more traditional South, trailed behind. Of 891 Unitarian and Universalist churches in 1850, only 23 existed below the **Mason-Dixon Line**.

Only the Quaker sect, one of the oldest religions in America, seems to have had a unanimous position on the political and social questions of the day—renouncing violence and supporting abolition. By 1850 Baptists, Presbyterians, and Methodists had split along sectional lines over doctrinal and organizational controversies exacerbated by the issue of **slavery**. Northern congregations thereby became more fervently anti-slavery. The other major church sects equally lacked a strong spirit of fellowship, and there appeared an increased tension in religious circles between social activism and private religious expression.

Mormonism, possibly the most important fringe religion in this period, was the great catchall of the evangelical movements. Patriarchs, angels, and demons seemed to punctuate the semi-Biblical rituals of Mormon metaphysics. At one time or another every Protestant heresy in America was preached by one or the other of the spokesmen for the Latter-day Saints, but polygamy was the cause for which the Mormons were most often persecuted. Mormons were so feared and hated that they were driven to isolation in the West in the prewar years. Nonetheless, Mormonism was among the most vigorous, adaptable, and individualistic of religions, carving a niche for itself in the wasteland and helping the nation to expand into the Southwest.

Added to this confusion were the **Catholics**. In the 1830s the Roman Catholic Church was possibly the only religion in America not divided over doctrine. The Roman Church was intolerant of criticism, unapologetically authoritarian, resolute, and unalterable in its structure. It was the oldest and best organized religion in the Western world, and it demanded the unquestioned obedience of its members to the will of the Pope. A "Protestant Crusade" to stem the growing influence of the Catholics began in the 1820s and increased in proportion to Catholic **immigration**, which grew fastest in the 1840s and 1850s. The **Nativist** movement, truly reactionary and discriminatory, was rooted in a traditional abhorrence of authoritarian Roman papism.

The Quaker religion openly welcomed black worshipers, but Catholics were able to maintain their position in the South only by making concessions to the etiquette of white supremacy. Separate black congregations also grew in number among many Protestant sects because the white congregations of their several denominations did not welcome them. A growing army of black ministers was thereby able to found parishes among the freemen and slaves of the South. The African Methodist Episcopal (A.M.E.) churches had the most prominent black ministers of the period. **Related Entries**: Catholics; Immigration; Protestantism; Slave Religion; Young, Brigham.

SUGGESTED READING: Ann D. Jordan, *The Baptists* (1990); James W. Lee, *The Illustrated History of Methodism: The Story of the Origin and Progress of the Methodist Church from Its Founding by John Wesley to the Present Day* (1900); Anne C. Rose, *Victorian America and the Civil War* (1994); Conrad Wright, *The Beginnings of Unitarianism in America* (1976).

REPUBLICAN PARTY: In 1854 Congress passed the **Kansas-Nebraska Act**. In so doing a serious misreading of the temper of the voters had taken place, and they were left simmering in anger at the old political parties. Significantly, this political upheaval came at a time when the old party system was already suffering from weakening voter support and poor party discipline. Yet in the wake of the disaster that followed the Kansas-Nebraska Act, interest in politics and political discussions became increasingly popular, and several new parties moved in to fill the void. Among these were the **Nativists**, or American Party, and the Republican Party.

The Republican Party benefited from the quick collapse of the Nativists, who were too reactionary in their anti-Catholic and anti-foreign agenda to maintain national prominence. The Republicans, in being slower to develop, avoided a similar meteoric rise and fall. While Nativists generally identified with social and cultural ideals, the motivations of the Republicans were purely those of political ambition. Even early Republicans were astute politicians. The party agenda called for a restructuring and expansion of government on all levels. The positions taken on **abolition, urbanization**, the extension of **suffrage**, and **free labor** were all carefully crafted to foster a positive public impression of the party and to increase its power and prestige.

The base of the party, however, remained rooted in anti-slavery, and attracted former Whigs, anti-slavery moderates, and those interested in gradualism and colonization. (**Abraham Lincoln** was one of these, being a strong advocate of foreign colonization of free blacks.) Free labor and anti-slavery seem to have been the most fundamental characteristics of the Republican belief system and identity. These embodied the ideals of a classless, socially mobile society within the framework of a harmonic and expansive economic system, all deeply rooted in personal prosperity and capitalism. While Northern **Democrats** espoused many of these same principles, Republicans were more optimistic about the future of a highly industrialized America, and were certain that the new society and culture of the North would ultimately supplant that of the South to the betterment of the nation as a whole.

The Republican Party benefited greatly from the rising tide of sectional resentment. The Kansas-Nebraska Act was a godsend for the Republican Party. They used the passage of the act, and the decision of the courts in the **Dred Scott** case which followed it, as symbols verifying the existence of a slave power conspiracy. Not only did they find such a conspiracy dangerous in itself, but they saw in it clear evidence that the old powers wished to spread **slavery** to every corner of the land. As a new party the Republicans were in the unique position of being able to stand as the defenders of an idealized Northern culture, untainted, as were the Democrats, by former associations with the South.

An important part of the Republican arsenal of ideals was its characterization of the Southern planter class as the "slave aristocracy," viciously suppressing the mass of Southern whites and all blacks, and denying them the benefits of true political democracy. The Republicans were able to transform the fears of papism, slave power, and the unrestrained expansion of slavery into issues that could be blamed on the Democrats, North and South.

In the 1856 presidential race the Republicans championed the slogan "Free Speech, Free Press, Free Soil, Free Men, Fremont and Victory." **John C. Fremont** may have been made a national hero for his role in mapping and exploring the West, but he was an unacceptable presidential candidate in the South. Governor **Henry Wise** warned that if Fremont won the 1856 election, **Virginia** would secede. As a new party, the Republicans did not have time to organize an electoral victory behind Fremont, who had a good deal of political baggage anyway. Nonetheless, by the end of the decade the Republican Party had become the foremost instrument of anti-slavery sentiment in the country, and this brought it adherents.

Abraham Lincoln's anti-slavery stance during his debates with **Stephen A. Douglas** in 1858 had catapulted the young lawyer into a position of leadership in the Republican Party. By realigning himself with the influential radical wing of the party, he went on to engineer the Republican Party's convention in 1860 and received the party's presidential nomination instead of **William H. Seward**, who was more moderate on the slavery issue.

Lincoln probably would not have won the presidency in 1860 had the election not become a four-way race. He won the election with just under 40 percent of the popular vote and 59 percent of the electoral votes. He carried eighteen states, yet, with the exception of coastal California, not one of them was below the **Mason-Dixon Line**. This result reinforced his position as a sectional leader rather than a national one. The party was so closely identified with anti-slavery that it seems certain that the election of any Republican in 1860 would have led to **secession** and ultimately to the Civil War. **Related Entries**: Abolition; Kansas-Nebraska Act of 1854; Lincoln, Abraham.

SUGGESTED READING: Frank L. Dennis, *The Lincoln-Douglas Debates* (1974); Don E. Fehrenbacher, ed., *Abraham Lincoln, Speeches and Writings, 1859–1865* (1989); Xandra Kayden, *The Party Goes On: The Persistence of the Two Party System in the United States* (1985).

RHETT, ROBERT B. (1800–1876): planter, **newspaper** editor, and secessionist. As early as 1828, Robert B. Rhett of **South Carolina** was urging resistance to the rule of the federal government. He was one of the earliest and most outspoken of the **Fire-eaters**. He introduced amendments to the Constitution to protect Southern rights, and in 1844 he led an abortive **nullification** movement against the **tariff**. Rhett used his **Charleston**-based newspaper, the *Mercury*, to plead with the Southern states to secede en masse in defense of **states' rights** and Southern culture. Failing this, he urged South Carolina to set the secession example by acting alone, believing that the rest of the South would follow once the deed was done. His long dedication to the cause earned him the appellation "Father of Secession." **Related Entries**: Fire-eaters; Newspapers; Secession.

SUGGESTED READING: Richard H. Sewell, *A House Divided: Sectionalism and the Civil War, 1848–1865* (1988); Emory M. Thomas, *The Confederacy as a Revolutionary Experience* (1991); Dorothy Denneen Volo and James M. Volo, *Daily Life in Civil War America* (1998).

RICE. *See* Agricultural Products.

RICHMOND: At the head of the James River, 100 miles south of **Washington DC**, was Richmond, **Virginia**. As the third largest city in the South, Richmond had proven an elegant state capital with fine buildings and traditional **architecture**. Although the city was cultivated and cosmopolitan, it was also the center of Virginia's economy, boasting mills, railways, and trading establishments. By 1860 there were two major Southern **railroad** systems joining the Gulf states to Virginia, one complete and the other unfinished. Richmond, the eastern terminus of both networks, had the only single line directly connected to Washington.

Richmond was the finest city in the South, and one of the better places in which to live in the entire country. Within a few months of **secession**, though, Richmond had been made the capital of the new Confederate nation, and its tenor changed dramatically. The city teemed with soldiers, wagons, and governmental officials. Defenses in the form of artillery emplacements, trenches, and earthworks rimmed its suburbs. The South's only major foundry, the Tredegar Iron Works, turned out cannon, rails, and plates for gunboats. But, most important, in a mere four years the once stately city would be a ruin comparable to the broken hulk of Berlin at the end of World War II. Its people would be described as looking "hungry, gaunt, ghastly, and yellow." Even the young were so pale and thin that it was "pitiful to see" (Miers, 1958). **Related Entries**: Geography; Virginia.

SUGGESTED READING: Earl S. Miers, ed., *A Rebel War Clerk's Diary* (1958); Emory Thomas, *The Confederate State of Richmond: A Biography of the Capital* (1998); Marie Tyler-McGraw, *In Bondage and Freedom: Antebellum Black Life in Richmond, Virginia* (1988).

RIVERBOATS: River steamers were used almost everywhere in the South to provide transportation for people, animals, and goods. The only limit to their use was the availability of a navigable waterway, and riverboats were often seen to regularly travel seemingly impassable routes filled with snags and overgrown with hanging vegetation. Nonetheless, it was the grandeur and glamour of the river steamers that gave them their characteristic place in the antebellum environment.

In 1849 Sir Charles Lyell, an English scientist visiting the South, wrote *A Second Visit to the United States of North America*, an account of his travels which included a fine description of a river steamboat of the period called the *Amaranth*. He rode the steamer up the Tombigbee River to the capital of **Alabama**.

The principle [*sic*] cabins run the whole of the ship on a deck above that on which the machinery is placed, and where the **cotton** is piled up. This upper deck is chiefly occupied with a handsome saloon, about 200 feet long, the ladies' cabins at one end, opening into it with folding doors. Sofas, rocking chairs, tables, and a stove are placed in this room, which is lighted by windows from above. On each side of it is a row of sleeping apartments, each communicating by one door with the saloon, while the other leads out to the guard, as they call it, a long balcony or gallery, covered with a shade or a verandah, which passes around the hole [*sic*] boat. The second class, or deck passengers, sleep where they can on the lower floor, where, besides the engine

The lower deck of Southern riverboats was often filled with bales of cotton. Riverboats often put into the shore to take on cargo and renew their supply of firewood. (From the authors' collection.)

and the cotton, there are prodigious heaps of wood, which are devoured with marvelous rapidity by the furnace, and are as often restored at the different landings, a set of Negroes being purposely hired for that work.

There were more than 200 western steamers in 1830, and at floodtide their traffic could block the river passage. Multidecked steamers had become common, and they grew larger and more luxurious with the years. Riverboats were just as romantic to the antebellum public as they are to us now. The "Golden Age" of river steamers was the 1850s, when their cabins were splendidly appointed with carved woodwork and furniture, crystal chandeliers, carpeting, and mirrors. Some boats were fitted with a steam calliope, on which popular tunes were played when approaching a city.

River steamers were designed to draw very little water. In other words, they could float in as little as two or three feet of water if not overly loaded. Some riverboat pilots bragged that a river steamer could run on dew if need be. The pilot was housed in an elevated structure on the roof of the steamer called a pilothouse. Its position afforded an uninterrupted view of the river. The pilothouse contained a large wheel for steering the rudder and controls for operating the engine. The boilers were generally placed in the bow of the boat to balance the weight of the engines, which were in the rear.

Steam engine technology often outpaced thermodynamic theory in this period. Until 1825 high-pressure boilers were made in a "box" shape by riveting iron or steel plates together. This design proved particularly prone to fatal boiler explosions. The worst maritime disaster to befall an American vessel was the riverboat boiler explosion that took place on the *Sultana* in 1865. There were more than 1,500 fatalities among the soldiers who were taking passage up the **Mississippi River** on the overloaded steamboat. Not until the adoption of the cylindrical fire tube boiler design was high-pressure steam made safer and more practical.

It was quickly found that two engines were better than one on most vessels, and from this fact came the distinctive twin smokestack design of river steamboats. To increase firebox draft under the wood-fired boilers, very tall smokestacks were used. In 1840 their standard height was more than fifty feet above the river surface. Two types of propulsion were developed, the twin side wheels and the stern paddle wheel. Screw propeller technology was in its infancy, and was rarely found on riverboats. The use of two separately connected engines driving independent side wheels had many advantages. It cleared much of the machinery from the center of the boat, and allowed the varying speeds of the engines to be used to increase the boat's maneuverability. Sidewheel steam tugboats operated into the twentieth century. **Related Entries**: Gambling; Rivers; Transportation.

SUGGESTED READING: John F. McDermott, *Before Mark Twain: A Sampler of Old, Old Times on the Mississippi* (1998); Norbury L. Wayman, *Life on the River* (1971).

RIVERS: The **Mississippi River** was the most profoundly important waterway in the South. Its course formed part of the political boundaries of **Kentucky, Tennessee, Missouri, Mississippi, Arkansas**, and **Louisiana;** but it was not the only important waterway in the South. The great valley of the Shenandoah River, one of the few rivers that flowed northeast, into the upper reaches of the Potomac at Harper's Ferry in **Virginia**, was one of the earliest routes through the mountains, and, as part of the Wilderness Trail, it was used to settle the interior areas of Tennessee and Kentucky. Major rivers of the Old South flowed through the piedmont to the tidewater, including the Potomac, the Rappahannock, the James, and the York in Virginia; the Roanoke and the Cape Fear in **North Carolina;** the Pee Dee and the Santee in **South Carolina;** and the Oconee, the Ocmulgee, the Altamaha, and the Savannah in **Georgia**. Along the Gulf coast **flatboats** used the Coosa and Alabama Rivers to float cargoes to Mobile. The Yazoo River wound its way through Mississippi, and the Tombigbee continued to have traffic on it into the era of **railroads**. These rivers served as connections to the interior in the early years of the Republic and were navigable up to the Fall Line, sometimes providing transportation more than 100 miles inland. **Related Entry**: Geography. Also consult the heading "Rivers" in entries on individual states.

SUGGESTED READING: Michael Allen, *Western Rivermen, 1763–1861: Ohio and Mississippi Boatmen and the Myth of the Alligator Horse* (1994); Leland D. Baldwin, *Keelboat Age on Western Rivers* (1980); John F. McDermott, *Before Mark Twain: A Sampler of Old, Old Times on the Mississippi* (1998).

ROADS: The very poor condition of the area's roads and turnpikes was one of the few circumstances in Southern life that most Southerners wanted to change. Many of the roads in the South were very narrow. An observer in 1860 described them as "mere ditches" surrounded by dense forests of second growth pine or virgin oak that would snarl the movement of any wagons that left the beaten path. With high humidity and abundant vegetation, the rain-soaked road surfaces of the South remained wet and were easily churned into a sticky morass that was barely passable. Early travelers to the area complained constantly about the condition of the roads. Plantation owners saw little reason to improve them, as the **rivers** initially served well enough for transport, and attempts to provide turnpikes were sometimes blocked by the politically powerful tidewater gentry.

The poor general condition of public roads caused turnpikes and toll roads to be common in this period. Toll keepers, who had placed a large gate or pike across the road to stop traffic every few miles, collected money for passage as compensation for the time and money they invested in maintaining the road. Municipalities often let concessions to private firms on roads of this sort and required that those who lived in the vicinity or who were on public business travel free. Some of the earliest turnpikes were corduroy roads. Here bundles of saplings and small tree trunks were laid across the muddiest parts of the road surface and covered with a thin layer of soil to act as a cushion. Although uneven and bumpy, this arrangement allowed wheeled vehicles pulled by teams of oxen or draft horses to pass without sinking into the mud. Corduroy was very hard on foot traffic and almost impossible for single horses carrying riders, who often opted to ride across the open fields. Plank roads, as the name suggests, were roads built with several layers of tarred wooden planking covered with dirt and angled to each side for drainage. The amount of planking laid in completing such an enterprise required no mean investment in capital and labor. Such roads, which were in vogue from 1845 to 1857, proved critical to the movement of freight and produce during periods of wet weather.

The Columbia Pike south out of Nashville, **Tennessee**, was a well-maintained road of macadam. This was a type of road made popular by a Scottish engineer of the same name. It was composed of several layers of compacted, broken cubes of stone which were compressed by the passing traffic. The roadbed was crowned in the middle and ditched on the sides for drainage. The major advantage of this road surface was its ability to ignore the effects of rain. The Valley Pike, the main road down the center

The veranda, mossy trees, ladies strolling along garden walks in hoop skirts while a riverboat makes its way downriver—these romantic images came to typify the antebellum South and were embraced by its aristocracy. (From the authors' collection.)

of the Shenandoah Valley, was also of macadam and proved a veritable highway for the South during the Civil War. **Related Entry**: Internal Improvements at Federal Expense.

SUGGESTED READING: W. J. Reader, *MacAdam: The MacAdam Family and the Turnpike Roads, 1798–1861* (1980); George E. Woodward, *Woodward's Victorian Architecture and Rural Art* (1867; 1978).

ROMANTICISM: The South did not have the unifying ethnic and geographic ties of New England. It was, rather, a series of sometimes overlapping topographies, pursuits, and people sharing a common style and outlook. The tidewater, the Smoky Mountains, and the banks of the **Mississippi River** present vastly different terrains. The pursuits of raising **cotton**, rice, and tobacco or carving a home from the mountain wilderness had their own unique challenges and needs. The population of the South included French, Germans, Scotch-Irish, English, Spanish, Africans, and Native Americans in proportions unknown in the North—anything but a homogeneous group. Yet with all this diversity, there was a commonality, a "South."

Perhaps it was the semitropical climate, the scented breezes, or the isolation, but a manner evolved that was relaxed and leisurely, yet explosive and precipitate. The **planter aristocracy** were a minority, but their drive developed into a self-made image that pervaded the region. A code of honor, which dictated polite behavior yet often masked a savage cruelty, unfolded into the systematic practice of **dueling**. Gentlemen like knights of old met on the field of honor while Southern ladies placed themselves under their chivalric protection.

The South came to view itself in terms of romance. The Romantic movement, which swept the South between 1760 and 1860, emphasized feeling, imagination, and nature. It embraced the past, drawing strongly on the styles and ways of ancient Greece and medieval times. It celebrated the pastoral. Southern intellectuals of the antebellum period were widely read, and they used Romantic allusions freely in their own writing. Antebellum Southern **architecture** relied heavily on the Greek temple design with its column and pediments, and Southern portrait **painters** used the same soft color palette, discriminating lighting, and historic subject and symbols as their European counterparts of the Romantic period. Even Southern government was more closely matched to the ancient Roman republic with its ruling elite than a true democracy. These beliefs provided the perfect cover for a region that clung to the old ways, failing to develop the industrialism of the North. It celebrated its failure and elevated it to a cult of chivalry and romance. **Related Entries**: Literary Development; Reading.

SUGGESTED READING: Harnett T. Kane, ed., *The Romantic South* (1961); Dorothy Denneen Volo and James M. Volo, *Daily Life in Civil War America* (1998).

RUFFIN, EDMUND (1794–1865): planter, **secessionist**, and politician. Edmund Ruffin served for many years as the head of the Virginia Agricultural Society, and from 1833 to 1842 he was the editor of the *Farmer's Register*. He was already of advanced age when he took up the torch of secession in midlife and allowed his quest to become an obsession. Ruffin devoted twenty years to the espousal of secessionist doctrine. He became a professional **Fire-eater** traveling widely, speaking to public gatherings, and writing prolifically on only this theme. Ruffin was in his mid-sixties by the time secession became a reality; but he was still active in the cause and had the honor of firing the first shot to hit Fort Sumter. His hatred of the North was monumental. At the end of the war, Ruffin wrapped himself in a Confederate flag and shot himself through the brain. **Related Entries**: Fire-eaters; Secession.

SUGGESTED READING: Richard H. Sewell, *A House Divided: Sectionalism and the Civil War, 1848–1865* (1988); Emory M. Thomas, *The Confederacy as a Revolutionary Experience* (1991); Dorothy Denneen Volo and James M. Volo, *Daily Life in Civil War America* (1998).

RURAL CEMETERY MOVEMENT: During the 1830s a phenomenon known as the rural cemetery movement began to emerge. The deplorable

The extraordinary beauty of Bonaventure Cemetery, outside Savannah, Georgia, prompted *Harper's Weekly* to note, "There is nothing like it in America or perhaps the world." Its parklike setting and wide carriage roads earned it unbridled praise, something seldom bestowed upon Southern achievement. (*Harper's Weekly* IV, no. 205, December 1, 1860.)

conditions in crowded and neglected city cemeteries created a desolate setting for loved ones making their final farewells. This coincided with a general concern that society was changing too rapidly. The once almost inseparable concepts of family, community, and church were being torn asunder. The home became an isolated and romanticized refuge from society's tumult. The rural cemetery created an idyllic place where peace and calm would reign and the family bond could remain forever unbroken. Even nomenclature began to change. The term "cemetery," from the Greek "sleeping chamber," replaced the earlier phrase, "burying ground." The rural cemetery created a sort of garden of graves. Cemetery paths meandered over landscaped hills and valleys. Benches were placed at grave sites, providing an inviting place of contemplation. The landscape offered air and light, safety and nature, joy and optimism. It facilitated acceptance of the physical separation of the dead from the living.

Rural cemeteries continued to expand into the 1850s. By the time of the Civil War, virtually every city of size in the South had its own rural cemetery. The primary concern of rural cemeteries was the burial of families. They were created to provide a safe, secure resting place where the remains of loved ones would not be moved, abandoned, or vandalized. Sections in cemeteries were designed to highlight family plots. The winding roads were built wide enough to accommodate family carriages. Enough roads were constructed so that many family plots would be able to have the highly desired roadside locations. Grave site visitations were akin to afternoons in the park.

Bonaventure Cemetery, located approximately four miles outside Savannah, **Georgia**, was described as "one of the most lovely cemeteries in the country." A contemporary observer noted in *Harper's Weekly* in December 1860, "Its melancholy loveliness once seen can never be forgotten." **Related Entries**: Romanticism; Slave Burial.

SUGGESTED READING: Dorothy Denneen Volo and James M. Volo, *Daily Life in Civil War America* (1998).

SCIENCE AND TECHNOLOGY. *See* Inventions.

SCOTT, DRED (DRED SCOTT DECISION) (1795–1858): About 1795 Dred Scott was born as a slave on a **Virginia** plantation. He was to grow up to be the most famous slave in America. Taken to **Missouri** in 1827, Scott was sold to an army surgeon, who used him as a valet and barber. For four years, two in Illinois and two in Minnesota, Dred Scott lived in these **free states**. Upon the death of his master, Scott was passed on to the man's widow and her new husband, an **abolitionist** congressman who persuaded him to sue for his freedom in the Missouri courts on the grounds that he had lived on free soil for four years. The state courts quickly gave him his freedom; but the case was appealed and reversed by the Missouri Supreme Court.

In 1857, in a celebrated case (*Dred Scott v. Sanford*), the U.S. **Supreme Court** decided that the **Missouri Compromise** was unconstitutional, and that a black slave taken to free soil "never ceased to be a slave" and so could not claim his freedom in a court because he lacked standing as a citizen with the right to sue. The 7–2 decision effectively denied the right of Congress to prohibit slaveowning anywhere within the United States. The opinion of the Chief Justice, **Roger B. Taney**, was probably the most significant. Taney suggested that blacks could not be citizens even if they were free. The Constitution had been made by and for white men only. Moreover, Taney found that it was "useless and mischievous for the opponents of **slavery** to quote the Declaration of Independence, for its great words were never intended to include Negroes." Slaves were "articles of merchandise," and their owners could take their property with them anywhere they pleased— in or out of **slave states** or free states. Not only was Scott not free, but no black, free or slave, could bring suit in a federal court.

Dred Scott, the most famous slave in America. (*Dred Scott*, by unidentified artist from a daguerreotype made in St. Louis, 1857, negative number 37000. © Collection of The New York Historical Society.)

The decision effectively meant that Congress could do nothing about the **extension of slavery into the territories**. The South rejoiced that the highest court in the land had endorsed their slavery doctrine. Nonetheless, the Northern **Democrats** and their leader, **Stephen A. Douglas**, who had hoped to bury the slavery issue through the use of **popular sovereignty**, were embarrassed. The decision was a public relations blunder of the first magnitude. The abolitionists, who had instigated the suit in the hope of setting a precedent, were abashed by their failure. An outburst of protest greeted the Dred Scott decision in the North, and the **Republicans**, who were the real winners in the case, made it a cornerstone of their successful 1860 presidential election campaign.

Dred Scott could have been freed at any point by his abolitionist owners, and he was set free by his owner soon after the Supreme Court decision. But there was little joy in this achievement for Scott. He worked for a short time as a janitor doing odd jobs and was finally given a position as a porter in Barnum's Hotel in St. Louis. He died of tuberculosis less than a year after receiving his freedom. **Related Entries**: Missouri Compromise; Supreme Court of the United States.

SUGGESTED READING: Charles M. Wilson, *The Dred Scott Decision* (1973); Martin Siegel, *The Taney Court, 1836–1864* (1995).

SCOTT, WINFIELD (1786–1866): soldier and candidate for the presidency. Winfield Scott began his career at the College of William and Mary in his home state of **Virginia**. He studied law privately, but was drawn to a military life. In 1807 he was personally approached by President **Thomas Jefferson** to accept a captaincy and raise a regiment of artillery. In the fall of 1811, he set out to join his command and cut one of the first wagon **roads** through the heart of the Southern Indian country to Baton Rouge. During the **War of 1812**, he served at the Battle of Queenstown (Canada), was taken prisoner, and was exchanged. He was made a colonel and planned the successful attack on Fort George, where he was wounded.

In 1814, at Lundy's Lane (probably the hardest fought battle of the war to take place on U.S. soil), Scott, now a brigadier general, had two horses shot out from under him and was so severely wounded that he had to be carried from the field. In a sea of ineffective and incompetent officers, Scott became an overnight idol to the country. Honors were heaped upon him, and President **James Madison** made him a major general; but his wounds prevented him from further immediate service. He took his place rather at the head of an army board charged with writing the first standard American drill manual, *Rules and Regulations for the Field Exercise and Maneuvers of Infantry* (1815). With the demobilization of the wartime army, Scott was left as one of the highest ranking officers in the nation. In 1835 he revised the manual *Infantry Tactics* for the army, and this work remained the standard down to the Civil War.

He once again saw active service in the **Black Hawk War of 1832** and was chosen by President **Andrew Jackson** to watch the nullifiers in **South Carolina** during the crisis in 1833. This assignment was to begin a yo-yo-like series of activities that served to show Scott's invaluable service to his country. He was sent by Jackson to make war on the Seminoles and Creeks in the Southeast. In 1838 he was ordered by President **Martin Van Buren** to the northeastern border between the United States and Canada where the activities of overzealous Canadian patriots were threatening to cause a war. Almost immediately, he was reassigned to conduct the Cherokees from **Tennessee** and South Carolina to new lands beyond the **Mississippi River**. Before reaching his destination he was recalled to the Canadian border. Scott hastened east, concurrently opening a correspondence with the lieutenant governor of New Brunswick that avoided additional bloodshed. In 1841 Scott was finally made general-in-chief of the army by President **John Tyler**.

As the **Mexican War** approached, Scott, now nearly sixty years of age, endorsed the more youthful **Zachary Taylor** to command the nation's forces on the Mexican border. Despite Taylor's tactical victories, Scott was ordered by President **James K. Polk** to bring the war to a conclusion. In March 1847, he landed 10,000 men below Vera Cruz and took the city. He then pushed forward toward Mexico City, and marched into the capital in little more than five months. His fastidious attire during this period brought him the sobriquet "Old Fuss and Feathers."

In 1839 Scott's name had first begun to be associated with politics. The **Whigs** had considered him as a possible presidential candidate in that year, but had nominated **William Henry Harrison** (another military man) in his stead. When Scott returned after the conclusion of the Mexican War, he was greeted with "unprecedented ovation." Congress voted him a gold medal and its thanks. In 1852 the Whigs gave him their nomination for the presidency. The campaign was essentially without issues and poorly run by Scott, who was overwhelmingly defeated by **Franklin Pierce**. He was never again seriously considered as presidential timber.

In October 1860, foreseeing the eventuality of civil discord, if not war, he pleaded with President **James Buchanan** to reinforce the Southern forts and posts, but his advice was ignored. At the outbreak of hostilities, therefore, there was little strategic direction given to federal forces beyond a roughly drawn plan by Scott to exhaust the resources of the Confederacy by blockading its ports and controlling the flow of goods on the Mississippi River. Known as the Anaconda Plan, the strategy was essentially geographic and offensive. The South considered it an invasion, and the plan most certainly had all of the required defining characteristics.

Although President **Abraham Lincoln** quickly replaced him as army commander, Scott lived to see that the plan he envisioned was essentially the one which won the war. When he died his burial was attended by the most illustrious men in the country. This is altogether fitting. Scott had been associated with every President from Jefferson to Lincoln, and he was intimately involved in the critical undertakings of most of them. **Related Entry:** Mexican War of 1846.

SUGGESTED READING: John S.D. Eisenhower, *So Far from God: The U.S. War with Mexico, 1846–1848* (1989); Charles W. Elliott, *Winfield Scott: The Soldier and the Man* (1937); Arthur D.H. Smith, *Old Fuss and Feathers: The Life and Exploits of Lt.-General Winfield Scott* (1937; 1977).

SEA ISLANDS PLANTATIONS: Along the Atlantic coast south of **Charleston** lies a region of sandbars, spits, and large fertile islands suitable for raising animals and crops. The most important of these islands are off the coast of **South Carolina**, and some minor islands are along the coasts of both **Georgia** and **Florida**. The whole region, known as the Sea Islands, is somewhat tropical in character and exceedingly flat, with **rivers** flowing almost on a level with the surrounding country.

Sixteenth-century Spanish explorers noted this quiet coastal backwater, and an unsuccessful French settlement was planted in the area. English plantations did not begin to appear on the Sea Islands until late in the seventeenth century. Much of the region required the building of drainage canals and the clearing of dense undergrowth and forests. The same alluvial characteristics that provided fertility and renewal also supplied an environment amenable to disease. Exposure to the local swamps was thought to be so dangerous that the laborers needed to dig the hundreds of miles of drainage canals necessary for the area to be productive could not be found among willing whites. Black **slavery**, therefore, became the fundamental form of all labor in the region. As the first settlers came from Barbados, the Sea Islands plantations quickly took on many of the worst characteristics of the **sugar** plantations of the West Indies. This meant, in many cases, a harsh existence for the slaves that worked in the region. By the Civil War no less than 80 percent of the population of the Sea Islands was composed of black slaves, a proportion of slaves to free laborers unrivaled almost anywhere in the **antebellum South**.

The planters who established themselves in the Sea Islands nonetheless found many inviting plantation sites, for the area drained by the local rivers was of considerable size—more than ten thousand square miles. While the environment was not as desirable as that of the **Virginia** tidewater, the South Carolina low country was, according to one observer, "the size of Belgium." The first English settlers called it the "sweet scented coast" because of the profusion of aromatic vegetation. Oak, pine, palmetto, cypress, and sweet gum grew on the large islands. A few miles inland there were huge stands of long-leaf pine which provided timber in abundance.

The rivers—slow flowing, shallow, and tortuous in their courses—provided **transportation** to the coast by shallow-draft vessels and steamboats, but they also poured thousands of cubic feet of silt-laden water into the ocean every minute, creating lines of shifting sandbars that made navigation difficult and dangerous for any vessel. With the exceptions of Charleston to the North and Savannah to the South, the only noteworthy port in the region was Beaufort, on Port Royal Island. Here the owners of the riverfront plantations fled by day in order to escape the nightly mosquitoes and swamp fevers.

Although the primary crop of this region was rice, the Sea Islands were noted for the production of luxury **cotton** with its long, delicate, and silky fibers. Sea Island cotton could not be grown profitably anywhere else in the world. Even so, Sea Island planters continuously experimented in an effort to improve the quality of their luxury cotton. By 1826 Kinsey Burden produced a superfine fiber by planting a tufted seed in heavily fertilized soil— a process quickly adopted by other growers. The world eagerly sought this superfine fiber to make laces and fine fabrics. Upcountry planters, unfortunately, found that their soil would not support the growth of a Sea Island variety of long-staple cotton. Even in the face of widely fluctuating cotton prices, this fact alone provided the low country gentry with a relatively stable market and a virtually inexhaustible source of wealth. **Related Entries**: Cotton; Geography.

SUGGESTED READING: Guion Griffis Johnson, *A Social History of the Sea Islands* (1930; 1969); Mary R. Bullard, *Robert Stafford of Cumberland Island: Growth of a Planter* (1886; 1995).

SEABROOK, WHITEMARSH BENJAMIN (1792–1855): Southern apologist. Whitemarsh B. Seabrook's pamphlet *A Concise View of the Critical Situation and Future Prospects of the Slaveholding States in Relation to Their Colored Population* (1823) revealed to its many readers forebodings of a worldwide attack on the institution of **slavery**, and he urged slaveholders to prepare for the encounter. More important, the pamphlet served to alert the tidewater planter, and all whites living in areas where the majority population was black, to the dangers posed by slaves "agitated" into a frenzy of revolt by **abolitionists** and by debates on **emancipation** in the U.S. Congress. Seabrook used the bloody descriptions supplied by "the wretched fugitives" of the 1808–1809 slave revolt in Haiti to paint a nightmarish picture of whites slain in their beds by Negroes bent on revenge. *A Concise View* appeared in all the **Charleston** papers in August and September 1823 as a reprint subsequent to the **Denmark Vesey** investigation. **Related Entries**: Fear of Slave Revolts; South Carolina Association; Vesey, Denmark.

SUGGESTED READING: William W. Freehling, *Prelude to Civil War: The Nullification Controversy in South Carolina, 1816–1836* (1966).

SECESSION (SECESSIONISTS): In the **nullification** crisis the South found a weapon with which to enforce its will on the national government—the threat of secession. The radical politicians of the South developed the concepts of **states' rights**, nullification, and secession to the level of political gospel during the decade of the 1850s. Secession thereafter dominated the rhetoric of Southern politicians. Yet many Southern leaders espoused immediate disunion sporadically, and usually only during election campaigns. Those who did otherwise, with some notable exceptions, did not achieve lasting prominence. The most unremitting secessionists were the **Fireeaters**, who spoke loudly and often on the subject of immediate disunion.

Secession was a political issue in the national elections in both 1852 and 1856, and **South Carolina** threatened to secede in both these years if the "wrong" presidential candidate won. Neither the election of **Franklin Pierce** of New Hampshire in 1852 nor that of **James Buchanan** of Pennsylvania in 1856 posed a great enough threat to cause any Southern state to secede. However, **Abraham Lincoln** was so closely associated in the Southern mind with secession that his election precipitated almost immediate disunion.

The hope for secession was founded upon the support of several states which would never leave the Union. (From the authors' collection.)

On the afternoon of December 20, 1860, South Carolina passed an Ordinance of Secession. Five additional Southern states quickly followed its example: **Mississippi, Florida, Alabama, Georgia**, and **Louisiana**. In February, **Texas** came on board. At first it appeared that only these seven states would secede, and early Confederate flags sported only seven stars. However, in April 1861, after the bombardment of Fort Sumter and Lincoln's call for 75,000 volunteers to defend the Union, **Virginia** joined its sister states. This news was followed in May and June by the secession of **Arkansas, North Carolina**, and **Tennessee**.

Secessionist sentiment in **Missouri** and **Kentucky** was somewhat split. As large areas of these states were quickly brought under federal control, actual secession was impractical. Eleven states had actually seceded; nonetheless, when the new Confederate battle flag was designed it had thirteen stars, the last two representing the fiction that Missouri and Kentucky were willing but unable to join the Confederacy. The use of thirteen stars was thought to reinforce the symbolic connections between the infant Confederacy and the American Revolution. **Related Entries**: Fire-eaters; Force Bill; Nullification.

SUGGESTED READING: William W. Freehling, *The Road to Disunion, Vol. 1: Secessionists at Bay* (1990); Richard H. Sewell, *A House Divided: Sectionalism and the Civil War, 1848–1865* (1988); Dorothy Denneen Volo and James M. Volo, *Daily Life in Civil War America* (1998).

SECTIONAL DISPUTES (SECTIONAL INTERESTS): During the antebellum period the polarization of the nation underwent a number of distinct phases. Initially the conflicting demands of the thirteen colonies were focused on inequity of power among the populous and sparsely populated states. Then the focus shifted to the wrangling of the political parties; and, in a final metamorphosis before the Civil War, the focus was on conflicts among the geographical sections of the country.

The **Whigs** and **Democrats**, the two oldest political parties in America, had reached agreement on several issues that had plagued the early republic. **Tariffs**, the **Bank of the United States**, and the regulation of internal commerce ranked high among these divisive issues. The power of the parties had displaced the individual states as the institutions of political discontent. In fact, the strangely heterogeneous interest groups that made up the early political parties were more afraid of governmental interference by an unbridled executive than of each other. During the 1840s the parties were careful to symbolically pair Northerners with Southerners on their presidential tickets.

However, the spoils of the **Mexican War of 1846** helped to fuse nascent sectionalism into a political reality. In a notable speech made in favor of the **annexation of Texas**, future Confederate Vice President **Alexander H. Stephens** argued that the South needed the added weight of **Texas** to preserve "a proper balance between the different sections of the country." By extension, the South found that it needed its "fair share" of all new territories in order to maintain a political balance in the federal government. Northerners, for their part, genuinely feared that **slavery** would take root in the territories if barriers were not raised to prevent it.

The decade of the 1850s was one of rapid economic and social change in America, and politics was gaining a more general audience than at any time since the Revolution. The Whigs and Democrats were searching for new issues that would mobilize the voters behind the old party structure. This attempt to underscore the meaning of the old parties had far-reaching consequences as political and social agendas began driving forward proposals that required strong federal action.

One unforeseen consequence of trying to bolster the old parties was that political conflict became largely geographical. For many years the North and South had been at loggerheads over republicanism, protectionism, incrementalism, and abolitionism. Southerners frequently expressed their dissatisfaction with such "isms." Nonetheless, with Western interests initially complementing their own, Southerners were able to control the government. However, when the West realigned itself with the North in the 1850s, the reaction was precipitate.

The forces of sectionalism were clearly evident in the aftermath of the **Kansas-Nebraska Act of 1854**, which allowed the residents of both territories separately to choose to be a slave state or free state. Although the measure was popular among Northern Democrats and the Southern Democrats gave it support, its passage ultimately caused a split in the party along geographical lines. Moderates in the North felt betrayed. Whigs abandoned their party in the North, while Southern Whigs joined the Democrats.

Outraged by the act, Northern voters began to speak of the existence of a "slave power conspiracy." They were also frustrated in their inability to elect more than a spattering of Northerners to the presidency to protect their rights and felt that they had been unfairly dictated to by the South. In response, moderates in the South began to harden their position and seriously consider disunion. Moreover, the events taking place in "**Bleeding Kansas**" and the schemes of fanatical abolitionists, like **John Brown**, tended to radicalize even the most moderate politicians.

Northern officeseekers, with their sights set on 1860, began calling for an assault on the traditions and honor of the South with all the enthusiasm that their rhetoric could convey. Such attacks fueled Southern indignation, created a desire for vindictive satisfaction, and retrenched the positions of the moderates. Southern radicals began to call for immediate disunion as the best means of protecting their sectional interests. "Both North and South seemed to be swayed by the demagogue," observed William Fletcher. The threat of **secession** thereafter dominated the rhetoric of the South, and the radical politicians of the South raised the concept of **states' rights** to the level of political gospel. Another Southerner, Carlton McCarthy, noted, "When one section of the country oppresses and insults another, the result is . . . war!" **Related Entries**: Agriculture; Extension of Slavery into the Territories; Internal Improvements at Federal Expense; Plantation Economy.

SUGGESTED READING: Richard H. Sewell, *A House Divided: Sectionalism and the Civil War, 1848–1865* (1988); Dorothy Denneen Volo and James M. Volo, *Daily Life in Civil War America* (1998).

SEMINOLE INDIANS. *See* Indian Relations with Slaves.

SEQUOYAH (1770?–1843): This inventor of the Cherokee alphabet was born in the Indian town of Taskigi, **Tennessee**, and was probably the child of Nathaniel Gist and a mixed-blood Native American woman. For some years he lived as a Native American and made a living as a hunter and fur trader. Handicapped by a serious accident, Sequoyah was forced to come into increasing contact with white civilization, and he became obsessed with the ability of whites to read and write. About 1809 he began to study the English language with the object of writing an alphabet in his native language. By 1821 he had devised a table of characters that represented more than eighty syllables in the Cherokee language, and, with the help of his six-year-old daughter, he was able to demonstrate the practicality of his system. His hope that his people might learn to read and write in their own tongue, accepted by his tribal elders but widely ridiculed by whites, was fulfilled. Sequoyah's development of the Cherokee alphabet stimulated the printing of books and newspapers in that tongue, and he was highly honored by his people. **Related Entry**: Indian Removal.

SUGGESTED READING: Jane A. Shumatz and W. David Baird, *Sequoyah: Inventor of the Cherokee Alphabet* (1993); Diane Shaughnessey and Jack Carpenter, *Sequoyah: Inventor of the Cherokee Written Language* (1998).

SEWARD, WILLIAM H. (1801–1872): statesman, governor of New York, secretary of state. Although drawn to the **Anti-Masonic Party** as a young man in the 1820s, William Seward was an unrelenting supporter of **John Quincy Adams** and a leader of the **Whig Party** for two decades. His first important elected office was in the New York senate in 1830. In 1834 he ran unsuccessfully for governor, mainly because his sentiments were too conventional. He opposed **nullification**, advocated **internal improvements at federal expense**, and supported the national bank. Nonetheless, when he assumed the role of governor in 1838, he had radicalized some of his positions. He supported the abolition of imprisonment for debt, the establishment of sectarian schools in which children would be instructed in their own language, and the end of **slavery** in some form. Notwithstanding these changes, abolitionist and radical reformers found that he did not wish to take positions that were not part of the political creed of his party.

Seward declined public office in 1842 because he had depleted his financial resources. During the next seven years he practiced law, but he never abandoned his interest in politics. He ardently championed the cause of Irish freedom and gained a following among Irish American voters. Seward was an expansionist, and this brought him into conflict with many who feared the **extension of slavery into the territories**. Yet he was able to keep his policies within the scope of his anti-slavery agenda. By 1848 he had become a solid anti-slavery advocate and was elected to the U.S. Senate. In 1850 he

William H. Seward, Alexander H. Stephens, Stephen A. Douglas, Simon P. Chase, and Charles Sumner, all major political figures of the late antebellum period. (From the authors' collection.)

took a firm stand against all compromise on slavery and favored the admission of California as a **free state**.

In the election of 1852 the Whig Party was completely routed. Seward turned to the new party of anti-slavery—the **Republican Party**, which had formed in response to the **Kansas-Nebraska Act of 1854**. He correctly predicted that slavery would be ended either "by gradual voluntary effort, and with compensation" or by violent civil war. In 1858 he termed the bloody struggle over **secession** that loomed between the increasingly antagonistic sections of the country "an irrepressible conflict between opposing and enduring forces."

The 1856 Republican presidential nominee was **John C. Fremont**, whom Seward supported in the hope that he himself would be the next Republican nominee. But this was not to be. The rising star of the Republican Party in 1860 was **Abraham Lincoln**, not William Seward. Nonetheless, when Lincoln took office he offered Seward the position of secretary of state. His conduct in this office was commendable. Not only was he able to deflect European recognition of the Confederate states, but he was able to strike just the right tone of friendship mixed with a dire warning of unwanted consequences when dealing with **emancipation** and the border states.

When Lincoln was shot in 1865, Seward sustained a brutal attack by would-be assassins in his own house; yet within a few days he was able to transact public business. Later that year he suffered an injury in a carriage accident from which he did not completely recover. Although he was crippled during his last term of office, he was an able administrator and is best known for the purchase of Alaska from Russia in 1867. Increasing paralysis overtook him thereafter, and he died in 1872. **Related Entries**: Lincoln, Abraham; Republican Party.

SUGGESTED READING: Ernest N. Paolino, *The Foundations of the American Empire: William H. Seward and U.S. Foreign Policy* (1973); John M. Taylor, *William Henry Seward: Lincoln's Right Hand* (1991).

SIMMS, WILLIAM GILMORE (1806–1870): poet, novelist, and Southern apologist. In the two decades preceding the Civil War, Simms dominated the literature of the South. The Charlestonian's astute awareness of time and the past, a deep sense of place, and his detailed depiction of characters make him truly representative of the antebellum literary man. His works provide valuable insight into the concerns and views of the people of his time and region and demonstrate how Southern **agriculture, slavery**, the frontier, diversity, and views on **states' rights** are the products of a unique civilization.

Beginning his career as a poet, Simms expanded into drama and criticism but is probably best known for his fiction. His major works draw upon his experiences in the coastal, low country plantation and provide the backdrop for his historical tales and romances, while the backwoods of the Gulf provide the setting for his mountain fiction. Simms' most important works may well be his tales and novelettes, which were first published in magazines or with cheap paper covers.

Simms' politics, like those of many of his literary contemporaries, spilled over into his professional life, and he became an apologist for slavery and **secession**, thus negating any broad appeal to which he might have aspired.

Some of his better known works include *The Scout, The Golden Christmas, The Damsel of Darien,* and *Border Beagles.* **Related Entry**: Literary Development.

SUGGESTED READING: Louis D. Rubin, Jr., general editor, *The History of Southern Literature* (1985).

SLAVE ARISTOCRACY. *See* Planter Aristocracy.

SLAVE BURIAL: Slaves were buried in their own graveyards. Contemporary journals describe them as simple sites with a variety of markers and headstones. Some graves were decorated with evergreens or shrubs, and on occasion railings enclosed family lots.

Death rituals among slaves retained images and meanings that tied them to their African roots. In death one "went home." To a slave, this symbolized freedom and, if anything, it was a reason to rejoice rather than to mourn. While graves were marked by simple wooden markers, they were decorated, much as they were in Africa, with the last items the deceased had used. Often these would be pottery or glass containers, medicine bottles, quilts, dolls, or toys. As a tangible symbol of the separation of the deceased from the world of the living, it was essential that these items be broken. Failure to do so was thought to invite a similar fate for the surviving family. Marble headstones, often with very fine tributes to the departed, were erected by some slaveholders for servants who were held most dear.

Funeral services required permission. It was not unusual for slaveowners to allot a portion of the work day to provide time for the funeral. Some even provided food for the celebration that followed. Others required that the funeral be held after the day's labor had been completed. The master and mistress of the plantation commonly attended the funerals of personal and household servants. If permission could be obtained, slaves from neighboring farms attended. Funeral sermons could be separated from burial by days, weeks, or months. This could be related to the African system of multiple funerals, or it could have been necessitated by slaveholder restrictions. Witnesses of night funerals described these services as solemn yet eerie, lit by pine knot torches and filled with mournful strains of slave hymns.

While slaves did not follow the mourning dress conventions of white society, some slaves were known to have had mourning attire. Such clothing was probably purchased after the death of the master, and the slave was then permitted to use it for personal losses. **Related Entries**: Rural Cemetery Movement; Slave Religion.

SUGGESTED READING: Harriet A. Jacobs, *Incidents in the Life of a Slave Girl, Written by Herself* (1861; 1987); Albert J. Raboteau, *Slave Religion: The "Invisible Institution" in the Antebellum South* (1978).

SLAVE CHILDREN. *See* Children Born as Slaves.

SLAVE CLOTHING: The clothing of slaves varied with the economic status of the slaveholder and with the tasks with which the slave was charged. Slaves who worked in the household were seen by visitors to the home, and therefore their appearance was a reflection on the slaveholder. Slaves who worked in the fields needed serviceable clothing that would survive the rigors of the work being done.

Clothing was usually issued twice a year. While some plantation owners purchased clothing for their slaves ready-made, most purchased cloth by the yard and had the clothing fashioned on site, quite a labor-intensive enterprise. Commonly the **plantation mistress** oversaw the process personally and was even involved in the cutting and sewing process. Very large plantations had slave women working as full-time seamstresses who undertook most of the labor. They would work from several basic sets of patterns, with individual ones for the very tall or very broad. Other operations allocated set amounts of yardage for the garments to be made and allowed the slaves to fashion the clothing themselves. Children would be given yardage commensurate with their size.

Plantation slaves were often clothed in coarse but durable "Negro cloth," which was produced from **cotton** in the mills of New England or in **wool** broadcloth imported from England. The fabric was sturdy and became as soft as flannel as it was washed. Blue, red, and gray were common colors. The slaves often dyed white suits tan or gray with willow bark or sweet gum. Cloth was fashioned into trousers and shirts for the men and boys. Slave women wore calico, woolen, or linsey dresses, head kerchiefs, and aprons. Both sexes were provided with straw hats and handkerchiefs which were used generally as head coverings or neck cloths. Men, women, and children were provided with red flannel underwear for the winter.

Shoes for slaves were difficult to procure at a reasonable cost. In the absence of a slave that was trained in shoemaking from raw leather, plantation owners resorted to buying shoes in bulk. There existed an entire trade dedicated to the manufacture of cheap shoes for slaves. These shoes rarely gave long use without the services of a cobbler. Although some effort was made to measure at least the length of their feet, most ex-slaves complained of rarely having had shoes that fit well. Slaves generally preferred to go barefoot in the fields, as did their white counterparts. Slaves who went barefoot in winter greased their feet with tallow to protect the skin. **Related Entry**: Fashion.

SUGGESTED READING: Eugene D. Genovese, *Roll, Jordan, Roll: The World the Slaves Made* (1974); Charles Joyner, *Down by the Riverside: A South Carolina Slave Community* (1984).

SLAVE COURTSHIP AND MARRIAGE: The slave family was an unstable institution. No Southern state recognized marriage between slaves. Marriage was considered a legal medium by which property was handed down. Since slaves had no property, the law saw no reason to recognize the union of slaves as binding.

Slaves coveted marriages blessed by clergy. Some morally scrupulous planters encouraged marriage in opposition to the immorality of open promiscuity. Others found that such a policy decreased the incidence of runaways and discouraged fighting among the slave population. A tradition of "jumping the broom" is thought to have developed by slaves denied a legally binding wedding ceremony, as a physical manifestation and finalization of their union. Female slaves did not take their husband's name; rather, they retained the name of the slaveowner. Weddings of slaves dear to the slave-holding family were often held in the "big house," with the master and mistress supplying castoff finery to attire the couple and providing ample provisions for a celebratory feast.

Slave courtship and marriage "abroad," as those between plantations were called, were generally discouraged due to the freedom they allowed slaves to travel beyond the owner's holdings. Small holdings and a dearth of available mates, however, made the practice more common. Husbands were generally issued weekend passes that permitted them to leave after a half day of work on Saturday to visit their wives and children abroad, and to return Monday morning.

During the federal occupation of **New Orleans**, more than 500 slave marriages were recorded as having taken place while couples had been slaves. Of these, fewer than 100 remained unbroken. While some unions lasted 20 to 40 years, the average length of a slave marriage was 5.6 years. Records indicate that 70 percent of these marriages ended due to death or personal choice, and only 30 percent were broken by the planters. Many planters went to considerable lengths to avoid breaking up families because of the great unrest it caused. Unfortunately, however, mortgage foreclosures, loan repayments, and inheritances brought many slaves to the auction block with no concern for the family unit. Executors of estates often divided slaves up into lots of equivalent value for distribution to heirs. Additionally, planters often made gifts of slaves to their children, especially as wedding presents.

Slave children did not belong to their parents and were generally considered the property of the mother's master. The father and the father's master, should he not hold the mother, were denied any standing in regard to the offspring of slave unions. The offspring of a slave and a free man was, therefore, a slave. The progeny of a slave and a free woman, however, was considered to be freeborn even if the woman were black. Even the children of a white master by a slave mother were born slaves. In the case of a dispute in this regard, with very few exceptions, whenever a slave's human rights came into conflict with a master's property rights, the courts invariably sided in favor of the master. **Related Entries**: Children Born as Slaves; Miscegenation.

SUGGESTED READING: Peter Kolchin, *American Slavery, 1619–1877* (1993).

SLAVE DRIVERS. *See* Overseers.

SLAVE DWELLINGS: Slave quarters were constructed by the slaves themselves to the specifications of the plantation owner. Accounts describe two-story as well as single-story dwellings, although many existing photographs depict single-story units similar to the British "hall and parlor" type found in England and Northern Ireland. Another popular style was the "double pen" wherein a one-room cabin had a second room added to it. The addition was commonly done on the other side of the chimney. In

Slave houses took a variety of forms and could be one or two stories. This one in Tennessee is made of brick. (Photo by James Volo.)

some cases, this may have accommodated a second family, although contemporary accounts clearly state that there were single-family dwellings in at least some instances. Average cabin size was eighteen by twenty-two feet. On large plantations, slave quarters were arranged in groups, with street names reminding one English visitor of a country village. One **South Carolina** plantation contained three such groupings, each containing twelve dwellings. The slaves were left pretty much to themselves in these areas, although some plantations located the **overseer**'s house prominently at the end of the street. Less affluent plantations provided only log cabins chinked with clay. Slave dwellings generally had porches. Some slave quarters had glass windows, while others had only shutters.

The interior arrangement of slave dwellings varied. While appearing very European on the outside, many were adapted on the inside to resemble two-room dwellings commonly found in Africa. The main room functioned as both a kitchen and dining area, the center of which featured some type of table and chairs or benches. Cooking and eating utensils were stored in chests or sideboards. Some slave quarters were decorated with cast-off furniture from the slaveowner's home. Slaves who possessed carpentry skills generally provided their families with above average furnishings. Walls were likely to be decorated with landscape prints obtained from traveling salesmen.

All of the rooms in slave dwellings were likely to be used as sleeping quarters at night. Some were furnished with serviceable beds, some had plank bunks, and some had nothing more than mattresses which would be rolled up out of the way during the day. Children were frequently accommodated in sleeping lofts. **Related Entry**: Architecture.

SUGGESTED READING: Charles Joyner, *Down by the Riverside: A South Carolina Slave Community* (1984); John Michael Vlach, *Back of the Big House: The Architecture of Plantation Slavery* (1993).

SLAVE ESCAPES: While the thought of and planning for escapes were undoubtedly widespread, many slave escapes were prompted by the anticipation of a beating or rumors of being sold. The obligations of motherhood kept female escapes lower than those of males, but escapes were made by both sexes. Some slaves traveled via the **Underground Railroad**, journeying along a variety of routes that led north, or south to other countries. Many fugitives, however, were alone, penniless, and left largely to their own resourcefulness.

In the border states such as **Maryland, Kentucky**, and **Tennessee**, slaves were more likely to be successful in their attempt to slip away to freedom; escape was far more difficult for those in the Deep South. These slaves often sought refuge in the wilderness, sequestered in caves for months and years, some banding together in what came to be known as maroon communities. Others secreted themselves in hiding places in sympathetic households willing to risk the conspiracy. The Seminole Indians also offered refuge to escaped slaves.

One of the most ingenious escapes was that made by Henry "Box" Brown, who was shipped by Samuel Smith in a two foot by three foot shipping crate to the office of black **abolitionist** William Still. Smith boxed up two additional slaves who were unsuccessful in their escape to freedom. Having initially hidden under the floorboards of a house and then in a den in a bamboo swamp, Harriet Jacobs finally sought refuge in her freed grandmother's storage shed attic in North Carolina. After Jacobs spent seven years in the dark and cramped attic, friends obtained passage for her on a northbound ship and she was able to complete her escape. Lear Green was a female slave who successfully traveled from Baltimore to Philadelphia inside a chest.

William Craft disguised his light-skinned wife, Ellen, as a white invalid gentleman while he acted the part of a male black servant. Ellen wore dark glasses and a poultice in a handkerchief to conceal her beardless cheeks. To avoid having to write, she kept her right arm in a sling. Ellen played the role of a sickly young man to the hilt and was befriended by fellow travelers who warned the fragile "young man" to watch his servant least he attempt escape.

Successful attempts were limited. Census reports for the twenty years prior to the Civil War recognize 1,000 slaves as having fled. Some slaves did run away, only to hide and return after an extended period of time. **Related Entries**: Indian Relations with Slaves; Underground Railroad.

SUGGESTED READINGS: William Craft, *Running a Thousand Miles for Freedom: or The Escape of William and Ellen Craft from Slavery* (1969); William Still, *The Underground Railroad* (1970).

SLAVE FOOD: Some slaves ate all their meals in their cabins, but on large plantations, meals were also served from a central kitchen. The latter was most common for midday meals because it provided the least amount of disruption in the workday. House servants often ate the same meal as the family after they had been served.

Slave rations were distributed weekly, usually on Saturday. The quality and amount varied from farm to farm. Economic fluctuations often caused **cotton** planters to cut costs, which translated into poorer quality rations, a pattern those involved in the lucrative nature of rice cultivation did not experience.

Yet **slave narratives** suggest that **food** was often abundant. Much of the food common to slave households was thought unwholesome or offensive to the delicate palates of whites. Whites normally did not eat chicken necks, gizzards, or feet. The small intestines of hogs were made up into chitlins; and coosh-coosh, a mixture of boiled cornmeal, syrup and bacon fat, was considered less than appealing. Nonetheless, ham and gravy, fried chicken, sweet potatoes, ashcake, and hoecake—all Southern standards—were found in slave kitchens. To supplement their diet slaves were allowed to grow their own vegetables and to catch fish, squirrels, raccoons, groundhogs, opossums, and rabbits. They also brewed locust or persimmon beer.

Salted codfish was a staple of the slave diet as it was inexpensive and easy to store. Cod was purchased from New England fishermen who considered it a "junk" fish. Salted cod was a familiar staple item in many European communities, especially those along the Atlantic and Mediterranean coasts, and there was a worldwide market for it. Nonetheless, **slavery** provided a large and continuing market close to home for the American fishermen, and almost all that they caught and prepared was sent south. Besides salted codfish, slaves were periodically issued molasses, salt pork, okra, peas, collard greens, turnips, and black-eyed peas. These foods supplemented their steady diet of cornmeal, fresh or dried corn, and potatoes or yams. Wheat flour, white bread, and beef were almost unknown to them.

The food provided for slaves was of poor quality by modern standards, and the diet was periodically unbalanced. Surprisingly, slaves seem to have been provided by this diet with sufficient calories and nutrients to allow for the heavy labor to which they were put. **Related Entry**: Food.

SUGGESTED READING: Eugene D. Genovese, *Roll, Jordan, Roll: The World the Slaves Made* (1974); Dorothy Denneen Volo and James M. Volo, *Daily Life in Civil War America* (1998).

SLAVE MARKET. *See* Buying and Selling Slaves.

SLAVE MUSIC: Music was an integral part of slave life. It existed as spirituals, laments, work chants, secular songs, and funeral dirges. In a way, these songs provided a certain release. The airs established a group consciousness and provided strength to withstand oppression. The chants created rhythms for repetitious tasks, easing the physical burdens of labor and relieving the tedium. Slave music furnished an outlet for repressed anger and served as a means of self-expression.

The slaves brought songs with them from Africa which by the nineteenth century had been adapted to English words and heavily influenced by the imagery of Bible stories taught to them by missionaries and evangelists.

Musical accompaniment commonly came from a banjo or fiddle. Masters would sometimes let slaves borrow these instruments for holidays and celebrations. Some such instruments were purchased by slaves themselves with extra earnings generated by gardens or crafts. Many instruments were handmade. A slave with particularly fine skills might carve his own fiddle, but it was more likely that ingenuity led them to improvise with materials at hand. Stringed instruments were made using horsehair and animal skins or bladders and gourds. Goat and sheep skins were stretched across a variety of objects to create drums. Other percussion instruments drafted sheep ribs, cow jaws, tree trunks, and old kettles and pans into their design. Animal horns could provide the raw material for wind instruments. **Related Entries:** Minstrel Shows; Slave Religion.

SUGGESTED READING: John W. Blassingame, *The Slave Community: Plantation Life in the Antebellum South* (1979); John Anthony Scott, *The Ballad of American Song: The History of the United States in Song and Story* (1967).

SLAVE NARRATIVES: The first examples of writing in the formal genres by blacks is seen in the 1820s. Some appeared as poetry, but certainly the slave narratives, which began to appear in the 1830s, had the greatest effect. While the influence of an anti-slavery editor is plainly visible in some, others are clearly the work of the avowed author. **Frederick Douglass'** *Narrative* (1845) has perhaps garnered the most fame. Other significant works were penned by **William Wells Brown**—America's first black novelist—Josiah Henson, and Henry "Box" Brown. Popular narratives were not the sole domain of men. Harriet A. Jacobs published *Incidents in the Life of a Slave Girl* in 1861. Slave narratives sold very well, supplying sensationalism and sentimentality to an audience that relished both.

Many slave biographies and narratives were based on oral interviews and were taken down in the 1920s and 1930s by historians desperate to document the details of slave life before its participants faded away. Under the sponsorship of the Federal Writers Project, the Virginia Writers Project, and other agencies, these narratives were given by people who were, on the average, over eighty years old, and had been children when the Civil War began. The validity of these records can be judged by contrasting them with other information found in the letters, diaries, and contemporary writings of the slaveholders, and in the collections of plantation records, Freedmen's Bureau documents, and other written material dealing with the slave trade and plantation management that survived the war. Each narrative must be subjected to the same type of evaluation by which all sources of historical information are judged.

Slave autobiographies, in particular, have been used extensively by historians because they are few in number. Under close scrutiny they often turn out to be carefully crafted propaganda pieces, rooted in truth, but designed by the **abolitionists** to appeal to all the dissimilar reform groups of the North. In the 1860s there was an explosion of hand-written testimony from slaves recently freed by federal troops.

Nonetheless, the data that were compiled are useful, particularly since the slaves could not be expected to leave much in the way of other written documentation. Many of the data collected took the form of anecdotal statements by former slaves assembled by well meaning, but not unbiased, investigators. It is not enough to say that all sources are biased. Some sources suffer from other limiting characteristics beyond their obvious intent, such as the author's selective memory, or his desire to make himself seem heroic. It is almost impossible to correct the data that we have for the prejudice of "untrained, negligent, or incompetent" nineteenth-century researchers (Stampp, 1980). Such data have been used, perhaps too uncritically, by scholars, authors, playwrights, and screenwriters to distort the picture of **slavery** beyond our ability to know the truth. **Related Entries**: Brown, William Wells; Douglass, Frederick; Slave Escapes.

SUGGESTED READING: Ira Berlin, ed., *Remembering Slavery: African Americans Talk About Their Personal Experiences of Slavery and Freedom* (1998); Harriet A. Jacobs, *Incidents in the Life of a Slave Girl* (1861; 1987); Belinda Hurmence, ed., *We Lived in a Little Cabin in the Yard* (1994); Kenneth M. Stampp, *The Imperiled Union* (1980).

SLAVE PATROLS: Slave patrols, made up of whites, monitored the **roads** and periodically checked the slave quarters. Often an outgrowth of the **militia**, the patrol was usually comprised of a captain and three others who were appointed for a period of a few months. Some states required these patrols, while others merely provided the authorization for local communities to raise them. **Alabama** and **South Carolina** were more dedicated to

Slave patrols questioned and detained all blacks, free or slave. Failure to obey the patrol could end in corporal punishment or even death. (Sketch by F. B. Schell of *Leslie's Illustrated Magazine*, June 1863.)

the practice than other states, most of which observed a degree of vigilance reflective of public sentiment at the time. All blacks were required to have a pass signed by the master or **overseer** when off the plantation and not accompanied by a white. A slave caught without such documentation was subject to detention, immediate and sometimes vicious punishment, or even death. Twenty lashes were almost expected in such a case.

Complaints against slave patrols came from masters and slaves alike. Masters who bought their way out of serving on the patrol were often replaced with **poor whites** who, not having a master's perspective, abused the slaves and hassled them in the slave quarters. Slaves grieved over such untoward punishment, often regarding their masters as their protectors against such practices.

Slaves instituted their own resistance measures. Warning systems were created to notify others of nearby patrols. Trapdoors and hiding places were built into slave quarters to help unauthorized travelers hide. To protect slave meeting places, vine ropes were tied across access roads to trip approaching riders, thus providing additional escape time. **Related Entries**: Black Codes; Punishment of Slaves.

SUGGESTED READING: Eugene D. Genovese, *Roll, Jordan, Roll: The World the Slaves Made* (1974).

SLAVE RELIGION: The slaves who first were brought to the Americas came from diverse cultural and religious backgrounds. Upon arrival at a plantation, they found themselves intermingled with other Africans who held a wide range of beliefs and practiced a multiplicity of rites. The desire to hold true to ancestral customs was a strong one, and some slaves would periodically steal away to neighboring farms to join with others from the same ethnic group. The diversity that abounded, however, produced an openness which transcended cultural differences with a common mystical relationship to God and the supernatural. African religious practices were marked by a communication with the natural world and a joyful expression of overt sexuality which shocked the prudish Protestants. Lacking an understanding of the African culture and having no desire to cultivate one, slaveholders did their best to strip slaves of their native religious culture. Effectively, however, these practices were merely driven underground to be practiced in secret.

By the close of the eighteenth century, and as an outgrowth of the Great Awakening, many whites felt it their duty to bring Christianity to the slaves. Evangelical, revivalist **Protestantism** leveled all men as sinners before God, regardless of wealth or color. An intense commitment to conversion was focused on slave communities. The comprehensiveness of such an undertaking was facilitated by the increasing number of second, third, and even fourth generation slaves who had fewer cultural and linguistic barriers to Christian instruction. Generally, the slave community was open to this movement. The emotionalism, congregational response, and plain doctrine of revivalist preaching were favorably disposed to the African religious heritage. Remnants of African dance and song found a home in the spirituals of evangelical Protestantism. The egalitarian perspective of this movement opened the way for black converts to participate actively in churches as preachers and even as founders. Slaves had the freedom to attend church side by side with their owners and in some instances to worship at independent black churches. Even so, the majority of slaves who had the opportunity to become church members in the first decades of the nineteenth century were household servants, artisans, and urban residents.

By the 1830s churchmen became increasingly committed to the idea of an aggressive program of plantation missions in order to reach rural slaves. The distance between plantations made ordinary pastoral care impossible. Planters were generally amenable to the concept of slave conversion in a theological sense, although two revolts led by slaves who found validation for their cause in Scripture produced huge setbacks in any latitude afforded slaves. Now planters were expected to join missionary societies and local churches with monetary support for the plantation missionaries. Proponents of the cause adopted the techniques of Bible and **temperance** societies to raise Southern consciousness by printing sermons and essays, adopting resolutions, and devoting entire conferences to the topic. Southerners began to see that Scripture could be used to sanction a kind of Christian social order based on mutual duty of slave to master and master to slave as found in Ephesians 6:5–9. As the decade advanced, growing uneasiness toward Northern **abolitionists** created an ambivalence in Southerners regarding slave instruction; however, the criticism leveled by Northern churches at those of the South only made Southerners more sensitive to their duty. Supporters of plantation missions continued to convince slaveholders that they had duties toward their slaves. **Plantation mistresses** in particular were urged to take an active role in slave instruction by reading sermons to them, including them in family prayers, and conducting Sabbath schools. Some household slaves were led in prayer each morning by the mistress. Slaveholders were encouraged to give their slaves the opportunity to tend a small garden plot, raise livestock, and accumulate money in the belief that as one class rose, so would the other. This even had economic appeal to some. The ideal of a Christian master-slave relationship fed the Southern myth of the benevolent planter-patriarch who oversaw the simple, helpless black. By the eve of the Civil War it was not unusual for slaves to outnumber whites at racially mixed churches.

This manifestation of the plantation missionaries' success was misleading and represented only one component of a slave's religious experience. In the secrecy of their cabins and amid brush or "hush arbors," slaves met free from the owner's gaze and practiced a religion that addressed issues other than a slave's subservience to his master. Freedom was often the subject of prayer. Through prayer, song, and "feeling the spirit" slaves gained renewed strength through hope. These informal prayer meetings were filled with spirituals which perpetuated a continuity with African music and performance. The drums that had once been a vital part of their spiritual expression were replaced by rhythmic hand clapping and foot-stomping known as "shouting." Rather than truly adopting Christianity, they had adapted it to themselves.

Generally, slaves faced severe punishment if they were found attending these prayer meetings. Gathering in deep woods, gullies, and other secluded places, they created makeshift rooms with quilts and blankets that had been wet down to inhibit the transmission of voices. A common practice was to place an iron pot or kettle turned upside down in the middle of the floor to catch the sound. The roots and perhaps the symbolism of this practice have been lost. On occasion, rags would be stuffed into the mouth of an overzealous worshiper. **Slave narratives** repeatedly speak to the uplifting nature of these meetings.

An underground culture of voodoo and conjuring was practiced in areas where there were large numbers of slaves from the Caribbean or where African snake cults—which involved the handling of serpents as part of their ritual—had been imported and adapted. The power of these priests or conjurers never reached the level it had in its native lands. **Related Entry**: Slave Burial.

SUGGESTED READING: Harriet A. Jacobs, *Incidents in the Life of a Slave Girl, Narrated by Herself* (1861; 1987); Charles Joyner, *Down by the Riverside: A South Carolina Slave Community* (1984); Albert J. Raboteau, *Slave Religion: The "Invisible Institution" in the Antebellum South* (1978).

SLAVE REVOLTS. *See* Fear of Slave Revolts.

SLAVE STATES: John Hayward's *Gazetteer of the United States* (1853) gives the following information about slave states in this period:

Slave States	Whites	Colored	Slaves	Total
Delaware	71,169	18,073	2,290	91,532
Maryland	417,943	74,723	90,368	583,034
Virginia	895,304	53,829	472,528	1,421,661
North Carolina	553,118	27,373	288,412	868,903
South Carolina	274,623	8,900	384,984	668,507
Georgia	521,438	2,880	381,681	905,999
Alabama	426,486	2,293	342,892	771,671
Mississippi	295,758	899	309,898	606,555
Louisiana	255,416	17,537	244,786	517,739
Tennessee	756,893	6,271	239,461	1,002,625
Kentucky	761,688	9,736	210,981	982,405
Missouri	592,077	2,544	87,422	682,043
Arkansas	162,068	589	46,982	209,639
Florida	47,167	925	39,309	87,401
Texas	154,100	331	58,161	212,592
D. of C.	38,027	9,973	3,687	51,687
Total	**6,223,275**	**236,876**	**3,203,842**	**9,663,993**

Related Entry: Free States.

SUGGESTED READING: John Hayward, *Gazetteer of the United States* (1853).

SLAVE VALUATION. *See* Value of Slaves.

SLAVERY: Slavery was one of the pivotal questions in dispute throughout the antebellum period. History inexplicably continues to blame the English for creating a system of "American" plantation slavery when the system is documented to have existed before the New World was discovered and more than a century before the English set foot in any colony of their own. The African slave trade was begun by Arab and Muslim traders in the fifteenth century, and the Portuguese adapted slavery to their immensely profitable **sugar** plantations in the islands of the eastern Atlantic before the discovery of the New World. Three-quarters of all the Africans brought to the New World were imported by Spain and Portugal.

Unfortunately, the early history of slavery in North America is poorly documented and inconclusive. It seems certain that none of the founders of the first English colonies anticipated a dependence on black slaves. While the first Negroes brought to the English colonies were formerly thought to have been exclusively slaves, recent research suggests that many of them were actually indentured servants or free craftsmen. It is equally clear, however, that distinctions were made between black and white laborers and servants in even the earliest English colonies.

The distinction between **free blacks**, black indentured servants, and black slaves quickly blurred. Free blacks seem to have preferred to live in an urban setting and were twice as likely to live in cities than slaves, who were primarily agricultural workers. In cosmopolitan areas free blacks and slave craftsmen found opportunities for employment, exposure to black culture and religion, and the company of other freemen. However, the majority of free blacks lived on the margins of poverty and were subject to detention and questioning by the authorities without cause. They were continually encouraged to sell themselves back into slavery.

By the beginning of the eighteenth century, race-based slavery firmly established itself in English North America in place of indentured service. Historians have been hard pressed to explain the sudden shift from white indentured labor to black slavery, as indentured servants were less expensive to maintain and generally more tractable workers. The absurd theory that the Negro race was better suited to the hot climate of the South than the white was put to rest by **John Quincy Adams** when he noted that Europeans cultivated the land in hotter climates in Greece and in Sicily than those in **Virginia** or the Carolinas. During the eighteenth century slave labor proved profitable only on large-scale plantations that produced a cash crop. **Related Entries**: Atlantic Slave Trade; Black Slaveowners; Buying and Selling Slaves; Children Born as Slaves; Emancipation; Extension of Slavery into the Territories; Fear of Slave Revolts; Federal Laws Governing Slavery; Overseers (Slave Drivers); Punishment of Slaves; Race Relations; Slave Burial; Slave Clothing; Slave Courtship and Marriage; Slave Dwellings; Slave Escapes; Slave Food; Slave Music; Slave Narratives; Slave Patrols; Slave Religion; Slave States; Slaves—Hired Out; Slaves—Task Labor.

SUGGESTED READING: Ira Berlin, ed., *Remembering Slavery: African Americans Talk About Their Personal Experiences of Slavery and Freedom* (1998); Harriet A. Jacobs, *Incidents in the Life of a Slave Girl* (1861; 1987); Belinda Hurmence, ed., *We Lived in a Little Cabin in the Yard* (1994); Kenneth M. Stampp, *The Peculiar Institution* (1956); Dorothy Denneen Volo and James M. Volo, *Daily Life in Civil War America* (1998).

SLAVES—AFRICAN COLONIZATION. *See* African Colonization.

SLAVES—ATLANTIC TRADE. *See* Atlantic Slave Trade.

SLAVES, BUYING AND SELLING. *See* Buying and Selling Slaves.

SLAVES, CHILDREN BORN AS. *See* Children Born as Slaves.

SLAVES—GANG LABOR: Gang labor was commonly used on large plantations. Plantations having fifty or more slaves generally divided their workers into two gangs. The most able-bodied men and sometimes women were known as plow-hands. Less capable workers were designated as hoe-hands. On some plantations trash-gangs were assigned to such light work as weeding and yard cleanup. This last group often included children, those of advanced age, or those with other limitations. The gang was generally headed by a slave driver, usually chosen from the male slaves of that gang. **Related Entries**: Plantation Economy; Slaves—Task Labor.

SUGGESTED READING: Edward D.C. Campbell, Jr., with Kym S. Rice, *Before Freedom Came: African-American Life in the Antebellum South* (1991).

SLAVES—HIRED OUT: Sometimes skilled slaves were hired out to work for artisans or others who were in need of their services. This practice made efficient use of the labor supply and generated additional income for owners who sometimes found themselves with surplus slaves. It was not uncommon for slaves to be hired out to pay for the schooling expenses of minor heirs or to meet other pecuniary needs of the owner's family. Slave hiring was more likely to occur nearer to cities, where the need was greater and the practice was better suited to the evolving industrial necessities of an urban economy.

Slaves worked in industries such as textile and iron manufacturing, tobacco processing, and mining. Most of these workers were male, and the majority were owned by the companies engaged in the industry, but as many as one in five were hired out by their masters on an annual basis.

Slaves were hired out to work in construction, carpentry, and masonry trades. Unskilled slaves were also hired out to work in brickyards. Because brickyards were often situated near swamps, even the most desperate free workers were loath to work there. Risk of malaria and respiratory problems prompted masters who hired out their slaves to such facilities to demand premium compensation. Period papers indicate that slaves employed in such hazardous environments drew double the rate for other slaves and as much as one-fourth of their value annually.

Some skilled slaves found substantial independence by offering themselves for hire. These slaves were only the most trusted. Their wages were paid to their masters. The practice was not without its negative aspects, however, as the person hiring the slave did not have the same personal or financial interest in the slave to temper working conditions. Hiring out also could separate a slave from his family and friends.

From time to time, white artisans, resenting the competition, called for ordinances to limit the practice of hiring out, but slaveowners felt that regulation infringed on their property rights. This practice was illegal in some Southern states. **Related Entries**: Plantation Economy; Slaves—Gang Labor; Slaves—Task Labor.

SUGGESTED READING: Peter Kolchin, *American Slavery, 1619–1877* (1993).

SLAVES OWNED BY BLACKS. *See* Black Slaveowners.

SLAVES—TASK LABOR: On large plantations the most common form of organized labor was that of the "gang." However, the cultivation of rice utilized a slave labor system different from other Southern crops known as task labor. The extensive hydraulic engineering needed to provide ditches and gates for flooding the crop did not require the labor gangs necessitated by **sugar** or **cotton** production. Slaves on rice plantations were assigned specific, individualized jobs. The task was delegated based on an average worker's ability to perform it in a single day's labor. Enterprising and skillful slaves were often able to complete their day's assignment and then apply themselves to the cultivation and marketing of their own crops or production of handicrafts. The slaves were subject to less direct supervision in this system and thus enjoyed greater independence. While the task labor system was developed on the rice plantations, it was also used by forward thinking plantation owners to produce other crops throughout the South. **Related Entries**: Plantation Economy; Slaves—Gang Labor; Slaves—Hired Out.

SUGGESTED READING: Edward D.C. Campbell, Jr., with Kym S. Rice, *Before Freedom Came: African-American Life in the Antebellum South* (1991); James L. Michie, *Richmond Hill Plantation, 1810–1868: The Discovery of Antebellum Life on a Waccamaw Rice Plantation* (1989).

SOIL EROSION. *See* Erosion of the Soil.

SOUTH CAROLINA: Highlights of a period description of the state from John Hayward's *Gazetteer of the United States* (1853) read as follows:

Surface and Soil: Along the sea-coast there is a chain of valuable islands, the soil of which is admirably suited to the growth of the best descriptions of **cotton**. The low country is well adapted to the culture of rice, of which large quantities are annually raised. Two sorts of cotton are raised, the long and short staple, nearly all of which are exported to the Northern States and to Europe. Among other vegetable products are the grains of nearly every variety; fruits of the best kinds, as figs, pomegranates, apricots, nectarines, cherries, pears, peaches, and melons. The sweet potatoes of South Carolina are renowned for their fineness of flavor. Tobacco and indigo are raised in large quantities. Tar, pitch, turpentine, and vegetable oils are among the important natural products of the state.

In this period illustration the State-House of South Carolina exhibits classical architecture and elegance typical of public buildings at the time. (From *Harper's Weekly* IV, no. 205, December 1, 1860.)

Rivers: The state is well supplied with watercourses. Some of the streams are of great extent, and afford navigation for steamers and small craft for considerable distances.

Education: The free school system is not yet fully incorporated within the institutions of South Carolina. Charity schools, however, for the elementary instruction of poor white children, are supported through both public and private means, in many parts of the state. A number of respectable academies or high schools, and many primary schools, are well sustained by the wealthy classes. There are three colleges of some note, a state medical college, of high character, a Baptist theological seminary and another supported by Lutherans.

Internal Improvements: There are three **railroads** and another is in progress. Several canals have been constructed, which, though of inconsiderable extent, are of great utility.

Manufacture: Some attempts to introduce the spinning and weaving of cotton have been introduced but with indifferent success. Agriculture and commerce are the chief supports of the state. The exports of **raw materials**, including cotton, rice, lumber, pitch, and tar are annually of great magnitude.

Minerals: Iron, lead, plumbago, and various ochres are obtained in considerable quantities. Gold is found in many parts of the state but mining operations are carried on with less spirit than [in] **North Carolina**.

Indians: No organized tribes, or large bands of native Indians, are at present residing within the state.

Population: For the past fifty years, the white population of the state has but slowly advanced in numbers, compared with the increase of the slave population. Of the 668,567 inhabitants at the last census, 384,948 were slaves. In the low country, the blacks outnumber the whites more than three to one; in the central parts, the whites are rather numerous; and in the upper country, the numerical difference between the two races is nearly reversed from that in the lowland.

Related Entries: Geography; Nullification; Secession; South Carolina Association.

SUGGESTED READING: John Hayward, *Gazetteer of the United States* (1853); Louis B. Wright, *South Carolina: A History* (1976).

SOUTH CAROLINA ASSOCIATION: In 1823, as a response to the **Denmark Vesey** conspiracy, tidewater planters led by **James A. Hamilton** formed the South Carolina Association in **Charleston**. The formation of this group has been described as one of the most revealing events of the antebellum period because of its long-term effects. The association was to become a permanent institution in **South Carolina** until the Civil War, and it served as a point of dissemination of **nullification** and **states' rights** propaganda as well as a training ground for armed resistance to the rule of the federal government.

The avowed purposes of the South Carolina Association were to strictly enforce the **Black Codes**, to keep a close eye on the activities of the slaves, and to insist on the enforcement of all laws pertaining to **free blacks**. Its initial success in reinstituting the enforcement of the **Negro Seaman's Law**, and in thwarting the protestations of the federal government in that encounter, caused the association to grow and spread to dozens of chapters throughout the state.

Governor Hamilton's great contribution to the continued life of the association was to make it an influential "political club" in an era when politics was becoming a national hobby. Membership was open to any white who could pay the one dollar fee, and the monthly meetings quickly became important social events. Non-slaveholders and small slaveholders were, by their membership, able to join with the tidewater gentry in the seeming equality of association functions. More important, white "mechanics"—woodworkers, metal smiths, and other tradesmen previously viewed with disdain by the **planter aristocracy** because of their close ties to manual labor—suddenly became respected white South Carolinians. Hamilton's association, while excluding almost no one who was white in reality, had all the outward appearances of an exclusive club; and men who had despaired of being accepted in such elite circles flocked to enter. The power of this process to marshal support among the vast majority of white Southerners should not be underestimated. Those who owned no slaves now came, by their membership in the association, to stand behind an agenda based on states' rights and the continuation of **slavery**, and against a strong central government and **abolition** even though they stood to gain little either way.

The association made political pamphlets and tracts available to its members monthly. It played an important role in circulating reprints of **White-marsh Seabrook**'s pamphlet *A Concise View of the Critical Situation and Future Prospects of the Slaveholding States in Relation to Their Colored Population* (1823). In his view, South Carolina needed to reserve the right "to enact laws, guarding against the corruption and consequent insubordination of her slaves." The association warned of an ever growing danger to white South Carolinians from their slaves. Its propaganda—some true and some planted for effect—claimed the existence of gangs of runaway Negroes in the upcountry swamps; the murder of white **overseers** by the slaves under their charge; the murder of a planter and a planter's daughter in two separate instances; and the slashing of two white men by a black who ran amok in the streets of Charleston. Moreover, a previously docile slave serving as a cook poisoned a feast attended by hundreds of whites, killing several and making scores deathly ill. As the association put it, "State Sovereignties [are] the ark to which we must ultimately look for our safety."

Hamilton was determined to keep the momentum of the association going by carefully planning its activities, but he also took care that its structure did not become too democratic. All political decisions were left to previously chosen delegates and not to the membership at large. During the tariff difficulties of 1832, he organized two separate statewide conventions, with delegates from almost seventy districts, to decide what legislative actions should be taken. Thousands of spectators attended these meetings, and they were favored with broadsides, political discourse, and militant speeches filled with high rhetoric.

Many in the association viewed their struggle in 1832 as a continuation of that of 1776 and took an active role in raising troops of citizen **militia**, appointing officers, and holding military reviews. So popular was the esprit de corps engendered by these affairs that many joined the association simply to be able to enjoy the camaraderie and chivalric atmosphere of the militia companies. The need to present a defensive front in its confrontation with the federal government caused the new state governor, **Robert Y. Hayne**, who had been elected to replace Hamilton, to set up a system of mounted militiamen throughout the state. These presumably could respond quickly to federal "invasion" without posing a threat to the government. Moreover, the state legislature gave the governor the power to buy arms and to conscript any South Carolinian between the ages of eighteen and forty-five. The legacy of a successful militia uprising against the overwhelming force of the regular British army in the Revolution, whether martial mythology or historical reality, was being reflected in the meetings of the South Carolina Association and was to have far-reaching effects in the organization of the

The extent of Southern hospitality on largely isolated plantations is manifest in this contemporary illustration. (From *Harper's Weekly*, November 1858.)

infant Confederate army in 1860. **Related Entries**: Force Bill; Hamilton, James A.; Vesey, Denmark.

SUGGESTED READING: William W. Freehling, *Prelude to Civil War: The Nullification Controversy in South Carolina, 1816–1836* (1966; 1992); James A. Hamilton, Jr., Papers, University of North Carolina Library Collection, Chapel Hill.

SOUTHERN HOSPITALITY: Born of necessity in a region where sweeping plantations produced few travelers and left the countryside bereft of small villages, Southern hospitality was the general custom wherein a traveler might ask for lodging at any private home happened upon as nightfall approached. The North developed towns and villages as it expanded, spawning numerous public houses and inns which could provide needed quarter to the traveler. The South, however, grew as counties, with travel accommodations appearing with great infrequency and mainly along the major commercial lines of travel. One diarist noted that during a six-month journey through the South, he came upon public houses less than once a week.

There was a considerable gap in expectations, however, between some Northern travelers and the hospitable provider. Period writings of Northerners document rude behavior and wretched fare. Southern readers deeply resented these stories, and some vowed to show any Yankee who approached seeking hospitality just how paltry situations could be. Part of this problem may have arisen from the fact that many Northerners were viewing the relationship with a dictionary definition in mind. To them, hospitality meant receiving and entertaining visitors without remuneration. Some Southerners saw the hospitality as the kindness of permitting a complete stranger to take shelter with them, and had no problem declaring the exact price expected in return upon being approached by a traveler. In 1860 a traveler in **Mississippi** recorded that he was usually received free of charge if the house belonged to people of means, or that he paid the customary charge of one dollar, for which he was furnished with supper, lodging, breakfast, and food for his horse. Southern travelers, especially those of "quality," may have been treated differently, for they commonly describe warm receptions which always found "room for one more" in even the humblest abodes and gracious hostesses who seemed able to repeat the miracle of the loaves and fishes.

Certainly, what elevated Southern hospitality to its current connotation would be the lavish presentations and courtesies extended to invited guests or to visitors who presented letters of introduction to prominent plantation owners. These guests could anticipate the assistance of servants in preparing their dress, luxuriant presentations of abundant food and drink, and free use of the plantation's amenities, such as horseback riding, libraries, and gardens. Period letters and journals often describe parties of multicourse meals, which one would imagine would be reserved for holidays or the most special occasions, taking place with regularity. One breakfast description included cornbread, buckwheat cakes, boiled chicken, bacon, eggs, hominy, fish, both fresh and pickled, and beefsteak all being served at a single sitting. Dinner offerings were likely to be equally impressive. An 1833 letter detailed a dinner that began with a very rich soup and continued with a saddle of mutton, ham, beef, turkey, duck, eggs with greens, potatoes, beets, and hominy. After the circulation of champagne came dessert, which included plum pudding and tarts followed by ice cream and preserves and peaches preserved in brandy. Lastly came figs, raisins, almonds and wine, port, Madeira, and a sweet wine for the ladies. **Related Entries**: Food; Holiday Celebrations.

SUGGESTED READING: Frederick Law Olmsted, *The Cotton Kingdom: A Traveler's Observations on Cotton and Slavery in the American Slave States* (1861; 1996); William Thorp, *A Southern Reader* (1955).

SOUTHERN PRESS. *See* Newspapers.

SPECIE: The term specie, or "hard" currency, refers to the use of gold or silver rather than paper money as legal tender for all transactions. Debates over paper money raged throughout the nineteenth century, and they were closely intertwined with disputes concerning banks. Many newly chartered banks threw themselves into the business with inadequate backing and inflated optimism. They made liberal loans and issued reams of paper currency—a practice allowed to banks at the time. In the 1820s the widespread use of paper money caused the money supply to increase 300 percent in less than a decade.

The resulting inflation stimulated business and created a demand for both domestic and foreign goods. Unfortunately, more was imported than exported, and an already unfavorable trade balance was made worse. In the 1830s speculators began to borrow paper money to make investments in government land, thereby fueling further inflation. Specie payment for government land soon became a political issue, and financial disaster threatened.

A wheat failure in 1835, requiring that America import grain from abroad, proved the precipitating event. The lack of confidence engendered by this unexpected circumstance caused European exporters to refuse credit to American importers and to demand hard money payments. In reaction to this, American businessmen also began to demand gold and silver for merchandise; but the bank vaults were empty—most of the gold and silver had been shipped abroad to pay America's foreign debts.

President **Andrew Jackson** intervened in July 1836. He issued an executive order known as the Specie Circular in which he declared that the government would require payments in specie for all federal land purchases, essentially putting a halt to the speculative buying and selling. The Distribution Act at the end of the year required banks to repay any borrowed government funds in specie. This was a heavy burden on almost all financial institutions, and by the spring of 1837 every bank in the country suspended specie payment to their depositors. The ensuing economic paralysis resulted in the Panic of 1837.

There was no escape from the depression into which the nation passed. Northern factory workers lost their jobs as manufacturers closed their businesses for lack of credit. Western farmers lost important markets in Europe, as mills and factories—especially in England—were unable to collect on American debts and went into bankruptcy. The South suffered as the demand for **cotton** crashed and cotton prices fell. Finally, many slaves found that they faced the auction block for the first time, and slave families faced permanent separation as even the most humane slaveowners were forced to raise cash by liquidating their investment in slave labor.

In 1838 the provisions of the Specie Circular were repealed by an act of Congress. But it was not until 1840 that President **Martin Van Buren**, who took office in 1837 as Jackson's anointed successor, was able to pass a Subtreasury Bill which allowed the government to shore up the economy by issuing Treasury notes to meet expenses and temporarily abandon a "hard" money approach to national financing. All government payments were to return to specie by 1843. In 1851 Congress adopted a three-cent coin, and in 1853 it authorized the coinage of three-dollar gold pieces while reducing the silver in all coins but the silver dollar. The question of paper currency or specie payments remained a divisive political issue until the adoption of the Gold Standard Act in 1900. **Related Entries**: Jackson, Andrew; Land Speculation.

SUGGESTED READING: John Steele Gordon, *Hamilton's Blessing: The Extraordinary Life and Times of Our National Debt* (1998); A. B. Johnson, *The Advanced Value of Gold* (1862).

SPOILS SYSTEM: The term "spoils" was applied to the practice of placing political supporters in government jobs by William L. Marcy, who defended it by saying, "To the victors belong the spoils." The spoils system is most closely identified with the accession of **Andrew Jackson** to the presidency in the election of 1828. It was actually his secretary of state, **Martin Van Buren**, who introduced the idea of the spoils system (long a staple of New York politics) into the federal bureaucracy.

The bulk of civil servants employed by the government since the turn of the nineteenth century had come to believe that their jobs were lifetime appointments. While Jackson found little corruption in government, he sensed a great deal of incompetence and began to replace the older office-holders with his loyal supporters. Fear spread immediately throughout the government service, and Jackson's actions met with vehement and outspoken protest. Nonetheless, Jackson's appointments were not as ruthless as his detractors may have suggested. In a list of 10,000 post office workers and petty bureaucrats, fewer than one in ten were actually replaced. **Related Entries**: Jackson, Andrew, Van Buren, Martin.

SUGGESTED READING: Charles G. Sellers, "Andrew Jackson Versus the Historians" *Mississippi Valley Historical Review* 44, no. 4 (March 1958); Charles G. Sellers, *Jacksonian Democracy* (1958).

STATES' RIGHTS: The Founding Fathers left undecided the question of whether the state or the national government was ultimately sovereign. While the Bill of Rights explicitly forbade federal involvement in state affairs, discontent and frustration with the inertia of the political process induced many Americans to demand federal intervention in a whole series of social initiatives including the **abolition** of **slavery**. A new type of "despotism" emerged from this imperative to reform. Although based on intellectual and emotional forces rather than on physical compulsion, **reform movements** were willing to suppress personal liberty, tradition, and even constitutional principles to correct the social ills in America.

By mid-century there were signs that the people were finding the unceasing intervention by government in their daily affairs tiresome. A remedy was needed, yet the voters eschewed an expression of personal rights and turned rather to states' rights. **Thomas Jefferson** warned in 1821 that the federal government should not be allowed to define the limits of its own powers. Many of his worst fears had come to be realized by mid-century. The **Supreme Court** had seen fit to express the doctrine of implied powers, which allowed for a broad interpretation of congressional powers under the Constitution. As a consequence many Americans wished their individual states to assert their sovereignty and rein in the federal government before it became too powerful.

The concept of states' rights was first elaborated by **James A. Hamilton** of **South Carolina** in the **nullification** crisis, but it was given its final form by **John C. Calhoun**. Southerners frequently invoked states' rights as a symbol in their turmoil over slavery in the 1850s, but the idea of limited federal power was much older than the slavery debates of the nineteenth century. States' rights advocates seem to have been able to keep the two questions of sovereignty and slavery distinct. Certainly New England Federalists had seen no link to slavery when they claimed their own states' rights during the opposition to the **War of 1812**. Nonetheless, in much of the North the questions of states' rights and the continuation of slavery became a single issue on which it was impossible to have divergent views. If slavery was to be eradicated, then states' rights must be sacrificed on the altar of abolition. **Related Entries**: Calhoun, John C.; Constitutional Convention; Nullification.

SUGGESTED READING: Drew Gilpin Faust, *The Creation of Confederate Nationalism: Ideology and Identity in the Civil War South* (1988); William W. Freehling, *Prelude to Civil War: The Nullification Controversy in South Carolina, 1816–1836* (1966; 1992); James R. Kennedy and Walter D. Kennedy, *The South Was Right* (1995).

STEPHENS, ALEXANDER H. (1812–1883): congressman and Vice President of the Confederacy. Alexander H. Stephens was one of those who was brought to prominence and power from outside the upper classes of Southern society. At the University of Georgia, a hotbed of political discussion, Stephens was exposed to the most pressing political topics of his day. He came away with a strong appreciation of **states' rights** and an aversion to protective **tariffs**. He believed that the right of **secession** was essential for keeping the national government within constitutional bounds. At university he made a lifelong friend of **Robert A. Toombs**, who was to become a noted defender of the Southern way of life.

Stephens' success at law allowed him to buy a small plantation home and successfully stand for a seat in the **Georgia** legislature as a Southern **Whig**. His outstanding advocacy of a **railroad** to connect Georgia with the grain-growing region of the old Northwest brought him to local prominence and paved his way to Congress in 1843. His first notable speech was made in

favor of the **annexation of Texas**. Stephens argued that the South needed the added political weight of **Texas** to preserve "a proper balance between the different sections of the country." Nonetheless, Stephens never failed to criticize the prosecution of the **Mexican War**.

In 1849 Stephens strongly resisted proposals to admit California as a **free state** but contented himself with an endorsement of the **Compromise of 1850**. Likewise, he took great pride in managing the passage of the **Kansas-Nebraska Act of 1854** by Congress, but he was disappointed when its passage quickly caused the disintegration of his party. In an effort to rescue their political positions, Stephens, Toombs, and **Howell Cobb** launched the Constitutional Union Party, which made some short-term gains but quickly collapsed. Thereafter, by vigorously denouncing the anti-immigrant and anti-Catholic positions of the **Nativist Party**, Stephens was able to shift to the **Democratic Party** without losing his seat in Congress.

He proved a kindly master to his own slaves, and many Negroes held him in the warmest esteem. He defended the institution of **slavery** on Biblical grounds, calling it a "stern necessity." Ultimately Stephens came to actively defend the Southern way of life, which he described as "the best system for the sustenance, advancement, and happiness of Negroes," and he endorsed the concept of reopening the **Atlantic slave trade** with Africa.

Brought finally to accept the necessity of Southern independence, Stephens declared that he was "openly, boldly and fearlessly" for disunion. It was Stephens who initially called for a secession convention of all the Southern states. His accurate analysis of the coming war stands out among the hundreds in the North predicting that the war would be settled in a single afternoon of battle: "You may think that the suppression of an outbreak in the southern States would be a holiday job for a few of your Northern regiments, but you may find to your cost, in the end, that seven millions of people fighting for their rights, their homes, and their hearth-stones cannot be easily conquered" (Schott, 1988).

Stephens, who had survived a train wreck on the way to the convention in **Montgomery, Alabama**, had not sought high position, but nonetheless was chosen Vice President of the Confederacy. He proved an unhappy member of the infant government, opposing the "excesses" of **Jefferson Davis**, the suspension of habeas corpus, and the adoption of conscription. He found the effects of war distressing and spent a good deal of time visiting the wounded and the prisoners on both sides. His belief in constitutional restraint and his hope for a negotiated peace brought him into conflict with Davis, and he cast a very small shadow over the operations of the government after 1863. **Related Entry**: Confederate Government.

SUGGESTED READING: Rudolph R. Von Abele, *Alexander H. Stephens: A Biography* (1971); Thomas E. Schott, *Alexander H. Stephens of Georgia* (1988).

STOWE, HARRIET BEECHER (1811–1896): author. Harriet Elizabeth Beecher was the daughter of anti-slavery activist Lyman Beecher, a

Congregational pastor in Litchfield, Connecticut. Her sister, Catherine, established the Western Female Institute in Cincinnati in 1832, and Harriet was employed there as a teacher. In 1836 she married the Reverend C. E. Stowe, a theological professor at the Lane Theological Seminary in Cincinnati. Both institutions were hotbeds of extreme anti-slavery sentiment. In 1849 Mrs. Stowe visited a plantation in nearby Kentucky and saw the life of the slaves in their ramshackle cabins. This visit was her only firsthand knowledge of **slavery**, and, with the exception of slavery, she seems to have had a fondness for Southern ways and lifestyle. Her brother, Edward Beecher, was to provide her with most of her "facts" about slavery, and he spurred her on with rhetoric about the injustices of the **Fugitive Slave Law**.

Stowe's first major published work was *The Mayflower, or Descendants of the Pilgrims* (1849). Shortly thereafter, she began to contribute anti-slavery essays to the *National Era*, a **newspaper** published in **Washington, DC**. From 1851 to 1852, *Uncle Tom's Cabin* took form in this paper as a serial. She established her fame with the publication of *Uncle Tom's Cabin* in book form in 1852. A second, less well known work on the same theme, *Dred, a Tale of the Dismal Swamp* (1856), sold 100,000 copies in England.

President **Abraham Lincoln**, referring to the immense popularity of *Uncle Tom's Cabin*, called Stowe "the little woman whose book made such a great war." The South considered Stowe's work a slander and regarded it as **abolitionist** propaganda. The *Southern Literary Messenger* declared her work "a criminal prostitution of the high functions of the imagination." In fact, Stowe was unable to refute charges that the book was filled with factual errors and had been based largely on the uncontested **slave narratives** found in an abolitionist tract by Theodore D. Weld. She authored about a dozen routine works of fiction and nonfiction during the two decades after the war, including a work in 1870 that accused Lord Byron of incest with his sister that resulted in a child. The feeling aroused against her in Britain because of this book was intense, and she was accused of scandalmongering. Only her anti-slavery prominence saved her reputation. Her old age was not prosperous, and a full ten years before her death she had lapsed into senility. **Related Entries**: Reading; *Uncle Tom's Cabin*.

SUGGESTED READING: Joan D. Hendrick, *Harriet Beecher Stowe: The Life* (1994); C. E. Stowe, *Life of Harriet Beecher Stowe, Compiled from Her Journals and Letters* (1889; 1991).

STRICT CONSTRUCTION OF THE CONSTITUTION. *See* Constitutional Interpretation.

SUFFRAGE: Historically, the South had been neither democratic nor purely aristocratic. Instead, Southern politics had reached a balance much closer to the classical Roman concept of the republic, a public order in which the power rested with an elite group of people who ruled for the good of all. Such a large proportion of the people were uneducated—it is estimated that 20 percent of white males were illiterate—that it was easy for the gentry, a distinct minority, to dominate their communities. In a period when the thought of giving the vote to white women of property brought charges of radicalism, a large part of the white male population was also excluded from voting by a variety of legal means, usually including property qualifications.

The South was not overly backward in this regard. Not until 1818 had Connecticut abolished its property qualifications for voting, and New York and Massachusetts had not followed suit until 1821. Rhode Island did not liberalize its voting requirements until 1842. However, in **North Carolina** the property qualifications for voting were not removed until 1857, and it was not until 1865 that all white males were free to vote in **Kentucky**.

Early in the century votes could be marshaled from among the unsophisticated electorate by the use of simple expedients. In *Journey to America*, **Alexis de Tocqueville**, a European observer of the American political system in the 1830s, noted, "To gain votes, one must descend to maneuvers that disgust men of distinction. One must haunt the taverns, drink and argue with the mob; that is what is called Electioneering in America" (Volo and Volo, 1998).

Educated by their leaders to unify behind the politics of **secession**, ordinary citizens quickly recognized that their support was crucial and that their physical assistance might be required on the battlefield. They therefore sought to trade their support for more meaningful reforms in government, and for social and political access denied to them in former years. Requirements for **office holding** and enfranchisement were changed, and limits on legislative prerogatives and judicial authority were enacted. Most local offices were slowly made elective instead of appointive, further democratizing the process.

By 1860 adult white males could vote in every state that would enter the Confederacy, and election turnouts often rose above 70 percent of the eligible voters. Nonetheless, the old aristocratic Southern families had a firm hold on the structure of local and state government. Plural voting—allowing a man to vote in each county in which he owned property—and voice voting allowed the gentry to maintain their control. Not until after the Civil War were these practices abolished. The mass of Southern voters generally applauded this reluctance, especially within the plantation districts, choosing to support their leaders in a defense of the traditional American way of life. **Related Entries**: Planter Aristocracy; Women's Rights.

SUGGESTED READING: Alfredo DeGrazia, *Public and Republic: Political Representation in America* (1985); Donald W. Rogers and Christine B. Scriabine, *Voting and the Spirit of Democracy: Essays on the History of Voting and Voting Rights in America* (1992); Dorothy Denneen Volo and James M. Volo, *Daily Life in Civil War America* (1998).

SUGAR (SUGARCANE): The African slave trade was begun by Arab and Muslin traders in the fifteenth century, and the Portuguese adapted **slavery** to their immensely profitable sugarcane plantations in the islands of the eastern Atlantic. After the discovery of the New World, as sugar production required a semitropical environment, its cultivation was initially limited to the West Indies. It later spread to the delta region of **Louisiana** and other hot and humid parts of the South. The production of sugar was particularly lucrative, but it was hard on the slaves, who suffered ghastly levels of mortality in the pest-infected humidity of the cane fields. Masters often sold unrepentant slaves to the disease-infested sugar plantations in lieu of punishment.

Nonetheless, if a large sugar grower were fortunate enough to have three good agricultural years in a row, he could become fabulously wealthy. Fortunes made in growing sugar in the eighteenth century had altered the entire structure of British society. At the end of the Seven Years War, Britain had surrendered all of French Canada in exchange for a few small West Indian sugar islands and believed that it had gotten the better part of the bargain. Sugar growers living in the South—there were fewer than 200 individuals due to the high cost of essential machinery—developed a class structure based on all the ideals of the high aristocracy. Many built manor houses that rivaled the great homes of Europe. Before the rise of **cotton**, profits from sugar provided a financial bulwark for the American South. The archaic plantation system would have faded into obscurity were it not for the cash sugar generated. **Related Entry**: Plantation Economy.

SUGGESTED READING: Joseph Carlyle Sitterson, *Sugar Country: The Cane Sugar Industry in the South, 1753–1950* (1953); Sidney W. Mintz, *Sweetness and Power: The Place of Sugar in Modern History* (1985).

SUMNER, CHARLES (1811–1874): lawyer, senator, and cabinet officer. After graduating from Harvard in 1830, Charles Sumner studied law at Cambridge University. In 1834 he began a law practice in Boston while simultaneously editing the *American Jurist*, a law quarterly of high reputation. From 1837 to 1840 he visited Europe, and after his return he published the *Vesey Reports*, a twenty-volume study of the 1822 **Denmark Vesey** slave conspiracy in **Charleston, South Carolina**.

Sumner began his career in politics as a **Whig**. His speech in 1845 on the growing conflict between the United States and Mexico caught the public's attention and was printed and circulated throughout the country and in Europe. He vociferously opposed the **annexation of Texas** and any measure that might expedite the **extension of slavery into the territories**. Ultimately he drifted from the Whig Party to join the Free Soil Party. In 1851 he gained the seat of **Daniel Webster** in the Senate, having been supported by the **Democrats** and the Free Soilers of Massachusetts who formed a coalition to elect him.

Restraint was unfortunately missing from much of antebellum politics. Here Representative Preston Brooks is shown caning Senator Charles Sumner in the Senate chamber. (From authors' collection.)

His first important speech before the Senate was against the **Fugitive Slave Law**. He attacked the **Missouri Compromise** and bitterly denounced the **Kansas-Nebraska Act**. His speech, "The Crime Against Kansas" (1856), occupied two full days, and was so bitter and forceful that it drove Representative **Preston S. Brooks** to assail Sumner with a cane as he sat writing at his desk in the Senate chamber. Sumner fell to the floor senseless, and he was disabled for quite some time by the injuries he received. The assault upon Sumner helped to solidify the growing resentment felt among anti-slavery forces in Congress against the autocracy exhibited by many Southern statesmen.

Reelected for a second term in the Senate, Sumner naturally affiliated with the **Republican Party** and exerted himself throughout the 1860 campaign for the election of **Abraham Lincoln**. On resuming his seat in the Senate he gave an anti-slavery speech later published under the title "The Barbarism of Slavery." Throughout the Civil War he supported every measure that might overthrow **slavery** and opposed every compromise with it. In 1865 he delivered the eulogy for Lincoln; and in 1873 he was censured by the Massachusetts legislature in a storm of disapproval for his surprising proposal that the Civil War battle honors be removed from the regimental colors of federal units who fought their fellow citizens in the South. Shortly thereafter he died suddenly. A contemporary noted that "Mr. Sumner was a man more

respected than loved, and could command more admirers than followers."
Related Entry: Brooks, Preston S.

SUGGESTED READING: David Herbert Donald, *Charles Sumner* (1996); Alan
M. Kraut, Jon L. Wellelyn, and Frederick Blue, *Charles Sumner and the Conscience
of the North* (1994).

SUPREME COURT OF THE UNITED STATES: One reason for the
durability of the **slavery** question was that Southerners controlled the Supreme Court. The period was dominated by the Court of Chief Justice **John
Marshall** (1801–1835), followed by that of **Roger B. Taney** (1836–1864).
Both Courts, often top-heavy with Southern justices, generally sided with
the South on questions of slavery. Pro-slavery Presidents and political leverage in the Senate gave practical control of all Supreme Court appointments
to the South throughout the antebellum period.

The Court of Chief Justice John Marshall was less friendly to the Southern
position than it might have been. Marshall's decisions created new legal
precedents that strengthened the power of the federal government over the
states while raising personal property rights above those of the state governments. Nonetheless, it stayed out of other matters such as **nullification**
and slavery.

The Taney Court was much kinder to the states, modifying many of Marshall's strict doctrines to their advantage and strengthening the power of
the states to police the individual. Taney established the principle that if the
state's interests and those of the individual came into conflict, then the law
would be most narrowly construed in favor of the state. A friendly Court
was seen by Southerners as an effective remedy to growing anti-slavery hysteria in the North. The most significant ruling made by the Taney Court
was the **Dred Scott** decision, which effectively repealed the **Missouri Compromise** and strengthened the **Fugitive Slave Laws. Related Entries**: Lemmon Case; Marshall, John; Scott, Dred; Taney, Roger B.

SUGGESTED READING: John Agresto, *The Supreme Court and Constitutional
Democracy* (1984); Adrienne Siegel, *The Marshall Court, 1801–1835* (1995); Martin
Siegel, *The Taney Court, 1836–1864* (1995).

TANEY, ROGER B. (1777–1864): Chief Justice of the **Supreme Court**. The antebellum period was dominated by the Supreme Courts of Chief Justices **John Marshall** (1801–1835) and Roger B. Taney (1836–1864). The Taney Court modified many of Marshall's strict doctrines to the states' advantage and strengthened the power of the state to police the individual. Most of the landmark decisions that came before the Court did so in the first decade of Taney's tenure. Taney established the principle that if the state's interests and those of the individual came into conflict, then the law would be most narrowly construed in favor of the state. He did much to soften the effect of Marshall's decisions in favor of **states' rights** while expanding the jurisdiction of the Court in the interests of the national economy.

The most significant decision made by the Taney Court was in the case of **Dred Scott**. The decision effectively repealed the **Missouri Compromise** and strengthened the **Fugitive Slave Laws**. In the first part of his opinion Taney declared that slaves and blacks descended from slaves could not be considered citizens as that term was used in the Constitution. In the second part, he held that the federal government lacked the power to exclude **slavery** from the territories (thus making the Missouri Compromise unconstitutional).

More important, Taney adopted three points of pro-slavery thought. The federal government had no power over slavery except to protect the rights of slaveowners. The federal government was the "trustee" of the states in the matter of the territories. And the respective legislatures could not exclude slavery during the territorial period. Taney was widely condemned by Northern interests who demanded that he overturn his decision, but he remained adamant. Although Taney's reputation has suffered from comparisons with his predecessor, John Marshall, it is quite certain that his reading of the law at the time was correct. **Related Entries**: Lemmon Case; Scott, Dred; Supreme Court of the United States.

SUGGESTED READING: Martin Siegel, *The Taney Court, 1836–1864* (1995); Bernard C. Steiner, *Life of Roger B. Taney: Chief Justice of the United States Supreme Court* (1922; 1997).

TAPPAN, ARTHUR (1786–1865) AND LEWIS (1788–1873): abolitionists. New Yorkers Arthur and Lewis Tappan were rich, successful, and influential men, and devotees of the new trend toward mixing abolition with Christianity. Recruited to the abolition movement by Theodore Weld, the brothers were financial mainstays of the New York anti-slavery movement. Moreover, they helped to found the Lane Theological Seminary in Cincinnati, a stronghold of the evangelical movement in the West, and they provided the financial resources for an anti-slavery religious community at Oberlin College. Their generous contribution to Oberlin was tied to an agreement that black students be immediately admitted, making the institute a focus for abolitionist Christians from all over the country. The financial support of the brothers for a wide range of anti-slavery activities was severely curtailed by the failure of Arthur's mercantile house and the loss of a large portion of the family fortune in the Panic of 1837.

Arthur Tappan assumed a higher profile than his brother as an anti-slavery leader when he secured **William Lloyd Garrison**'s release from jail in Baltimore after his conviction for libeling a slave ship owner. Threats of violence and acts of harassment were directed toward Tappan by anti-abolition forces in both the North and the South. Northern bankers and insurers considered him a poor financial risk, as anti-abolition mobs might damage or destroy his place of business. A group of Southerners offered a bounty of up to $20,000 to anyone who would kidnap him.

Lewis Tappan abandoned his Calvinist roots to become the treasurer of the nascent American Unitarian Association. He was a supporter of the American Board of Commissioners for Foreign Missions and of the American Bible Society. In 1833 he established the American Anti-Slavery Society in New York, but split with the Massachusetts-based abolitionists over ancillary issues raised by the more radical Garrison. In 1834 a mob broke into Lewis' home in New York and made a bonfire of its furnishings in the street. Thereafter, deploring the violent rhetoric of the radical abolitionists and urging instead a devotion to passive resistance, he worked increasingly for the Negro through the American Missionary Association and the Foreign Anti-Slavery Society, and through support of the **Underground Railroad**. He was intimately involved in financing the defense of the *Amistad* Africans. **Related Entries**: Abolitionists; *Amistad;* Garrison, William Lloyd; Underground Railroad.

SUGGESTED READING: Alice Dana Adams, *The Neglected Period of Anti-Slavery* *in America, 1800–1831* (1973); Page Smith, *The Nation Comes of Age*, Vol. 4 (1981); Lewis Tappan, *The Life of Arthur Tappan* (1871; 1971).

TARIFF OF ABOMINATIONS. *See* Tariffs.

TARIFFS (TARIFF OF 1828): Tariffs were a major bone of political contention in the antebellum years, and they remained a hotly contested source of dispute well into the twentieth century. The Tariff of 1828 was called the "Tariff of Abominations" because it levied a duty of 40 percent on most manufactured goods imported into the country. This extremely high rate was instituted to drive up the price of imported goods. Domestically produced goods would be correspondingly less expensive and more attractive to the consumer. For this reason, tariffs with high duties were called protective tariffs.

High protective tariffs were not equally beneficial to all Americans, and among Southern planters, agricultural exporters, and international shipping interests they were deemed economically ruinous because they adversely affected the foreign commerce on which they relied. Certainly the politicians on both sides understood this, but the members of Congress were pressured by their self-serving constituents to protect certain industries from foreign competition. As the mills and factories involved were located predominantly in the Northeast, the use of protective tariffs quickly became a **sectional dispute**. Anti-tariff leaders argued that while protective duties forced the prices of imported goods to rise, they also increased the price of domestic manufactures. The additional cost in either case was actually being passed on to the consumers. Northern manufacturers and workers recouped the tariff in higher profits and wages, but Southern planters and agricultural workers received no compensating benefits.

All of the preceding arguments were too elaborate and sophisticated for most Americans to understand at the time, and even today the economic arguments are daunting. The ideas that a protective tariff could hurt **cotton** growers if retaliatory foreign duties were imposed on exported produce and that American agricultural exports could be hurt by lagging European demand were not easy concepts to communicate to the majority of voters. Not until 1830, in the midst of a deep and prolonged agricultural depression, did Southern politicians find a way to rally popular support to their anti-tariff position.

George McDuffie of **South Carolina** explained exactly why the protective tariffs were detrimental to the Southern economy. He described in disarmingly simple terms how the tariff duties were being paid by all Southerners directly. His analogy of the theft of forty out of every one hundred bales of cotton by the federal government in the form of tariffs was a vast oversimplification of the actual ramifications of the tariff on the economy. Nonetheless, the "Forty Bales" concept was of immense political importance, and it had a great impact on individuals in the South. Once McDuffie had established the theory, it popped up everywhere. **James A. Hamilton**, governor of South Carolina, used it to explain why rice prices had fallen, and even the most unsophisticated planter could employ it to explain why his debts persisted even though his harvests increased. One South Carolina politician praised the effectiveness of the Forty Bale Theory as an instrument of propaganda, saying, "You are as persuaded as if you saw it—that the manufacturer actually invades your barns, and plunders you of 40, out of every 100 bales [of cotton] that you produce."

The tariff would be highly protective for more than a decade. Its 1832 reincarnation was so unacceptable that it caused South Carolina to take action. The **Nullification Convention** of that year coalesced the nullifiers and **states' rights** proponents into a force that could not be ignored by the federal government, and it turned many of the followers of **John C. Calhoun** from nationalists into **secessionists**. A compromise tariff, engineered by **Henry Clay**, but not fully implemented until 1844, ended the immediate crisis and averted the very real threat of bloodshed over the issue. Under the new bill thousands of manufactured goods were put on a sliding scale of tariff duties that brought the overall rates down to 20 percent over a period of nine years. Although some leading industrialists attacked the compromise, there was surprisingly little real opposition. The South Carolina convention had used **nullification** to win some significant concessions from the federal government and had found a new weapon in its war over states' rights—secession. **Related Entries**: Calhoun, John C.; Hamilton, James A.; Nullification; Secession.

SUGGESTED READING: David F. Ericson, *The Shaping of American Liberalism: The Debates over Ratification, Nullification, and Slavery* (1993); William W. Freehling, *Prelude to Civil War: The Nullification Controversy in South Carolina, 1816–1836* (1965; 1995); Edwin L. Green, *George McDuffie* (1936).

TAYLOR, ZACHARY (1784–1850): soldier and twelfth President of the United States (1849–1850). Zachary Taylor was to have a military career of forty years, but with few exceptions, most of his early experiences (1806–1832) were in quiet garrison duty on the frontier. He saw action in the **War of 1812** in Indiana Territory, where his company of 50 men defended itself against 400 Indians. He fought in the **Black Hawk War** and was then given command of 1,100 men to fight the Seminoles in **Florida**. He was made a general after the Battle of Lake Okeechobee but failed during the next three years to eradicate the Indian problem.

In anticipation of the **annexation of Texas**, Taylor was ordered to advance to the Rio Grande. In April 1846, a party of American dragoons pressing forward into Mexican territory was ambushed, and several were killed. President **James K. Polk** asked Congress for a declaration of war as soon as he heard of the attack. With 6,000 men Taylor pressed the war forward to Monterrey; but he was severely criticized by the administration for his leniency in victory and would have been superseded had he not been popular at home. Meanwhile, General **Winfield Scott** had led an expedition to the capital at Mexico City. Taylor claimed that Polk and Scott were conspiring to ruin his growing reputation with the American people. Only his dramatic victory at Buena Vista saved his career.

There is no doubt that Taylor desired a political career. In his own correspondence he hinted that if the people spontaneously called on him to be President he would accept. He was nominated by the **Whigs** in 1848. In the subsequent campaign, Taylor expressed himself freely on the problems of the day. He believed that the South had the right to take up arms to defend **slavery** where it already existed. Although from a slaveowning family, he had no sympathy for extremists on either side of any issue. "I am a Whig," he wrote, "not an Ultra Whig." The **newspapers** found his statements filled with "noncommittal platitudes."

Taylor carried exactly half of the states in the election, seven in the North and eight in the South. His inaugural speech emphasized military preparedness, a return of honesty to government, continued encouragement of the economy, and compromise over **sectional issues**. He tried to balance his cabinet, giving four of seven posts to slaveholding Southerners, but he chose no one of outstanding ability. Within six months he was making replacements with more partisan supporters.

In the summer of 1849, Taylor toured the North, assuring people that they need not worry about the **extension of slavery into the territories**. This frightened the South, and in April 1850 a delegation of Southern politicians called on him to warn that he would lose the support of the Southern wing of his own party if he admitted California and New Mexico as **free states. Alexander Stephens** and **Robert Toombs** even suggested that **secession** might be in the wind.

Before the measures that came to be known as the **Compromise of 1850** could be enacted, Taylor died. On July 4, 1850, he had attended a ceremony connected with building the Washington Monument. The day was hot, and Taylor was observed drinking copious quantities of cold water and milk. That night he was feverish and very ill. Cholera had swept the North and Southwest in both 1849 and 1850, and when Taylor died on July 9 this was given as the cause. Since that time, and until recently, rumors of poison surrounded his death. However, in 1997 samples of tissue taken from his corpse failed to reveal any foul play concerning his death. **Millard Fillmore** became President upon his death. **Related Entry**: Mexican War of 1846.

SUGGESTED READING: John S.D. Eisenhower, *So Far from God: The U.S. War with Mexico, 1846–1848* (1989); Elbert B. Smith, *The Presidencies of Zachary Taylor and Millard Fillmore* (1988).

TEACHERS: Teaching remained a male-dominated vocation throughout the first half of the nineteenth century, especially in the South. Even though teaching was a respectable profession, women who taught were often pitied for their obvious dire financial situation. It was generally felt that the disciplinary demands of **education** required a strong, preferably male, hand.

At the secondary level, teachers taught only the subjects in which they had been schooled and had subsequently mastered. Since most teachers at this level had been college educated, the course work tended to be classical in its emphasis.

Many teachers, especially private tutors and "old field school" teachers, were imported from the North, a practice many Southerners became increasingly uncomfortable with as war loomed, especially in consideration of the strong Northern positions some teachers expressed against the Southern way of life. **Related Entries**: Education; Military Schools.

SUGGESTED READING: Lawrence A. Cremin, *American Education: The National Experience, 1783 Through 1876* (1980).

TELEGRAPH. *See* Inventions.

TEMPERANCE: From colonial times, a moderate use of strong drink was considered acceptable by all but the most radical portions of the population. In the absence of potable water, Americans consumed alcohol in prodigious quantities. Nonetheless, alcohol quickly became a target of nineteenth-century social reformers. The dangers of immoderate drinking were real, and alcoholism could end in disaster. Many men actually drank away their wages, leaving their wives and children destitute. For the alcoholic, suicide became a cliché. Strong drink was often cited as a cause of eternal damnation and earthly licentiousness, as well as spouse abuse and rape.

In fact, the temperance movement was very closely allied with women's issues and may have mirrored a rising tide of female discontent with their place in the social order. Women took up the temperance struggle by forming prayer groups and railing against saloons. A melodramatic scene printed on the cover of *Harper's Weekly* in 1858 showed a young wife and her children, their alcoholic father missing, turned out of their tenement into the cold.

Alcohol was viewed as both the cause and the balm of the economic despair found among the ethnic poor in the urban slums. Yet immigrant families, following European custom, often used alcohol as a cultural prerogative. Seen as the root cause of their problems by temperance activists, a regular appearance in the local tavern was considered the ultimate characteristic of the confirmed drunkard. Conversely, temperance was equated with love, purity, truth, fidelity, marital stability, economic prosperity, social position, and religious salvation.

The temperance crusaders, undaunted by the rebuff of most of Southern society, nonetheless produced a good deal of propaganda. **Newspapers** ran stories of drunken street brawls and bitter domestic scenes brought on by alcoholic consumption. Illustrations portrayed the general doom of the drunkard in its many guises; and slaveowners, cast in a cultural role which required that they imbibe prodigious quantities of alcohol, were accused of beating and killing their slaves in a drunken stupor. The temperance movement was set back for a time by the defection of activists to the **abolitionist** cause. Yet the temperance reformers increased the stakes of their game and insisted on total abstinence from alcohol in any quantity or strength and supplemented their demands with calls for its legal prohibition. Temperance forces succeeded in passing prohibition legislation in a half dozen Northern states, but many of these laws were subsequently found to be unconstitutional. **Related Entry**: Reform Movements.

SUGGESTED READING: Barbara L. Epstein, *The Politics of Domesticity: Women, Evangelism, and Temperance in Nineteenth Century America* (1981).

TENNESSEE: Highlights of a period description of the state from John Hayward's *Gazetteer of the United States* (1853) read as follows:

Surface and Soil: The soil, with the occasional exception of tracts among the high lands, is very fertile. Vast groves of pines furnish material for the extensive manufacture of tar, resin, spirits of turpentine, and lampblack. The mulberry is so plentiful and thrifty that the silk culture might be pursued with great profit. Peach and other fruit trees and the vine are cultivated with ample success. Besides **cotton**, excellent wheat, Indian corn, tobacco, potatoes of every kind, and all the usual varieties of vegetables are raised in good quantities.

Rivers: There are many large navigable streams in addition to the Mississippi and Tennessee Rivers. The East Tennessee possesses a vast amount of water power, admirably fitting it for a manufacturing country.

Education: The system of free education seems yet to be fully understood or appreciated by the people of this state. Still, the inhabitants support somewhat over 1000 common or primary schools, 200 or 300 academies, some of which are of respectable rank and six or eight collegiate institutions of varied character and standing.

Internal Improvements: There are five **railroads**, including branches now being constructed, of which only about 30 miles are yet in operation.

Manufacture: These consist chiefly of goods for domestic consumption. There are cotton and woolen factories, iron works, machine shops, ropewalks, mechanics' establishments of all descriptions, potteries, distilleries, breweries, a great number of flour mills, and grist mills.

Minerals: Salt springs are numerous and there is an abundance of marble, gypsum, various pigments, nitrous earths, &c.

Indians: Most of the tribes which have heretofore occupied the territory have passed across the great dividing stream, and taken up their residence upon the lands in the Indian Territory, in accordance with treaty stipulations.

Population: The population has been found, at every decennial census, to have increased prodigiously. It now has reached 1,002,625 of which nearly a fourth are slaves.

Other: The right of suffrage is not denied to colored persons, who are by law not competent witnesses in courts of justice.

Related Entry: Geography.

SUGGESTED READING: Wilma Dykeman, *Tennessee: A History* (1984); John Hayward, *Gazetteer of the United States* (1853).

TERRITORIES. *See* Extension of Slavery into the Territories.

TEST BOND CASE: In July 1831 Isaac Holmes and Alexander Mazyck decided to test the constitutionality of the **tariff** in the courts. In a well-publicized effort the two lawyers—leading members of the **nullification** party—imported a bale of Yorkshire Plains from Britain. In lieu of paying the tariff duties on the cloth in cash, they made out a bond for the amount payable to the collector of the port of **Charleston**. Bonds had long been accepted for the payment of debts, both personal and business; and they were commonly used for the payment of state and federal taxes by planters who would get almost all of their money when their crops were sold at the end of the growing season.

In order to demonstrate the damage done to Southerners by the high tariffs, the men sold the bale of cloth on the open market at a loss. When the bond came due, they refused to honor it, claiming that the duties were unconstitutional. James Pringle, who was the collector of the port, turned the case over to the federal district attorney for **South Carolina**, Edward Frost. Frost thought the tariff was oppressive but was not willing to forego enforcement of the law. Therefore, he resigned rather than prosecute the case. When President **Andrew Jackson** heard of Frost's resignation, he lost his temper and exploded in a rage, calling the resignation an act of treason. Jackson viewed the Test Bond Case as a serious development in the battle between the federal and state governments. "The Union shall be preserved," he wrote to **Martin Van Buren**. Although the amount of the bond was a mere twenty dollars, Jackson deemed the case a great danger to the continuation of the national government.

The case was tried in Charleston by Thomas Lee, federal judge who was a **Unionist**. The defendants chose as their attorney **George McDuffie**, an ardent nullifier, who arrived in Charleston with an escort of more than 200 supporters cheering and celebrating in a party atmosphere. The government chose **James L. Petigru**, a leading Unionist, to prosecute in the place of Frost. McDuffie opened the case with a demand for a jury trial in the hope that a finding by twelve citizens of South Carolina in favor of his clients would serve to nullify the tariff. Judge Lee allowed the jury trial over the objections of Petigru. Nonetheless, when McDuffie began to argue the constitutionality of the tariff to the jury, Petigru objected, and Lee sustained the objection. All questions of law, Lee claimed, were the prerogative of the judge. The jury served only as finders of fact, not as interpreters of the law. This decision made any further protestations by McDuffie futile. The jury was forced by the judge's instructions and the evidence to find that the bond was legal and payable.

The Jackson administration viewed the result as a success. Nonetheless, the jury had not brought in a verdict on the tariff, and even the judge had not ruled on the constitutionality of the law, only that the case revolved around whether or not the bond was genuine and entered into freely. The Test Bond Case was a blow to the proponents of **nullification**, as it forced them to expand their opposition from the courts to the establishment of a state convention for the purpose of vetoing the federal law. Conservatives dreaded such an assembly, fearing that it would end in disunion and armed confrontation. For many of the same reasons, radicals applauded it. **Related Entries**: McDuffie, George; Nullification; Petigru, James; Tariffs.

SUGGESTED READING: David F. Ericson, *The Shaping of American Liberalism: The Debates over Ratification, Nullification, and Slavery* (1993); William W. Freehling, *Prelude to Civil War: The Nullification Controversy in South Carolina, 1816–1836* (1965; 1995); William H. Pease, *James Louis Petigru: Southern Conservative, Southern Dissenter* (1995).

TEXAS: Highlights of a period description of the state from John Hayward's *Gazetteer of the United States* (1853) read as follows:

Surface and Soil: The state is well wooded throughout. Fruits and garden vegetables are cultivated with ease. The products of the field consist of **cotton**, (the great staple), maize, wheat, rye, barley, and other grains, **sugar** cane, and potatoes of each kind. Indigenous plants are indigo, vanilla, sasparilla, and many medicinal shrubs. As a grazing country, Texas is exceeded by few or none of her sister states. Vast numbers of cattle, horses, mules, sheep, and swine are raised upon the prairie lands, receiving or requiring little human care. Buffaloes and wild horses range the prairies in immense droves; and the deer, the bear, and other game are very abundant.

Rivers: Texas has numerous **rivers**, all flowing towards, and ultimately emptying into the Gulf of Mexico. These bays, being commonly obstructed by sand bars or narrow strips of land, do not afford convenient harbors, except for vessels of small draught. The Rio Grande del Norte is a notable stream of some 1800 miles in length, and is already becoming a great commercial channel, though occasionally impeded by shoals and rapids.

Education: The subject of public **education** has, as yet, occupied no great share of the public mind. Some schools of tolerable repute are supported in the most populous settlements. The state contains fewer free persons over the age of 20 who can neither read nor write, in proportion to the whole population than any other of the Southern States of the Union.

Internal Improvements: Texas can yet boast of very few such advantages in the shape of **railroads** or canals.

Manufacture: Nothing of great importance in this branch of industry. The inhabitants have been principally confined to **agriculture** and the preparation of their products for market as **raw materials**.

Minerals: Excellent coal, and iron ore abound in most inland districts. There are multitudes of salt springs and lakes from which large supplies of salt are procured.

Indians: The territory is still infested by hordes or remnants of tribes of savages, most of whom subsist by predatory incursions, often of the most destructive and sanguinary character. Efforts are in constant progress to reduce these marauders, by various methods, to a state of comparative peace and amity; but until the country shall become more densely populated, the desirable result will not probably be effected.

Population: The civilized inhabitants of Texas comprise emigrants from all other states, descendants of the original Spanish settlers, and persons in whom Mexican and Indian blood is blended. The former class, in all probability, compose a majority of the present population, which by the census of 1850, was as follows: whites, 154,100; free colored, 331; slaves, 58,161.

Other: No law for the **emancipation** of slaves can be passed, without consent of owners, and the payment of full compensation. The introduction of slaves as merchandise may be prohibited. Owners of slaves may be compelled by law to treat them with care and kindness; and in cases of refusal or neglect, the slaves may be taken and sold for account of the owners. Slaves may have a trial by jury when charged with crimes greater than petit larceny, and are protected against abuse or loss of life equally with the whites, excepting when engaged in a revolt.

Related Entries: Geography; Houston, Samuel; Texas, Annexation of.

SUGGESTED READING: Joe B. Frantz, *Texas: A History* (1976); John Hayward, *Gazetteer of the United States* (1853); Frederick Law Olmsted, *The Cotton Kingdom: A Traveler's Observations on Cotton and Slavery in the American Slave States* (1861; 1996).

TEXAS, ANNEXATION OF: In 1836 an army of Texans (Texicans) led by the former governor of **Tennessee, Sam Houston**, wrested all of the territory of **Texas** from the Mexican republic of General Antonio Lopez de Santa Anna. In 1837 the Republic of Texas, with Houston as President, was established under a constitution modeled on that of the United States which included guarantees to slaveowners of noninterference. Men and money poured into Texas during its War of Independence from every state in the Union, but predominantly from the Southern states. Although the revolution had been largely accomplished by former citizens of the United States, many Texans highly valued their newly won independence.

The imminent annexation of Texas in 1845 was inextricably linked to the political question of the **extension of slavery into the territories**. It was widely feared that all of Texas would be slave territory. Cheap, or almost free, land in Texas destroyed any hope of acquiring laborers who were free; and the widespread production of **cotton** was going to require slave labor.

Northern interests were greatly concerned over the proposed annexation of a pro-slavery territory, as it was feared that Texas might be carved into a large number of small slave states—each with two senators—which would upset the delicate balance of sectional interests in the national government for decades. Congress was flooded with protests against annexation. Southern interests viewed the admission of Texas expectantly, but both **Andrew Jackson** and **Martin Van Buren** failed to countenance any proposal for its admission.

In 1840, when President **William Henry Harrison** caught a cold during his inauguration and died, Vice President **John Tyler**, a **states' rights** advocate from **Virginia**, was suddenly catapulted into the Executive Office. Tyler had been nominated by the **Whigs** simply to balance their ticket, and they were alarmed when it became known that he wanted to annex Texas. The Whigs almost immediately read Tyler out of the party, and in the spring of 1844, **John C. Calhoun**, now Tyler's secretary of state, concluded a treaty with the Republic of Texas to enter the Union. Although Calhoun thought the moment propitious, Northern forces in Congress were successful in portraying the annexation as a slaveowner's plot, and the treaty was soundly rejected, with the votes breaking down along sectional lines.

In the 1844 election, the Whigs ignored Tyler and nominated **Henry Clay**. The **Democrats** nominated the first dark horse candidate in presidential election history, the loyal Democrat **James K. Polk**. Polk proved an adept politician and ran on a platform that stressed the need to admit both Texas and the **Oregon Territory** to the Union simultaneously. Clay opposed annexation; but he seriously misread the temper of the voters, who were more exhilarated by the idea of **manifest destiny**, with the country stretching to the Pacific, than they were fearful of the extension of slavery. This cost Clay the election.

Although Polk had won election by a slim margin, Tyler declared the result a popular mandate for Texas annexation and rushed a resolution through both houses of Congress in February 1845 admitting Texas even before Polk had taken office. The measure provided that Texas would not be carved into more than five separate states at any time and that the **Missouri Compromise** line would extend westward above the former Lone Star Republic. Once in office, Polk claimed the entire Oregon Territory, which had been shared with Great Britain, using the slogan "Fifty-four Forty or Fight!"—a reference to the northern boundary of the territory. However, the annexation of Texas brought war with Mexico, and Polk was forced to compromise with the British in extending the northern boundary of Oregon along the 49th parallel. Northern and western expansionists were outraged by the compromise, fearing that the nation had been given over to the dreaded power of the slave interest. **Related Entries**: Houston, Samuel; Mexican War of 1846; Polk, James K.

SUGGESTED READING: John S.D. Elsenhower, *So Far from God: The U.S. War with Mexico, 1846–1848* (1989).

THEATER: In the sociable and pleasure-seeking environment of the South theater enjoyed high prestige. The isolated plantations of the colonial South provided an assortment of **amusements**. Among these were plays given by roving groups of semi-professional or even amateur actors. Nonetheless, those who fancied more than an occasional theatrical enjoyment were forced to resort to reading books of plays.

Yet as Southern cities grew, planters and farmers came in from their outlying holdings to take advantage of the social and cultural benefits the cities offered. Alexandria, **Charleston**, Savannah, **New Orleans**, Mobile, and **Richmond** all had fine theaters. The early theaters could accommodate no more than a few hundred patrons. Of course, only a small number of people had the cash to support such a venture in any case.

In 1716 Williamsburg, **Virginia**, became the first colonial capital to have a regular theater. Charlestonians erected the New Theater in 1736, being careful to keep the price of admission just high enough to allow attendance by only the best of society. Charlestonian theatergoers, reinforced by the refugee planters from the slave revolts of the West Indies, had amazingly sophisticated tastes. The town witnessed the first opera performed in the colonies, Colley Cibber's *Flora*. In New Orleans fashionable balls and masquerades were held in the St. Phillip Theater. This fine building could accommodate over 700 people. In 1832 theatergoers moved on to the Theatre d'Orleans, a grand structure that cost $80,000 to erect. French and English plays were given here, and grand opera was introduced in 1837. The plays of Shakespeare, Sheridan, Goldsmith, and Farquhar alike found a new popularity and attracted large audiences. In 1851 the St. Charles Theater hosted a dozen performances by Swedish singer **Jenny Lind**.

A great many plays were written by American playwrights in the antebellum period, but few were worthy of distinction. A playwright could expect as little as $500 for a new play, and $100 for an adaptation. Nonetheless, Robert M. Bird wrote fifty-four plays. Among these was *The Gladiator* (1831), based on the life of Spartacus and very popular in the North because of its anti-slavery theme. Southern playwrights generally congregated in Charleston. Among them was George Washington Parke Custis, who wrote *The Indian Prophecy* (1827), *The Eighth of January* (1834), and the much celebrated *Pocahontas* (1836). Other popular plays were Robert Conrad's *Jack Cade* (1835) and George Henry Boker's *Calaynos* (1849), *Leonor de Guzman* (1853), and *Francesca Da Rimini* (1855). The last was loosely based on Dante's *Inferno* and may have been the best play of its type in the period.

Acting in the legitimate theater was a respectable profession. The antebellum stage was filled with excellent actors, among them Edmund Kean,

Edwin Booth, Edward Davenport, James Wallack, and Charles Burke. Among the actresses were **Fanny Kemble**, Mary Ann Duff, Anna Mowatt, and Laura Keene. Below the principal professional actors were a group of paid hirelings, and below that, volunteer amateurs. Actors worked out the **dueling** and physically demanding scenes on their own. Female characters were expected to flaunt their sexual proclivities and shrewdness behind a facade of witty repartee and polite formality, while male characters were to be played as either too calculating or too suggestive. These productions have been called "stand up and talk theater" because the sets and props were so minimal.

Edwin Forrest was a very successful American actor. He gave more than 1,000 performances of *The Gladiator*. His portrayal of Othello in 1826 became the standard by which actors were measured thereafter. Charlotte Cushman, who played her first role in 1835, dominated the actresses in much the same way that Forrest did the actors. In 1842 Charles Dickens attended the Marshall Theater in Richmond to see Joseph Jefferson, considered the greatest living actor of his day. Jefferson was well known to audiences in the nation's capital and throughout the South, especially for his portrayal of an indolent Rip Van Winkle, a role he played for thirty-eight years. Had Dickens visited the Marshall Theater in 1859 he might have seen a twenty-one-year-old actor, John Wilkes Booth, who was playing a supporting role for $20 a week in *Beauty and the Beast*.

Among the variations of legitimate theater were the "tableaux vivants," with actors and actresses striking attitudes from famous sculptures or paintings as through great picture frames. Tableaux had been a popular expedient of the diversion-starved denizens of the isolated plantation houses. In the cities they were often enjoyed by the bawdier set and composed of young volunteer actresses displaying their charms—though never revealing more than the latest fashion in low-cut gowns. As the volunteers often included some of the most eligible young women from among the urban population, the practice seems to have been free of social stigma.

Social satire was a strong theme in American drama, and reformers were well aware of its impact. Immediately after the release of the novel *Uncle Tom's Cabin* (1852) half a dozen stage adaptations appeared (one of them produced by P. T. Barnum). The play had a tremendous influence on the public. Although it was considered a slander by the South, huge audiences came to view it in the North. In a similar vein *The Octoroon* (1859) by Dion Boucicault, based on Mayne Reid's successful novel *The Quadroon* (1856), combined a theme of tragic love between a white man and a free mulatto woman with a knife duel, a steamboat explosion, a slave auction, and two murders. The success of *Uncle Tom's Cabin* and *The Octoroon* reflected the extent of the involvement of Northern society in the **slavery** controversy. **Related Entries**: Literary Development; *Uncle Tom's Cabin*.

SUGGESTED READING: Mary C. Henderson, *Theater in America* (1986; 1996); Arthur Hornblow, *The History of the Theater in America* (1912; 1972).

THREE-FIFTHS COMPROMISE: During the **Constitutional Convention** of 1787 it was thought to be impossible for the Constitution to be ratified without the support of the Southern states. As the Northern states were much more populous, the South disliked the concept of congressional representation based solely on white population. If representation was to be so based, Northern interests would always outnumber those of the South in Congress. If taxation was to be based on the importation of property, the South would be at a disadvantage again as each state imported slaves that could be taxed.

The Three-fifths Compromise, suggested by **James Madison**, was an arbitrary but reasonable concept that broke the constitutional deadlock. The government would count each slave as three-fifths of a person for the purpose of representation. At the same time it would limit the import tax to $10 per head, and reserve the right to prohibit the importation of slaves by 1808 (which it did).

The South thereby gained additional weight in Congress which was quite close to what it would have had if all slaves had been counted as whole persons. In 1811, for example, the compromise gave the Southern states eighteen more representatives than they would have had without the agreement. **John Quincy Adams** correctly complained that "slave representation has governed the nation." During the **abolition** debates the compromise again came into dispute, with anti-slavery forces claiming that a "slave power conspiracy" controlled the government. **Related Entries:** Constitutional Convention; Madison, James.

SUGGESTED READING: Howard A. Ohline, "Republicanism and Slavery: Origins of the Three-fifths Clause in the United States Constitution," *William and Mary Quarterly* 28 (1971): 563–594.

TIMBER. *See* Flatboats and Keelboats; Raw Materials.

TOBACCO. *See* Agriculture.

TOCQUEVILLE, ALEXIS DE (1805–1859): French statesman and writer. In 1831 a young French aristocrat by the name of Alexis de Tocqueville visited the United States and traveled throughout the nation for more than eight months, covering 7,000 miles and observing, asking questions, and recording the answers. When he returned to France, Tocqueville wrote one of the most useful books for historians about the United States in the antebellum years, *Democracy in America*. Tocqueville was able, during his visit, to identify a growing split in the American nation, pitting nationalism against **sectional interests**. By 1850 this work had gone through thirteen editions.

Tocqueville was impressed by the way Americans had applied the principles of liberty and equality to the needs of a new nation. He said little about **slavery** except that the trend was toward universal equality and that the nation and the world were inescapably tied to the ultimate acceptance of democratic principles.

Upon his return to France, he was elected to the French Chamber of Deputies and served briefly as a foreign minister. Strangely, he voted against the ultra-democratic principles of the 1848 revolution. In 1851 he retired from public life to write a history of the old royal government and revolution in France. **Related Entry**: Education.

SUGGESTED READING: J. P. Mayer, ed., *Journey to America*, by Alexis de Tocqueville (1960); George W. Pierson, *Tocqueville in America* (1959).

TOOMBS, ROBERT A. (1810–1885): politician, soldier, and Southern apologist. A talented, forthright, and devoted defender of the Southern way of life, Robert A. Toombs served as a U.S. senator from **Georgia**, a general in the Confederate army, and secretary of state in the Confederate government. Toombs was the fifth child of a well-to-do **cotton** planter. Originally educated at the University of Georgia, he withdrew from that institution under questionable circumstances and completed his law education in Schenectady, New York.

A successful law practice allowed Toombs to invest his considerable wealth in a cotton plantation and slaves in Georgia. Elected to the Georgia state legislature in 1837, Toombs promptly made himself an outstanding member of the state **Whig** Party, but he failed to involve himself in national questions until he was elected to Congress in 1844. He was initially a conservative member, taking strong positions only against the aggressive stance of the federal government with regard to the **Oregon Territory** boundary question and against involvement in the **Mexican War**. In light of future events, it is ironic that Toombs was described by a colleague as "a Southern man with Northern principles."

The **Wilmot Proviso** brought Toombs into the **sectional disputes** that raged in Congress at mid-century. He soon became an aggressive leader in the defense of the South and did much to secure the compromise measures that were passed in 1850. His "Hamilcar Speech," demanding a share for the South in the territorial opportunities offered by the acquisition of land after the Mexican War, was one of a forensic series that made him famous.

Toombs was reluctantly persuaded to join the **Democratic Party** by his close friend, **Alexander Stephens**, and served as a senator from Georgia—a position he held until January 1861, when he made a farewell speech to the Senate. In the interim, Toombs had decried the inability of the country to definitively settle the question of **extending slavery into the territories**, approved of the **Kansas-Nebraska Act of 1854**, and submitted a bill for the prompt admission of Kansas to the Union in an effort to stem the ongoing violence that came to be known as "**Bleeding Kansas.**"

Toombs took an active part in the **secession** congress and wrote a moving address to justify the adoption of the Ordinance of Secession. He was disappointed in his desire—and expectation—to be made President of the Confederacy, but accepted the post of secretary of state. As a moderate and diplomatic man, he opposed the attack on Fort Sumter as an unnecessary provocation of the North. He grew contemptuous of **Jefferson Davis'** conduct of the war and applied for a military position.

At Antietam in 1862, his brigade steadfastly held a critical position, bringing him recognition for his bravery and capacity. Toombs expected immediate promotion. When it was not forthcoming, he resigned from the regular army and never tired of criticizing the Confederate military effort, and Jefferson Davis in particular. He opposed the "excesses" of the **Richmond** government, the suspension of habeas corpus, and the adoption of conscription. Toombs' critical epitaph for the Confederate army was "Died of West Point." **Related Entry**: Confederate Government.

SUGGESTED READING: Ulrich B. Phillips, *The Life of Robert Toombs* (1913); William Y. Thompson, *Robert Toombs of Georgia* (1966).

TOWNSHIPS: The early settlement of the Atlantic seaboard was done in a relatively haphazard manner largely dictated by accidents of the terrain. Municipal and colonial boundaries were often in dispute in the eighteenth century because boundaries were set along the uncertain courses of **rivers** and streams or measured from large trees or other arbitrary landmarks. This circumstance did not arise from a lack of care in locating the boundaries, for early surveyors were quite as precise in their work as they are today. Charles Mason and Jeremiah Dixon, two English surveyors, spent five years, from 1763 to 1768, determining the boundary between Pennsylvania and **Maryland** and unwittingly divided the nation into North and South. With great accuracy they measured out "233 miles, 17 chains, and 48 links" through almost virgin forests. Surveys of the **Mason-Dixon Line** in 1849 and again in 1903 found only the smallest discrepancies.

In 1784 the infant American government decided to institute a standard township plan, integrated into the Northwest Ordinance, which envisioned each township to be composed of a giant square, six miles on a side. This area was conveniently divided into thirty-six squares, each with an area of one square mile, known as sections. A square mile has an equivalent area of 640 acres. The sections could be further subdivided into half sections (320 acres) and quarter sections (160 acres).

In every township four sections were put aside for government use, and the income from one more was dedicated to **education**. The rest could be sold to settlers. While a full section made a fairly large farmstead, a quarter section of 160 acres was generally thought to be a minimal family enterprise. The quarter section could be further quartered into 40 acre fields and wood-lots. The first 40 acre division supported the family home, a vegetable garden, chicken coops, an orchard, and grazing for the domestic animals. The second field could support a herd of cattle, a flock of sheep, or a cash crop. While the third field was left in hay and rotated in and out of production, the fourth division was usually left as a woodlot to provide firewood or lumber. Under this somewhat oversimplified plan a farm family could expect to provide food and fuel for itself and to accumulate a little cash selling **wool**, meat, **cotton**, or indigo. Of course, there was not enough land in a quarter section to divide among one's children, and the entire enterprise commonly went to the eldest son. Nonetheless, the township plan envisioned in the Northwest Ordinance continued to be used for community planning for over 200 years. **Related Entries**: Agriculture; County Government; Mason-Dixon Line; Westward Movement.

SUGGESTED READING: Judith St. George, *Mason and Dixon's Line of Fire* (1991).

TRAIL OF TEARS. *See* Indian Removal.

TRANSPORTATION: Personal travel in the antebellum period exhibited a great range of diversity. Stagecoaches, wagons, boats, and trains were all being used simultaneously. In the course of a single trip many combinations of different forms of transportation might be employed. As the period began, carriages and wagons were the primary means of personal and commercial transportation. This led to the development of many turnpikes and highways paved with boards known as plank **roads** that avoided the persistent mud which mired all wheeled vehicles.

As the period wore on, canals came into fashion, especially for transporting merchandise. Early canals were often built parallel to or in close proximity to natural waterways that were otherwise unnavigable. Many Southern canals were built through swamps and marshlands, both draining the surrounding land and providing sufficient depth of water for small craft and barges. Others were built slightly higher than the nearby waterway or in a manner that incorporated a waterway or lake into its length.

The most celebrated canal projects of the period were the Louisville and Portland Canal, finished in 1831, which enabled Ohio River barges to pass the Falls of the Ohio; the Chesapeake and Ohio Canal, completed in 1850 and extending west from Georgetown in the general direction of Pittsburgh; and the Erie Canal in New York, completed in 1825, connecting the Hudson River with the Great Lakes. The latter cost over $7 million to build, but had rapidly redoubled the investment from the tolls charged for its use. The phenomenal success of the Erie Canal attracted imitation and investment, and in the second and third decades of the nineteenth century capital placed in canals far outstripped investments in any other projects, reaching a peak in 1840. Thereafter, interest became focused on the construction of **railroads**.

Turnpike concessionaires, canal investors, teamsters, and stagecoach operators were bitter enemies of railroad development. Stories were spread by these forces of the dangers of railways. Boilers—as anyone could see from similar disasters on steamboats—were a great danger. Noisy locomotives frightened horses, purportedly dried up dairy cows, and caused hens to stop laying eggs. Moreover, the sparks from the smokestacks would set fire to forests and fields along the railroad right-of-way. These were strong arguments against railways, and some of them were true. Railway operators took note of the genuine dangers by fitting their smokestacks with spark-suppressing screens and placing bales of hay or **cotton** as a protective barrier on a flatcar behind the engine to separate the passenger cars from the boiler. Notwithstanding its detractors, a railroad building mania swept the country in the 1840s and continued unabated through the war years. By the 1850s, railroads had generally driven the turnpikes out of business. Canals were long-lasting once they were built, and could compete with railroad freight rates as they required little energy to move large loads. But they could not match their speed of transportation.

In the South, men were particularly fond of riding astride. Walking almost any distance was viewed with complete disdain. A contemporary observer noted that Southern males, from early childhood, rode everywhere and would mount their horses to go only a short distance down the street. Southerners could not be made to dispense with their horses even under the most trying economic or meteorological conditions. Moreover, they often furnished their servants with four-footed transportation in order to provide care for their own mount. While these sometimes took the form of an ancient mule or jenny, it was not uncommon for a black slave to be provided with a fairly good mount.

The female gentry traveled mostly by carriage or chaise. Southern roads, composed in large part of lesser used lanes between plantations, proved too narrow and overhung with branches to make coaches practicable. Nonetheless, well-heeled city dwellers sometimes supported a coach as a sign of their affluence even though they never left the urban districts in it. The gentry would go into debt to maintain their own carriage and team; and great pride was taken in being seen in a fine conveyance, pulled by matched horses and manned by a properly attired driver and footman. A visitor to **South Carolina** noted, "No coach moves in **Charleston** without a Negro before and a Negro behind." Rented vehicles were considered by many among the elite as an embarrassment to those who could not afford to own a carriage, and those who resorted to them were viewed with contempt. **Related Entries**: Internal Improvements at Federal Expense; Railroads; Roads.

SUGGESTED READING: Robert C. Black, *The Railroads of the Confederacy* (1952); W. J. Reader, *MacAdam: The MacAdam Family and the Turnpike Roads, 1798–1861* (1980); Ronald E. Shaw, *Canals for a Nation: The Canal Era in the United States, 1790–1860* (1990); Peter Way, *Common Labour: Workers and the Digging of North American Canals, 1780–1860* (1993).

TRAVEL AND VACATIONS: In the **antebellum South** the upper-class families from the coastal regions tried to absent themselves during the malaria and yellow fever seasons that came with the intolerably hot and humid weather of the Southern summer. Nineteenth-century medicine also suggested that the taking of mineral waters had beneficial effects on the health of those who could afford a month at the springs. Throughout the South it was the habit of the plantation families to remove themselves inland to a seasonal cottage, a resort, or a city with a finer climate than that of the miasmic swamps or of the tidewater. It has been estimated that the gentry of **South Carolina** alone spent more than a half million dollars a year outside the state on such trips. The city of Chattanooga in the hill country of **Tennessee** was known for its sulfur springs and attracted a good deal of patronage among the gentry. The United States Hotel at Saratoga Springs, New York, was one of America's most popular luxury **hotels** and a favorite destination of many wealthy Southern families. Here were found rich merchants from **New Orleans**, wealthy planters from **Arkansas, Alabama**, and Tennessee, and the more haughty and polished landowners from **Georgia, North Carolina**, South Carolina, and **Virginia**.

However, in the Old South from the 1830s to the mid-1850s a particularly popular and affordable trip was the "Springs Tour." The region of western Virginia that straddles the Alleghenies abounded in various natural springs. Around these a number of fashionable resorts were to be found, connected by good turnpikes and dependable stagecoach lines. The location was convenient to the best families of the South and within the financial means of the moderately blessed ones. From the Virginia tidewater one traveled due west, and from Tennessee and the Carolinas one headed straight north. The best known springs at the time were the Warm, the Hot, the White Sulphur, the Red Sulphur, the Blue Sulphur, the Sweet, and the Salt—all located in a seventy-five-mile square within a respectable distance of most coastal plantations. In six to eight weeks, adherents could cut back and forth through this area, staying at the different resorts without logging more than 200 miles from the time they entered the area.

The hotels and cottages that served this clientele varied in their appointments and hospitality. The resort of Colonel John Fry at Warm Springs featured a large ballroom, and stag horn bar, cooled wine—and a Negro bartender to serve it—besides well-appointed rooms for his guests. Other places were disgracefully overcrowded, having poor food, insufficient blankets, and two people to a bed. So many private carriages entered the area that there was insufficient space in the barns; and coaches, teams, Negro coachmen, and servants often were left to find shelter under the trees, almost completely open to the weather.

The mineral-laden waters that attracted all this attention were commonly taken internally to correct real or supposed intestinal ailments, dyspepsia, or general aches and pains. The warm and hot springs were commonly fitted with pools or tubs for soaking. Doctors and chemists often charted a particular itinerary for their patients that would, in their opinion, provide the proper "cure," but many happy travelers followed their own designs in the hope of stumbling upon Nature's antidote. One physician was so assured of having discovered the proper order of "treatment" that he published a pamphlet on the subject in which he attested to having become marvelously improved after several years of following his regimen; but his early death proved an embarrassment to his theory.

For most travelers there were no hard or fast rules for the Springs Tour, but common wisdom called for about a week at each location. The first stop was invariably a short stay at the Warm Springs, and everyone converged on the Sweet Springs during the last week of August or the first of September. The day began with a drink at the springs—a ceremony repeated throughout the stay. As the older generation settled in for the day, the daughters made music and the sons attempted to court them. Sometimes an excursion was organized, but relaxed boredom was the custom. Breakfast, dinner, and afternoon tea broke up the day, and the evenings were given over to dancing. While the women gossiped and loafed, the men talked politics, played chess, billiards, or cards, and smoked and drank prodigiously. Most travelers ended the season with a final week at the Warm Springs, having invested six weeks of their time in gossip, socializing, and soaking while having consumed brandy juleps, ham, mutton, ice cream, and approximately twenty-six gallons of mineral water. **Related Entries**: Geography; Medicine.

SUGGESTED READING: Carl Bridenbaugh, *Baths and Watering Places of Colonial America* (1946); Stan Cohen, *Springs of the Virginias* (1981).

TREATY OF GUADALUPE HIDALGO (1848): The treaty of Guadalupe Hidalgo ended the **Mexican War**, which had started in 1846 over the **annexation of Texas**. It recognized all U.S. claims to Texas, established the Rio Grande border, and ceded to the United States California, New Mexico, and most of the present states of Utah, Nevada, Arizona, and Colorado. In return the United States paid $15 million to Mexico and assumed an additional $3 million of Mexican debt. **Related Entries**: Mexican War of 1846; Scott, Winfield; Taylor, Zachary; Texas.

SUGGESTED READING: John S.D. Elsenhower, *So Far from God: The U.S. War with Mexico, 1846–1848* (1989).

TRIANGULAR TRADE. *See* Atlantic Slave Trade.

TUBMAN, HARRIET (c. 1821–1913): former slave and conductor on the **Underground Railroad**. Harriet Tubman's name has come to be synonymous with the Underground Railroad. As a thirteen-year-old field slave in rural **Maryland**, she sustained a serious head injury while defending another slave from a whipping. Her subsequent recovery, which took several months, led the religious young woman to think a great deal about the injustice of **slavery**. In 1844 she married John Tubman, a **free black**, and while remaining a slave, moved to his cabin. About five years later, rumors circulated that Harriet and her brothers might be sold. Harriet made her way to Pennsylvania, traveling by night and leaving her husband behind.

While working as a domestic in Philadelphia, she met black **abolitionist** William Still, chairman of the Philadelphia Vigilance Committee. Still was a leader of the Underground Railroad, and later became its historian. Harriet heard a rumor that her sister and two children were going to be sold from their plantation. Armed with a rifle and the knowledge of the safe places along the Underground Railroad supplied by Still, Harriet led them to safety. Harriet began making repeated trips to lead fugitive slaves north. Tubman made over fifteen trips, assisting nearly 300 slaves, including her parents and six of her ten brothers. A $40,000 bounty was offered for her apprehension by slaveholders, but she eluded capture. Tubman's exploits as a "conductor" on the Underground Railroad earned her the nickname "General Tubman."

During the Civil War, Tubman served as a nurse and provided the North with valuable information about the terrain of the South. Following the war and the death of her first husband, she married Nelson Davis, a black veteran, but kept the name Tubman. She worked for aid and schooling for freed slaves. Later she turned her home in Auburn, New York, into a farm for the poor and aged. **Related Entries**: Black Anti-slavery Activists; Underground Railroad.

SUGGESTED READING: Sarah Bradford, *Harriet Tubman, the Moses of Her People* (1886; 1994).

TURNBULL, ROBERT J. (1775–1833): writer and Southern apologist. Turnbull was a hero of the **nullification** campaign of 1828 in **South Carolina**. He was the author of a series of essays published in the **Charleston Mercury**. Herein, Turnbull presented a powerful case for strict constitutional construction. The essays were combined in *The Crisis* (1828), which was described as "the first bugle-call to the South to rally." Turnbull argued that "acquiescence" to attractive federally sponsored programs for **roads** and canals, or the toleration of less attractive federally imposed **tariffs**, would create a precedent whereby the national government might gain a "Constitutional right to legislate on the local concerns of the States" which was formerly denied to it by the Tenth Amendment and other language in the founding document. This language explicitly restricted Congress to the delegated powers.

Fundamentally, what Turnbull sought to ensure was the continuation of the institution of **slavery**. He felt that the "general welfare" clause of the Constitution, if allowed for **internal improvements at federal expense**, might be just as easily be construed to allow other forms of interference within the state. Turnbull therefore urged South Carolina, as a sovereign entity, to forcibly resist any federal law that encroached on its rights. "[Will] the institutions of our forefathers . . . be preserved . . . free from the rude hands of innovators and enthusiasts, and from the molestation or interference of any legislative power on earth but our own?" He declared, "Let us say to Congress, 'Hands Off'—mind your own business" (*The Crisis*, 1828). Turnbull saw clearly that when the concerns of the states and the federal government met on unresolved or ambiguous ground, it was through the mechanism of incrementalism that the rights of the states could most easily be violated. **Related Entry**: Nullification.

SUGGESTED READING: Turnbull Manuscripts, University of North Carolina Library Collection, Chapel Hill; David F. Ericson, *The Shaping of American Liberalism: The Debates over Ratification, Nullification, and Slavery* (1993); William W. Freehling, *Prelude to Civil War: The Nullification Controversy in South Carolina, 1816–1836* (1965; 1995).

TURNER, NAT (1800–1831): black leader. Born to an African woman on the plantation of Benjamin Turner in Southampton, **Virginia**, Nat Turner was deeply impressed with the superstitious beliefs of his mother. She told him that a birthmark he bore signaled that he was a prophet, destined for some great work. Turner, a precocious child, learned to read at an amazingly early age. He experimented with making paper, pottery, gunpowder, and maps, skills he probably gleaned through reading. Nat used his intelligence to impress the other slaves as well as to play upon their fears and superstitions, ultimately gaining recognition as a leader.

Whether he was a Baptist preacher or a devout believer who claimed that he prayed continually in response to having a spirit speak to him is not clear. His "calling," however, ultimately caused him to become detached from society and to experience visions of violence and bloodshed.

Turner awaited a natural phenomenon which he felt would be a true sign. In February 1831 an eclipse occurred. Nat immediately confided his plan for a revolt to a fellow slave, Hark Travis, and four other comrades from a neighboring plantation. On August 13 an even more portentous event occurred. An unexplained atmospheric event, labeled "Blue Days" by some, appeared over Virginia and **North Carolina**. For three days the sun appeared to be surrounded by a dense fog. Turner decided to delay no longer. August 21 was set as the fated day. Armed with one hatchet and one broadaxe, Turner and his associates set out at 2 A.M. upon their bloody mission. The plan called for killing every white person they saw, be it man, woman, or child, and it was to commence on the Travis plantation.

They took a collection of guns and muskets from the home and butchered the residents in their beds. Mounting horses from the stable, they moved on to the next house to reenact the grisly drama. At some places the slaves joined them; at others they fled. Uncooperative slaves were forced to join the mayhem so that they could not raise an alarm. As the night wore on the mob grew to somewhere between sixty and one hundred slaves.

The insurrection ran into difficulty when they were surprised by a group of white men who had received news of the uprising. The rebel throng fled in all directions, and Nat hid in the woods, intending to take up the revolt on the following day. However, this proved to be the finale of the murderous revolt. The uprising left thirteen men, eighteen women, and twenty-four children dead.

Turner escaped and eluded capture for over two months. Finally, on October 30, he was spotted and captured by Benjamin Phipps. Turner was tried on November 5, 1831. He confessed to his attorney, Thomas R. Gray, that he was responsible for the deeds yet pleaded not guilty because he felt no guilt. Six days later, he was hanged along with three of his companions. When all was over, fifty-three slaves were brought up on charges; of these, seventeen were executed, and twelve were transported out of state.

Confessions of Nat Turner was published by Gray and devoured by an anxious public in both the North and the South. Doubtless it was thought of as quite a thriller. The preface contained the testimony of six judges and a clerk who attested to the fact that Turner acknowledged the details as true during his trial. Some people felt that Gray had embellished portions since it was he who had extracted the story from his client. Nonetheless, the pamphlet sold an unprecedented 50,000 copies.

Following the initial terror of the Turner revolt, there was a brief period of overconfidence by whites who felt that their ever vigilant military forces combined with the cohesive white population would deter any future slave revolts. It did not take long, however, for the reality of their situation to take hold. Restrictive laws were passed against slaves and **free blacks**. Publishing, distributing, or importing any anti-slavery material became a capital offense in North Carolina. Verbal exhortations exacted the same severity. Public sentiment became inflamed to the point that a frenetic intolerance of any views against the system prevailed.

Nat Turner did nothing to hasten the prospects of **emancipation** for the slaves in the South. In reality, his revolt caused them to be bound tighter than ever to even more uneasy masters. **Related Entries**: Black Codes; Vesey, Denmark.

SUGGESTED READING: Joseph Cephas Carroll, *Insurrections in the United States, 1800–1865* (1969); Nicholas Halasz, *The Rattling Chains* (1966); William Styron, *Confessions of Nat Turner* (1993).

TURPENTINE. *See* Raw Materials.

TYLER, JOHN (1790–1862): governor of **Virginia**, senator, and tenth President of the United States (1841–1845). John Tyler was the first Vice President to ascend to the Executive Office at the death of a sitting President. The **Whig Party** was severely damaged by **William Henry Harrison**'s early death and the ascendancy of the less politically compatible Tyler to the presidency. Tyler, a former Democrat, was a maverick out of step with the party. He had been the only senator to vote against the **Force Bill** in the **nullification** crisis. He denied the right of the federal government to limit the spread of **slavery**, and believed in **state's rights**. President Tyler quickly gained the enmity of the Whig Party leader, **Henry Clay**. Within a year all but one of Tyler's cabinet had resigned, to be replaced with **Democrats** or Whigs with strong Southern leanings.

It was not anticipated that Tyler's administration would result in much constructive legislation. Nonetheless, he made a remarkable record, especially in the area of naval and maritime legislation and the establishment of a telegraph system for the Weather Bureau. His greatest achievement was the passage of the Webster-Ashburton Treaty, which settled the northeastern boundary of the nation with Canada.

In 1844 he narrowly escaped death when a large naval gun exploded during a trial on board the warship *Princeton*. Notwithstanding the popular sympathy this engendered, Tyler found it impossible to run for reelection on his own. The Whigs would have no part of him, and the Democrats chose **James K. Polk**, whom Tyler supported. When Polk won election by a slim margin on a platform that favored the **annexation of Texas**, Tyler declared the result a popular mandate for its acquisition and rushed a resolution through both houses of Congress in February 1845 admitting Texas even before Polk had taken office.

As an ex-President, Tyler retired to his plantation. The father of seven and a widower since 1842, Tyler remarried and had seven more children. His second wife, Julia Gardiner, was the daughter of one of those killed in the 1844 explosion. The family lived quietly in rural Virginia until the outbreak of the Civil War. Thereafter, Tyler became a member of the Virginia **secession** convention. He served in the provisional Congress of the Confederacy, and believed that the South should take the offensive militarily against the Union. He was elected to the Confederate House of Representatives but died in 1862 before he could take his seat. **Related Entry**: Texas, Annexation of.

SUGGESTED READING: Lucille Falkof, *John Tyler, Tenth President of the United States* (1990); Robert Seager, *And Tyler Too: A Biography of John and Julia Gardiner Tyler* (1963).

UNCLE TOM'S CABIN: When **Harriet Beecher Stowe** published *Uncle Tom's Cabin* in 1852, the book sold 300,000 copies in America and Britain in one year. Stowe's fictional work stressed the evils of **slavery** and presented a picture of total brutality. Mrs. Stowe had little personal knowledge of slavery. The factual basis for the story was found in Theodore D. Weld's radical **abolitionist** tract *Slavery as It Is: The Testimony of a Thousand Witnesses*, which was published in 1839. *Uncle Tom's Cabin* was immensely more effective in preaching the anti-slavery message in the form of a novel than the earlier tract had ever dreamed of being.

Stowe provided two accounts of the origins of this book, but it seems quite certain that the death of Uncle Tom was written first and the surrounding details of Little Eva and other characters were added at a later date. The character of Eliza Harris, who crossed the icy Ohio with her baby in her arms, seems to have been based on an actual person, and Stowe seems to have been made familiar with the story through her brother, Edward Beecher. The book was made into an equally popular play which found audiences nearly to the end of the century.

The South considered Stowe's work a slander and regarded it as abolitionist propaganda. **Mary Boykin Chesnut**, a southern woman familiar with slavery and slaves, wrote that she could not read a book so filled with distortions, as it was "too sickening" to think that any man would send "his little son to beat a human being tied to a tree." Chesnut goes on to suggest, using other literary references, that Stowe's work portrays as much fiction as Squeers beating Smike in Dickens' *Nicholas Nickleby* or the gouging of Gloucester's eyes in Shakespeare's *King Lear*. "How delightfully pharisaic a feeling it must be, to rise up superior and fancy [to] we [who] are so degraded as to defend and like to live with such degraded creatures around us . . . as Legree" (Woodward, 1981). In fact, Stowe was unable to disprove

E. L. DUNNE'S BAND AND ORCHESTRA

We present More New, Strong, Interesting ORIGINAL FEATURES than all other Uncle Tom's Cabin Companies that are traveling. COMFORTABLE SEATS FOR 1000 PEOPLE

Little **RUTH**

THE WONDERFUL CHILD ARTIST AS

EVA

THE LARGEST UNCLE TOM'S COM-PANY EVER ORGANIZED

NIGHT Performance **ONLY**

COME TO THE GROUNDS EARLY---SEE **FREE** **OUTSIDE EXHIBITION** 7:30 P.M.

DOORS OPEN AT 7:30 P. M. PERFORMANCE AT 8:00 P. M.

Renditions of *Uncle Tom's Cabin* drew huge audiences. This advertisement for a performance boasts that it can comfortably seat 1,000 people. (A playbill from the authors' collection.)

the charge that the book was filled with factual errors, although she attempted to do so in a subsequent work.

Nonetheless, amicably disposed Northerners found the passages describing the murderous brutality of Simon Legree indicative of the typical behavior of Southern slaveowners. The significance of the story, as of many of the attacks on the institution of slavery, lay in its ability to dramatize and emotionalize the issue. Writing and speech making on the subject of slavery in particular—and of Southern culture in general—were becoming increasingly stereotypical, and the stereotypes, even when presented in novels, were taking on a reality in the minds of the people as the Civil War approached. **Related Entries**: Literary Development; Punishment of Slaves; Stowe, Harriet Beecher.

SUGGESTED READING: C. E. Stowe, *Life of Harriet Beecher Stowe, Compiled from Her Journals and Letters* (1889; 1991); C. Vann Woodward, *Mary Chesnut's Civil War* (1981).

UNDERGROUND RAILROAD: The Underground Railroad facilitated many hundreds of slave escapes and was one of the most remarkable clandestine operations in American history. Its network, imagined to consist of numerous conductors, tracks, switching yards, and stations, became more widespread and efficient as the Civil War approached. No anti-slavery activity was as dramatic as that of slaves successfully escaping to free soil. The cumulative effect on public opinion of hundreds of anti-slavery poems, essays, and speeches paled in comparison to the unceasing flow of blacks fleeing the South for the North. Immediately after the Panic of 1837, when the **abolition** movement fell upon slack financial times, the stories of escaped slaves, like that immortalized by **Harriet Beecher Stowe** a decade and a half later in *Uncle Tom's Cabin* (1852), helped to buoy the spirits of the anti-slavery faithful.

According to a contemporary author (W. M. Mitchell writing in 1860), the term "Underground Railroad" originated in 1831 when a slaveowner frustrated by the continued escape of his bondsmen exclaimed that the abolitionists must have a **railroad** by which they helped slaves escape. The continued reference to stations, tracks, and depots suggests a system much better organized than was the actual case. The only tangible requisite components of the Underground Railroad were its people, who acted as conductors and guides and came from all walks of life and many levels of society. Although widely viewed as composed of dedicated Quakers, no single religion predominated. Many Underground Railroad agents were white, and many more were black. Most conductors assisted escaping slaves by hiding them in their homes, barns, or root cellars along well-established escape routes. The system provided disguises, transportation, counterfeit documents, money, and local guides to get the slaves to free soil. White abolitionists ventured into the South at the risk of their own lives to encourage slaves to flee and get them started on their way. Such persons were threatened with legal prosecution resulting in jail or fines. Rewards of over $10,000 were offered for such persons, dead or alive. Black agents could expect little less than death, if caught.

After the **Fugitive Slave Laws** were strengthened as part of the great **Compromise of 1850**, escaped slaves were often pursued into the **free states** by slave hunters. A panic took hold among **free blacks** and escaped slaves living in Northern cities that they would be rounded up and herded south into a renewed state of bondage. These fears were not completely unfounded, and abolitionists saw a need to remove the escapees from the country (usually to Canada), provide them with false identities as freemen, or purchase their freedom. The American Anti-slavery Society had been careful to provide funds to black abolitionist speaker and escaped slave **Frederick Douglass** for this purpose.

While the success of the Underground Railroad in psychological terms was appreciable, its success in absolute human terms has also been well determined. Southerners complained of losing hundreds of thousands of dollars in slave property every year. Slaveowners in the border states were particularly vulnerable. The borderlands of Ohio were possibly the busiest terminals on the entire Underground system. Maryland had 80 to 100 slaves escape annually at a cost of more than $80,000; Virginia lost in excess of $100,000; and South Carolina more than $200,000. Southerners estimated during the 1850 debates that they had suffered more than $15 million in losses due to the Underground Railroad. This monetary value represented the escape of 30,000 individuals, or about 1 percent of the more than 3 million slaves held in bondage at the time.

Several escaped slaves became dedicated to the cause of abolition and to the Underground Railroad in particular. The most famous escaped slave was certainly Frederick Douglass, who became an active abolitionist, publisher, and speaker in the North. **Joseph P. Parker**, a former slave and foundry worker, who had bought his own freedom, returned to the South to act as a conductor and guide for more than 100 of his fellow blacks. Finally, **Harriet Tubman**, who returned to the South more than a dozen times, conducted more than 300 individuals to freedom in a career that spanned fifteen years. **Related Entry**: Fugitive Slave Law of 1850.

SUGGESTED READING: Stuart Seely Sprauge, ed., *His Promised Land: The Autobiography of Joseph P. Parker, Former Slave and Conductor on the Underground Railroad* (1996).

UNITARIANS. *See* Religion and Religious Revivalism.

UNIVERSITIES. *See* Education.

URBANIZATION: Cities as distinct as Providence, Rhode Island, and Chicago, Illinois, experienced amazing rates of growth in the antebellum period due to their importance in trade. A number of small coastal towns became booming cities by mid-century in response to America's rise to maritime greatness in the Clipper Ship era. Boston, Salem, Portland, and New Haven, for example, were all active coastal trading cities in 1850. Boston alone was the terminus for no fewer than seven **railroads**. Pittsburgh, Cincinnati, Louisville, Memphis, Natchez, and St. Louis were all growing because of their location on navigable **rivers**. The number of towns having more than 10,000 people increased from six to more than sixty in less than half a century.

The cities which had been the largest at the turn of the century remained so and experienced the greatest rates of population growth. By 1850, New York City boasted a population of more than half a million people. Philadelphia, Boston, Newport, Baltimore, **New Orleans**, and **Charleston**—all large cities in the colonial period—had each grown to hold hundreds of thousands. Moreover, the physical size of most cities increased, sometimes doubling or tripling in area as they spread into the "suburban" countryside.

Immigration from abroad had an incalculable effect on the nature of

American society in the antebellum period. A remarkable influx of foreigners outstripped the physical expansion of the cities and stressed their infrastructure to the limit. Poverty, disease, crime, and ignorance were condensing in the slum districts of Northern cities as immigrants drew together in the security of their own communities. Reformers believed that the standard of living among these immigrants had to be improved if the squalor of the cities was not to become a permanent feature of American society. Many attributed widespread social nonconformity among these immigrants to social degradation, rather than to the social injustices of the American system.

In the cities of the Northeast the disparities between the immigrant and the native born, the wealthy and the impoverished, and the educated and the ignorant were growing. Urbanization brought crowding and disease. Technological advancement led not only to labor-saving devices and better systems of **transportation** and communications, but also to unemployment, railroad derailments, steamboat explosions, and factory disasters. Increasing industrialization exploited white labor on a level that seemingly rivaled the evils of **slavery**.

By comparison, Southern cities grew along the perimeter of the region's heartland and tended to materialize after the surrounding area was well settled. Outside of the almost self-sufficient plantations, small towns in the rural South offered few amenities, and consequently they often appeared shabby and run down to visitors unfamiliar with rural life. With slaves occupying most of the menial jobs, there was little in the South to attract immigration, and Southern cities tended to avoid the development of slums and ghettos. Nonetheless, Baltimore, New Orleans, and Charleston witnessed unprecedented growth by the end of the period. These cities grew as planters and farmers came in from their outlying and relatively isolated holdings to take advantage of the social and cultural benefits cities offered, but they also sported a large itinerant population of traders, bargemen, and clerks. **Related Entries**: Plantation Economy; Reform Movements.

SUGGESTED READING: Carl Abbott, *Boosters and Businessmen: Popular Economic Thought and Urban Growth in the Antebellum Middle West* (1981); Lisa C. Tolbert, *Constructing Townscapes: Space and Society in Antebellum Tennessee* (1999).

VALUE OF SLAVES: Although absolute values are impossible to ascertain, the total value of slaves owned in the South has been estimated at $4 billion. In 1860 the estimated value of all the slave property in **Virginia** alone was more than $300 million. From Virginia—a major supplier of slaves to other areas of the South—more than one-quarter million slaves were "sold south" in a single decade. In the decade of the 1850s small planters complained that the price of a prime field hand—said to be $2,000—had driven them from the marketplace.

Slave market records suggest that this $2,000 figure was an exaggeration. In 1860 young black men aged nineteen to twenty-four could bring between $1,300 and $1,700 in the market; young women between sixteen and twenty, from $1,200 to $1,500. Slaves with skills brought higher prices. Blacksmiths, wheelwrights, and furniture makers sold at a premium, as did particularly comely young women. Children, the aged, and the unskilled brought considerably less. A healthy child four months old was considered to be worth $100 in **North Carolina**. Nonetheless, the average price for a slave, taking all ages and sexes into account, has been estimated to have approached $1,500. It should be noted, to place these values in perspective, that a white **overseer** on a moderately sized plantation could expect to receive a salary of only $200 to $500 for an entire year's work. **Related Entries**: Atlantic Slave Trade; Emancipation.

SUGGESTED READING: Brion Davis, *Slavery in the Colonial Chesapeake* (1994); Ervin L. Jordan, Jr., *Black Confederates and Afro-Yankees in Civil War Virginia* (1995); Kenneth M. Stampp, *The Peculiar Institution* (1956); Jenny B. Wahl, *The Bondsman's Burden: An Economic Analysis of the Common Law of Southern Slavery* (1998).

VAN BUREN, MARTIN (1783–1862): politician, senator, Vice President, and eighth President of the United States (1837–1841). Martin Van

Buren was born in Old Kinderhook, New York (from which the term "OK" originated during his presidential bid). Until 1821 he was enmeshed in state politics, serving as a state senator and attorney general. In that year, Van Buren was elected to the U.S. Senate, where he was an active supporter of William Crawford in the 1824 presidential election. He tried, unsuccessfully, to produce a deadlock in the House of Representatives when the race was sent there for decision. Van Buren was a bitter opponent of **John Quincy Adams**, and this bitterness drove him toward **Andrew Jackson**.

Nonetheless, as a senator, Van Buren's political agenda steadfastly reflected what he thought was best for New York. He opposed and obstructed legislation that would have allowed the federal government to build **roads** and canals in other states, as they would deflect trade from the Erie Canal and New York.

Upon his return to **Washington** in 1828 he was invited by President Jackson to enter his cabinet as secretary of state. Van Buren immediately became one of Jackson's most influential cabinet members. It has been observed that it was Van Buren's idea to introduce the **spoils system** (long a staple of New York politics) to the federal bureaucracy. So completely did he win the President's confidence that Jackson proclaimed him "a true man with no guile." In 1831 Van Buren persuaded the President to allow him to resign as secretary of state so that Jackson could reorganize his cabinet and eliminate the supporters of **John C. Calhoun**.

Van Buren's tact and good political sense caused Jackson to choose him as a running mate in 1832. In the course of the campaign, and as presiding officer of the Senate, he aided Jackson in defeating a bill to recharter the **Bank of the United States**, in opposing **nullification**, and in limiting **internal improvements at federal expense**.

Van Buren was Jackson's anointed successor as the **Democratic Party**'s candidate for the presidency in 1836. Although he had endorsed the prohibition against the **extension of slavery** in the **Missouri Compromise of 1820**, by 1831 he had announced himself as a strong defender of the right of **slave states** to control the institution of **slavery** within their borders. Moreover, he condemned the activities of the **abolitionists** and voted in 1836 to ban abolitionist propaganda from the U.S. mails. Although there were some defections to Southern candidates in the election, Van Buren convinced enough Southern voters of his good will to win the electoral vote handily.

President Van Buren's administration was greeted with pressing problems almost immediately. The rumblings of the Panic of 1837 struck just as Van Buren was taking office. His term of office was burdened with a terrible economic depression, to which continued crop failures and low prices for **cotton** were added. Moreover, Van Buren suddenly became inept at keeping himself out of controversy. He refused to annex **Texas** because he wanted no war with Mexico, and he was opposed to extending slavery into any newly acquired territories. The **Whigs**, sensing weakness in the White House, evaded these issues, ran a brilliant and innovative campaign, and triumphantly elected **William Henry Harrison** in 1840. Van Buren even lost his home state of New York.

Van Buren was the leading candidate for the 1844 Democratic nomination, but he had committed political suicide by opposing the **annexation of Texas**. His party therefore brought forward **James K. Polk** as a dark horse candidate. Ironically, in 1848, the Free Soil Party, a group of anti-slavery politicians, nominated Van Buren for President on a platform opposing the extension of slavery in the new territories that had been added to the nation by Polk. Van Buren ran unsuccessfully in 1848. He accused the Democrats of selling out to the "slavocracy," but was himself accused of duplicity when he came out in favor of the compromise measures of 1850. He returned to the Democratic Party in 1852 trusting that **Franklin Pierce** would set the country aright. Indignant at the passage of the **Kansas-Nebraska Act of 1854**, he became increasingly pessimistic about the future of the Union. He was deeply shocked and despondent over the actual outbreak of civil war, and he died at the age of seventy-nine after months of suffering with an advanced case of asthma. **Related Entries**: Jackson, Andrew; Democratic Party; Texas, Annexation of.

SUGGESTED READING: Donald B. Cole, *Martin Van Buren and the American Political System* (1984); Robert V. Remini, *Martin Van Buren and the Making of the Democratic Party* (1959).

VESEY, DENMARK (DENMARK VESEY CONSPIRACY) (1767–1822): free black and anti-slavery radical.

The man who caused the greatest clamor over **slavery** in the 1820s was a skilled black freeman named Denmark Vesey. Although the slave revolt Vesey and his supporters planned was completely crushed in 1822, its consequences for blacks throughout the South were overwhelmingly tragic.

Denmark Vesey, of mixed race, was born into slavery. As a young man who showed intelligence and diligence, he was trained by his master as a carpenter. Early in the nineteenth century, Vesey was able to purchase his freedom with the winnings from a lottery jackpot. With his freedom and financial future assured, Vesey—described by contemporary observers as "brilliant, well traveled and well read"—turned his talents toward a crusade against slavery. He conducted this campaign with an unfortunate mix of sarcasm, indignation, and Biblical references. His diatribes were powerful and convincing, but they were also filled with rage and violence. Vesey often likened Negroes to the Children of Israel in the Promised Land, and he called for slaves to rise up and massacre their masters.

Vesey's fellow conspirators—numbering probably no more than 100 blacks—came almost exclusively from the city of **Charleston** and included an odd shaman-like character in the person of Gullah Jack, who added a touch of tribal mysticism to Vesey's preaching. The plot was significantly similar to that put into motion a generation later by the equally ruthless **John Brown**. Both schemes relied on the carelessness of the authorities in guarding the public armories. Vesey planned to attack a local military store that had a large stock of muskets and powder, as well as the Charleston Arsenal. He and his lieutenants then planned to distribute arms to their followers, to raise the black population, and to hold Charleston Neck against all white counterattacks. Thereafter, the plan dissolved into a vague scheme to sail from Charleston to friendly hands in San Domingo in the Caribbean.

As the plot was five years in preparation, it is not surprising that it was discovered. In May 1822 a house servant told the authorities that he had been approached to join the conspiracy by William Paul. Paul, a minor player by all accounts, was arrested immediately and implicated others. Vesey and his lieutenants were not immediately apprehended. So firm were the whites of Charleston in their supposed security that the ringleaders had openly moved about the city unmolested for several weeks after the plot had come to light, reflecting the lack of credence given the initial allegations by the authorities.

Ultimately, the closeness of the thing had dawned on the authorities, thereby prompting the chief civil officer of the city, Intendant **James A. Hamilton**, and the sitting governor, Thomas Bennett, take action. In the next two months, hundreds of blacks were detained and questioned. The possibility of communication between Vesey and the blacks of San Domingo sent a shudder of fear through the entire South. The latter had run a successful but bloody massacre of the French inhabitants of that island, and defeated seasoned French troops sent there to quell the revolt. Although the plot was probably not as widespread as the officials thought, no fewer than thirty-five Negroes, including Vesey, were hanged, and thirty-seven others were banished from the state. Free blacks in the American South were immediately viewed with greater apprehension than previously. Consequently, all blacks had their privileges curtailed, and new sanctions were immediately added to the **Black Codes** not only in South Carolina, but across the South.

A series of arsons known as the Charleston Fire Scare of 1826 followed on the heels of these repressive steps. For more than six months unknown arsonists nightly put torches to Charleston's buildings. As many as five fires were set on a single evening, and there was ample evidence of careful planning. The Fire Scare served to renew the distressing emotions of the Vesey plot and to maintain a belief that the slaves were willing to start a race war.

The trauma of living through a time of imminent violence, perpetrated by some of the most trusted bondsmen in the city of Charleston, hardened the opinion of many moderates against **abolition**. The Vesey conspiracy was seen as the "fruit of abolition." More important, the Denmark Vesey conspiracy set Southerners on the road of interdicting the mails and otherwise restricting the distribution of abolitionists' propaganda. Southern forces in Congress used the threat of similar revolts to quash any discourse on slavery in the halls of government, saying that such debates helped to incite slaves to murder, rape, and plunder. **Related Entries**: Brown, John; Gag Rule; Hamilton, James A.; Turner, Nat.

SUGGESTED READING: Robert S. Starobin, *Denmark Vesey: The Slave Conspiracy of 1822* (1979); Philip Spencer, *Three Against Slavery: Denmark Vesey, William Lloyd Garrison, Frederick Douglass* (1972).

VICTORIANISM IN AMERICA: On June 20, 1837, the world was at peace and young Queen Victoria ascended the throne of Great Britain. Victoria and her husband, Prince Albert of Saxe-Coburg, became both the darlings and leading lights of the Western Anglo world. The cut of Victoria's clothing—dowdy at best—quickly became the fashion in both Britain and America, and Albert almost single-handedly established the protocol of wearing trousers on state occasions. Nonetheless, it was the couple's dedication to self-control, social order, and absolute values that most affected American society.

As Victorianism evolved it progressed from **romanticism** to modern fundamental **Protestantism**, wherein the steady labor of the work ethic prevailed. Victorians saw regularity in the performance of tasks as the road to social discipline and order. With the general availability of the pocket watch, men increasingly lived their lives by the clock. Factory workers were expected to work in shifts dictated by the public clocks that came to be prominently displayed on towers, in the streets, and on the factory walls. The idea of being "on time" represented a significant change in the lifestyle of most city dwellers.

Although society became increasingly humanitarian and secular, it came in conflict with many traditional institutions. Characterized by the activism of the "haves" for the "have-nots," Victorians increasingly demanded social reforms for those who were oppressed. Philanthropic reforms, while benevolent, were largely institutional in nature and focused almost solely on the visibly degraded elements of society, including paupers, drunkards, orphans, illiterates, slaves, prostitutes, and prisoners. The poor, as an example, would receive public aid only while confined within the workhouse, where they would be taught order, discipline, and responsibility. Ironically, Victorians, without the slightest sense of hypocrisy, viewed the aftermath of the **abolition** of **slavery** as an arrangement in which freed slaves would be *forced* to work.

Victorian men's work increasingly took place in the special atmosphere of business premises such as factories or offices. Fathers commonly left the home to work for ten to fourteen hours, and their children rarely saw them during daylight. This tendency to "go to work" rather than to work at home led to the virtual removal of men from the home environment, leaving it the sole province of the female. The modern Victorian home increasingly came to focus almost solely on the wife and children. The evolution to a female-dominated household may help to explain the growing formalism and rigid authoritarianism Victorian fathers demanded when they were present.

Victorian women were expected to confine their own aspirations to those that fit within their husband's sphere. Selflessness, volunteerism, and family were the prominent features of Victorian society for women. Large families (possibly emulating the nine children of Victoria and Albert) were in fashion. One of the prominent features of Victorianism was the mutual reliance between fathers and daughters. While fathers and sons, and mothers and daughters, often came into conflict, young women found it difficult to break free of the affectionate ties they had with their fathers. In turn, Victorian men created business or career opportunities for their sons and sons-in-law but made companions of their unmarried daughters. In all cases they demanded unquestioning obedience from them. **Related Entries**: Kinship; Planter Aristocracy.

SUGGESTED READING: Anne C. Rose, *Victorian America and the Civil War* (1992).

VIRGINIA: Highlights of a period description of the state from John Hayward's *Gazetteer of the United States* (1853) read as follows:

Surface and Soil: The eastern section is generally low country, with a soil partly sandy and partly alluvial, abounding in swamps and unproductive tracts, and for the most part, especially towards the sea-coast and along the margins of rivers, noted for the prevalence of fatal **epidemics** during the season from August to October. In the mountainous district the soil becomes more fertile. Between the numerous ridges there lie extensive valleys presenting soil of the richest quality. The chief products are wheat, Indian corn, and tobacco. **Cotton** is also cultivated in the alluvial district; and in other quarters hemp and **wool** are among the chief staples. All the varieties of grain, vegetables and fruit peculiar to the climate are raised.

Rivers: Some of the finest **rivers** in America flow within its boundaries, the most important of which are the Potomac, Rappahannock, James and Kanawha Rivers. Its sea-coast and principal rivers afford many excellent harbors.

Education: In 1809 a fund "for the encouragement of learning" was established by law, to be derived from all fines, escheats, and forfeitures; and this fund was augmented, in 1816, by the addition of a very large share of the claim on the general government for military services during the then recent war. The benefits of common schools were bestowed, with various degrees of success, upon large numbers of indigent children, who would otherwise, in all probability, have grown up in deplorable ignorance, vice, and misery. A further system of primary schools was authorized in 1820. There are numerous academies, or rather private schools; some of these are of a respectable rank, but they are designed chiefly for the children of those who can afford to dispense with the public bounty. A large number of academies and high schools are devoted exclusively to the **education** of females. Of the still higher orders of educational seminaries, the most prominent are the University of Virginia, the College of William and Mary, Washington College and Hamden Sidney College. There are several theological institutions of comparatively recent date.

Internal Improvements: Among the most important undertakings are the construction of a series of canals and dams for the improvement and extension of the navigation of [the] James, Kanawha and New Rivers. Another great work is the Dismal Swamp Canal, whereby the waters of the Chesapeake Bay are connected with those of Albemarle Sound. Sundry **railroads** have recently been opened.

Manufacture: The manufactures of the state are confined principally to the preparation of its staples for market, or for domestic consumption.

Minerals: Iron, lead copper, gypsum, salt, anthracite and bituminous coals are among the most plentiful and profitable.

Other: Every white male, 21 years of age, and possessed of a freehold valued at $25, or being a housekeeper, or head of a family, and having paid taxes, is qualified to vote for state or other officers; but subordinate officers, soldiers, marines, or seamen, in the national service, as well as paupers, and men convicted of infamous crimes, cannot exercise the right of suffrage.

Related Entries: Geography; Suffrage; Wool.

SUGGESTED READING: John Hayward, *Gazetteer of the United States* (1853); Frederick Law Olmsted, *The Cotton Kingdom: A Traveler's Observations on Cotton and Slavery in the American Slave States* (1861; 1996); Louis Rubin, Jr., *Virginia: A History* (1984).

VIRGINIA AND KENTUCKY RESOLUTIONS: Even in the early days of the American Republic, there were grave doubts about the ability of the federal government to discipline itself in the exercise of its powers. The contrast between the federal/state system of sovereignty envisioned and established by the **Constitutional Convention** in 1787 and the actual working relationship between the federal and state governments quickly became obvious to any observant American. It did not take long for the states to come into conflict with those who wanted to extend the powers of the federal government.

Thomas Jefferson and **James Madison** combined in 1798 to define the limits of legitimate federal power in the Virginia and Kentucky Resolutions. In the resolutions Jefferson and Madison tried to demonstrate that the states were not united on the principle of unlimited submission to their general government, but were the exclusive or final judges of the extent of the powers delegated to it.

In the antebellum political debates, Southerners widely quoted the Virginia and Kentucky Resolutions (both in and out of context) to support the concept of **states' rights**. Madison clearly considered the application of these doctrines by those friendly to **nullification** or **secession** a misrepresentation of his opinions. He and Jefferson had proposed no more than cooperation among the several states in securing the repeal of unfair federal laws or the amendment of the Constitution. **Related Entry**: Constitutional Interpretation.

SUGGESTED READING: James R. Kennedy and Walter D. Kennedy, *The South Was Right* (1995).

VIRGINIA DYNASTY. *See* Executive Branch/Presidency.

WAR HAWKS: The term War Hawk is usually reserved for the two dozen most outspoken proponents of the **War of 1812** from among those who made up the war party in the twelfth Congress. In the congressional elections of 1810 and 1812 a number of young representatives were elected who were wildly in favor of prosecuting a war against the British. Among these were **John C. Calhoun** and **Henry Clay** (who was elected Speaker of the House). Clay and his supporters were interested in expanding the nation. During the winter of 1811–1812 the War Hawks consistently made fiery speeches declaring that a thousand **Kentucky** riflemen could take all of Canada. They expected the war to be short, as the British were expending most of their energy fighting Napoleon in Europe. An increase in Indian depredations in the Old Northwest, widely believed to have been incited by the British, lent a spark of justification to their cause. Sensing a war spirit in the West and South (including the frontier regions of Vermont and Pennsylvania), the War Hawks were able to convince President **James Madison** to declare war in June 1812. The War Hawks were aggressively opposed by the Federalists of New York, New Jersey, and most of New England. When Canada was not taken in two months as predicted by the War Hawks, the failure was laid at the door of the Federalists for their lack of support for the war effort. **Related Entry**: Harrison, William Henry.

SUGGESTED READING: Harry Fritz, "The War Hawks of 1812," *Capital Studies* 5 (Spring 1977); David S. Heidler and Jeanne T. Heidler, *Encyclopedia of the War of 1812* (1997).

WAR OF 1812: As **Thomas Jefferson**'s chosen successor, **James Madison** had little trouble entering the Executive Mansion as the fourth President of the United States in 1809. Nonetheless, he was to experience eight difficult and troubled years in office. Opposed in many areas by the members of his own cabinet, Madison was faced with an immediate crisis in foreign relations. The Napoleonic Wars were in full swing in Europe, and both Britain and France had interrupted international maritime commerce with wartime measures and countermeasures that were harmful to American trade. Lacking all but a skeletal navy, Madison's predecessor, Jefferson, had attempted to resolve the problem by providing for coastal defenses, including sixteen state-of-the-art fortresses and a fleet of about 200 gunboats, to defend American harbors. Jefferson then placed an embargo on all American trade by closing the nation's ports; but this policy left American ships rotting at their moorings and American sailors without employment.

In 1810 Congress authorized Madison to open trade with Britain and France provided that when one or the other lifted its restrictions, trade would be cut off with the other. On the strength of an assurance by Napoleon that the objectionable French measures would be raised, Madison issued a proclamation of nonintercourse ending all commerce with Britain. At the time Napoleon was the master of the European continent; but Britain retained control of the seas, had bases in nearby Canada, and enjoyed the allegiance of many tribes of Native Americans. Britain's European ally, Spain, held much of the southern border of the United States. The possibility of a new frontier war loomed behind Madison's decision to cut off British trade. Nonetheless, in June 1812 the President sent a special message to Congress asking that a declaration of war be made against the British.

Although Madison used British incitement of the Indians to hostilities and the impressment of American seamen by British ships as causes for going to war, the Federalists, especially those in New England, opposed him. Strong support for the war came from Southerners and those in frontier communities. Congressional **War Hawks** saw an amazing opportunity to fulfill a long-held wish to seize both Canada from Britain and what remained of Spanish **Florida** from its European ally, Spain, in the coming cataclysm. Nonetheless, the war along the Canadian border was initially mismanaged; one of America's vaunted frigates, the *Chesapeake*, was drawn forth and defeated by a British warship, the *Shannon*, within site of Boston harbor; Mr. Jefferson's gunboats proved to be useless; and the capital at **Washington, DC**, was captured and burned. Madison's enemies in his own party thwarted any attempt to seize Florida, and there was little enthusiasm left thereafter, even among Southerners, for creating more Northern states from Canadian territory. Federalists threatened Madison with the **secession** of the New England states in the final months of the conflict if he did not sue for peace. Ironically, the Federalist Party would not survive this confrontation.

With the armistice in December 1814, Madison found that not a single war aim had been attained. Notwithstanding these setbacks, history has dismissed the dismal failure of American arms in "Mr. Madison's War" for the less bitter illusions of success offered by the victories of the U.S. frigate

A street scene before the White House in Washington, DC, in the 1840s. (From a period text in the authors' collection.)

Constitution; the successful defense of Fort McHenry (one of Jefferson's fortresses, whose flag was the Star Spangled Banner); and the minimal successes on Lake Erie and Lake Champlain and at Fort Erie. None of these had proved decisive. The only truly decisive engagement of the war was the defeat of the British regulars at the **Battle of New Orleans**—significant in that it was to catapult **Andrew Jackson** to national prominence. **Related Entries**: Battle of New Orleans; *Constitution*; Jackson, Andrew.

SUGGESTED READING: David S. Heidler and Jeanne T. Heidler, *Encyclopedia of the War of 1812* (1997).

WASHINGTON, DC: The federal capital at Washington was highly valued as a symbol by nineteenth-century Americans. Carefully laid out in a district allocated from within the boundaries of **Maryland** in order to salve the pride of the South, the nation's capital city had been under construction since the turn of the century. Americans pointed proudly to the imposing structure of the U.S. Capitol Building, as well as the General Post Office, the Bureau of the Treasury, the Smithsonian Institution, and the Executive Mansion as representative of a vigorous young nation preparing to take its place among the leading countries of the world.

Unfortunately, Washington was also symbolic of other things. The plans for the city, like the basic founding concepts of the nation itself, were as pretentious as they were visionary. The city had fallen to the British in 1814 and had been burned. Although rebuilding had started immediately, even in 1860 the plans for the city, and the nation itself, lay unfulfilled and disordered. Sprawling along the banks of the Potomac with the "Old City" of Alexandria, **Virginia**, across the water, the great buildings of the new capital remained incomplete even after the expenditure of vast sums of money and six decades of effort. The Capitol, an imposing architectural edifice, lay unfinished with its original dome removed—a scaffolding and a towering crane representative of restructuring and rethinking. The wings of the building were "stretched bare and unfinished, devoid even of steps." The imposing obelisk of the Washington Monument, at that time, lay as a mere foundation. Blocks of marble, lumber, cast iron plates, and the tools of workmen strewn about the district gave quiet testimony to the fact that the plan for the nation's first city, like the social and political plan for the American nation itself, was incomplete and open to revision. **Related Entry**: War of 1812.

SUGGESTED READING: Margaret Leech, *Reveille in Washington* (1941; 1991).

WEBSTER, DANIEL (1782–1852): politician, cabinet officer, and senator. Daniel Webster's early career in New Hampshire was in law, but his fine intellect and natural eloquence made his entry into politics inevitable. He was a thoroughly aristocratic **Whig** throughout his career. From 1813 to 1817 he was a member of the House of Representatives and an opponent of President **James Madison** and the **War of 1812**. From 1817 to 1823 Webster was out of politics and devoted himself to his law practice, and he therefore took no part in the framing of the **Missouri Compromise of 1820**. He reentered Congress in 1823, and was chosen by his state legislature for the Senate in 1827. It was in the Senate chamber that Webster had his greatest influence on national policy. He was disappointed, but resigned to his political fate, when he was passed over in both 1836 and 1840 as a candidate for the presidency.

Throughout his career Daniel Webster spoke strongly for a broad interpretation of the Constitution (*see* **Constitutional Interpretation**); and he proposed a rationale for a strong federalism similar to that which **John C. Calhoun** was to provide for the state **nullification** arguments. Nonetheless, Webster's role in history was to use his brilliant mind and splendid ability as a speaker to argue temperately about the issues of his day, and then only to meet a crisis or avert dissension. His politics were deliberately designed to "beat down the . . . equal extremes" raging on both sides of any question (Shewmaker, 1991). While he personally found **slavery** distasteful, he did not think it as bad as disunion. When the strict constructionist **John Tyler** ascended to the presidency after the death of **William Henry Harrison** in 1844, Webster was the only member of the cabinet (he was secretary of

Daniel Webster speaking before the Senate. (From the authors' collection.)

state) who did not abandon his post. He retired in 1842 to private life, but was back in the Senate in 1845. This was a dark time for him politically, as he disliked slavery and tried to limit it without creating a combative atmosphere in the Senate. This was a difficult task at a time when politics was so lacking in restraint. The **Mexican War of 1846** proved troubling for him also, as he opposed the war's prosecution, but lost a son in the ensuing combat. He worked closely with **Henry Clay** to provide for the compromise measures of 1850.

Webster's final office was that of secretary of state under **Millard Fillmore**, a position he held until his health failed. He died in 1852 after giving a long dissertation on religious matters to those at his bedside. His continued endorsement of moderation in critical situations probably helped to postpone the Civil War for a decade. **Related Entries**: Constitutional Interpretation; Nullification; Webster-Hayne Debate.

SUGGESTED READING: Robert V. Remini, *Daniel Webster: The Man and His Time* (1997); Kenneth E. Shewmaker, ed., *Daniel Webster, "The Completest Man"* (1991).

WEBSTER-HAYNE DEBATE: In 1830 there was a great debate between **Daniel Webster** and **Robert Y. Hayne** in the Senate over the disposition of public lands on the western frontier. The contest lasted two weeks and made state **nullification** a national issue. The Webster-Hayne encounter was the first of the great forensic epics to catch the imagination of the American public in the antebellum period. The last of them may have been the Lincoln-Douglas debates in 1858. Well-dressed men and women, in a holiday atmosphere, crowded the Senate galleries to hear the debate. Hayne, dressed in a homespun **cotton** and linen suit, appropriately symbolizing the traditional simplicity of Southern life, was a counterpoint to the "manufactured" broadcloth suit with turnback tails worn by Webster. For his part, Webster's commanding size, smoldering eyes, and craggy face were more than a complement to Hayne's debonair deportment and youthful features.

In the debate Hayne defended the concept of individual state sovereignty, declaring that there was no greater evil "than the consolidation of this government" under the unrestrained rule of federal law. A group of sovereign states melted down into a single *united states* could not be consistent with freedom. The constitution had been ratified by individual state conventions called for the purpose, and those conventions had the power to nullify any act of the federal government. Concurrently, Hayne openly accused the politicians of New England, as a group, of "disloyalty" for their lackluster support of the **War of 1812**, reopening a sectional wound more than a decade old.

Daniel Webster's reply, which took six hours to deliver and filled seventy-three printed pages, presented his own conception of the federal union and defended New England's position with regard to the war with Britain. The New Hampshire senator asserted that the Union was established with specific powers and obligations, not by the states, but by the people in general; and he declared that the states could not assume the power from the people to dissolve it. Moreover, he declared that the constitutional process had divided the right of sovereignty between the state and federal governments, and had left federal law the "supreme law of the land." Webster ended his speech with the impassioned phrase: "Liberty and Union, now and forever, one and inseparable."

Both Hayne and Webster came to the debate with a good deal of political baggage. As a representative of the **South Carolina** radicals, who were trying to maintain a majority in Congress with a South-West coalition, Hayne had to argue the case against high **tariffs** without alienating the West. His strategy was to avoid defending nullification directly (the concept had been roundly criticized by all the states except South Carolina in 1828). He planned, instead, to place his emphasis on the open access to public lands that would lead to a quick repayment of the national debt and eliminate the need for the tariffs altogether.

In answer to Webster's remarks, Hayne, who was acutely aware of the political consequences of his performance, characterized Negroes as "subhuman" in order to salve the irrational racism of his constituents. The end of **slavery**, a side issue in Hayne's view, would condemn **free blacks** to an existence that was "poor, wretched, vile and loathsome." Moreover, he was maneuvered by Webster into arguing the merits of state nullification at length. Hayne's statements won him local approbation and the governorship of his state when he left the Senate; but they also weakened the South-West alliance to the point that the radicals were forced to put their future energies into countering a possible majority tyranny by establishing a fundamental minority right of veto.

Webster, however, was forced to defend his many antiwar statements from the period of the **War of 1812**, including some that sounded very much like they supported **states' rights**: "The solemn duty of the state governments," he had said in 1814, "was to protect their own authority against the usurpations of the national government"—a statement made by Webster in opposition to the military conscription for a war that was unpopular with his constituents. Webster's contribution to the political process during the debate was to turn Hayne's advocacy for a right of minority veto into a wedge that split the South-West coalition. Webster understood that the West cared more for majority rule than it did for cheap land.

Webster was generally credited with having routed Hayne in the debate, and his remarks were memorized and recited by thousands of school children in the North for decades. Webster had somehow caught the meaning of the new American nation in a way that continued to elude Hayne and other Southern apologists. **Related Entries**: Legislative Branch/Congress; Nullification; South Carolina Association.

SUGGESTED READING: Theodore D. Jervey, *Robert Y. Hayne and His Times* (1970); Robert V. Remini, *Daniel Webster: The Man and His Time* (1997); Kenneth E. Shewmaker, ed., *Daniel Webster, "The Completest Man"* (1991).

WESTWARD MOVEMENT: Historians have identified at least six different "Wests" in America's history. The area of the old Northwest and the Great Lakes was once the West, and the earliest West, in the eyes of the South, extended from the Appalachian Mountains to **Missouri, Louisiana**, and **Texas**. The mountain man's West was in the eastern foothills of the Rocky Mountains, while the Mormons founded a West in the Great Basin of Utah. The farthest west of the Wests were coastal California and the **Oregon Territory**.

Among the earliest frontiersmen to push west were the trailblazers and farmers of the eighteenth century who went into western New York and the mountains of Pennsylvania, **Virginia**, the Carolinas, **Tennessee**, and **Kentucky**. This was when the "West" was still in the East. By 1770 more than 400,000 people had pushed out from the Atlantic seaboard and into the forests of the Middle Atlantic and Southern states. An entire generation of men and women had advanced the frontier south toward Texas and west toward Illinois and the banks of the **Mississippi River** before 1800. These early frontier families faced a number of obstacles in making this penetration.

The roads west were often crowded with wayfarers. Stagecoach inns, like the one in this Currier and Ives print, were popular rest stops. (From the authors' collection.)

Besides the natural resistance of the wilderness and the Appalachian Mountains, they faced the French and later the British in the old Northwest, the Spanish and the French in **Florida** and Louisiana, and the native Indian population almost everywhere.

The military roads forged by British generals Edward Braddock and John Forbes during the final French and Indian War (1754–1763) initially served as arteries to western Pennsylvania. Braddock's road began in Alexandria, Virginia, passed through Winchester, Virginia, and several small settlements in **Maryland**, and entered Pennsylvania near the border of present-day West Virginia. Of course, Braddock had suffered an ignoble reverse and had lost his life in the campaign. Workmen improving Braddock's Road in 1824 dug up a skeleton with officer's insignia, believed to be his, which had been hastily buried during the retreat.

Forbes left from Philadelphia and moved west through Pennsylvania from Raystown (Bedford, PA). Ignoring Braddock's more sensible route, which followed the natural flow of the local rivers, he hacked a "Great Wagon Road" through the virgin Pennsylvania wilderness. In many places the road ran in a straight line for miles, ignoring the up and down topography of ridges and valleys. Forbes claimed he had been duped into using the Raystown route by Pennsylvanians who hoped to use it to corner the Ohio Valley trade. Indeed, after the withdrawal of the French from the region, the Forbes Road attracted numerous inns and stagecoach stops along its length, and became characterized by the Conestoga freight wagons that plied its length.

In 1775 Daniel Boone led Kentucky-bound settlers along the Wilderness Trail through the Cumberland Gap (named by Thomas Walker, a Virginian who first explored the area in 1750). The Old Walton Road ran from Frenchman's Broad Creek in the Great Smoky Mountains to Nashville, Tennessee, and many pioneers used the Warrior's Path to travel from the Cumberland Gap to the Scioto River, which flowed north toward the Great Lakes. Like the Warrior's Path and the **Natchez Trace** from Louisiana to Tennessee, most of these routes into the interior were initially well-established Indian trails through the forests.

These footpaths were slowly improved to allow for the passage of wagons. In 1796 Congress authorized the construction of **Zane's Trace**, a road from western Virginia to Kentucky which became a major westward route for settlers in the upper South. By 1810 Kentucky, Tennessee, and Ohio had amassed a staggering population of over 500,000 using these routes. A national highway to the West was begun with federal funds in 1806 and extended from Cumberland, Maryland (1811), to Wheeling, [West] Virginia (1818), to Vandalia, Illinois (1850).

The major trails to the Pacific West were the Oregon Trail, the California Trail, and the Santa Fe Trail (to New Mexico and Southern California). Most emigrants in the 1840s set their sights on Oregon prior to the discovery of gold in California. In 1840 fewer than 100 hardy souls took the Oregon Trail, but by 1845 this number had reached 5,000 annually. The discovery of gold caused the number to increase tenfold, with 40,000 emigrants in 1849 and 55,000 in 1850 (the peak year of emigration prior to the opening of the transcontinental **railroad**).

The one major group that chose to forego these destinations was the Mormons. Having been persecuted in Ohio, Missouri, and Illinois, the advance parties sent out by the Mormons hurried into the Great Salt Lake Valley of Utah, leaving more than 13,000 refugees waiting in Iowa and Nebraska for the signal to move west. Meanwhile millions of European immigrants avoided the fertile soil and untouched resources of the Deep South, passing along its northern borders and carrying their skills into a far different West largely to escape the contamination of race-based **slavery**. **Related Entry**: Extension of Slavery into the Territories.

SUGGESTED READING: Thomas D. Clark, *Frontier America* (1969); John P. Hale, *Trans-Allegeny Pioneers 1748 and After* (1971); Mary Ellan Jones, *Daily Life on the American Frontier* (1998); Robert E. Reigel, *America Moves West* (1956).

WHIG PARTY (WHIGS): The name "Whigs" was taken by the early National Republican Party of **Thomas Jefferson** to emphasize its opposition to the "tyrannical and king-like" administration of President Andrew Jackson. The name was symbolic of the successful opposition to George III in the American Revolution. Jackson, unshaken by the analogy, maintained his popularity with the people and served from 1828 to 1836. The Whigs also opposed Jackson's anointed successor, **Martin Van Buren**, but with little passion, refusing to align themselves behind a single candidate. Instead each regional caucus selected and supported their own man.

Consequently, the Whigs spent four unhappy years under Van Buren preparing to run a stronger presidential candidate in 1840 against Van Buren, who was weakened by the Panic of 1837, which ushered in a severe economic depression. Factories closed, banks failed, and men were out of work. The successful 1840 Whig campaign was the first modern political effort in history. This time the Whigs chose **William Henry Harrison** as their sole candidate based largely on his military reputation, "frontier" character, and good showing in the previous presidential election. The campaign for General Harrison was, according to Charles M. Ormsby, a contemporary observer, "one of unexampled excitement, characterized by immense popular gatherings, political songs, the use of symbols, and the participation of both sexes to a degree hitherto unknown in America" (*A History of the Whig Party*, 1860).

The Whigs had carefully paired their "frontier Indian fighter" with **John Tyler** of Virginia to attract the Southern vote, but the party drew up no platform because it could not agree on any issue other than the desire to defeat Van Buren. At Whig rallies hard cider flowed freely. The Whigs had found in Harrison the perfect new-style candidate—one that had vote-getting appeal.

Yet the party was severely damaged by Harrison's early death and the ascendancy of the less politically compatible Tyler to the presidency. Within a year all but one member of Tyler's cabinet—**Daniel Webster** being the lone holdout—had resigned to be replaced with **Democrats** or Whigs with strong Southern leanings.

The Whigs strongly opposed the **annexation of Texas** and sided with the anti-slavery forces against the **extension of slavery into the territories**. In 1845 they were unable to defeat the Democratic dark horse candidate **James K. Polk**, but in 1849 they successfully ran former general and Mexican War hero **Zachary Taylor** for the White House. Once again the party was fated to receive an unwarranted blow when Taylor died in mid-term. **Millard Fillmore**, his Vice President, was to be the last Whig to occupy the Executive Mansion.

During the 1840s, the Whigs and Democrats, the two oldest political parties in America, had reached agreement on several issues that had plagued the early republic. In the next decade the Whigs searched for new issues that would mobilize the voters. This attempt was to have far-reaching consequences. The party was particularly devastated by the **Kansas-Nebraska Act of 1854**. The Southern wing of the Whig Party, sympathetic to compromise on the **slavery** issue, bolted from the party, thereafter aligning themselves with the Southern Democrats; and the party, already weak after years of deterioration, was left in disarray.

A serious misreading of the temper of the voters had taken place. Many Whigs thereafter turned to the new **Republican Party**, but **Abraham Lincoln**, a former Whig, did not rush to join. In 1854 in a speech in Peoria, Illinois, he began to speak out against the Kansas-Nebraska Act. Yet, instead of casting his fortunes with the openly anti-slavery Republicans, he mistakenly continued to identify himself with the nearly defunct Whig Party. Viewed as an old party candidate, he lost the 1854 Senate seat in a close race. Immediately thereafter, he transferred his allegiance to the Republicans and helped to organize the party in Illinois. In this manner the metamorphosis of the party from Jeffersonian Republicans to Whigs to the Republican Party of Lincoln was completed in little over a half century. **Related Entries**: Harrison, William Henry; Kansas-Nebraska Act of 1854; Webster, Daniel.

SUGGESTED READING: E. M. Carroll, *Origins of the Whig Party* (1970); Michael F. Holt, *To Rescue Public Liberty: A History of the American Whig Party* (1999).

WILMOT PROVISO: During the **Mexican War of 1846**, anti-slavery forces in Congress understood that any land ceded to the United States would most likely be slave territory. David Wilmot, a Democrat from Pennsylvania, offered an amendment to an appropriations bill sponsored by President **James K. Polk**, who was asking for money to negotiate a Mexican boundary settlement. Wilmot proposed that "neither **slavery** nor involuntary servitude shall ever exist in any part of the territory" acquired from Mexico. Southern forces led by **John C. Calhoun** and **Jefferson Davis** opposed the amendment. Although the Wilmot Proviso passed several times in the House of Representatives in 1846–1847, the Senate, controlled by pro-slavery factions, always voted it down. Despite its failure to pass, the Wilmot Proviso raised serious constitutional and political questions.

Americans were increasingly divided over the **extension of slavery into the territories**. Slavery advocates said that Congress had no right to interfere with slavery in any manner. Moreover, they claimed an absolute obligation on the part of Congress, under the Constitution, to protect the slave property of all Americans in the territories. Slavery might be forbidden only after a territory had become a state, and then only by an act of the state itself. Moreover, the South had contributed to winning the Mexican War (some considered the war a purely Southern victory), and Southerners ought to be allowed to settle with slaves in the conquered territories. The Wilmot Proviso led to the formation of the Free Soil Party, which was committed to preventing the extension of slavery in the territories. **Related Entries**: Missouri Compromise of 1820; Popular Sovereignty.

SUGGESTED READING: Chaplain W. Morrison, *Democratic Politics and Sectionalism: The Wilmot Proviso Controversy* (1967).

WISE, HENRY ALEXANDER (1806–1876): editor, congressman, and governor. Best known as the governor of **Virginia** at the time of **John Brown**'s trial in 1859, Henry A. Wise began his career as a lawyer in **Tennessee**. As a member of Congress for Virginia he was a firm proponent of **states' rights** and a supporter of **slavery**. He served briefly as a diplomatic representative to Brazil before becoming the governor of Virginia.

In the period after John Brown's unsuccessful raid on Harper's Ferry, Virginia, Wise received several requests from Northern **abolitionists** to visit Brown in his Charlestown, Virginia, jail cell. A notable exchange took place between the governor and Lydia M. Child, who was a popular writer of domestic treatises, a friend of Brown, and an abolitionist. When word of Brown's failure and imprisonment reached Boston, Child informed Wise of her determination to go to Virginia to nurse him (Brown was slightly wounded during his capture). James Redpath, Brown's first biographer, observed that Wise's answer to Child's request "was respectful, but crafty and characteristic." Her visit, responded Wise, would be "a mission merciful and humane." Further, he recognized her right to visit Charlestown and assured her that the visit "would . . . be respected, if not welcomed." However, he warned the lady that "a few unenlightened and inconsiderate persons, fanatical in their modes of thought and action . . . might molest you, or be disposed to do so, and this might suggest the imprudence of risking any experiment on the peace of a society very much excited by the crimes with whose chief author you seem to sympathize so much." Declaring that Virginia and Massachusetts were not at war, Wise assured the lady of his readiness to protect her: "I could not permit an insult, even to a woman . . . who whetted knives of butchery for our mothers, sisters, daughters, and babes." The governor's answer chilled Mrs. Child's enthusiasm for the trip, and a letter to her from John Brown, who had been apprised of the exchange, prevented it (James Redpath, *The Public Life of Captain John Brown*, 1860).

Wise received seventeen affidavits submitted by friends and neighbors of Brown declaring, in so many words, that John Brown was insane and had come from a family where insanity was rampant. Although this was probably true at the time of the raid, Governor Wise withheld his clemency, allowing Brown to go to the gallows on December 2, 1859. Wise went on to become one of the more colorful brigadier generals in the Army of Northern Virginia. Surviving the war without a major wound, he died in 1876 without ever accepting amnesty. **Related Entry**: Brown, John.

SUGGESTED READING: Craig Simpson, *A Good Southerner: The Life of Henry A. Wise of Virginia* (1985).

WOMEN'S RIGHTS (WOMEN'S SUFFRAGE): The genesis of the women's rights movement can be found in the campaign to end **slavery**. It is often traced specifically to the February 21, 1838, speech made by **Charleston**-born **Sarah Grimké** before the Massachusetts state legislature. This was quite a remarkable occurrence because in 1838 women could neither vote nor run for public office. Sarah was joined by her sister, **Angelina Grimké**, and together these two upper-class women became the first Southern female anti-slavery activists in America. The Grimkés soon found that they met with resistance not only by championing the anti-slavery movement but also as women intruding into the male-dominated **reform movement**. Eventually, the sisters moved north, closer to the other movers and shakers of the **abolition** movement. The sisters were attacked repeatedly for their unfeminine behavior. In a *Liberator* piece, Angelina asserted that women should not only speak out on slavery, they should be heard on all the laws of the land, an idea that would not gain very much support for some time to come.

In the antebellum period every venue, from ministers to magazines, imbued the notion of womanhood with all the characteristics of **romanticism**. However, with technological advancement, women were beginning to experience some freedom from the endless toil of producing the bulk of a family's domestic needs. Their place as an equal guarantor along with the husband in providing living essentials was becoming a thing of the past in increasingly urban areas. Women were seen more as consumers than producers. Womanhood was becoming increasingly defined as "domestic, maternal, religious, cultured, idle and subservient."

It is quite ironic that the women's rights movement should begin with these South Carolinians, since the issues they raised gained momentum with the factory girls of New England and found voice with such other pioneers such as Elizabeth Cady Stanton, Lucy Stone, **Abby K. Foster**, and Susan B. Anthony. At the Women's Rights Convention held in Seneca Falls, New York, in 1848, Southern women were most noted for their absence. The romantic notion of womanhood was befitting the chivalric attitudes of the **planter aristocracy**, and women in the poorer classes were still laboring in a system where they were full economic partners in producing the necessities of family survival. **Related Entries:** Grimké, Angelina and Sarah; Romanticism; Suffrage.

SUGGESTED READING: Elizabeth Frost and Kathryn Cullen-Dupont, *Woman's Suffrage in America* (1992); Winston E. Langley and Vivian C. Fox, *Women's Rights in the United States: A Documentary History* (1994); Donald W. Rogers and Christine B. Scriabine, *Voting and the Spirit of Democracy: Essays on the History of Voting and Voting Rights in America* (1992); Sylvia Strauss, *Traitors to the Masculine Cause: The Men's Campaign for Women's Rights* (1982).

WOOD. *See* Raw Materials.

WOOL: In 1607 a group of men familiar with sheep raising and cloth manufacture introduced sheep to the colony of **Virginia**. As early as 1662 the colony attempted to stimulate the manufacture of woolens by passing laws for the encouragement of that industry; however, it was not until 1692 that the first fulling mills were constructed. Although exact records do not exist, it appears that a considerable amount of woolen broadcloth was produced, because Governor Nicholson advised Parliament to prohibit the making of cloth in the colonies. As the colonial period drew to a close, Virginia had numerous fulling mills in various locations.

By 1790, although **cotton** was "king," **South Carolina**, having offered premiums for making wool-cards and for woolen cloth, had a fulling mill for dressing fine and coarse woolens. The spinners and weavers of this area were settlers from Britain who had considerable skill in dyeing, fulling, and pressing wool. In 1833 the **tariff** placed duties on wool broadcloth but exempted the cheap, raw wool which was used in the production of **slave clothing. Related Entries**: Livestock; Slave Clothing.

SUGGESTED READING: Mildred Gwin Andrews, *Men and Mills: A History of the Southern Textile Industry* (1988); Ernest McPherson Lander, *The Textile Industry in Antebellum South Carolina* (1969).

YANCEY, WILLIAM L. (1814–1863): Southern apologist. William L. Yancey of **Alabama** was one of the most eloquent of the **secession** apologists. Yancey had lived as a youth in the North and never tired of using his personal experiences to reinforce the perception of the moral and cultural degradation of Northern cities. In the 1830s, he became convinced that the South could no longer protect itself from the degrading Northern influences that seemed to be gaining control of Congress. When the **Democrats** refused to include a pro-slavery plank in their 1848 election platform, Yancey became an ardent and unapologetic secessionist, urging immediate disunion. He hammered relentlessly on the themes of Southern unity of action and immediate disunion. The Southern states, he said, "all united may yet produce spirit enough to lead us forward, to call forth a Lexington, to fight a Bunker's Hill, to drive the foe from the city of our rights." It was Yancey, in the spring of 1860, who engineered the split in the Democratic convention that all but ensured the election of an anti-slavery candidate. He thereby knowingly ensured disunion and opened the way for **Abraham Lincoln** to enter the White House. **Related Entries**: Fire-eaters; Secession.

SUGGESTED READING: Richard H. Sewell, *A House Divided: Sectionalism and the Civil War, 1848–1865* (1988); Emory M. Thomas, *The Confederacy as a Revolutionary Experience* (1991); Dorothy Denneen Volo and James M. Volo, *Daily Life in Civil War America* (1998).

YELLOW FEVER. *See* Epidemics.

YEOMAN TRADITION: Nowhere was the overwhelmingly rural nature of society more deeply ingrained in the antebellum period than in the South. In the social hierarchy, just below the **planter aristocracy** was a large group of small farmers who exhibited the social characteristics of the English yeomanry of past times. These small landowners, like those in feudal times, aspired to emulate their social betters by raising their standard of living at the expense of black labor. Southerners were reared in an atmosphere that supported a reasonable expectation that they could become substantial slaveowners. By draining swamps, manuring their fields, and planting cash crops, they hoped, in the early days of the century, to increase their incomes to the point where they might be able to afford the purchase of a slave or two. Thereafter the yeoman farmer hoped to become part of the slaveholding gentry and stabilize his new social position by marrying his daughters above their social station.

The South was a structured society tied to tradition and continuity, but economic security, once the hallmark of plantations, was no longer a certainty as the century wore on. Yeoman farmers had so worn out their land that they cast their lot with the expansionists who were moving into the territories. Many migrated with their manners and culture into other states: **Kentucky** and southern Ohio, **Mississippi** and southern Indiana, and **Texas**. Some with modest holdings were able to maintain their standard of living by establishing cash crops of tobacco, hemp, **cotton**, and meat for the market.

Working in the fields with their sons, sometimes side by side with a few slaves, yeoman farmers were a far cry from the **"poor whites"** with whom they are often confused. The yeoman farmer could see eye to eye with the planter aristocracy on the political issues surrounding **slavery**. Even if he did not own any slaves, the yeoman farmer hoped to own them, and therefore had a stake in the continuation and expansion of slavery. When the price of field hands rose to $2,000, the yeoman farmers largely supported a reopening of the **Atlantic slave trade** with Africa in order to decrease the price of black laborers, but this position proved too radical for the more conservative large plantation owners.

The yeoman farmers turned out in large numbers to support the Confederacy, but were ill-disposed to conscription or any legislation that excused the large slaveowners from service. Yeoman support for the war—largely dependent on the perceived value of continued slavery—did not extend to the generally mountainous areas of western **Virginia** and eastern **Tennessee**, nor was it strong in portions of **North Carolina** where there was an abundance of cheap white labor. **Related Entries**: Helper, Hilton Rowan; Poor Whites.

SUGGESTED READING: R. B. Brown, *Closing the Southern Range: A Chapter in the Decline of the Southern Yeomanry* (1990).

YOUNG, BRIGHAM (1801–1877): religious leader. Although the Mormon religion (Church of Jesus Christ of the Latter-day Saints) was started in 1823 by Joseph Smith, who saw himself as a present-day prophet, Brigham Young is more closely associated with the church leadership in the antebellum period. Mormonism, possibly the most important fringe religion in this period, was the great catchall of the evangelical movements. Patriarchs, angels, and demons seemed to punctuate the semi-Biblical rituals of Mormon metaphysics. At one time or another every Protestant heresy in America was championed by one or the other of the spokesmen for the Latter-day Saints.

Mormons based their religion on the Book of Mormon, a new scripture purportedly translated by revelation from golden plates originally written by a person named Mormon who had escaped with others from Jerusalem in a prehistoric time before Christ made his way to the North American continent. Here he set down certain records that he and his fellows had brought with them from Israel. Mormon condensed and inscribed the records on these golden plates before his death. Tradition said that his son Moroni hid the plates in the hill of Cumorah near Palmyra, **Missouri**, hundreds of years before the discovery of America. The Lord purportedly spoke directly to Joseph Smith revealing their contents. The resulting Book of Mormon restored all the ancient orders—elders, teachers, apostles, and deacons—and all the ancient rights including baptism by immersion, the sacraments, and modern-day revelation; but a return to polygamy was the cause for which the Mormons were most often persecuted.

Brigham Young was a convert to the Church of Jesus Christ of Latter-day Saints in 1832. Within months of his conversion his wife died, and Young turned all of his energies to the work of his new religion. Originally from New York State, as a missionary for his religion Young traveled the country trying to make converts. He moved to Kirtland, Ohio, at the urging of Joseph Smith, who advised that all the "Saints" do so. Brigham brought his little knot of converts with him from New York and found that dozens of such groups were pouring into Kirtland. Here, in a form of religious socialism, a good part of the possessions of each newcomer was turned over to the church treasury.

At this time the Missouri Saints were experiencing trouble with their neighbors largely because they were mostly Northerners and treated the region as their own promised land. Anti-Mormon mobs formed to drive them from their neat, prosperous farms. This was to be the first of many persecutions suffered by the Mormons. Not long thereafter, Joseph Smith formed an army of 250 men who were to march to Missouri to help their fellow Saints. Young was one of these. Unfortunately, this army of God was struck down by cholera and ordered back to Ohio.

In 1834 Young, who had two small daughters from his first marriage, married again. He was selected as one of the Twelve Apostles who stood next to the three-man presidency of the church headed by Smith. This group decided to move the church to Missouri and support the desperate Saints there who were suffering from burnings and beatings following the inability of the Mormon army to aid them. Once in Missouri, Smith and his companions were arrested by Missouri governor Lilburn Boggs, and the Mormons were warned to leave the state. Young, who had quite accidentally missed being arrested, found himself responsible for almost 12,000 homeless and destitute people. He made arrangements to purchase land on the banks of the **Mississippi River** in Illinois in the name of the church and moved his charges there.

Meanwhile, Joseph Smith and his companions managed to escape jail in December 1839 and joined the Saints in Illinois. Here Smith unfolded his plan for Nauvoo, the "beautiful" city of the Saints. However, the unhealthy effects of the local swampland caused about half the people of Nauvoo to come down with malaria and other fevers. Meanwhile Young was sent to England to foster the church. After almost a year, he returned to energize the Apostles and improve Nauvoo. Slowly the city grew and prospered.

However, other groups in Illinois became fearful of the large, well-equipped military force the Mormons maintained for their protection. They began to see Joseph Smith as a danger both economically and politically. In 1844 the Mormons decided to run Smith for the U.S. presidency. This decision led almost immediately to Joseph Smith's assassination at the hands of a mob in Carthage, Illinois, the abandonment of Nauvoo, and the removal of the Saints to Iowa. Brigham Young, braving the storm of internal church politics, assumed the leadership of the Twelve Apostles and the church presidency in 1847, which put practical control of the Mormons in his hands.

In 1848, having decided to leave the United States to escape further persecution, Brigham Young turned west to the great American desert. Having been persecuted in Ohio, Missouri, and Illinois, advanced parties of Mormons hurried into the Great Salt Lake Valley of Utah, leaving more than 13,000 refugees waiting in Iowa and Nebraska for the signal to move west. By 1849 Young's vision of a Mormon empire in the west had taken root. Exactly two years after they had entered the valley, the Mormons had built a city and established themselves across the Great Basin. Brigham Young successfully maintained a Mormon influence in the West until his death in 1877. **Related Entry**: Religion and Religious Revivalism.

SUGGESTED READING: Paul D. Bailey, *The Armies of God* (1968); Richard L. Bushman, *Joseph Smith and the Beginnings of Mormonism* (1984); Edwin D. Follick, *The Cultural Influence of Mormonism in Early Nineteenth Century America* (1963); Kenneth W. Godfrey, ed., *Women's Voices: An Untold Story of the Latter-day Saints* (1982); Ray Benedict West, *Kingdom of the West: The Story of Brigham Young and the Mormons* (1957).

ZANE'S TRACE: Zane's Trace, which became a major westward route for settlers of the Southern interior, was a road named for Colonel Ebenezer Zane, who founded Fort Henry at Wheeling Creek in western **Virginia**. In 1777 Indian attacks killed forty-one settlers at Wheeling, but the families rebuilt their homes and continued with their lives. There was a great need to improve the system of Indian footpaths that led to the interior to allow for the passage of wagons as the community prospered. In 1796 Congress authorized the construction of Zane's Trace, a wagon road from Wheeling to **Kentucky**. From here emigrants could float down the Ohio on **flatboats**. Because of wilderness roads like Zane's Trace, between 1800 and 1810 Kentucky, **Tennessee**, and Ohio amassed a population of over 500,000 people. **Related Entry**: Westward Movement.

SUGGESTED READING: Robert E. Reigel, *America Moves West* (1956).

Chronology of the Antebellum Period

1781–1783

- Articles of Confederation and Perpetual Union are ratified by the original thirteen states.

- Treaty of Paris ends the American Revolution, and Britain recognizes U.S. independence.

1784–1785

- Congress finds that it is unable to raise revenue, and the limitations of the Articles become almost immediately apparent.

1786–1788

- Congress enacts the Northwest Ordinance, providing that the Northwest Territory be divided into three to five states when sufficiently populated.

- Congress calls for a **Constitutional Convention** to repair the Articles. The delegates draft and sign the Constitution of the United States.

- **Delaware**, Pennsylvania, and New Jersey ratify the Constitution.

- **Georgia**, Connecticut, Massachusetts, **Maryland, South Carolina**, and New Hampshire ratify the Constitution, for a total of nine states, putting the document into effect.

- George Washington is elected first President.

- **Virginia** and New York ratify the Constitution after heated debate.

- Rhode Island and **North Carolina** refuse to ratify the Constitution.

- Anti-Federalists propose a Bill of Rights.

- District of Columbia is formed from land donated by Maryland and Virginia.

1789

- Federalist Party is formed.
- Federal Judiciary Act creates the **Supreme Court**.
- Congress adopts the Bill of Rights.
- New York City becomes the national capital.
- North Carolina ratifies the Constitution.

1790

- Rhode Island ratifies the Constitution.

1791

- The states ratify the Bill of Rights.
- Vermont becomes the fourteenth state.

1792

- The Democratic Republican Party (not the 1854 Republicans), led by **Thomas Jefferson**, forms in opposition to the Federalists.
- Kentucky becomes the fifteenth state.

1793

- Congress passes the first **Fugitive Slave Law**, making it illegal to aid runaway Negro slaves or to prevent their arrest.

1794

- Whiskey Rebellion in western Pennsylvania protesting an excise tax on liquor is crushed by **militia** under Gen. Henry "Light Horse Harry" Lee (father of **Robert E. Lee**).

1795

- Naturalization Act allows immigrants to become citizens.
- Treaty of San Lorenzo with Spain establishes the **Florida** boundary and gives the United States free navigation of the **Mississippi River**.

1796

- **John Adams** is elected second President.
- **Tennessee** becomes the sixteenth state.

- Congress authorizes the construction of **Zane's Trace**, a road from western Virginia to Kentucky.

1797

- France interferes with neutral American shipping.

- XYZ Affair exposes the extortion of U.S. ministers by French authorities in Paris.

1798

- United States opens undeclared naval war on armed French vessels.

- Alien and Sedition Acts restrict domestic political opposition and allow the arrest of dangerous aliens.

- **Virginia and Kentucky Resolutions**, espousing **nullification** of the Alien and Sedition Acts by the several states (**states' rights**), are written by Thomas Jefferson and **James Madison**.

- Mississippi Territory established by Congress.

1799

- Alexander Hamilton publishes *Report on the Subject of Manufactures* describing the state of American industry.

1800

- Thomas Jefferson and Aaron Burr tie in electoral votes for the presidency.

- **Washington, DC**, becomes the national capital.

- Congress divides the Northwest Territory into Ohio and Indiana.

- Spain cedes the Louisiana Territory to France.

1801

- House of Representatives chooses Jefferson as President and Burr as Vice President.

- **John Marshall** becomes Chief Justice of the Supreme Court.

1802

- Congress establishes the U.S. Military Academy at West Point.

- Congress repeals the Judiciary Act, which allowed the appointment of 200 "midnight judges" by John Adams.

1803

- Ohio becomes the seventeenth state.

- United States makes the **Louisiana Purchase** from France.

- Meriwether Lewis and William Clark begin their explorations.

- Supreme Court establishes the principle of judicial review by declaring an act of Congress unconstitutional in *Marbury v. Madison*.

1804

- Hamilton is killed by Burr in a pistol duel.

- Black slaves declare independence in Haiti after defeating a large French army in a bloody revolt.

1805

- Michigan Territory is formed by Congress.

- Ice is successfully shipped from New England to the West Indies.

1806

- Jefferson orders Burr's arrest for treason.

- Congress restricts the importation of British goods.

1807

- British impress American seamen from the U.S. frigate *Chesapeake*.

- Congress passes the Embargo Act, prohibiting any foreign trade.

- Burr is tried for treason and acquitted.

1808

- Congress prohibits the importation of African slaves.

- Enforcement of the Embargo Act creates a disastrous depression in American shipping.

- James Madison is elected fourth President.

1809

- Illinois Territory is formed by Congress.

1810

- Madison resumes trade with France on the assurances of Napoleon.

- Southerners revolt against Spain and briefly form the Republic of West Florida.

- United States annexes West Florida.

1811

- Western **War Hawks** in Congress increase their protest against British interference with U.S. shipping.

- **William H. Harrison** suppresses Indian resistance in Indiana Territory at the Battle of Tippecanoe.

- First boat to steam down the Mississippi River reaches **New Orleans**.

1812

- Congress declares war on Britain (**War of 1812**).

- Gen. William Hull surrenders an American army to the British at Detroit.

- Tecumseh persuades the Northwest Territory tribes to join the British.

- U.S. frigate *Constitution* defeats British frigates *Guerriere* and *Java* in separate ship-to-ship contests.

- U.S. frigate *United States* captures British frigate *Macedonian*.

- Madison is reelected President.

- **Louisiana** becomes the eighteenth state.

- The remnant of the Louisiana Purchase becomes the Missouri Territory.

1813

- British attempt to blockade American coastal ports.

- British take Fort Niagara and burn Buffalo, New York.

- Americans capture York (Toronto).

- U.S. Capt. Oliver Hazard Perry defeats the British fleet on Lake Erie.

- British abandon Detroit.

- Gen. Harrison defeats the British at the Battle of the Thames River.

- Indian power collapses when Tecumseh is killed at Thames River.

1814

- Gen. **Andrew Jackson** defeats the Creek Indians at the Battle of Horseshoe Bend, **Alabama**.

- U.S. fleet defeats the British fleet on Lake Champlain, NY.

- British bombard Fort McHenry in Baltimore.

- British capture **Washington, DC**, and burn the Capitol and the White House.

- Antiwar Federalists at the Hartford, Connecticut, convention threaten to have New England states secede.

1815

- Gen. Jackson defeats the British at the **Battle of New Orleans**.

- Treaty of Ghent ends the War of 1812.

1816

- **James Monroe** is elected fifth President.

- Indiana becomes the nineteenth state.

- Congress enacts the first protective **tariff** to raise revenue.

1817

- Mississippi Territory is divided into Alabama Territory and the twentieth state, **Mississippi**.

- Seminole Indians attack white settlers in Florida and Georgia.

1818

- Connecticut abolishes property qualifications for voting.

- United States and Britain establish the U.S.-Canadian border to the Rocky Mountains at the 49th parallel but not for Oregon.

- Gen. Jackson invades Florida to punish the Seminole and executes two British citizens.

1819

- Spain, told to control the Indians or give up the remainder of Florida, cedes the region to the United States and sets the western boundary of the Louisiana Purchase in the Adams-Onis Treaty.

- Supreme Court upholds the right of Congress to establish a national bank and establishes the doctrine of implied powers in *McCulloch v. Maryland*, a blow to strict construction of the Constitution.

- Depression of 1819. Banks foreclose on more than 50,000 acres of farm-land in **Kentucky** and Ohio.

- Alabama becomes the twenty-second state.

1820

- Congress agrees to the **Missouri Compromise**. Maine is admitted as a free state (twenty-third); Missouri is admitted as a slave state (twenty-fourth).

- Monroe reelected President.

- Government offers as little as eighty acres of land to settlers for $1.25 an acre.

1821

- Jackson made military governor of Florida.

- Stephen Austin establishes the first American settlement in **Texas** with the approval of the Mexican government.

- New York and Massachusetts abolish property qualifications for voting.

1822

- Florida is organized as a territory.

- **Denmark Vesey**'s slave rebellion uncovered in **Charleston**, South Carolina. Vesey and thirty-four others are executed.

- South Carolina adopts the Negro Seaman Law, which places all free Negro seamen under arrest until their ships leave port.

1823

- Monroe Doctrine warns Europe to stay out of the affairs of the Western Hemisphere.

- **Cotton** mills in Massachusetts begin producing cloth with water-powered machinery.

1824

- United States agrees to 54°40' for the lower limit of Russian possessions in North America.

1825

- With the electoral support of **Henry Clay**, the House of Representatives chooses **John Quincy Adams** as President over Andrew Jackson, who had initially received the most votes.

- **Democratic Party** is formed with Jackson at its head.

- Creek Indians refuse to cede their lands to Georgia.

- Congress adopts the **Indian removal** policy.

- The Erie Canal opens an important route connecting New York State with the Ohio and Mississippi Valleys.

1826

- Both Thomas Jefferson and John Adams die on July 4.

- Creek Indians agree to removal.

1827

- United States and Britain agree to joint occupation of Oregon.

- Congress gives the President the right to call out the militia.

- The first black **newspaper**, *Freedom's Journal*, is published in New York.

1828

- Andrew Jackson is elected President.

- The "Tariff of Abominations" is passed.

- South Carolina declares the tariff unconstitutional (nullification).

1829

- Jackson introduces a "**spoils system**" and forms the "Kitchen Cabinet."

1830

- **Robert Y. Hayne** debates **Daniel Webster** over states' rights and the nature of the Union.

- Congress adopts the Indian Removal Act, sending Indians to Oklahoma Territory.

- *Godey's Lady's Book* is published.

1831

- **Nat Turner** leads a slave revolt in Virginia.

- The **Anti-Masonic Party** is formed.

- Supreme Court upholds the removal of the Cherokee from Georgia.

1832

- **Black Hawk War** with the Sauk Indians of Illinois.

- Jackson reelected President.

- South Carolina **Nullification Convention** nullifies the 1828 and 1832 tariffs.

- Cholera **epidemics** sweep American cities.

1833

- Oberlin College is established as an **abolitionist** center.

- American Anti-Slavery Society is formed.

- **Slavery** is abolished in the British Empire.

- Jackson removes government funds from the National Bank.

- The **Force Bill** is adopted against South Carolina nullifiers.

- Jackson sends arms to South Carolina Unionists.

1834

- **Whig Party** is formed.

- Jackson is censured by the Senate for killing the National Bank.

- First Methodist mission and farming settlement is founded in Oregon.

- Cyrus McCormick patents the mechanical reaper.

- Anti-abolition riots break out in Northern cities.

1835

- Texas revolts against Mexican rule.

- An unsuccessful attempt is made to assassinate Jackson.

- The Seminole Indian War begins with the massacre of U.S. troops.

- Gold is found on Cherokee land in Georgia.

- Samuel Colt invents the revolving pistol.

1836

- Mexican general Santa Anna massacres Texans at the **Alamo** and at Goliad.

- **Samuel Houston** defeats Santa Anna at the Battle of San Jacinto, and Texas becomes an independent republic.

- **Arkansas** becomes the twenty-fifth state.
- Wisconsin Territory is formed by Congress.
- William H. McGuffey publishes the first of his standard elementary school readers.
- Jackson publishes the Specie Circular, requiring payments in specie (gold or silver) for all federal land purchases.
- **Martin Van Buren** is elected President.

1837

- A general economic depression becomes the Panic of 1837.
- Gen. **Zachary Taylor** defeats the Seminoles at the Battle of Okeechobee.
- Supreme Court membership is increased from seven to nine justices.
- Victoria becomes the Queen of England.

1838

- U.S. troops forcibly remove the Cherokee from Georgia (Trail of Tears).
- Congress adopts the **gag rule**, limiting discussion of anti-slavery.
- Some Northern states pass Personal Liberty Laws to obstruct the capture of fugitive slaves.
- The **Underground Railroad** is developed.
- Samuel F.B. Morse introduces the Morse Code.
- Iowa Territory is formed by Congress.

1839

- The *Amistad*, a slave ship, is found off Long Island, New York.
- Louis Daguerre invents the daguerreotype, the first successful form of **photography**.

1840

- Congress passes the Subtreasury Bill in an effort to stem the effects of the ongoing Panic of 1837.
- **William Henry Harrison** is elected President.

1841

- **John Tyler** becomes President when Harrison unexpectedly dies of pneumonia.

- All of Tyler's cabinet resigns with the exception of Daniel Webster.

- The *Amistad* Africans are freed by the Supreme Court.

- **Immigration** to the United States from Ireland and Britain approaches 300,000 over the previous ten years.

1842

- Rhode Island liberalizes voting requirements.

- Seminoles defeated and removed to Oklahoma.

- **John C. Fremont** leads an exploration of Oregon.

1843

- The great migration on the Oregon Trail begins.

- Congress finances a telegraph line between Baltimore and Washington, DC.

- Fremont begins his second expedition.

1844

- Samuel F.B. Morse sends first telegraph message: "What hath God wrought!"

- Composer **Stephen C. Foster** gains recognition.

- Dominicans successfully revolt against the Haitian government by forming the Dominican Republic.

- **James K. Polk** is elected President.

1845

- Florida becomes the twenty-seventh state.

- Texas accepts annexation to become the twenty-eighth state.

- The potato crop in Ireland fails, producing the Great Famine.

- Mexico begins military operations to stop the **annexation of Texas**.

- U.S. Naval Academy opens at Annapolis, Maryland.

1846

- The **Mexican War** begins.

- Gen. **Zachary Taylor** defeats the Mexicans at Palo Alto, Resaca de la Palma, and Monterrey (Mexico).

- U.S. naval forces occupy Monterey, California, and San Francisco, California.

- Oregon boundary is set at the 49th parallel.

- Congress exempts lands acquired from Mexico from the **Wilmot Proviso**.

- Smithsonian Institution is established by Congress.

- Iowa becomes the twenty-ninth state.

1847

- Irish immigration reaches 100,000 in a single year.

- Liberia (Africa) becomes a free and independent republic for former slaves with the aid of the American Colonization Society.

- Gen. Zachary Taylor defeats Santa Anna at Buena Vista.

- Gen. **Winfield Scott** captures Veracruz, defeats the Mexicans at Cerro Gordo, Churubusco, Molino del Ray, and Chapultepec, and enters Mexico City.

- California comes under U.S. control.

1848

- **Treaty of Guadalupe Hidalgo** ends the Mexican War.

- Wisconsin becomes the thirtieth state.

- Zachary Taylor is elected President.

- **Women's rights** convention held in Seneca Falls, New York.

- Gold discovered in California.

1849

- Congress establishes the Minnesota Territory.

- California requests admission as a free state.

- California Gold Rush.

- Cholera epidemic sweeps the South.

1850

- **Millard Fillmore** becomes President upon the death of Taylor.

- Senator Henry S. Foote of **Missouri** threatens Senator **Thomas Hart Benton** with a pistol in the Senate chamber.

- **Compromise of 1850** allows California into the Union as a **free state**.

- New Mexico and Utah are formed as territories.
- Fugitive Slave Law is strengthened and the slave trade is abolished in the District of Columbia.
- Cholera epidemic sweeps the Midwest.

1851

- Maine enacts a prohibition on alcoholic beverages.
- Isaac Singer patents the continuous-stitch sewing machine.

1852

- **Franklin Pierce** is elected President.
- **Harriet Beecher Stowe** publishes *Uncle Tom's Cabin*.
- Horse-drawn steam fire engines are invented.
- Safety matches are invented.

1853

- Washington Territory is formed by Congress.
- **Gadsden Purchase** from Mexico fills out U.S. continental borders.
- Yellow fever epidemic sweeps through New Orleans, leaving thousands dead.
- Baltimore and Ohio Railroad is completed to the Ohio River, and the New York Central Railroad is formed.

1854

- **Kansas-Nebraska Act** is passed by Congress.
- The modern **Republican Party** is formed.
- Massachusetts Emigrant Aid Society sends anti-slavery settlers to Kansas.
- The Ostend Manifesto suggests that the United States should seize Cuba.
- **George Fitzhugh** publishes *Sociology for the South, or The Failure of Free Society*, defending slavery.
- **Nativist** or Know-Nothing Party wins local offices in New York, Massachusetts, and Delaware.

1855

- **Stephen Douglas'** concept of **popular sovereignty** makes Kansas such a battleground of opposing forces that it is called **Bleeding Kansas**.

- Christian Sharps produces an efficient breechloading rifle.

- U.S. government adopts the conical minié ball as a standard bullet for its firearms.

- Frank Leslie publishes his first *Illustrated Newspaper*.

1856

- Pierce recognizes the pro-slavery legislature of Kansas Territory.

- Pro-slavery "border ruffians" attack and burn Lawrence, Kansas.

- Radical abolitionist **John Brown** kills five pro-slavery men in Kansas.

- Senator **Charles Sumner** is caned by Representative **Preston Brooks** in the Senate chamber.

- **James Buchanan** is elected President.

1857

- Supreme Court decides against **Dred Scott**, declaring the Missouri Compromise unconstitutional and declaring that Congress has no right to limit slavery in the territories.

- **George Fitzhugh** publishes *Cannibals All!, or Slaves Without Masters*, which contends that slavery is a positive good.

- Economic depression sweeps the country.

- North Carolina removes property qualifications for voting.

- **Frederick Law Olmsted** designs Central Park in New York City.

- Kansas elects a free state legislature, but pro-slavery delegates draw up the Lecompton Constitution, protecting slavery.

- Federal troops try to restore peace in Kansas Territory.

- Buchanan accepts the Lecompton Constitution.

1858

- Minnesota becomes the thirty-second state.

- **Abraham Lincoln** and Stephen Douglas debate during a run for the Senate.

- People of Kansas reject the Lecompton Constitution, and Kansas becomes a free territory.

- A religious revival sweeps the nation accompanied by prayer meetings in the cities and camp meetings on the trail.

- U.S. troops suppress the Mormon militia and restore order to Utah Territory.

1859

- Lincoln makes a speech at the opening of Cooper Union Institute.

- Oregon becomes the thirty-third state.

- Cotton production in the United States reaches 2 billion pounds per year.

- John Brown seizes the U.S. arsenal at Harper's Ferry, hoping to start a slave rebellion in Virginia.

- Col. Robert E. Lee captures John Brown.

- John Brown is hanged for murder, treason, and conspiracy.

1860

- Lincoln is elected President.

- South Carolina secedes from the Union.

- South Carolina seizes the U.S. arsenal at Charleston.

1861

- Mississippi, Florida, Alabama, Georgia, Louisiana, and Texas secede and join South Carolina in forming the **Confederate government** at **Montgomery, Alabama**.

- **Jefferson Davis** and **Alexander H. Stephens** are elected President and Vice President of the Confederacy.

- Confederate forces fire on Fort Sumter, in Charleston harbor, forcing federal troops to surrender.

- Virginia, Arkansas, North Carolina, and Tennessee secede.

- Confederate capital moves to **Richmond, Virginia**.

- Lincoln proclaims a blockade of Southern ports.

- Congress abolishes flogging in the U.S. Army.

- Robert E. Lee resigns from the U.S. Army and joins his state, Virginia, after turning down the command of federal forces.

- Gen. Winfield Scott is given command of the federal army.

- Telegraph wires connect New York and California.

- Kansas becomes the thirty-fourth state.

- West Virginia leaves Virginia to be admitted to the Union as the thirty-fifth state (1863).

- Congress creates the territories of Dakota, Colorado, and Nevada.

- Mathew Brady begins a photographic record of the Civil War.

- Confederate forces rout federal troops at the Battle of Bull Run (Manassas, VA).

1862–1865

- The Civil War is fought, resulting in more than 600,000 deaths.

- Gen. Robert E. Lee surrenders at Appomattox, Virginia, in April 1865.

- Lincoln is assassinated in April 1865 by John Wilkes Booth.

- Gen. Stand Wati (a Native American) is the last Confederate commander to surrender, in June 1865.

Index

Boldface page numbers indicate location of main entries.

About the Authors

JAMES M. VOLO is a teacher, historian, and living history enthusiast. He has been an active historic reenactor for more than two decades, participating in a wide range of living history events, including television and screen performances. With Dorothy Denneen Volo, he is co-author of *Daily Life in Civil War America* (Greenwood, 1998).

DOROTHY DENNEEN VOLO is a teacher and historian. She has been an active living history reenactor for twenty years and has been involved in numerous community historical education projects. With James M. Volo, she is co-author of *Daily Life in Civil War America* (Greenwood, 1998).